THE NEW BOOK OF KNOWLEDGE ANNUAL

THE
NEW BOOK
OF
KNOWLEDGE
ANNUAL

The Young People's Book of the Year

Grolier Incorporated, Danbury, Connecticut

1991
Highlighting Events of 1990

ISBN 0-7172-0622-X
ISSN 0196-0148
The Library of Congress Catalog Card Number: 79-26807

STAFF

CONTENTS

CONTRIBUTORS

BIERHORST, John
Author, *The Mythology of Mexico and Central America; The Mythology of South America; The Naked Bear: Folktales of the Iroquois; Doctor Coyote: A Native American Aesop's Fable*
AZTECS
INCAS
MAYA

BOSCH, Gulnar K.
Professor Emeritus of Art History, Florida State University; Curator, Oriental Art, Jacksonville Art Museum
ISLAMIC ART AND ARCHITECTURE

FARAH, Mounir A.
President, The Middle East Outreach Council; Senior author, *The Human Experience: A World History;* Co-author, *Global Insights: People and Culture; The Middle East: The Myth and the Reality*
ISLAM

HAHN, Charless
Stamp editor, *Chicago Sun-Times*; Co-author, *British Pictorial Envelopes of the 19th Century*
STAMP COLLECTING

KURTZ, Henry I.
Author, *The Art of the Toy Soldier; John and Sebastian Cabot*
THE BATTLE OF WATERLOO
THE BATTLE OF WOUNDED KNEE

LAYTON, Donald L.
Professor of History, Indiana State University
IVAN

MEISTER, Michael W.
Professor, History of Art Department, University of Pennsylvania; Editor, *Encyclopedia of Indian Temple Architecture; Discourses on Siva; Making Things in South Asia*
ART AND ARCHITECTURE OF INDIA

PASCOE, Elaine
Author, *South Africa: Troubled Land; Neighbors at Odds: U.S. Policy in Latin America; Racial Prejudice; The Horse Owner's Preventive Maintenance Handbook*
AROUND THE WORLD

RAGLAND, Ronald L.
Chief, Neuroradiology, University of Massachusetts Medical Center

DIAGNOSTIC IMAGING

ROLLER, Duane H. D.
Professor, History of Science and Curator, History of Science Collections, the University of Oklahoma

INVENTIONS

SEELY, Clinton B.
Department of South Asian Languages and Civilizations, the University of Chicago; Author, *A Poet Apart: A Literary Biography of the Bengali Poet Jibanananda Das*

LITERATURE OF INDIA

SHOEMAKER, Earl A.
News editor, Krause Publications (*Numismatic News*)

COIN COLLECTING

SLOANE, Leonard
Author, *The New York Times Book of Personal Finance*

INCOME TAX

SOLOMON, Charles
Author, *Enchanted Drawings: The History of Animation*

ANIMATION ·

TESAR, Jenny
Author, *Introduction to Animals* (Wonders of Wildlife series); Series consultant, *Wonders of Wildlife*

AMERICA'S ROYAL PALACE
HEDGEHOGS
IGUANAS
MOLES
SHREWS

TOSH, Nancy
Editor, *Crafts 'n Things* magazine

POPULAR CRAFTS

WOODEN, Howard E.
Director Emeritus, the Wichita Art Museum; Author, *Collected Essays on 101 Art Works; American Art of the Great Depression: Two Sides of the Coin*

IMPRESSIONISM

IN THE PAGES OF THIS BOOK...

How closely did you follow the events of 1990? Do you remember the people who made news during the year? What about the trends—what was in and what was out? Who won in sports? What were the top songs, films, and television shows? What important anniversaries were celebrated? All these helped make up your world in 1990—a year that was like no other.

Here's a quiz that will tell you how much you know about your world—about what took place during the past year and about other things, as well. If you're stumped by a question, don't worry. You'll find all the answers in the pages of this book. (The page numbers after the questions will tell you where to look.)

In January, 1990, Japan became the third nation, after the United States and the Soviet Union, to send a spacecraft to (the moon/Jupiter/ Mars). (*17;131*)

On April 22, millions of people throughout the world celebrated _____ by taking part in parades, marches and other events concerning environmental issues. (*23;114*)

What current rock group has so many teenage fans that their popularity is being compared to that of the Beatles? (*261;264*)

Pete Sampras, a 19-year-old tennis player from California, became the youngest men's singles champ in (U.S. Open/Wimbledon/French Open) history. (*181*)

In June, scientists in Brazil announced the discovery of the black-faced lion tamarin, a new kind of (squirrel/monkey/bird). (*86*)

In July, U.S. Supreme Court Justice _____ resigned; and _____ was named to succeed him. (*28;67*)

Spike-haired, smart-mouthed Bart is part of what very popular, but strange, family? (*256*)

An international crisis began on August 2, when Iraq invaded the neighboring nation of (Kuwait/Iran/Israel). (*12;30;40*)

A recent survey showed that young people between the ages of 13 and 15 spend most of their money on _____ and _____. (*226*)

In 1990, mystery fans celebrated the 100th anniversary of the birth of the Queen of Crime. Who was this world-famous, best-selling author? (*254*)

The rock duo Milli Vanilli lost their Grammy Award when it was revealed that they hadn't actually (played the instruments/done the singing/written the music) on their hit debut album. (*269*)

In October, the Nobel Peace Prize was awarded to _____ for his efforts in ending the Cold War and promoting international peace. (*35;48*)

What long-eared, carrot-chomping Hollywood celebrity celebrated his 50th birthday in 1990? (*262*)

In 1990, the (New York Knicks/Detroit Pistons/Chicago Bulls) won their second consecutive NBA championship. (*170*)

The majestic elephant, which has been called ''Nature's great masterpiece,'' is being killed in great numbers for its valuable _____. (*70*)

Thousands of people have discovered that they can go ice skating in July and surfing in January if they participate in two new sports. What are they? (*163;183*)

Recent studies have shown that kids are (less/more) physically fit than they were a decade ago. (*124*)

Jessica Tandy won the 1990 Academy Award as best actress for her role in _____, which also won best-picture honors. (*248;260*)

Some people call it ''painting the sky.'' Others call it ''dancing with the wind.'' What do *you* call this popular activity? (*132;134*)

Africa's last territory, (Rwanda/Zambia/Namibia), became an independent nation in March. (*20;60*)

Once again, the _____ proved their dominance in hockey when, in 1990, they won the Stanley Cup for the fifth time in seven years. (*176*)

A square-jawed detective of the 1930's was the hero of what big summer movie hit? (*261*)

Germans held massive celebrations on October 3 when East and West Germany became one nation again. The capital of reunited Germany is (Bonn/Berlin/Frankfurt). (*34;55*)

High-speed supertrains are being developed that never touch the track—they float above it. The technology that makes this possible is called maglev, which means _____. (*113*)

Which TV shows won Emmys as the best comedy series and the best drama series in 1990? (*270*)

Preliminary results of the 1990 U.S. census put the population in America at about (150/250/350) million people. (*193*)

During 1990, many countries issued commemorative stamps marking the 150th anniversary of the world's first postage stamps, the Penny _____ and the Two-Penny _____. (*142*)

These pizza-eating, martial-arts experts scored a major hit in 1990 with their first film. Who are these unlikely heroes? (*224*)

The 1990 World Cup in soccer was won by (Argentina/West Germany/Italy). (*164*)

Britain gained a new prime minister in November when _____ was chosen to succeed Margaret Thatcher, who resigned after eleven years in office. (*37;65*)

What was the trouble with Hubble in 1990? (*23;128*)

In June, the U.S. Supreme Court ruled that a Federal law making it a crime to burn or deface the American flag was (unconstitutional/constitutional). (*26*)

In baseball, the _____ made a surprising sweep of the Oakland A's to win the 1990 World Series. (*166*)

Many Soviet citizens got their first taste of American fast food in January when (Burger King/McDonald's/Wendy's) opened a restaurant in Moscow. (*17*)

In December, French and British construction workers shook hands to celebrate a major ''breakthrough.'' What happened? (*39*)

THE WORLD IN 1990

U.S. soldiers march through the sands of the Saudi Arabian desert. After Iraq invaded and annexed the neighboring country of Kuwait in August, 1990, several hundred thousand U.S. troops were sent to the Persian Gulf as part of a multinational force. Their goal was to block further Iraqi aggression and, if necessary, force Iraq out of Kuwait.

THE YEAR IN REVIEW

The year 1990 began on a note of hope that had first been sounded late in 1989, when a wave of freedom and democracy toppled Communist governments in Eastern Europe. It closed on a note of suspense, with soldiers from the United States and other countries facing Iraqi troops in the deserts of the Persian Gulf region.

The Persian Gulf crisis began in early August, when Iraq invaded neighboring Kuwait. It quickly developed into one of the year's biggest stories. Countries around the world condemned Iraq's aggression in the important, oil-rich Gulf region. The United States sent several hundred thousand troops to Saudi Arabia to block a further Iraqi advance. And the United Nations imposed stiff sanctions on Iraq, banning trade and freezing Iraqi assets abroad, in an effort to pressure Iraqi leader Saddam Hussein into leaving Kuwait. Meanwhile, other countries joined the United States in sending troops to the region and in enforcing the U.N. sanctions with a naval blockade.

But the Iraqi troops remained in Kuwait. And several thousand foreigners, including hundreds of Americans, were held hostage in Iran and Kuwait. In November, the United States announced that it would nearly double the number of its troops in Saudi Arabia. And the United Nations Security Council passed a resolution stating that if Iraq didn't leave Kuwait by January 15, 1991, U.N. members might use any means—including military force—to force it out.

In early December, soon after the resolution was passed, Iraq released the foreign hostages. Both sides continued to build up their troops, however. At year's end, a last-ditch effort to solve the crisis diplomatically was under way.

An important feature of the Persian Gulf crisis was the unity with which the world reacted to it. The Soviet Union and the United States, rivals since the end of World War II, joined in condemning the Iraqi invasion. This was a symptom of a major change in world affairs: the collapse of Communism and the end of the Cold War.

Changes in Communism had begun in the late 1980's, as Soviet leader Mikhail Gorbachev introduced greater political and economic freedom in an effort to save his country's failing economy. The Soviets also relaxed their hold over Eastern Europe. And late in 1989, the world witnessed an astounding series of events. One by one, Communist governments in Eastern Europe gave in to demands for freedom and democracy and stepped down.

Change continued in 1990. Perhaps the most important event of the year was the reunification of Germany, which had been divided into two countries—Communist East Germany and democratic West Germany—since the end of World War II. On October 3, the two were finally joined as East Germany was in effect absorbed by West Germany.

The United States and the Soviet Union also signed new arms-control agreements during the year. And, for his role in all these developments, Gorbachev was awarded the Nobel Peace Prize. Yet it was clear that the road from Communism to democracy would be a difficult one. Throughout Eastern Europe, countries faced severe economic problems and growing political division, including rivalry between ethnic groups. Problems were no less serious in the Soviet Union, where people faced food shortages and where, in some places, ethnic rivalry erupted in violence. The individual republics that make up the Soviet Union called for greater freedom; some even demanded complete independence.

While events in the Persian Gulf and the Communist world dominated the headlines for much of the year, there were important developments in other parts of the world. In South Africa, the white minority government at last seemed to be taking steps toward ending apartheid, its policy of racial segregation and discrimination. Black leader Nelson Mandela, imprisoned for 27 years, was freed in February. And, marking the end of a long struggle, the former South African territory of Namibia achieved full independence in March.

In Nicaragua, voters turned out the ruling Sandinista party and elected a new president, Violeta Barrios de Chamorro. The Sandinistas, a leftist group that had led the country since 1979, had been opposed by a U.S.-backed rebel force, the contras. That conflict seemed at an end. There were also encouraging signs for peace in several other long-running conflicts. In Cambodia, four groups that had been fighting a long civil war agreed on a framework for peace. And late in the year the government of Lebanon appeared to be gaining some control over the vicious factional fighting that has long torn that Middle Eastern country. In Israel, however, the government continued to struggle with an uprising among Palestinian Arabs in the West Bank and the Gaza Strip, territories that Israel has occupied since its 1967 war with Arab countries.

In an event that took many people by surprise, British Prime Minister Margaret Thatcher resigned in November. Thatcher, who was known for her conservative policies, firm will, and support of the United States, had led Britain for more than eleven years. She stepped down after losing the support of her Conservative Party, which chose John Major to replace her and thus become the new prime minister.

In the United States, it seemed clear by year's end that the economy was entering a period of recession. Sharp increases in oil prices, caused by the Persian Gulf crisis, and years of huge federal government budget deficits added to the economic woes. So did widespread failures of savings and loan associations. Deposits in the savings banks were insured by the government, but solving the problem was expected to cost as much as $500 billion in taxpayers' money. Meanwhile, Canada also faced an economic downturn. And the country struggled with a constitutional crisis that stemmed from calls by Quebec Province for greater independence.

The year also saw growing concern about a problem shared by people around the world: destruction of the environment. April 22 was designated Earth Day 1990. Some 200 million people worldwide marked the day in various ways, calling attention to environmental problems that range from pollution to global warming. Although these problems were often overshadowed during the year by political events such as the Persian Gulf crisis, it was clear that solving them would be one of the most important—and most difficult—tasks that the world has ever faced.

3 Manuel Antonio Noriega, the former ruler of Panama, surrendered to the United States. Noriega had been ousted in December, 1989, when U.S. troops invaded Panama. He had taken refuge in the Vatican embassy in Panama City for eleven days. When he voluntarily left the embassy, he was taken into custody by U.S authorities in Panama and arrested on charges that he had helped drug traffickers. Noriega was flown to the United States to stand trial on the charges.

7 It was reported that recently discovered dinosaur fossils may disprove the long-held theory that *Tyrannosaurus rex* was the largest meat-eating dinosaur. The fossils, found in Colorado, were of a dinosaur named *Epanterias amplexus*. They indicated that this dinosaur was as big as the biggest *tyrannosaur*. *Epanterias* lived 30 million years before the *tyrannosaur*. It weighed about four tons and was nearly twice as long as a school bus. Its jaws were expandable, like those of a snake, enabling it to eat an animal as big as a cow in a single gulp.

15 The Soviet government declared a state of emergency in the republic of Azerbaijan and sent 11,000 troops to restore order. Since 1988 there had been violent clashes in the republic between two ethnic groups—Muslim Azerbaijanis and Christian Armenians. The conflict had recently escalated into a virtual civil war.

Recently discovered fossils indicate that *Epanterias* was as large as *Tyrannosaurus*. The dinosaurs are compared here with *Allosaurus* (a smaller cousin of *Epanterias*), an Indian bull elephant, and a football player.

MOSCOW'S GOLDEN ARCHES

Soviet consumers can now enjoy one of the mainstays of many Americans' diets: the "Beeg Mek." On January 31, McDonald's opened its first restaurant in the Soviet Union. Located on Pushkin Square in Moscow, it's the biggest McDonald's in the world. It has 27 cash registers and 700 seats and can serve more than 15,000 customers a day. Soviet citizens were delighted with the beautiful restaurant and the tasty food. But best of all they liked the friendly, polite service of the teenagers who waited on them. The food seemed inexpensive to Western tourists: a Big Mac, French fries, and cola cost about 5 rubles —less than one dollar in U.S. currency. But this was a great deal of money for the average Soviet citizen, who earns about 10 rubles a day. Still, many Soviets considered McDonald's food a treat when compared with the poor quality and high cost of food at Soviet restaurants.

 The space shuttle *Columbia* completed the longest mission in the history of the shuttle program, returning to Earth after almost eleven days in space. One of the mission's highlights was the retrieval of a failing scientific satellite, which was brought back to Earth in *Columbia*'s cargo bay. The mission crew consisted of Daniel C. Brandenstein, Bonnie J. Dunbar, Marsha S. Ivins, G. David Low, and James D. Wetherbee.

 Japan launched a rocket with two satellites to the moon. Previously, only the United States and the Soviet Union had sent spacecraft to the moon. The satellites were to be released into lunar orbit for scientific observations.

FEBRUARY

2 Andrei Lukanov was named premier of Bulgaria. He succeeded Georgi Atanasov, who resigned after four years in office.

4 In national elections in Costa Rica, Rafael Calderón Fournier of the Social Christian Unity Party was elected president. He succeeded Oscar Arias Sánchez, president since 1986.

9 It was reported that scientists at Yale University had identified the world's oldest known flowering plant. Called the Koonwarra plant, it was an herb about an inch (2.5 centimeters) tall. Its tiny flower was probably greenish or beige. The plant lived 120 million years ago and is known only through fossils found in the Koonwarra area of southeastern Australia. It is believed that almost all of today's flowering plants are descendants of the Koonwarra plant.

25 In national elections in Nicaragua, Violeta Barrios de Chamorro of the National Opposition Union was elected president. She defeated the incumbent president, Daniel Ortega Saavedra of the Sandinista National Liberation Front, the party that had ruled Nicaragua since 1979.

This enlarged photo shows a fossil of the tiny Koonwarra—the world's oldest known flowering plant.

Free at last: Nelson Mandela (with his wife, Winnie).

WALK TO FREEDOM

South African black nationalist leader Nelson Mandela, who spent 27 years in jail for his efforts to end white minority rule, was freed on February 11. During his years in prison, Mandela had helped focus worldwide attention on the struggle for racial equality in South Africa.

Blacks outnumber whites in South Africa by more than five to one, but whites have ruled the country since its early days. In 1948, apartheid—"separateness"—became the government's official policy. Everyone was classified according to race. This classification determined who could vote, where people could live, which schools they could attend. The main goals of Mandela and many other people, including his fellow members of the African National Congress (ANC), have been to end apartheid and establish black majority rule.

Mandela was born on July 18, 1918, into a royal family of the Xhosa. He received a law degree from the University of South Africa in 1942 and later helped set up South Africa's first black law firm. In 1944 he was one of the founders of the ANC Youth League, a group that became a leading force in protests against the government. He was arrested twice for his protest activities in the 1950's. In 1960, the government banned the ANC and other black protest groups. But Mandela continued his crusade, helping to form a military wing of the ANC and begin a guerrilla campaign. He was arrested in 1962 and, two years later, sentenced to life in prison for sabotage and conspiracy to overthrow the government.

Even in prison, however, Mandela continued his opposition to the government. His dedication helped bring international pressure on South Africa to free political prisoners and end apartheid. The government finally began to move in this direction in 1989. The ANC and other black protest groups were legalized a week before Mandela's release.

Out of jail at last, the 71-year-old Mandela faced a difficult task: to work with both black and white leaders to find a solution to the racial strife that has long divided his country.

4 The space shuttle *Atlantis* completed a four-and-a-half-day secret military mission. It was widely reported that a spy satellite was launched over the Soviet Union. The mission crew consisted of John O. Creighton, John H. Casper, David C. Hilmers, Richard M. Mullane, and Pierre J. Thuot.

11 Lithuania, one of the Soviet Union's fifteen republics, declared itself independent. It announced that it would restore the statehood it had held from 1918 to 1940, when it was annexed by the U.S.S.R. The Soviet Union said that the declaration of independence was "illegitimate." (In the following months, the Soviet government strongly sought to pressure the republic into suspending the declaration. And neighboring Baltic republics Estonia and Latvia, likewise annexed by the Soviet Union in 1940, also began moves toward independence.)

13 In the Soviet Union, the parliament voted to increase the powers of the president. Under the new system, power has been transferred away from the Communist Party to the government. And the new presidency includes broad executive powers similar to those of Western government leaders. (On March 15, the parliament elected Mikhail S. Gorbachev, the only candidate, to the new-style presidency.)

Ertha Pascal-Trouillot became president of Haiti. She succeeded Prosper Avril, who resigned after eighteen months in office.

In national elections in Grenada, an island nation in the Caribbean, the National Democratic Congress won the most seats in parliament. Nicholas Braithwaite, the party's leader, became prime minister. He succeeded Ben Jones, who had held the position for three months.

14 In Mongolia, the Communist Party replaced its entire leadership and named Gombojavyn Ochirbat the new general secretary. He succeeded Dzhambiin Batmunkh, who had been party leader since 1984. The Communist Party also voted to give up its monopoly on power.

18 East Germany held its first free parliamentary elections. An alliance of conservative parties, backed by West Germany, received the most votes. (On April 12, Lothar de Maizière became premier of the non-Communist government. He succeeded Hans Modrow, who had held the post since November, 1989.)

21 Namibia, Africa's last territory, became an independent nation, ending 75 years of South African rule. Sam Nujoma, leader of SWAPO, the main Namibian nationalist movement, became the nation's president.

Scientists have developed a technique to make some species of bamboo flower in the lab. If they can repeat this process with other species, pandas—which feed mainly on bamboo—may be saved from becoming extinct.

BAMBOO BREAKTHROUGH

Scientists in India announced in March that they had found a way to make young bamboo plants flower and produce seeds in the laboratory. The breakthrough was expected to help the many people in tropical nations who depend on bamboo, which is one of the most widely used plants in the world.

Bamboo is the tallest of the grass plants. It grows more than 100 feet (30 meters) tall, with stalks up to 12 inches (30 centimeters) thick. Most of the 500 known species live in tropical or subtropical climates. Forests of bamboo are extremely important to the economies of tropical nations. The woody stems are used for houses, furniture, baskets, fishing poles, water pipes, boat masts, and scaffolding for building skyscrapers and ships. The tender shoots and grain can be eaten. The leaves are used as food for livestock.

Bamboo is a fast-growing plant. But many species flower only at intervals of 30 years or more. And at that time, all the plants of a particular species—all over the world—burst into bloom. After they flower, the stalks die. Underground parts of the plants survive, and in time they give rise to new stalks. Seeds give rise to new plants, too. But it may take five to ten years before there are stalks that can be cut and used by people.

The discovery of a way to make bamboo plants bloom in the lab means that people can get the plants to produce seeds in several weeks rather than in the normal 30-year time span. Scientists also hope to use the discovery to develop new kinds of bamboo that will grow faster and resist diseases.

7 John M. Poindexter, national security adviser under former President Ronald Reagan, was convicted of criminal charges in connection with the Iran-contra affair. The affair involved the secret sale of weapons to Iran in 1985 and 1986. Profits from the sale were used to provide military aid to rebels in Nicaragua known as the contras, at a time when such aid was specifically forbidden by Congress. Poindexter was the highest-ranking official convicted in connection with the scandal. He was found guilty on five charges of conspiracy, perjury, and obstruction of Congress. (On June 11, Poindexter received a six-month prison sentence. It was the first prison term for any of the seven people convicted as a result of the Iran-contra affair.)

8 In a runoff election in Hungary, the center-right Hungarian Democratic Forum won the most seats in parliament. Jozsef Antall, the party's leader, became premier. He succeeded Miklos Nemeth, who had been premier since 1988. Antall thus became head of the country's first freely elected government in 43 years. (On May 2, parliament chose Arpad Goncz the nation's president. He succeeded Matyas Szuros, who had been president since October, 1989.)

In national elections in Greece, the conservative New Democracy party won the most seats in parliament. The head of the party, Constantine Mitsotakis, became premier. He succeeded Xenophon Zolotas, who had been premier since late 1989.

This cartoon takes a humorous look at the serious issue of the endangered environment. Earth Day was celebrated on April 20.

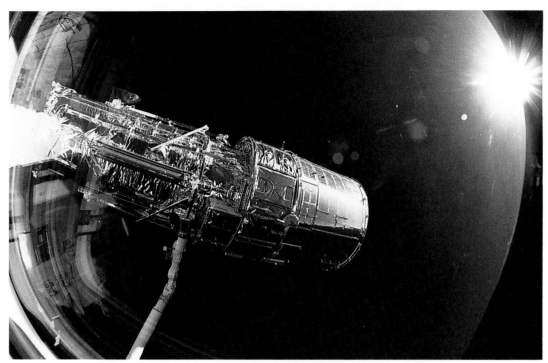

Discovery's robot arm is used to launch the Hubble Space Telescope. A major flaw discovered in June prevented the telescope from properly functioning.

16   In Nepal, Krishna Prasad Bhattarai was named prime minister. He succeeded Marish Man Singh Shrestha, who had held the position since 1987.

22   Robert Polhill, an American held hostage by terrorists in Lebanon since January, 1987, was freed. On April 30, a second American hostage, Frank Reed, was released by his kidnappers. He had been abducted in September, 1986. (Later in the year, three Europeans were released, leaving six Americans and seven Europeans still held hostage by Palestinian and pro-Iranian groups.)

Millions of people throughout the world participated in Earth Day festivities. The event, which marked the 20th anniversary of the first Earth Day, was celebrated by parades, concerts, marches, clean-up campaigns, workshops, and other activities designed to increase people's awareness of environmental issues.

29   The space shuttle *Discovery* completed a five-day mission. The crew consisted of Charles F. Bolden, Jr., Steven A. Hawley, Bruce McCandless 2nd, Loren J. Shriver, and Kathryn D. Sullivan. The mission's highlight was the launch of the Hubble Space Telescope, a $1.5 billion instrument designed to look at the far reaches of the universe. The cosmic telescope was expected to have a clarity ten times greater than an Earth-based telescope. (On June 27, it was reported that a flaw had been discovered in the Hubble's mirror system, preventing cameras from making sharp, clear images. This severely limited the ability of the telescope to study distant objects such as black holes, or to obtain images of planets around other stars.)

MAY

4   Constantine Karamanlis was chosen president of Greece by the nation's parliament. He succeeded Christos Sartzetakis, who had been president since 1985. (Karamanlis had previously been president from 1981 to 1985.)

15   *Portrait of Dr. Gachet*, a painting by Dutch artist Vincent van Gogh (1853–90), was sold for $82.5 million. The price was the highest ever paid for a painting at auction. The previous record price was $53.9 million, paid in 1987 for van Gogh's *Irises*.

20   In Rumania's first free national elections in more than 50 years, Ion Iliescu was elected president. Iliescu had been serving as interim president since December, 1989, following the ouster and execution of President Nicolae Ceauşescu.

22   Pro-Western North Yemen and pro-Soviet South Yemen merged, forming the Republic of Yemen. The new country, on the Arabian peninsula at the entrance to the Red Sea, is slightly smaller than France. Sana became the political capital of the country; Aden became its economic capital. Ali Abdullah Saleh, who had been president of

Portrait of Dr. Gachet, by Vincent van Gogh, was sold for a record $82.5 million. The painting was a portrait of van Gogh's physician, and it was completed just six weeks before the artist's death, in 1890.

REMEMBER THE *LUSITANIA*

May 7, 1990, marked the 75th anniversary of an event that helped draw the United States into World War I—the sinking of the British luxury liner *Lusitania.*

Back in 1915, the war was raging in Europe as Britain and its allies fought Germany and its allies. The United States was officially neutral. The *Lusitania*'s 1,257 passengers and 667 crew members were in high spirits as they set sail from New York City on May 2, bound for Liverpool, England. Their steamship was the world's largest and fastest liner, known as the Empress of the Sea.

The day before, on May 1, Germany had placed a notice in U.S. newspapers warning that the war zone included the waters around the British Isles. Nevertheless, it seemed that the *Lusitania*'s trip would be a smooth and sunny one. On May 7, as the passengers finished lunch, they glimpsed the green fields and white cottages of southern Ireland.

Suddenly, a torpedo from a German submarine ripped through the side of the *Lusitania*, and the ship began to capsize. Within twenty minutes the Empress of the Sea had sunk. Among the 1,198 who died were 124 Americans. The unprovoked attack was widely condemned. Germany claimed that the *Lusitania* was armed and carrying ammunition to the British. Britain said the *Lusitania* was unarmed and carried only a small amount of rifle ammunition.

Support for Britain increased after the attack, and "Remember the *Lusitania*" became a common slogan. Two years later, on April 6, 1917, the United States declared war on Germany.

North Yemen, was chosen president of the unified country. Haider Abu Bakr, who had been president of South Yemen, was named premier.

27 In national elections in Colombia, César Gaviria Trujillo of the Liberal Party was elected president. He succeeded Virgilio Barco Vargas, who had been president since 1986.

JUNE

8 Explosions aboard the *Mega Borg*, a Norwegian supertanker carrying 38 million gallons of oil, caused a fire that threatened to produce a massive oil spill in the Gulf of Mexico. But firefighters controlled the blaze, limiting leakage to about 4 million gallons of oil. In addition, scientists sprayed oil-eating bacteria across a large area of the floating slick—the first open-sea test of this method of controlling oil pollution.

10 In a runoff presidential election in Peru, Alberto Fujimori, head of the Change 90 movement, was elected president. He succeeded Alan García Pérez, who had been president since 1985.

11 The U.S. Supreme Court ruled that a recently passed Federal law making it a crime to burn or deface the American flag was unconstitutional. The justices said that the law suppressed freedom of speech, which is protected under the First Amendment. The federal law had been passed following a public outcry over a 1989 Supreme Court ruling that struck down a Texas law against flag burning, also because it violated First Amendment guarantees.

21 A powerful earthquake struck northern Iran. More than 40,000 people were killed, 60,000 were injured, and 400,000 were left homeless.

The massive earthquake that struck Iran destroyed or severely damaged more than 100 villages.

Gorbachev and Bush relax at Camp David between summit sessions.

THE WASHINGTON, D.C., SUMMIT

U.S. President George Bush and Soviet President Mikhail S. Gorbachev met in Washington, D.C., May 31 to June 3. It was their second summit meeting and the fifteenth such meeting between U.S. and Soviet leaders.

During the four-day meeting, Bush and Gorbachev signed an agreement to end production of chemical weapons and eliminate all but 5,000 tons of their existing stockpiles. They also approved the framework of a new treaty to reduce strategic (long-range) nuclear weapons. Trade between the two nations was another major issue discussed. The two leaders signed an agreement designed to lead toward granting the Soviet Union "most-favored-nation" status, which provides the lowest possible tariffs on goods entering the United States. Another agreement was designed to make it easier for U.S. and Soviet commercial ships to deliver goods to ports in each country. The men also signed or announced agreements on grain sales, student exchanges, scientific and technical cooperation, and civil aviation.

Following the summit meeting, Gorbachev and his wife, Raisa, visited the states of Minnesota and California, meeting with business leaders, politicians, and ordinary citizens. Prior to the summit meeting, the Gorbachevs had visited Canada, where they had met with Prime Minister Brian Mulroney. It was Gorbachev's first visit to Canada as Soviet leader.

In southern California, a series of brush fires destroyed more than 500 homes. The greatest damage occurred in Santa Barbara, where a fire believed to have been started by an arsonist destroyed some 400 homes. Severe drought and hot winds contributed to the spread and severity of the fires.

JULY

2   In Saudi Arabia, more than 1,400 Muslim pilgrims were killed during a stampede in a crowded pedestrian tunnel leading to the holy city of Mecca. The accident occurred during the annual *hajj*, or pilgrimage, which marks the high point of the Islamic year. Every Muslim is expected to make the pilgrimage at least once in his or her lifetime, and some two million Muslims from all over the world were in Mecca and the adjoining tent city of Mina at the time of the accident. Most of the victims were Indonesian and Malaysian pilgrims.

6   Petar Mladenov resigned as president of Bulgaria after three months in office. Prior to that, he had briefly held the post of Communist Party leader. (On August 1, the nation's parliament chose Zhelyu Zhelev president—the first non-Communist president in more than forty years.)

11   In Houston, Texas, the leaders of the seven major industrial nations ended their 16th annual summit meeting on world economic issues. The countries represented were Britain, Canada, France, Italy, Japan, West Germany, and the United States. The major topics under discussion were easing restrictions on international trade, giving economic aid to the Soviet Union, and dealing with the threat of global warming (the greenhouse effect). The three-day meeting resulted in compromises but no major agreements on the issues.

16   A major earthquake struck the main island of the Philippines. More than 1,600 people were killed and 3,000 were injured.

20   U.S. Supreme Court Justice William J. Brennan, Jr., resigned. Brennan had served on the Court for nearly 34 years and was considered the leader of the liberal members. (On July 23, President George Bush nominated David H. Souter, a judge on the Federal Court of Appeals in Boston, to succeed Brennan. On October 2, the Senate confirmed the nomination.)

26   It was reported that a team of U.S. archeologists had discovered a tiny statue that was once an ancient figure of worship. Said to be an example of the biblical ''golden calf,'' it is believed to be about 3,500 years old and the only one of its kind ever found. Such idols were worshipped in Canaan, an ancient land between the Mediterranean Sea and the Jordan River. The calf figurine was discovered during excavations of Canaanite ruins near Ashkelon, Israel. About the size of a human hand, the calf is made primarily of bronze; it was probably kept polished to a high sheen so that it looked like gold.

This tiny statue of a "golden calf" was discovered in the rubble of a buried temple in Israel. About 3,500 years old, the figurine was found in almost perfect condition. In ancient times, the calf was probably displayed emerging from the pottery vessel shown behind it.

AUGUST

2 Iraqi troops invaded the neighboring nation of Kuwait and seized control of the country and its rich oilfields. The Kuwaiti government headed by Sheik Jabir al-Ahmad al-Sabah fled to Saudi Arabia. The following day, Iraqi troops moved into position for a possible attack on Saudi Arabia. On August 6, the United Nations Security Council voted to impose a trade embargo on Iraq and occupied Kuwait. On August 7, President George Bush ordered American troops to Saudi Arabia to defend its oilfields from Iraqi attack. On August 8, Iraq declared that it had annexed Kuwait, a move declared "null and void" by the U.N. Security Council the next day. During the following weeks, other nations—including Britain, France, Syria, and Egypt—sent troops to Saudi Arabia. Hundreds of thousands of foreign workers fled Iraq and Kuwait, but thousands of Americans and other Westerners were held hostage by Iraq. On August 25, the U.N. Security Council voted to allow the use of force to halt shipping to and from Iraq, to prevent violations of the trade embargo. By the end of the month, most of the nations of the world were aligned in condemning the Iraqi invasion.

20 In Quebec, Canada, Army troops were sent to the towns of Oka and Chateauguay, where hundreds of armed Mohawk Indians were manning barricades. The barricades had been set up in March and July to protest the planned expansion of a golf course onto land that the Mohawks claimed as ancestral territory. The federal government had agreed to purchase the disputed land and allow the Mohawks to use it. But the Mohawks set additional conditions for removal of the barricades. During the summer, Indian groups across Canada had blocked highways and rail lines to show support for the Quebec Mohawks. (On September 26, the Mohawks surrendered without any concessions to their demands.)

25 Chinese officials announced the discovery of the burial site of an emperor of the Han Dynasty—one of the greatest civilizations of ancient times. Located near the ancient capital of Xian, the 2,100-year-old network of underground vaults was uncovered during road construction. The vaults contained tens of thousands of terra-cotta statues of men, boys, and horses, each about 2 feet (60 centimeters) tall. It is believed that the figures were buried with Emperor Jingdi, who ruled from 157 B.C. to 141 B.C. The figures were described as being masterfully carved and of great artistic quality.

When Iraq invaded Kuwait, President George Bush sent thousands of American troops to the Saudi Arabian desert to defend the country's oil fields from a possible Iraqi attack. The U.S. forces found themselves in unfamiliar surroundings where they had to adapt to excessive heat and unusual living quarters—such as this camouflaged tent.

SEPTEMBER

9 U.S. President George Bush and Soviet leader Mikhail Gorbachev met in Helsinki, Finland, to discuss Iraq's invasion of Kuwait. The two leaders agreed ''that Iraq's aggression must not be tolerated'' but that they hoped to resolve the crisis peacefully.

10 Following more than eight months of civil war, President Samuel K. Doe of Liberia was killed by rebel forces led by Prince Johnson. Doe had been president since seizing power in a coup in 1980. Johnson declared himself Liberia's new ruler. But he wasn't recognized by many other Liberians, including the head of another rebel faction that controlled much of the nation.

12 France, Britain, the Soviet Union, and the United States—the four nations that defeated Germany in World War II—signed a treaty giving up their rights to occupy Germany. The agreement restored full sovereignty to East and West Germany, and it paved the way for the reunification of the two Germanys.

18 The 45th annual session of the United Nations General Assembly opened at U.N. headquarters in New York City. Guido de Marco of Malta was elected to serve as assembly president for one year.

Young people from various nations don native costumes at the U.N.'s World Summit for Children.

The renovated entrance to the new Ellis Island Immigration Museum. For 32 years, Ellis Island served as the "gateway to America" for millions of people.

REOPENING THE GATEWAY TO AMERICA

On September 9, Ellis Island, a small, 27-acre (11-hectare) island in New York Bay southwest of Manhattan, was reopened and dedicated as the Ellis Island Immigration Museum. The new museum contains documents and other items relating to 400 years of American immigration.

From 1892 to 1924, Ellis Island was the major immigration station for the United States. More than twelve million people, mostly poor Europeans, passed through the "gateway to America." They were examined and either admitted to the United States or deported. At the height of its activity, the station processed as many as one million people a year.

The $156 million renovation of Ellis Island was paid for in part by 197,588 immigrants and relatives of immigrants who donated $100 or more. The names of these immigrant families are engraved in the American Immigrant Wall of Honor at the new museum. Hundreds of former immigrants attended the dedication ceremonies. In addition, 46 new citizens were sworn in by Associate Justice Antonin Scalia of the U.S. Supreme Court.

 More than 70 presidents, prime ministers, and other world leaders gathered at the United Nations in New York City for the World Summit for Children. It was the largest gathering of government leaders in modern times. The purpose of the meeting was to focus world attention on the plight of young people, especially children in the poorer countries and in the inner cities of industrialized nations. The leaders agreed to work together to fight disease, malnutrition, and illiteracy among children.

OCTOBER

3 After 45 years of separation, West Germany and East Germany were reunited into a single nation. In effect, East Germany was absorbed into West Germany, and the East German government went out of existence. Berlin became the capital of the new Federal Republic of Germany. West German leaders, including President Richard von Weizsäcker and Chancellor Helmut Kohl, kept their posts in the new government.

8 In Jerusalem, Israeli police killed 21 Palestinian protesters and wounded more than 100 others. The clash occurred at a holy site known as the Temple Mount to Jews and Haram al-Sharif (Noble Sanctuary) to Arabs. Israeli officials said that the Palestinians had started the incident by throwing stones down on Jewish worshippers praying at the nearby Western Wall, or Wailing Wall. Since 1987, Palestinians have been rebelling against Israeli rule in the occupied territories—the West Bank and the Gaza Strip. The October 8 death toll was the highest in a single incident in the rebellion, which is called the *intifada* ("uprising").

The German flag: The black, red, and gold banner of West Germany became the flag of all Germany when the country was finally reunited on October 3—after 45 years of separation.

THE 1990 NOBEL PRIZES

Chemistry: Elias James Corey of the United States, for developing methods that simplify the production of complex substances such as plastics, pesticides, and pharmaceuticals.

Economics: Harry M. Markowitz, Merton H. Miller, and William F. Sharpe of the United States, for their investment theories, which form the basis of financial economics.

Literature: Octavio Paz of Mexico, for his lyrical, surrealistic poetry and impassioned essays on Mexican society.

Peace: Mikhail S. Gorbachev, president of the Soviet Union, for his efforts to end the Cold War with the West and promote international peace. He was the first Communist leader to win the Peace Prize.

Physics: Richard E. Taylor of Canada and Jerome I. Friedman and Henry W. Kendall of the United States, for their work confirming the existence of quarks —subatomic particles that are the basic building blocks of all matter.

Physiology or Medicine: Joseph E. Murray and E. Donnall Thomas of the United States, for their pioneering work in the transplantation of human organs and cells from one person to another.

---

10 The space shuttle *Discovery* completed a four-day mission. The primary objective of the mission was to launch the Ulysses spacecraft, which will study the polar regions of the sun. The mission crew consisted of Richard N. Richards, Robert D. Cabana, Thomas D. Akers, Bruce E. Melnick, and William M. Shepherd.

13 In Lebanon, army general Michel Aoun surrendered power in his fight for control of the country. Aoun had headed Christian military forces that for nearly a year had fought the Syrian-backed Muslim government. It was hoped that Aoun's surrender would bring an end to the fifteen-year-old Lebanese civil war, which had killed more than 150,000 people.

24 Elizabeth H. Dole resigned as U.S. Secretary of Labor. (On December 14, President George Bush nominated Lynn Martin to succeed Dole.)

In national elections in Pakistan, the conservative Islamic Democratic Alliance won the most seats in parliament. The party's leader, Nawaz Sharif, became prime minister. He succeeded Benazir Bhutto, who had been prime minister since late 1988. Bhutto had been dismissed by President Ghulam Ishaq Khan and accused of corruption and misconduct in office.

27 In national elections in New Zealand, the conservative National Party won a majority of seats in parliament. The party's leader, Jim Bolger, became prime minister. He succeeded Mike Moore, who had held the position for two months.

NOVEMBER

3 Gro Harlem Brundtland became premier of Norway. She succeeded Jan P. Syse, who had resigned after a year in office. Brundtland had previously been premier in 1981 and from 1986 to 1989.

9 Mary Robinson was elected president of Ireland. She became the first woman ever to hold the office and the first president since 1945 who wasn't a member of the governing Fianna Fail party. Robinson succeeded Patrick J. Hillery, who had been president since 1976.

Chandra Shekhar became prime minister of India. He succeeded Vishwanath P. Singh, who had resigned after eleven months in office.

20 The space shuttle *Atlantis* completed a five-day secret military mission. The primary objective of the mission was reportedly the launch of a spy satellite over the Persian Gulf area. The mission crew consisted of Richard O. Covey, Frank L. Culbertson, Jr., Charles D. Gemar, Carl J. Meade, and Robert C. Springer.

British Prime Minister Margaret Thatcher, known for her conservative policies and strong will, resigned after more than eleven years in office. She was the longest-serving British prime minister of the 20th century. Thatcher announced her resignation after she failed to win reelection as leader of the ruling Conservative Party on the first ballot. Rather than face defeat on the second ballot, she decided to give up the party leadership and thus the leadership of Britain.

U.S. President George Bush joined American troops in Saudi Arabia for Thanksgiving.

21 The leaders of 34 European and North American countries signed the Charter of Paris for a New Europe. The treaty proclaimed the end of the Cold War—the period of confrontation but no actual fighting that followed World War II. During that time, Europe was divided into West and East blocs. The new charter pledged a commitment to democracy and human rights, and it established a secretariat to be headquartered in Prague, Czechoslovakia.

22 President George Bush spent Thanksgiving visiting some of the 230,000 American troops in Saudi Arabia. In his speeches, Bush stressed that the United States was prepared to use force to oust Iraqi troops that had invaded neighboring Kuwait in August.

26 Goh Chok Tong became prime minister of Singapore. He succeeded Lee Kuan Yew, who became prime minister in 1959, when Singapore became an independent nation.

27 In Britain, the ruling Conservative Party chose John Major to be its new leader and the nation's prime minister. Major succeeded Margaret Thatcher, who resigned after having been prime minister since 1979.

29 The United Nations Security Council voted to allow the United States and its allies to oust Iraq from Kuwait by force if Iraqi troops weren't withdrawn by January 15, 1991.

DECEMBER

1 In Chad, President Hissein Habré was overthrown in a coup. Idris Deby, leader of the rebel forces, succeeded Habré, who had been in power since 1982.

2 In national elections in recently united Germany, the Christian Democratic Party won the most seats in the new parliament. The party's leader, Helmut Kohl, thus kept his position as the nation's chancellor. The elections were the first free all-German elections since 1932.

5 Shahabuddin Ahmed was named president of Bangladesh. He succeeded Hussain Mohammad Ershad, who had resigned. Ershad had been president since a 1982 coup.

7 Dimitar Popov was named premier of Bulgaria. He succeeded Andrei Lukanov, who resigned after ten months in office.

9 For the first time in Poland's history, the people voted directly for president. Lech Walesa, leader of the Solidarity movement and winner of the 1983 Nobel Peace Prize, was elected president. He succeeded Wojciech Jaruzelski, who had been president since 1985.

11 The space shuttle *Columbia* completed a nine-day mission. The primary objective of the mission was to operate a set of powerful telescopes inside the shuttle. The mission crew consisted of Vance D. Brand, Guy S. Gardner, Jeffrey A. Hoffman, John M. Lounge, Robert A. R. Parker, Samuel T. Durrance, and Ronald A. Parise.

In the first class taught from space, astronauts aboard *Columbia* beam a science lesson to 41 students from four southeastern states. Classrooms were set up at two NASA centers.

THE CHUNNEL CONNECTION

Deep below the English Channel, French and British construction workers shook hands on December 1, to celebrate the breakthrough of the Channel Tunnel. Popularly known as the Chunnel, the tunnel will connect Folkestone, England, and Coquelles, France, when it is completed in 1993. It will cut travel time between London and Paris from 12 hours to only 3 hours.

Digging for the Chunnel—the largest construction project in Europe—began exactly three years earlier, on December 1, 1987. Most of the digging was accomplished by using two huge boring machines guided by lasers, which set out from the opposite shores. The final rock separating the two sections of the tunnel was cut away by workers using hand-held pneumatic drills.

The Chunnel will be about 30 miles (48 kilometers) long. It will actually contain three tunnels. The tunnel where the breakthrough occurred will be used for maintenance. Two other tunnels will carry trains—one for traffic toward England, the other for traffic toward France. In addition to passenger and freight trains, there will be shuttle trains that will ferry cars, trucks, and buses between the two countries.

12 Lauro F. Cavazos resigned as Secretary of Education. (On December 17, President George Bush nominated Lamar Alexander to succeed Cavazos.)

16 In Haiti's first fully democratic elections in its 186-year history, Jean-Bertrand Aristide was elected president. Aristide, a priest who had campaigned as a champion of the poor, succeeded Ertha Pascal Trouillot, president since March, 1990.

Iraq invaded Kuwait in 1990, and several hundred thousand U.S. troops found themselves in an unlikely place—in the desert protecting Saudi Arabian oilfields.

THE PERSIAN GULF CRISIS

The largest U.S. military force to operate overseas since the Vietnam War stood poised for action in the Persian Gulf region at the end of 1990. The force, some 400,000 strong and joined by troops from other countries, was sent after Iraq invaded the tiny Persian Gulf nation of Kuwait in August.

The Iraqi invasion of Kuwait sparked an outcry around the world. Iraq, one of the strongest military powers in the Middle East, acted with brutal disregard for the rights of its small neighbor. Moreover, seizing Kuwait gave Iraq control of 20 percent of the world's known oil reserves and put its troops in a position to threaten the even richer reserves of Saudi Arabia.

THE INVASION

Under dictator Saddam Hussein, Iraq had grown into a major Middle East power. From 1980 to 1988, it had fought a war with Iran, its neighbor to the east. The war had ended in a stalemate. But it left Iraq with a battle-hardened army of about a million soldiers—the largest in the Arab world—and some highly advanced weapons systems, including missiles and chemical weapons. Sad-

dam Hussein continued to build up his forces after the war, and it was rumored that he was developing nuclear weapons.

The invasion of Kuwait grew out of a dispute over oil and territory. Iraq was an oil-exporting country with substantial reserves. But the war with Iran had battered its economy and left it with debts of $80 billion, much of which had been lent by Saudi Arabia and Kuwait. A drop in oil prices made the situation more difficult by reducing Iraq's income from oil.

Saddam Hussein accused Kuwait and some other members of the Organization of Petroleum Exporting Countries (OPEC) of pumping too much oil, thus driving down the price. He also said that Kuwait was drawing more than its share from a vast oil field that lies beneath both countries. He demanded payments and debt relief totaling about $44 billion. And he revived an old boundary dispute, demanding control over territory that would give his country greater access to the Persian Gulf. When Kuwait didn't immediately agree to his demands, Iraqi forces invaded on August 2.

The Iraqi troops had no difficulty overcoming the far smaller Kuwaiti forces. The Kuwaiti ruling family fled the country. (Kuwait, an emirate, had been ruled by the same family for about 250 years. The emir at the time of the invasion was Sheik Jabir al-Ahmad al-Sabah.) The Iraqi forces then moved south and massed on Kuwait's border with Saudi Arabia.

The invasion was immediately condemned by countries around the world. The United Nations demanded that Iraq withdraw from Kuwait and voted to impose a stiff trade embargo and other economic sanctions against Iraq. And within days of the attack, the United States sent its first ground forces and warplanes to Saudi Arabia, to block a possible Iraqi invasion of that country.

The United States also sent Navy ships to the Persian Gulf region and announced that it would back up the U.N. embargo by imposing a blockade on Iraqi ports. Ships would be prevented, by force if necessary, from carrying goods in and out of Iraqi ports.

But Iraq didn't back down. Instead, it increased its troops in Kuwait and announced that it had annexed the country, making Kuwait a province of Iraq. Iraqi forces reportedly assaulted and killed Kuwaiti citizens and looted the country, even taking equipment from hospitals. Many Kuwaitis were forced from their homes, and eventually as much as half Kuwait's population fled the country. So did thousands of foreigners, many of them workers from Egypt, India, and other countries. Most made their way to emergency camps set up along the Iraq-Jordan border, where they waited in squalid conditions for transportation home.

Meanwhile, Iraq demanded that foreign embassies in Kuwait close. Those that refused, including the U.S. embassy, were surrounded, and supplies of food, water, and electricity were cut off. And thousands of people from other countries, especially Westerners, were rounded up and taken hostage by the Iraqis. Many were taken to important military and industrial sites in Iraq. The Iraqis hoped to prevent attacks on these sites by placing hostages there as "human shields."

THE BUILDUP

The world reaction to the invasion represented a rare show of unity. For one of the few times in recent history, the United States and the Soviet Union stood together in condemning Iraq. And the U.S. troops and ships were soon joined by forces from other countries.

In the Arab world, however, Iraq's action produced a division. Saudi Arabia, Egypt, and other moderate Arab countries condemned the invasion. So did Syria, Iraq's western neighbor and its major rival. These countries sent troops to Saudi Arabia or supported the growing international force there in other ways.

But Saddam Hussein won the admiration of many Arabs by presenting himself as a champion of the poor against oil-rich states like Kuwait. To some, he seemed the only Arab leader able to stand up to the West. He also tried to broaden the issue, claiming that the question of Kuwait couldn't be settled unless other Middle East questions, such as Israel's occupation of territory claimed by Palestinian Arabs, were settled at the same time. Although he had never been a religious leader, he called on Muslims to rise up in a holy war against foreigners and "corrupt" Arab states.

American troops often trained in gas masks because of the possibility that Iraq might use its chemical weapons.

ARAB COUNTRIES OF THE MIDDLE EAST

The Arabs of the Middle East have much in common. Most, for example, are Muslims. But when Iraq invaded Kuwait, a split was created in the Arab world. Arab countries took different stands on the invasion, reflecting their individual views and circumstances.

Egypt. A major Middle East power, Egypt has often rivaled Iraq for influence in the region. It opposed the invasion and sent troops to defend Saudi Arabia from possible Iraqi attack. Egypt is a relatively poor country, and it receives about $2 billion a year in U.S. aid. A parliamentary republic led by President Hosni Mubarak, it is the only Arab country to recognize Israel.

Lebanon. Since the 1970's, Lebanon has been decimated by civil war between Christian and Muslim factions. This strife continued in 1990. The Lebanese government, which is dominated by Syria, opposed the Iraqi invasion and supported the countries that sent troops to Saudi Arabia's defense.

Syria. Under the firm control of dictator Hafez al-Assad, Syria has long been one of Iraq's most powerful rivals in the Middle East. It condemned the invasion of Kuwait and sent troops to aid Saudi Arabia. The Syrian government is known for its ruthless suppression of dissent and has been accused of aiding terrorists in attacks on the West. The country has some oil reserves, but it isn't a major oil producer.

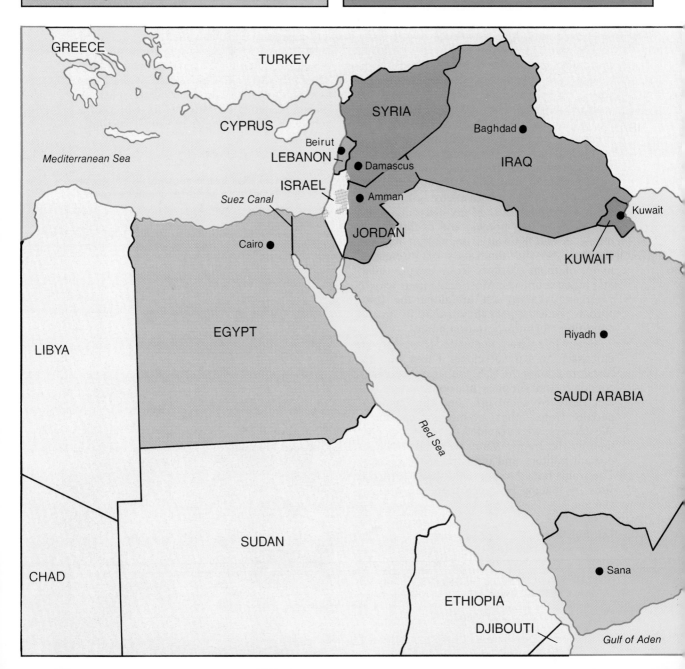

Jordan. A trading partner of Iraq, Jordan was caught in the middle of the crisis. Its ruler, King Hussein, agreed to abide by U.N. sanctions against Iraq but opposed military action and tried to act as a mediator. The sanctions hurt Jordan's economy, and the country was burdened by thousands of people fleeing from Iraq and Kuwait.

Saudi Arabia. A monarchy led by King Fahd of the Saud family, Saudi Arabia has vast oil reserves and was directly threatened by the invasion. Although it had distanced itself from the West in the past, it permitted a huge buildup of Western military forces on its soil and agreed to help pay for the force. The government requires strict observance of Islamic customs; women, for example, go veiled in public and are barred from many activities.

Iraq. Under dictator Saddam Hussein, Iraq was seeking to become the dominant power in the region. In the 1980's, during a long war with neighboring Iran, it built up a huge army and advanced weapons systems. The government was known for brutal repression and had even used chemical weapons against a group of its own citizens, the Kurds. Although Iraq has huge oil reserves, its economy is weak and most Iraqis are poor. Saddam Hussein was seen by some Arabs as a champion of the poor against the oil-rich Arab states.

Kuwait. A small country with vast oil reserves, Kuwait was ruled by the al-Sabah family from the mid-1700's until Iraq's 1990 invasion. Kuwait had supported Iraq in its war with Iran; but when that conflict ended in 1988, Kuwait became involved in a dispute with Iraq over oil reserves and territory.

Bahrain. A small Persian Gulf state with minor oil reserves, Bahrain condemned the Iraqi invasion. This country, an emirate with a hereditary ruler, is the site of an important U.S. naval base. After the invasion, it permitted U.S. and British combat aircraft to be stationed on its soil.

Qatar. Another oil-producing Persian Gulf emirate, Qatar took a firm stand against Iraq and, like Bahrain, permitted the deployment of Western warplanes within its borders. The country is known for its strict observance of Islamic customs.

United Arab Emirates. A group of seven small city-states governed by hereditary rulers, the United Arab Emirates has huge oil reserves. It, too, condemned Iraq and allowed the United States to deploy warplanes in its territory. One of the wealthiest Arab states, it also agreed to help pay for the multi-national force formed to opposed Iraq.

Oman. Oman, which has long had close relations with Britain, was firmly against the Iraqi invasion and also accepted the deployment of U.S. and British combat planes. Oman exports oil, but its reserves aren't as large as those of some other countries in the region.

Yemen. In May, 1990, North Yemen (which had ties with the West) merged with South Yemen (a Marxist state) to form a single country. A relatively poor country with some oil reserves, Yemen leaned toward Iraq in the crisis but said that it would observe the U.N. sanctions. Relations with Saudi Arabia were strained when the Saudis expelled hundreds of Yemenis who were working there.

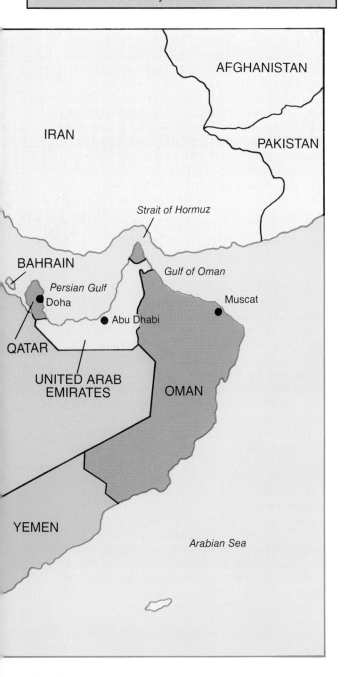

Thus Libya, Jordan, the Palestine Liberation Organization (PLO), and several of the poorer Arab countries didn't condemn the invasion. They called for Arab leaders to meet and work out a compromise. But these efforts were unsuccessful—Iraq refused to give up its claims on Kuwait, while Kuwait and its allies firmly refused to give up territory or grant other concessions as a result of Iraq's aggression.

As weeks stretched into months, both sides built up their forces. Iraq signed a peace treaty with Iran, which allowed it to move troops away from its eastern border and station them in the south. They dug into defensive positions along the Kuwait-Saudi border.

By late October, the United States had sent more than 200,000 troops to take part in the operation, known as Desert Shield. Most were stationed in the Saudi desert. They included reserve units that were called up for the crisis, as well as full-time soldiers. Among them were substantial numbers of women, who were barred from combat but

When Iraq seized its wealthy neighbor Kuwait, it gained control of 20 percent of the world's known oil reserves.

filled many support roles. The sight of female soldiers in fatigues was new to many Saudis. In Saudi Arabia's Islamic culture, women are heavily veiled and are forbidden to drive cars and perform many kinds of work.

The U.S. forces were joined by about 60,000 Saudi troops and smaller numbers from France, Britain, Kuwait and the other Persian Gulf states, Syria, Egypt, Pakistan, Bangladesh, and Morocco. Argentina sent a token force, and Czechoslovakia sent a small unit skilled in defense against chemical weapons. In addition, 95,000 Turkish troops were massed on Iraq's northern border. More than a dozen countries, including Canada and the Soviet Union, joined the naval blockade. And a number of countries, including Saudi Arabia and Japan, offered billions of dollars to pay for the operation and to aid countries that were hurt by the economic sanctions.

The soldiers stationed in the Saudi desert found the duty hard. Daytime temperatures soared as high as 120°F (49°C). Water—as much as 6 gallons (23 liters) per soldier each day—had to be trucked in. The soldiers were weighed down by fighting gear. Faced with the threat of Iraq's chemical weapons, they frequently trained in gas masks and heavy protective suits. Moreover, the powdery desert sand caused military equipment to break down. Even navigating in the flat, monotonous landscape was difficult.

THE THREAT OF WAR

As the troops waited in the desert, the economic sanctions began to take hold. Iraq's income from oil was cut off, and imports of food and other essentials were reduced to a trickle. The United Nations strengthened the sanctions by banning most air traffic to and from Iraq. But Iraq showed no sign of leaving Kuwait, although it released some foreign hostages.

In November, President George Bush announced that up to 200,000 more U.S. troops would be sent to the Gulf, to give the force offensive capability. That sparked a debate on whether the time had come to use force. Some people argued that the international troops couldn't remain in the desert indefinitely, waiting for the sanctions to work. Besides, the sanctions were hurting countries that had traded with Iraq. And the cut-off of Iraqi oil exports, coupled with the threat of war, had made oil prices soar.

SADDAM: A BRUTAL DICTATOR

By invading Kuwait, Saddam Hussein seemed to be making a bid to dominate the Arab world. But the 53-year-old Iraqi president (who is commonly referred to by his first name) had already gained a reputation as a brutal and ambitious dictator.

Born in 1937 to a peasant family, Saddam was orphaned at an early age and was raised by an uncle. As a young man, he joined the Baath Party, a political group that supports Arab nationalism. He was among a group of party members who tried to assassinate Iraqi dictator Abdel Karim Kassem in 1959. The plot failed, and he fled to Egypt. But when the Baath Party seized power in a coup in 1968, he returned and became the second most powerful person in the government. Eleven years later, he became president.

Saddam brought stability to Iraq through severe repression. He eliminated political opponents; simply criticizing his rule could bring death. He also built up Iraq's military strength, developing missiles and chemical weapons. In 1981, Israel bombed and destroyed an Iraqi nuclear reactor that it said was being used to develop nuclear weapons. Saddam used chemical weapons in his eight-year war with Iran and to put down unrest among a group of his own citizens, the Kurds.

Having eliminated his critics, Saddam was said to be isolated and to lack a clear picture of the strength of world opposition to his invasion of Kuwait. There was talk that Iraqi army officers who saw the situation more clearly might overthrow him, to prevent a war that Iraq would likely lose. But after years of repression, there was no organized Iraqi opposition. And Saddam had already survived several assassination attempts.

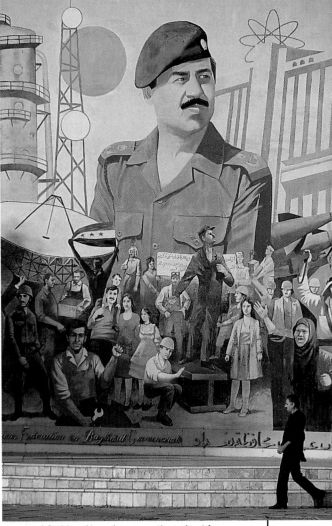

Murals of Saddam Hussein appear throughout Iraq.

Others argued that the sanctions should be given more time and that military action, if it proved necessary, should be directed by the United Nations. There was debate, too, about the U.S. goals. The United States said that it was in the Gulf region to restore the Kuwaiti government and establish peace and security. But it wasn't clear if establishing peace and security meant overthrowing Saddam. And keeping Mideast oil in friendly hands seemed to be another goal.

In late November, the United Nations set a deadline for Iraq's withdrawal from Kuwait: January 15, 1991. After that, U.N. members would be free to use any means,

even force, to drive Iraq out. Soon after, Iraq released its remaining foreign hostages, including about 800 Americans. At the same time, however, Iraq continued to build up its troops. There was a last-ditch effort to arrange high-level talks between Iraq and the United States, but the two sides couldn't agree on dates for the talks. Thus fears of war remained strong.

One thing was clear: If war came, thousands of people would be killed. Yet to let Iraq's invasion stand would be to turn aside as a brutal aggressor destroyed an independent country and reached for a stranglehold on the region's vital oil supplies.

Supporters of a separate Quebec cheer after the failure of the Meech Lake accord.

CANADA'S MEECH LAKE ACCORD

In the summer of 1990, Canada faced a constitutional crisis. At issue was a dispute between the provinces that had deep historical roots. The dispute cast a shadow over the country's future, threatening to break up the federation that has linked Canada's provinces and territories for 123 years.

The specific cause of the dispute was a constitutional amendment known as the Meech Lake accord, which was first proposed in 1987. But the underlying issue was the desire of Quebec province to guarantee its right to a "distinct society"—a society based on French customs, culture, and language, in contrast to the English-speaking society of the rest of Canada.

TWO CANADAS

The part of Canada that today forms Quebec was colonized by France in the 1600's. But France had rivals in the New World, and its greatest rival for the area that would become Canada was Britain. The rivalry led to fighting, and in 1759, during the French and Indian (Seven Years) War, the British captured Quebec city from the French. Four years later, France ceded its Canadian holdings to Britain.

At first, the British tried to impose their laws and customs on the former French territory. But they soon realized that the loyalty of Lower Canada (as Quebec became known) would best be kept if its people were allowed to maintain their traditional way of life. Thus French remained the main language, and Roman Catholicism the main religion. Property rights and civil laws (but not criminal laws) were based on the French legal system rather than the British.

Over the next century, as Canada grew and became increasingly independent from Britain, there were often frictions between French- and English-speaking Canadians. Quebeckers firmly resisted any attempt to blend their culture into a common Canadian one. But in the 1860's, during the U.S. Civil War, many Canadians worried that Canada might split up into separate states. The result was a new constitution, the British North America Act, which was drawn up by Canadians and passed by the British Parliament in 1867. It provided for a central government that would have certain powers, such as the regulation of trade. Other powers, such as the administration of justice, were left to the provinces.

The following years saw many power struggles between the federal and provincial governments. Because the constitution was controlled by the British Parliament, many of these disputes were settled by the British government. Even after Canada gained complete freedom from Britain under the Statutes of Westminster in 1931, Britain kept the right to amend the Canadian constitution because the Canadians hadn't agreed on a formula for amending it themselves.

After full independence, the federal government sought new powers, especially in areas of taxation and in funding social programs. But on the whole, the provincial governments retained more powers than the state governments in the United States. And Quebeckers, increasingly worried that their French-speaking society would be absorbed by the rest of Canada, often led in the push for more provincial powers.

In the late 1960's, the federal government responded to some of Quebec's concerns and took steps to make Canada a bilingual society, with French and English on equal footing. But some Quebeckers wanted to go much further—they wanted to separate from Canada completely. The issue sparked violence. In 1970, a Quebec separatist group kidnapped a British trade official and murdered a provincial cabinet official. Prime Minister Pierre Elliott Trudeau (himself a Quebecker) called in troops and suspended civil rights to quiet the situation.

But the problem continued. In 1976, the Parti Québécois, which supported separation, won Quebec's provincial election. The next year the province passed a law making French its official language. Meanwhile, the new provincial premier, René Lévesque, promised a referendum that would let Quebeckers decide whether the province should pursue the question of separation from Canada. But in the referendum, held in 1980, Quebeckers voted by a 20-point margin not to do so. Most felt they would be better off, economically and politically, as part of the federation.

In this atmosphere, the provinces and the federal government began new efforts to repatriate, or take control of, the Canadian constitution. The compromise they worked out included a complicated formula for amending the constitution. The constitution was also to include a charter guaranteeing basic individual rights, although provinces would be allowed to pass laws that violated the charter. In 1982, as a result of this agreement, Canada finally gained control of its constitution from Britain.

QUEBEC DEMANDS AN AMENDMENT

One by one, each of the provinces adopted the new constitution—except Quebec. Before it would sign, Quebec demanded that the constitution be amended to recognize its special cultural status. As a result, in 1987, the federal and provincial governments drew up an agreement called the Meech Lake accord (after the lake near Ottawa where it was forged). It declared Quebec to be a "distinct society," gave Quebec the right to set policy in certain cultural areas, and also granted all provinces the right to veto constitutional changes.

To become a constitutional amendment, the Meech Lake accord was to be passed by each of the provincial legislatures by June 23, 1990. At first it seemed that this wouldn't be a problem; after all, the provincial premiers had all agreed to the plan. But soon some of the provinces began to raise objections. They complained that French-speaking Quebeckers were being granted privileges that Canada's other minority groups, including Indians, Eskimos, Chinese, and Ukrainians, didn't enjoy. In 1988, when Quebec passed a law restricting the use of English on signs, some English-speaking Canadians complained that their rights were being violated.

As the 1990 deadline approached, two provinces—Manitoba and Newfoundland—held out against the amendment. There was a last-ditch flurry of efforts by the provincial leaders and Canadian Prime Minister Brian Mulroney to work out a compromise. But Quebec refused to consider any changes in the original agreement, and the proposed amendment died.

The failure of the Meech Lake accord reopened the question of Quebec's future. After the referendum of 1980, the separatist movement had seemed to lose strength. The Liberal Party, which supported union with Canada, had led the Quebec government since 1985. But in 1990, support for separatism appeared to be growing once again. People began to talk of an independent Quebec, perhaps tied to Canada in some sort of economic association.

In the fall, Quebec premier Robert Bourassa appointed a commission to study the question. But it seemed clear that, whatever course Quebec chose, difficult times were ahead for both French- and English-speaking Canadians.

Soviet leader Mikhail Gorbachev was the prime mover in the collapse of Communism in Eastern Europe. He was awarded the Nobel Peace Prize in 1990.

THE COLLAPSE OF COMMUNISM

From the end of World War II through the 1980's, tension between two competing systems—Communism and democratic capitalism—dominated world affairs. Communist countries, led by the Soviet Union, attempted to spread their system around the world. The democracies, led by the United States, tried to block that spread. Both sides built up huge arsenals of nuclear and other weapons, and the fear that war would break out between them was constant. Because it

never did, the long struggle became known as the Cold War—a war without fighting.

Then, late in 1989, the world witnessed a series of amazing events. In Eastern Europe, which had long been dominated by the Soviet Union, repressive Communist governments gave way to popular demands for greater freedom and democracy. And as these governments fell from power in country after country, the Soviet Union did nothing. Even within the Soviet Union, demands for reform were bringing major changes.

In 1990, these historic events continued. It seemed that the world was seeing nothing less than the collapse of Communism and the end of the Cold War.

IN THE SOVIET UNION

The events that led to the collapse of Communism began in 1985, when Mikhail Gorbachev came to power in the Soviet Union. He faced a rapidly growing economic crisis. In the Communist system, the government controls all aspects of the economy, deciding what will be produced and setting wages and prices. But after years of this control, there were severe shortages of even basic items such as food and housing.

Gorbachev sought to solve the problem with new policies. For the first time in years, the government allowed people to speak out and criticize the system. This policy was called *glasnost*, or "openness." With a policy called *perestroika*, or "restructuring," Gorbachev tried to lessen state control of the economy.

The restructuring soon spread to the political system as well. In 1989, for the first time, voters were actually given a choice of candidates in elections for a national legislature, the Congress of Deputies. And in early 1990, the Communist Party officially gave up the "leading role" in government that it had been guaranteed by the Soviet constitution. The government was reorganized, and Gorbachev was named to a new and more powerful presidency.

Trouble in the Republics. More changes came in February and March as the Soviet Union's fifteen divisions, or republics, held local elections. In these contests, opposition parties were allowed to compete for the first time in about 70 years. The days leading up to the voting saw the country's first mass demonstrations in support of democracy. And in contests for city councils and republic legislatures in many areas, candidates who urged reform unseated long-time Communist officials.

In the Baltic republics—Lithuania, Latvia, and Estonia—voters chose candidates who supported not just reform but independence from the Soviet Union. (The Baltic republics were independent from 1918 to 1940, when they were taken over by the Soviet Union.) And when the newly elected legislators took office, they began to put their campaign promises into action. Lithuania declared itself independent in March, and Estonia and Latvia took steps toward independence.

The Lithuanian action brought a sharp reaction from the Soviet government, which cut supplies of oil and gas to the republic and sent troops to patrol the streets of Vilnius, the capital. The crisis eased in June, when Lithuania suspended its declaration and began to negotiate with the Soviet government for gradual independence.

There was trouble in other republics, too. In several—Armenia, Azerbaijan, Kirghizia, Moldavia—violence broke out between ethnic groups. The government sent in troops to quell some of these conflicts.

The spirit of rebellion seemed to be spreading throughout the country. In May, Boris Yeltsin, a radical reformer who often opposed the central Soviet government, was chosen president of Russia, the largest and most important republic. And as the year went on, republic after republic declared itself sovereign, meaning that its laws would take precedence over the laws of the central Soviet government. Even Russia and the Ukraine, the Soviet Union's breadbasket, took this step.

A Growing Crisis. Politically, the Soviet Union seemed at times to be on the verge of falling apart. And the country's economic crisis was worsening, too. In 1990, the government began to permit private ownership of homes, farms, and businesses for the first time since the Communists had come to power. But these and other economic reforms were slow to take hold.

Some people opposed the reforms, fearing the unemployment and price increases that were likely to come as state control of the economy was loosened. Others said the government wasn't pushing reform fast enough. Gorbachev was even jeered by demonstrators at the 1990 May Day parade, an annual event that honored Communism. And in fact, the Soviet leader seemed to waver back and forth on how to proceed.

As the economic problems worsened, food shortages developed. In October, Gorbachev announced a sweeping plan to deal with the crisis by phasing out central government control of the economy. But because the plan had no timetable and was vague on key points, some republics rejected it and said they would follow a more radical plan.

With winter approaching and public unrest growing, Gorbachev was given emergency powers in November. He proposed a new "treaty of union" that would give the republics more freedom. Meanwhile, shortages grew worse. The Soviets asked for and began to receive emergency shipments of food, medicine, and other supplies from the West. And the United States lifted a fifteen-year-old ban on loans to the Soviets so that they could buy U.S. food. Despite the aid, however, there were mounting fears that Communist hard-liners might try to regain control of the country.

Within the Soviet Union, rebellion was rampant. The Soviet republic of Lithuania declared itself independent, bringing a sharp reaction from the government.

The Soviet Union's economic crisis also worsened during the year. Here, a group of protesters pitch tents outside the Kremlin in Moscow to dramatize their plight.

EAST AND WEST

As the Soviet Union struggled with its internal problems, reform continued in the countries of Eastern Europe. And it became clear that the changes in the Communist world meant the beginning of a new era in relations with the Western democracies.

NATO and the Warsaw Pact. Soon after World War II, the democratic West and the Communist East had formed two defensive alliances, the North Atlantic Treaty Organization (NATO) and the Warsaw Pact. NATO and Warsaw Pact troops were drawn up in opposing camps in Western and Eastern Europe, alert for war. But in 1990, the alliances announced the end of their conflict.

In this, they were acknowledging what seemed inevitable. As Eastern European countries moved toward democracy, they became less and less likely to join the Soviets in an attack on the West. Czechoslovakia, Poland, and Hungary demanded that Soviet troops stationed on their soil be withdrawn. When East and West Germany were reunited in October, Soviet troop withdrawals were also part of the plan. The Soviets even permitted reunified Germany to become a member of NATO.

NATO made changes, too—scrapping a plan to update its nuclear weapons, and planning to reduce and reorganize its troops. In the future, NATO leaders said, the organization's military role would shrink, while its political role would grow.

Arms Control. The two sides also made progress on arms control. In June, at a summit meeting in Washington, D.C., Gorbachev and U.S. President George Bush signed an agreement that would nearly eliminate both countries' stockpiles of chemical weapons. And in November, NATO and the Warsaw Pact adopted the most comprehensive treaty on conventional (non-nuclear) arms in history. There was also progress toward a new agreement on long-range nuclear weapons.

Confirming the events of the year, leaders of the United States, Canada, and 32 European countries signed a historic agreement in Paris in November. Called the Charter of Paris for a New Europe, it proclaimed the end of the "era of confrontation" that followed World War II. And for his role in the events, Gorbachev was awarded the 1990 Nobel Peace Prize. But his country's problems remained severe, and this cast a shadow on the prospects for international peace.

NATO and the Warsaw Pact ended their long conflict. The Warsaw Pact even destroyed some of its tanks.

Symbol of the times: A Rumanian official sits on a toppled statue of Lenin—the "father of Communism."

CHANGES IN EASTERN EUROPE

In the former Soviet-bloc countries of Eastern Europe, where people had long suffered under Communism, change continued in 1990:

Poland. In 1989, Poland's Communist government had agreed to share power with Solidarity, the independent labor union that long opposed Communism. And in 1990, the new Solidarity-led government began a program of "shock therapy" for the country's ailing economy. But while shortages of food and other essential items eased, prices and unemployment rose sharply.

In September, President Wojciech Jaruzelski—the last Communist in the government—said he would step down. A presidential election was held in December, and the winner was Solidarity leader Lech Walesa, who had won the 1983 Nobel Peace Prize for his opposition to Communism.

Czechoslovakia. Czechoslovakia's first free elections since 1946 were held in June, and a coalition of citizens' groups won a majority in parliament. The coalition supported Vaclav Havel, who had led the peaceful revolution against Communism in 1989. Havel had been named interim president, and in July, 1990, the new parliament formally elected him to a two-year term. The government then began to deal with the problems left by years of Communism. But there was disagreement about how quickly reform should come. And friction developed between the country's two main ethnic groups, the Czechs and the Slovaks.

Hungary. Hungary, which declared itself a republic in 1989, also held parliamentary elections in 1990. Six different parties fielded candidates in the April vote. A conservative coalition led by the Hungarian Democratic Forum won the most seats; its leader, Jozsef Antall, became premier. In May, parliament elected Arpad Goncz, a writer and leading opponent of Communism, as president.

Hungary's economy was among the most promising in Eastern Europe. But here, too, rising prices and unemployment led to growing dissatisfaction.

Rumania. In 1989, Rumania was the scene of a violent revolution in which Communist dictator Nicolae Ceauşescu was overthrown and executed. The new government, led by Ion Iliescu, included many former Communists. Iliescu's party won a landslide victory in elections in May, 1990, but it was charged that the government had manipulated the results. And when anti-government protests broke out in Bucharest, the capital, Iliescu suppressed them with force. The government later admitted it was using members of Ceauşescu's secret police to keep order. These incidents led Western nations to deny Rumania economic aid.

Bulgaria. In multiparty parliamentary elections in June, Bulgaria's Communist party—renamed the Bulgarian Socialist Party—won the most seats. Bulgaria thus became the only Eastern European country in which Communists won a free election. But in July, anti-government demonstrations forced President Petar Mladenov to resign. Parliament chose Zhelyu Zhelev president—the first non-Communist president in about 40 years. Meanwhile, there was new friction between Bulgarians and ethnic Turks. And the country's economy worsened to such an extent that, in November, Prime Minister Andrei Lukanov was also forced to resign.

October 3, 1990: Germany is one nation again and jubilant crowds gather at the Brandenburg Gate—long a symbol of the division of East and West Berlin.

GERMANY: A COUNTRY REUNITED

At 12:01 A.M. on October 3, 1990, after 45 years of separation, East Germany and West Germany were reunited. It was the climax of a series of dramatic events that brought the two Germanys, divided at the end of World War II, together at last.

Just a year earlier, few people would have imagined that the reunification of Germany was likely. But in 1989, change began to shake the Communist countries of Eastern Europe—including East Germany. Repressive Communist governments buckled to pressure for reform and democracy. It was this sweeping movement that, eventually, made German reunification possible.

The new Germany seemed likely to be one of the most important countries in Europe—and the world. Yet, after years of life under opposing political and economic systems, Germans faced some difficult adjustments.

A DIVIDED GERMANY

Compared to other European countries, the German nation was formed late in his-

tory. In 1871, a group of separate German states was unified by force by Otto von Bismarck, chancellor to the Prussian ruler William I. Germany quickly became one of Europe's strongest powers. Germany's ambitions eventually led to World War I (1914–18), in which it was defeated by Britain, France, and the United States.

The harsh peace terms exacted from Germany at the end of World War I hurt the country's economy and made many Germans resentful. This contributed to the rise of the Nazi dictator Adolf Hitler in the 1930's. During World War II, Hitler's armies overran most of Europe. The Nazis were notorious not only for their aggression but for their brutality and the atrocities they committed. During the war years, they killed some six million Jews, along with thousands of Gypsies and other minorities.

In 1945, Hitler was defeated by the chief Allied Powers: Britain, France, the Soviet Union, and the United States. War-torn and devastated by heavy bombing, Germany was divided into four occupation zones. The Soviets controlled the easternmost zone, and the other Allies controlled zones in the west.

Tensions soon developed between the Allies. As a Communist country, the Soviet Union had little in common with the Western allies. The Soviets were dedicated to the spread of Communism, while the three other powers hoped to see democracy flourish in Germany. This split marked the beginning of the Cold War, which would dominate world events for many years.

As a result of these tensions, there was no peace conference at the end of the war. Cooperation between the Allies ended completely in 1948, and the question of Germany's future remained unsettled. As they had elsewhere in Eastern Europe, the Soviets set up a Communist state in East Germany (the German Democratic Republic) in 1949. Meanwhile, the three western zones were combined to form West Germany (the Federal Republic of Germany).

Under a democratic government and with economic help from Western countries, West Germany began to recover from the devastating effects of the war. It developed a healthy, booming economy based on free markets and private enterprise. In the 1950's, it strengthened its ties to other Western countries by joining the North Atlantic Treaty Organization (NATO) and the European Economic Community (Common Market).

East Germany remained linked to the Soviet Union, joining the Warsaw Pact and Communist economic groups. Its government controlled the economy and most aspects of life. Recovery from the war was slow. And after Soviet forces crushed a revolt in East Germany in 1953, the system became even more tightly controlled.

Faced with a life of drabness and repression, many East Germans left for the West. By 1961 they were leaving at the rate of 1,000 a day, and East Germany had developed a serious labor shortage. The East German government abruptly decided to stop the flood by sealing its entire border with West Germany. Barbed wire was strung along the border, and machine-gun-carrying soldiers patrolled it. On each side, Germans were cut off from friends and family.

THE BEGINNING OF CHANGE

For the next 28 years, divided Germany remained a symbol of the tensions of the Cold War. But slowly, change began to come to the Communist world. It started in the Soviet Union, which took small steps toward greater democracy and economic freedom in the late 1980's. Soon it became clear that the Soviets would no longer enforce the Communist rule of Eastern Europe with armed force. In country after country of Eastern Europe, demonstrators demanded freedom. And in country after country, they won it.

East Germany's Communist rulers remained firmly opposed to change. But in mid-1989, thousands of East Germans began to escape to the West through Hungary, which had relaxed its border controls. And East Germans who stayed behind took to the streets in huge protests. In October, East German leader Erich Honecker was forced to resign, along with most of his government.

And then something else remarkable happened: On November 9, East Germany opened its border with West Germany. Soon it was clear that the Communist rule of East Germany had collapsed. And the reunification of Germany, which had seemed so distant only months before, suddenly seemed inevitable.

At first people thought that reunification would take many years to achieve. But several factors forced the pace to quicken. After years of failed Communist policies, the East German economy was near collapse. And East Germans were pouring into West Germany in huge numbers. West Germany was hard pressed to provide them with housing, jobs, and social services. Maybe faster reunification would end the flood of refugees and help the East German economy.

But reunification raised complicated questions. In East Germany, changing to a market economy would mean that many inefficient, state-run businesses would close, bringing widespread unemployment. Government workers, too—including members of East Germany's infamous secret police—would be out of work.

There were questions that involved other countries as well. Some of Germany's neighbors, especially Poland, feared that a united Germany might try to reclaim territory it had lost in the war. And while relations between the Soviet Union and the West were improving, there were still tensions. Soviet troops were stationed in East Germany, and NATO forces were stationed in West Germany. The United States and other Western powers

East German children eagerly examine West German toys. There were great differences in the quality of the goods produced in the two countries.

Then, on July 16, the Soviet Union dropped its objection to German membership in NATO. In an agreement negotiated by West German Chancellor Helmut Kohl and Soviet President Mikhail Gorbachev, the Soviets also agreed to withdraw their troops from Germany over a three- to four-year period. In exchange, Kohl agreed that Germany would help pay for the withdrawal, would limit its own troop strength, and wouldn't allow NATO troops or nuclear weapons in what had been East Germany.

The last hurdle to full unification had been cleared. On September 12, the World War II Allies and the two Germanys signed a peace treaty that would restore sovereignty to a future united Germany. And on October 3, West Germany and East Germany at last joined to form a single nation.

AFTER UNIFICATION

Helmut Kohl was named the first chancellor of the new Germany. And on December 2, 1990, Kohl won the first free all-German elections in 58 years. His government, and all Germans, faced a future that was bright but far from trouble-free.

West Germany had developed one of the strongest economies in the world. But East Germany's roads, railroads, and telephone system needed rebuilding. Banks had to be compensated for the currency exchange. Huge amounts would have to be paid in unemployment and other social benefits for East Germans who were thrown out of work by the switch to a market economy. These and other costs of unification, such as paying for Soviet troop withdrawals, were expected to be well over $200 billion—a staggering sum.

There were social problems, too. East Germans feared that they would be treated as second-class citizens. West Germans worried that East Germans, already working for low wages, would take their jobs. Some West Germans complained that East Germans were too used to being taken care of by the state and were unwilling to work hard. East Germans complained that West Germans were cold and cared only for material things.

Most people agreed that Germany would be able to put these problems behind it and that, when it did, it would be one of the most important countries in Europe. In fact, some

said that Germany should decide whether to remain in NATO (which meant that it probably would remain). The Soviets wanted a united Germany to be neutral.

In February, the two Germanys and representatives of the four World War II Allies met in Ottawa, Canada, and agreed on a framework for reunification. First, East and West Germany would agree on the domestic aspects. Then they would meet with the Allies to settle the international questions.

As this "two-plus-four" process got under way, events moved forward with dizzying speed. East Germany's first free elections were held in March, and a coalition led by the Christian Democratic Union swept the vote. Since the Christian Democrats were also in power in West Germany, this helped smooth the path to unification. Both Germanys soon agreed to honor the postwar border with Poland. And on July 1, they officially merged their economies. East Germans were able to exchange their nearly worthless currency for West German marks.

BERLIN—AGAIN THE CAPITAL

As the two Germanys united in 1990, no city had greater reason to celebrate than Berlin—because no city had suffered more during Germany's troubled years.

Before World War II, Berlin was Germany's capital and one of Europe's most famous cities, known for its beautiful boulevards and buildings and for its sophistication. But the city suffered terribly in the closing days of the war, when bombing reduced wide sections to rubble.

When the Allied Powers divided Germany into occupation zones after the war, Berlin (which was in the Soviet sector) was also divided into four zones, with the Soviets controlling East Berlin. Then, in June, 1948, the Soviets attempted to force the Western allies out of West Berlin. All land routes into the city were blocked by Soviet troops. For eleven months, the Western allies flew food and other supplies to the city in a massive airlift.

Eventually, the Soviets backed down. But Berlin's troubles were far from over. When East Germany closed its border with West Germany in 1961, the East Germans built a towering concrete wall that divided Berlin in two. People were allowed to cross only at tightly controlled checkpoints, and few were let through. The Berlin Wall became a stage for heroism and tragedy as determined East Germans tried to escape to freedom in the West. Many succeeded. But many others didn't, and some were killed in the attempt.

To most of the world, the Berlin Wall was a symbol of Communist repression. U.S. President John F. Kennedy expressed the feeling of the free world when he visited West Berlin soon after the wall was built and announced, "I am a Berliner." Even when tensions between East and West eased in the 1970's, the Wall stood as a grim reminder of the deep opposition between the two sides.

There matters stood until 1989, when Berlin, along with the rest of East Germany, became caught up in the changes that were sweeping through the Communist world. On the night of November 9, a rumor spread through the city: the East German government had opened its borders

Westerners went East and Easterners went West, and everyone found out what was behind the Berlin Wall.

with the West. East Berliners went to the Wall to see if the rumor was true—and found that it was.

Once again, Berliners could move freely through their city. Within days, thousands were pouring back and forth, and East German troops had begun to tear down the infamous 29-mile (47-kilometer) wall. The parts that remained became the scene of joyful celebrations. Gradually, subway lines and other links between the two parts of the city were reopened.

With reunification, Berlin once again became the capital of Germany. The city's Reichstag building became the seat of Parliament, as it had been before the country was divided. And as united Germany's black, red, and gold flag was raised at the Reichstag just after midnight on October 3, bells pealed and fireworks exploded in the night sky. Berliners all over the city celebrated the end of their long ordeal.

people feared that Germany would dominate Europe. They looked to the past—to the Germany of World Wars I and II.

But people who looked to the future saw that a united and democratic Germany, with close ties to other European countries, could be a valuable member of the world community. Thus, as Germans celebrated on October 3, people around the world wished them well.

Workers remove a sign from Silverado Banking, a savings and loan association in Denver, Colorado. The Silverado was one of many S&L's that have recently failed, costing the government billions of dollars.

A TROUBLED ECONOMY

After nearly a decade of good times, the United States economy faced a swarm of troubles in 1990. These ranged from a growing number of personal and business bankruptcies to failing banks and massive federal budget deficits. Added to these problems was the fact that after years of growth, the economy as a whole was slowing down.

Many people believed that the country was entering a recession—a period in which the output of goods and services declines and unemployment rises. Signs of recession were cropping up everywhere. In many areas, jobs were hard to find, and wages weren't increasing. Real estate prices, which rose during the 1980's, were flat or falling in many places.

In fact, although the U.S. economy as a whole grew at a slow rate during 1990, about a third of the states were said to be in or near a recession. And the economic problems that made headlines in 1990 helped raise fears of a country-wide recession.

BANKRUPTCIES

During the early 1980's, many people began to increase their debts. They took out mortgage loans to buy homes and consumer loans to buy cars and other expensive items. For some people, making the payments on these loans became a heavy burden. This was especially so as the economy began to slow down. Some people found that their earnings didn't increase as much as they had expected. Others lost their jobs and could no longer meet the payments on their loans.

A growing number of people solved this problem by declaring bankruptcy. In bankruptcy proceedings, a court takes over a person's finances and determines how his or her debts will be paid. There are several forms of bankruptcy, but usually assets such as a home are sold to pay the debts. In the 1980's, the rate of personal bankruptcies was twice what it had been in the 1970's and almost four times what it had been in the 1930's, when the United States was in the grip of the Great Depression. Many people expected that if the economy continued to slow, the rate would increase still more.

Business bankruptcies were also on the rise. Like individuals, many businesses had gone on a borrowing binge in the 1980's. Some borrowed huge sums to take over other companies and then found that they couldn't earn enough to pay the debt. One example was the Campeau Corporation of Canada, which piled up some $7.5 billion in debts as it bought major department store chains throughout the United States. The stores included some of the best-known and most successful in the country—Bloomingdale's, Jordan Marsh, Burdines, and Bon Marche. But although they were profitable, the stores couldn't bring in enough to pay Campeau's debts. In early 1990, Campeau declared bankruptcy, and tried to sell some of the stores.

THE SAVINGS AND LOAN CRISIS

The financial problems of businesses and individuals seemed almost pale beside those of the U.S. savings and loan associations (S&L's). S&L's are banks that traditionally have concentrated on offering interest-bearing savings accounts and mortgage loans. After the Great Depression, when many banks failed and people lost their savings, the U.S. government set up an insurance system to guarantee deposits in S&L's. At the same time, new regulations were imposed on them.

In the early 1980's, however, many of the federal regulations were lifted. The idea was that with less regulation, S&L's would be better able to compete with commercial banks. They could pay higher interest, offer more services, and make a broader range of loans. At the same time, the government raised its limit on deposit insurance from $40,000 to $100,000 per deposit.

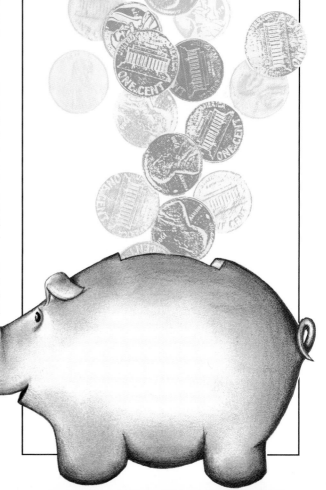

BEN FRANKLIN'S GIFT

"A penny saved is a penny earned," Benjamin Franklin wrote in *Poor Richard's Almanack*. Franklin took his own advice, too. And in 1990, the states of Massachussetts and Pennsylvania, and the cities of Boston and Philadelphia, benefited from his thriftiness.

Franklin, who died in 1790, set aside the sum of 2,000 pounds sterling for the two cities and their respective states in his will. The money, worth about $1 million in today's terms, was to be used to help young apprentices such as he had once been get started in their trades. The catch was that most of the money couldn't be touched for 100 years, and the rest for 200 years. Over all that time, the money earned interest. And in 1990, the remaining bequest was worth $6.5 million.

Franklin's will didn't require that the final sums be spent as he wished, and there were lots of ideas about how it might be used. But, with the United States facing growing economic problems two hundred years after Franklin's death, his gift delivered a sharp lesson on the value of saving money.

While most S&L's remained profitable, many quickly got into trouble by using their guaranteed deposits to invest in risky deals. Then, when the risky loans went bad, they didn't have enough money in reserve to cover their losses. Besides mismanagement, there were also cases of fraud on the part of bank officials.

The trouble surfaced first in the Southwest, where real estate values fell in the mid-1980's. But by the late 1980's it was clear that S&L's in many parts of the country were failing. The government stepped in, taking over failing banks, selling their assets, and paying up their insured deposits. Officials estimated that more than 1,000 S&L's, 40 percent of the total number, might eventually fail and that the cost of bailing them out might rise to the staggering sum of $500 billion—$5,000 for every U.S. household. Meanwhile, tighter regulations were imposed on the S&L's that were continuing to operate.

THE FEDERAL BUDGET

Like individuals and businesses, the federal government borrowed heavily during the 1980's. But the *national debt* dwarfed any private debt—by the mid-1980's, it had soared over $2 *trillion* and was still growing.

The government got into debt the same way that people do—by spending more money than it took in. Each year the government takes in money from taxes and other revenues and spends it on programs that range from defense to school lunch subsidies. When revenues are less than the spending called for in the government's budget, it borrows the difference. This yearly amount is called the *budget deficit.*

In the 1980's, under President Ronald Reagan, the United States increased spending on defense. Rather than raising taxes to cover the spending, Reagan sought to cut spending on domestic programs. But the government was never able to cut enough from these programs, which altogether account for only a small part of the budget. Deficits continued to mount. And as they did, the government was forced to spend more just to pay the interest on its loans.

In 1985, Congress passed a law requiring the government to set goals and gradually reduce the yearly budget deficits. By 1993, the yearly deficit would be eliminated and the budget would be balanced. (Even then, however, the $2 trillion national debt would still exist.)

If these goals weren't met, the budget-deficit law required spending to be cut automatically from both military and domestic programs. The government managed to meet the goal each year until 1990. But it did so largely through accounting procedures, such as putting certain programs "off budget" so that they didn't show up in the figures, and by selling federal assets.

In 1989, a remarkable event—the collapse of Communism—raised hope for the budget deficit. People thought that, with Communism no longer a threat, the United States might be able to cut military spending. The money taken from defense, nicknamed the "peace dividend," could be used to reduce the deficit and perhaps to restore some of the social programs that had been crippled by spending cuts.

But in 1990, a series of events changed the picture. It became clear that the government would need much more money than had been thought for the savings and loan crisis. Hopes for big defense cuts were dashed when the United States mounted a huge and expensive military operation in the Middle East, to counter the Iraqi invasion of Kuwait. The Middle East crisis also raised the price of oil. That made a recession more likely—businesses and individuals would have to spend more on energy and would thus spend less on other things. And in a recession, the government's revenues were likely to be lower.

President George Bush had campaigned in 1988 on a pledge of "no new taxes." In 1990, however, he conceded that revenues might have to be increased—instead of the $64 billion-deficit allowed by the deficit-reduction law, the deficit was expected to be more than $290 billion.

After much debate, Congress and the Bush administration agreed to cut spending on a range of programs and raised taxes on gasoline, tobacco, alcoholic beverages, luxury purchases, and certain other items. They also increased taxes on incomes over $100,000. This plan was supposed to reduce the deficit by $43 billion its first year and by nearly $500 billion over five years.

South Africa took some steps toward ending its system of apartheid in 1990. In January, Nelson Mandela, a leader of black resistance, was released after 27 years of imprisonment. He toured the United States (*above*) and Canada in June and was met by huge, cheering crowds.

AROUND THE WORLD

Dramatic changes in southern Africa and Central America made the headlines in 1990. Here is a roundup of those and other events around the world.

SOUTH AFRICA

South Africa took encouraging steps in 1990 toward ending the system of white minority rule that has long held sway there. But at the same time, the country was torn by violence.

Whites have dominated South Africa since colonial times, in the 1700's. In 1948, the National Party came to power and began to establish a rigid system of racial discrimination called apartheid. Under this system, blacks had no political power. Housing, education, employment, and all aspects of life were strictly segregated. For blacks, the results were poverty, poor education and social services, and lack of opportunity.

For years, black protests against these policies were suppressed, often brutally. Black groups were outlawed, and individuals were jailed. With no political voice, some turned to violence and guerrilla tactics.

In recent years, however, the international outcry against apartheid has grown. Many countries restricted trade with South Africa and imposed other economic sanctions in an effort to pressure the government into changing its policies. Although South Africa eased some of the restrictions of apartheid, the basic policy remained. But finally, the government began to move toward reform.

In February, 1990, several banned black

Namibia, Africa's last colony, became independent in March. It had been ruled by South Africa for 70 years.

political organizations, including the African National Congress (ANC), were legalized. Then, on February 11, ANC leader Nelson Mandela was released from 27 years of imprisonment. Mandela's forceful personality and refusal to compromise with the government had made him a symbol of black resistance, and his release was hailed as a sign of progress.

The government and the ANC began talks aimed at finding a way to change South Africa's constitution and grant political power to blacks. The government agreed to the principle that every person, black or white, should have an equal vote in elections. But it wanted safeguards to protect minority rights in whatever new political system was

developed. As the talks continued, the ANC announced that, as a sign of good will, it would suspend the guerrilla operations it had mounted against the government in the past.

Both Mandela and South African President F. W. de Klerk visited North America later in the year. In June, Mandela was cheered by huge crowds of supporters during a tour of the United States and Canada. In September, De Klerk became the first South African president to be received at the White House since World War II.

But South Africa's progress was clouded by divisions among both whites and blacks. Conservative whites were alarmed by talk of reform, and some said that they would fight to keep their position in society.

Violence between blacks complicated the picture, too. The causes of the violence were complex and unclear. Early in the year, fighting between black groups was most severe in Natal province, in the southeast. Many people there were Zulus (South Africa's largest ethnic group) and members of Inkatha, a conservative political organization. They clashed with members of the ANC, who included many Xhosas and members of other ethnic groups. The struggle between the two factions wasn't new. From 1987 through mid-1990, some 5,000 people lost their lives in these conflicts.

As 1990 went on, however, the violence among blacks spread to other areas. In Soweto, the sprawling black township outside the city of Johannesburg, some 800 people were killed between early August and mid-September. And the violence took a new turn: Bands of armed blacks attacked other blacks randomly, with no clear reason.

The ANC charged that a mysterious "hidden hand"—perhaps a conservative white group—was fanning the flames of violence in the hope of blocking reform. The government promised to do more to control the violence and to find the causes behind it. But it seemed that South Africa's road to reform would be long and difficult.

NAMIBIA

Africa's last colony, Namibia, gained independence on March 21, 1990. South Africa had ruled this territory (also known as South-West Africa) since the end of World

War I. For the last 23 years of that time, the United Nations had called repeatedly for Namibia's independence. And a rebel group, the South-West African People's Organization (SWAPO) had waged a guerrilla war against the South Africans.

Independence finally came through an agreement reached in 1988 with the help of the United States. Under the agreement, a U.N.-supervised cease-fire was declared and troops were withdrawn. Late in 1989, Namibians elected an assembly that developed a new constitution.

SWAPO won 57 percent of that vote. And on independence day—as Namibia's blue, red, green, white, and gold flag was raised at a ceremony in Windhoek, the capital— SWAPO leader Sam Nujoma became the country's first president.

SWAPO had long advocated a socialist state, in which the government would run the economy. But the new country's constitution, worked out in negotiations with other groups, set up a Western-style democracy. And after independence, Nujoma called for private investment in addition to government economic controls. The new government felt that this would best help Namibia become economically, as well as politically, independent.

LIBERIA

Through most of 1990, a civil war raged in Liberia, a West African country that has a long history of ties to the United States. Liberia was founded in 1847 by freed slaves from the United States. Their descendants governed the country until 1980, when Samuel K. Doe, a master sergeant in the Liberian National Guard, took control of the government. Doe's rule was marked by human rights abuses, and tensions between Liberia's sixteen different ethnic groups mounted during the 1980's.

The war broke out late in 1989, when rebel leader Charles Taylor launched an attempt to overthrow President Doe. The fighting soon became widespread. Government troops killed civilian members of tribal groups that were thought to support the rebels, and rebels killed members of tribal groups that supported the government.

By August, about 5,000 people, mostly

Newspapers roll off the press in Nicaragua, announcing that Violeta Barrios de Chamorro won the presidency.

civilians, had died. They included hundreds of refugees who had taken shelter in a church. Taylor's rebels controlled most of the countryside. The capital and chief port, Monrovia, was held partly by Doe and partly by another rebel group, led by Prince Johnson, which had broken with the main rebel force.

On August 5, U.S. Marines were flown into Liberia and began to evacuate American and other foreign citizens after rebels threatened to take foreign hostages. Soon after, West African nations sent a peacekeeping force to Liberia. But the force was unable to stop the fighting, and in September President Doe was captured and killed by Johnson. Doe's supporters went on a rampage after his death, killing civilians and burning buildings in Monrovia. With other forces closing in around them, however, it seemed unlikely that they could hold out for long.

Late in November, Johnson, Taylor, and Doe's supporters agreed to a cease-fire. There were hopes that negotiations between the three factions would soon begin. But at year's end, the outlook for peace remained unclear.

NICARAGUA

In a vote that took many people by surprise, opposition groups in Nicaragua won a landslide victory over the leftist Sandinista government in national elections on February 25. Two months later, Violeta Barrios de Chamorro took office as president of the Central American country, replacing Sandinista leader Daniel Ortega Saavedra.

The vote seemed to end a long and troubled period of Nicaraguan history. The Sandinistas had come to power in 1979, after a civil war in which Nicaraguan dictator Anastasio Somoza Debayle was overthrown. Many moderates supported them at first. In fact, Chamorro had been part of the first Sandinista government. But as the Sandinistas moved to silence dissent and impose socialist policies, they lost that support. They were also accused of supplying arms to leftist rebels in neighboring El Salvador.

In the early 1980's, the United States began to support a group of Nicaraguan rebels known as the contras. It also imposed economic sanctions on Nicaragua. These policies were controversial, and Congress halted military aid to the contras in 1988. But fighting continued. And meanwhile, failed government policies and the U.S. sanctions devastated the Nicaraguan economy.

Finally, the Sandinistas agreed to hold free elections. The 1990 vote was supervised by a team of international observers that included former U.S. president Jimmy Carter. Chamorro's coalition, an alliance of opposition groups that ranged from moderates to Communists to former supporters of Somoza, won 55 percent of the vote. The Sandinistas received 41 percent.

The United States lifted its economic sanctions and began to send aid. The contras agreed to lay down their arms and disband.

But the new president had her work cut out for her. Recognizing that the Sandinistas still had support in the country, she retained some officials of the old government, including the chief of the army. This caused some people to worry that the Sandinistas might try to regain power by force.

The Sandinistas were also accused of stirring up unrest and organizing a series of strikes and demonstrations that plagued the new government in its first months. They remained firmly opposed to some of Chamorro's policies, such as returning to private ownership land and businesses that had been taken over by the government during their years in power.

But with Communism and socialism giving way to democracy in many parts of the world, there were also signs that the Sandinistas were rethinking their past policies. Thus there was hope for a less troubled future in Nicaragua.

CAMBODIA

After two decades of conflict, the factions in Cambodia's civil war agreed to a United Nations peace plan in September, 1990. While many details remained to be worked out, the agreement was seen as a hopeful sign.

Cambodia's long conflict began in the early 1970's, when the country was torn by fighting between the U.S.-backed government and the Khmer Rouge, a Communist guerrilla group. The war was part of a regional conflict that included the Vietnam War. After the United States withdrew its troops from the region in 1975, the Communists came to power.

In Cambodia, the Khmer Rouge ruled brutally. People were forced to resettle on collective farms, and more than a million died of starvation or disease or were executed by the government. Many Cambodians fled to refugee camps in neighboring Thailand. Then, in 1979, the Khmer Rouge were driven from power by the Vietnamese, who invaded Cambodia. The Vietnamese set up a new government, while the Khmer Rouge began to fight a guerrilla war from bases along the Thai border. They soon formed a coalition with two non-Communist Cambodian opposition groups.

Khmer Rouge guerrillas sit on a pile of artillery shells at a base near the Cambodian–Thai border. The Khmer Rouge, who brutally ruled Cambodia in the late 1970's, are one of several factions involved in that country's long civil war.

In 1989, Vietnam announced that it was withdrawing its troops from Cambodia (some Vietnamese military advisers remained, however). Fighting intensified, and there were fears that the Khmer Rouge might return to power. In 1990, the Khmer Rouge began to move refugees from Thailand into sections of Cambodia that they controlled. In these "liberation zones," the people had little food, shelter, or medical care and were at risk from malaria and other diseases.

But meanwhile, there were new international pressures for a solution. China, which had long supported the Khmer Rouge, called for a United Nations settlement. The Soviet Union, which had supported the government installed by Vietnam, also favored a settlement. And the United States, which had backed the two non-Communist opposition groups that were allied with the Khmer Rouge, changed its policy. For years the United States had recognized the opposition as Cambodia's rightful government. But in July, 1990, it ended that recognition.

These developments helped lead to the U.N. peace plan that was accepted in September. Under the plan, a council made up of members of the Cambodian government and the three opposition groups would govern the country under U.N. supervision until free elections could be held. A U.N. peacekeeping force would organize a cease-fire and the elections.

Further details were to be worked out in negotiations that were scheduled to begin in Paris later in the year. While much remained to be done, there was hope that Cambodia might finally have peace.

ELAINE PASCOE
Author, *South Africa: Troubled Land*

NEWSMAKERS

Former U.S president **Jimmy Carter**, who served from 1977 to 1981, continued to make headlines in 1990. Since leaving office, Carter, 66, has been far from idle. He has helped build homes for the homeless (*left*), promoted agricultural and health-care reforms in developing countries, and acted as a mediator in international disputes and human rights cases. He has also served as an independent observer to guarantee the fairness of elections in several countries, including the 1990 elections in Nicaragua.

When **L. Douglas Wilder** was sworn in as governor of Virginia in January, 1990, he became the first black elected chief executive of a state. Wilder, 58, brought 20 years of government service to the job, having been both a state senator and lieutenant governor. As a moderate who appealed to blacks and whites alike, he was also being mentioned as a possible Democratic vice-presidential candidate in 1992.

John Major succeeded Margaret Thatcher as prime minister of Britain and leader of the ruling Conservative Party in November. Major, 47, had an unusual background for a British political leader: He had quit school at 16 and worked as an office clerk, laborer, and bus conductor before entering banking and then politics. As Thatcher's protegé, Major rose rapidly through Conservative Party ranks during the 1980's. He was expected to continue many of her policies.

In the closing days of 1989, as Communism collapsed in Eastern Europe, **Vaclav Havel** was chosen president of Czechoslovakia. For more than 20 years, Havel, a playwright and philosopher, had been one of the leading opponents of the Czechoslovakian Communist government. He had been jailed three times but had steadfastly refused to keep silent or flee to safety in the West. His courage in helping to lead Czechoslovakia to freedom won him admiration around the world.

"This is the dawn of a new republic," **Violeta Barrios de Chamorro** declared as she was sworn in as president of Nicaragua in April, 1990. In February elections, Chamorro's UNO coalition had defeated the Sandinistas, the leftist party that had held power for over a decade. Chamorro, 60, had once been part of the Sandinista movement. Her husband, a journalist and a leading opponent of the Nicaraguan dictator Anastasio Somoza Debayle, was assassinated in 1978, and that event helped spark the uprising that brought the Sandinistas to power. But Chamorro broke with the Sandinistas as their policies became more restrictive.

Rose Fitzgerald Kennedy, the head of one of America's leading political families, turned 100 on July 22, 1990. Her nine children included President John F. Kennedy and Senator Robert Kennedy, both of whom were assassinated. She is also the mother of Senator Edward M. Kennedy, shown with her below in an earlier photo.

Justice **William J. Brennan, Jr.,** retired from the U.S. Supreme Court in 1990. Brennan, 84, had served for nearly 34 years. He was known as one of the Court's leading liberals and a steadfast defender of individual liberties. Brennan wrote many decisions supporting free speech, equal rights, and the right to privacy. In recent years, as the Court became more conservative, he had often dissented from its rulings.

David H. Souter, 51, replaced Brennan on the Supreme Court. Souter, who was sworn in in October, had served as attorney general and a state judge in New Hampshire and had recently been appointed to the federal bench. Little was known about his views on some hotly debated issues, such as abortion, that are expected to come before the Court. But he was expected to reinforce the Court's conservative trend.

ANIMALS

The trumpetfish below is an underwater hitchhiker. It is catching a ride through a tropical reef on the back of a Spanish hogfish. The trumpetfish isn't being lazy— swimming with another fish lets it sneak up on its prey. Relationships between different animals are common in nature, and they help animals survive.

SAVE THE ELEPHANTS

A huge form takes shape in the dim light of an African dawn: an elephant, slowly moving toward the bank of a river. Cautiously, the great beast lifts its trunk and sniffs the air for danger. Then it rumbles a signal, and other elephants appear on the riverbank. Soon all are drinking and bathing contentedly—snorting, rolling in the mud, and playfully squirting water over themselves.

Standing about 10 feet (3 meters) tall and weighing as much as 6 tons, elephants are the largest land animals. They are famous for their intelligence as well as for their size and strength. People have long admired them—in the 1600's, the English poet John Donne called the elephant "Nature's great masterpiece" and "the only harmless great thing." Yet today these magnificent animals are in danger of disappearing forever.

Part of the threat comes from the growth of civilization: Much of the elephants' natural habitat has been taken over by people for use as farm and grazing land. Even more serious, however, is the widespread slaughter of elephants by hunters. Most of the animals are killed for one reason—their ivory tusks, which are valued for making jewelry and other items.

Now, however, people are taking action to save the elephants. The steps include new efforts to protect the animals from poachers and an international ban on ivory trade, which was adopted by many countries late in 1989.

A MAJESTIC ANIMAL

There are two kinds of elephants: African elephants, which live in parts of Africa south of the Sahara, and Asian elephants, which live in India, Sri Lanka, and Southeast Asia. And there are a number of differences between them.

African elephants are larger and have bigger ears and flatter heads than their Asian cousins, for example. The back of the Asian elephant is convex, or arched, while the African elephant has a dip behind the shoulders. And African bulls (males) and cows (females) both have well-developed tusks, which are actually enormous curving teeth. Asian bulls and cows have only short tusks, and many cows have none at all.

There are differences in temperament, too. Asian elephants have long been tamed by people and used as riding and work animals. In the past, they were used in battle. Today they are still used as work animals, mainly in logging—an elephant can drag two tons and lift 600 pounds (270 kilograms) with its trunk and tusks. And Asian elephants are the elephants you see in the circus. African elephants, on the other hand, are wilder and are rarely tamed.

Despite these differences, wild Asian and African elephants live in much the same way. Most elephants travel in herds of ten to fifty individuals, roaming over a wide area in search of plants to eat and water for drinking and bathing. The herd is made up mostly of cows and young elephants, or calves. Adult males generally travel alone, and when two meet, they may fight.

An elephant eats constantly, consuming as much as 500 pounds (225 kilograms) of food a day. The animals can strip bark from trees with their tusks and even uproot trees to get at the tasty green leaves. In this way, herds of elephants help keep the African plains open and free of brush. They also use their great tusks to dig open water holes. This is helpful to the other grasslands animals.

An elephant herd is led by an experienced cow. This cow and the other older females, or matriarchs, teach the younger ones how to find food and water, what migration routes to take, and other important elephant knowledge. Calves live with the group as long as fourteen years, learning these skills.

The members of the herd are usually related, and they form a closely knit group. Mothers make sure their babies keep up as the herd travels, using their trunks and heads to nudge the little ones along. Other cows act as elephant aunts, helping to look out for the calves. If a calf is attacked or injured, the herd will gather around to defend or help it. The concern that elephants show for others of their kind is one of the traits that has endeared them to people.

ELEPHANTS IN DANGER

While Asian elephants have been considered endangered animals since the early 1970's, concern for African elephants has grown recently. By some estimates, the number of African elephants was cut in half between 1979 and 1989, shrinking from nearly 1.3 million to about 625,000. At this rate, some people think, African elephants will be wiped out in another twenty years.

What's behind their dwindling numbers? In many areas of Africa, elephants range over land that's needed for agriculture. A herd of elephants moving through a farmer's fields can destroy crops in short order. Thus farmers see the animals as huge pests, and they shoot them or drive them away.

To protect the animals, many African countries have set aside reserves for elephants. By law, the animals may not be killed in the reserves. And the killing of animals that wander off the reserves is limited by law.

In most places, however, the elephant herds have shrunk dramatically in spite of the reserves and laws that are supposed to protect them. And the main reason is that poachers (illegal hunters) have continued to kill the animals for their ivory.

The poachers use military-style automatic weapons to kill the great beasts. They especially hunt the bulls, which have the biggest tusks. This affects the entire elephant population—as the number of bulls declines, the

Young elephants live with members of the herd for many years. They learn how to survive from the more mature females. Thus when the older elephants are slaughtered by hunters, the young elephants may never learn how to find food and water.

cows have fewer opportunities for mating, and so there are fewer calves.

When poachers can no longer find enough bulls, they turn their guns on the mature females in the herds. Often they mow down entire groups of elephants, young and old, simply to get the large tusks of the matriarchs. By some estimates, poachers kill about 200 African elephants a day.

When a herd is attacked by poachers, even the elephants that escape the bullets may not survive. When a mother elephant is killed, for example, her baby will starve or die of thirst before it will leave her side. And when the most mature and experienced matriarchs of a herd are killed, the younger elephants may never learn how to find good water holes and food sources.

The poachers have continued this slaughter because of the great demand for ivory. The tusks of a single elephant can bring more money than many Africans earn in a year. Most of the tusks are smuggled out of Africa to Hong Kong and other places in the Far East, where the demand is especially high. There the ivory is carved into all kinds of items, from sculpture and jewelry to buttons, dice, and piano keys.

Concern about the fate of the elephants caused a number of countries, including the United States, Canada, most Western European nations, and Japan, to halt imports of ivory in mid-1989. And later that year, 76 countries backed an agreement banning trade in ivory. At the same time, they named the African elephant an endangered species. The ban caused an immediate drop in the demand for ivory.

Some countries refused to go along with the ivory ban. These were mostly countries such as Zimbabwe and Botswana, where the elephants have been well protected. In fact, the animals are so well protected that the herds sometimes grow too large. Too many elephants damage the environment, stripping the land of vegetation and making food scarce for all animals. Then the government must "cull the herds"—kill some of the elephants—to protect the environment.

These countries aren't wealthy, and they would like to sell the ivory from their *legally* hunted elephants. But many people worry

Many elephants have been killed for their valuable ivory tusks, which are carved into jewelry, figurines, and other trinkets. A world ban on ivory trading in 1989 caused a huge decrease in the demand for carved ivory.

that the buyers of ivory won't bother to ask how it was obtained. Thus, they say, poaching and smuggling will continue as long as *any* trade in ivory is allowed.

The ivory ban is to last until 1992, when the countries involved will review it. Meanwhile, African countries are taking other steps to protect the elephants. They are stepping up patrols against poachers and cracking down on corrupt officials who have closed their eyes to ivory smuggling. Some are fencing off reserves in areas where elephants come in conflict with farmers. And wildlife groups are spreading the word about the dangers the animals face, urging people not to buy ivory items. Their hope is that the magnificent elephant can be saved.

WHAT AM I?

Here's an animal you're not likely to see —even if you travel to every zoo in the world! This peculiar-looking mystery creature has fur, feathers, scales, a tough hide, claws, and hooves, all at the same time. It has a big hump and two different pairs of wings on its back. Its four legs don't match, and its tail is enormous. And it has floppy ears, branching antlers, big eyes that bug out on top of its head, and a *very* strange nose.

All the same, when you begin to examine this curious creature more closely, it may look familiar—or, at least, parts of it will. Surely you've seen that hump somewhere before . . . and that funny-looking tongue must remind you of something. In fact, this odd creature is made up of parts of other animals, some of them exotic and some quite common. It could be the creation of a mad scientist—but it has really been put together as a game for you.

Can you identify the thirteen different animals that were used to make this mystery creature? Find each of the numbered parts, and see if you can guess what animal it comes from. (The answers are given below.)

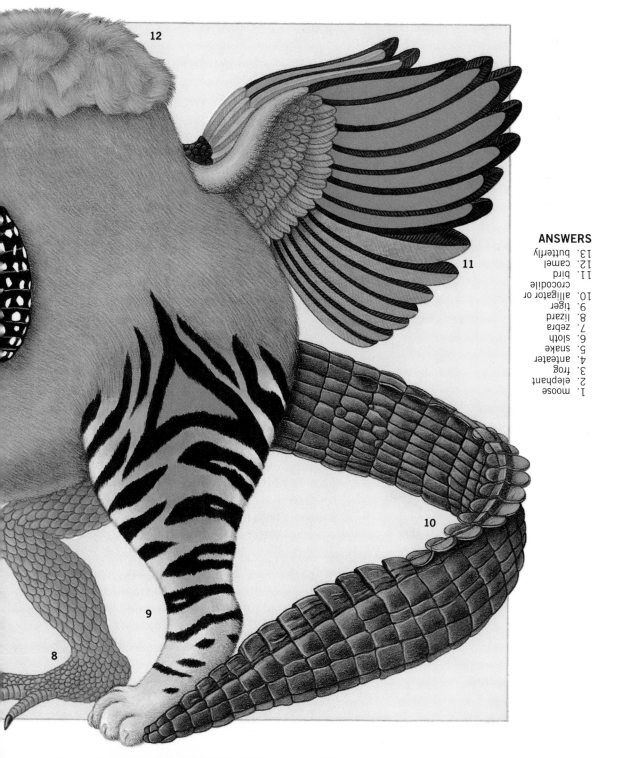

ANSWERS

1. moose
2. elephant
3. frog
4. anteater
5. snake
6. sloth
7. zebra
8. lizard
9. tiger
10. alligator or crocodile
11. bird
12. camel
13. butterfly

Clownfish and sea anemones are partners in a special relationship that benefits both animals. These partnerships are common in nature, and they help animals to survive.

ANIMAL PARTNERS

Sea anemones are animals that look like flowers, with dozens of brightly colored tentacles that wave about in the water. The tentacles deliver a deadly poisonous sting—and when an unfortunate fish blunders into them, it's usually killed and eaten by the anemone. But one fish is an exception to this rule: clownfish live right among the tentacles without being harmed.

Sea anemones and clownfish are partners in a relationship that benefits both animals. The clownfish cleans away debris from among the anemone's tentacles. And this debris is often food for the clownfish. In addition, the relationship gives the fish protection: Few predators will risk the anemone's sting to pursue them.

How does the clownfish avoid being

stung? Before it tries to swim among an anemone's tentacles, the clownfish will brush lightly against the anemone. It does this repeatedly, quickly swimming away each time. Scientists think that by doing this, the fish builds up an immunity to the anemone's poison. But the fish must remember which anemone to go back to—if it swims into the wrong one, it won't be immune.

The sea anemone and the clownfish are far from unique in their teamwork. Partnerships between two different kinds of animals are common in nature. They are called *symbiotic relationships*. And these partnerships help both animals to survive.

CLEANERS

Many animal partnerships, like that of the anemone and the clownfish, are based on the exchange of cleaning services for food and other benefits. And a great many of these relationships involve fish and other water

The little cleaner wrasse at right and the cleaner shrimp below aren't afraid of their big partners. They specialize in clearing away parasites and other debris from the larger fish—and they get a free meal in the process.

creatures. Most of these animals can't groom themselves the way cats, monkeys, and many other land animals do. They depend on other creatures to do it for them.

The cleaner wrasse is a specialist in this job. These small fish are brightly colored, which makes them easy to spot. They set up cleaning stations in the ocean and attract clients with a sort of dance, swimming head down and waving their bodies from side to side.

Larger fish line up at the cleaner wrasse station, each waiting for its turn to be cleaned. The cleaners' clients include many fish that are predators—but the cleaners themselves are rarely eaten. As the larger fish wait calmly, the little cleaners swim right into their mouths and gill cavities to clear away parasites, fungi, and debris, getting a free meal in the process.

Many other ocean creatures perform cleaning services. One of them is the remora, or suckerfish. This bold fish travels with the shark, one of the most feared ocean preda-

tors. The remora has a large sucker on top of its head with which it attaches itself firmly to the shark. (Some remoras attach themselves to other large ocean creatures, even whales.) As the shark swims along, the remora travels all over its body removing debris. It gets food and protection—and an occasional feast. Sharks are messy eaters, and when the shark feeds, the remora detaches itself and gobbles up the leftover bits.

An unusual animal partnership is that of the huge sperm whale and a small shore bird, the gray phalarope. The sperm whale is a mammal and must come to the surface to breathe. When it does, part of its huge body breaks the surface of the water for a few seconds. The little phalarope swoops down, lands on the whale's back, and quickly pecks up parasites before the whale dives again. Phalaropes normally live near the shores of Africa and Latin America. But they have been known to follow whales far out to sea.

One of the strangest partnerships involves the Nile crocodile and a bird called the

This remora is "stuck on" the shark. The bold fish has a large sucker on top of its head, which it uses to attach itself to the shark and travel around with it. The remora cleans debris from the shark's body and gets food and protection in return.

The cattle egret is often seen hopping around the feet of large animals such as rhinos. The grazing animal helps the egret catch its food, and the egret warns the large animal of danger.

Egyptian plover. The crocodile cruises the muddy waters of African rivers and lakes. As it does so, leeches and other pests fasten onto the soft tissues of its mouth. Bits of food become trapped between its teeth.

This reptile is also a fearsome predator, up to 12 feet (3.6 meters) long, with sharp teeth and huge, powerful jaws. Most animals keep a sharp lookout for the crocodile and avoid it. But when the Egyptian plover spots a crocodile sunning itself on a riverbank, with its jaws gaping wide open, the bird hops right into the croc's open mouth! Does the crocodile eat the bird? No. Instead of snapping up what would seem at first glance to be a free snack, the crocodile just lies there as the bird hops in its mouth and removes the leeches and debris, giving the croc a free tooth-cleaning. In return, the bird gets a meal. The bird also acts as a lookout for the crocodile as it naps on the riverbank. And for as long as the cleaning goes on, the bird has the protection of this powerful predator.

FEATHERED FRIENDS

Birds like the Egyptian plover are involved in partnerships with animals of many kinds. In the Mediterranean Sea, for example, several kinds of gulls get help with housecleaning chores from the common wall lizard.

The birds build their nests in crevices along the rocky shores of islands. Insect pests soon move in, troubling parent and young birds alike. But wall lizards clamber among the nests, eating the insects. The lizards are just the right size to make a meal for the gulls—but the birds ignore them as they go about their job.

Other birds work in partnership with grazing animals. One of the most familiar of these is the cattle egret. In Africa, this elegant white bird can be seen hopping around the feet of antelope, zebras, elephants, and other large animals. But it has expanded its range to the Americas, where it is often seen among herds of cattle.

The grazing animals help the egret catch its food—insects, especially grasshoppers. As the animals move through the grass, insects hiding there are disturbed and pop up into the air. The egret spots them and gobbles them up. In exchange, the egret warns the grazing herd of approaching dan-

79

Cleaning services, in return for food, are also provided by the oxpecker. This little bird spends almost its entire life riding around on the back of a large animal, feeding on the ticks that it finds there.

ger—by hopping up on an animal's back, calling, and flapping its wings. If the animal is slow to respond, the egret will even peck on its head to get its attention.

Egrets also perform some cleaning services for grazing animals, removing insect pests from their coats. But another bird—the oxpecker—is a specialist in this job. Oxpeckers live in Africa, where they spend almost their entire lives riding around on the backs of large animals, such as warthogs and buffalo. The birds sleep, sunbathe, and even mate on the animals' backs. Their main food consists of the ticks that they find there and remove. The birds leave their hosts only to nest or, briefly, if they are disturbed. Like cattle egrets, oxpeckers will warn their host animal of danger, drumming on its head to make it hurry away.

Cowbirds are native to North America, where they live with herds of cattle. Like cattle egrets, they keep the animals free of insect pests and feed on insects kicked up by the animals. Cowbirds once followed the great herds of bison that roamed across the North American plains. Because the herds were constantly on the move, the birds developed an unusual way of raising their young: Cowbirds lay their eggs in other birds' nests, leaving the job of hatching and raising the young to an unsuspecting stranger.

ALLIES IN DEFENSE

If you've seen films of animals grazing on the plains of Africa, you may have noticed that some kinds of animals seem to hang around together. Ostriches can often be spotted near herds of zebras. Around waterholes, impala often can be found with baboons. The animals may seem to be ignoring each other, but they are actually working together for mutual protection.

Zebras and ostriches, for example, help alert each other to the approach of predators. The ostrich has excellent eyesight, and its long neck helps it see far away. It may spot enemies before the zebra can. But the zebra has an excellent sense of smell. It may scent enemies before the ostrich can see them. By working together, the animals increase their chances of escaping.

The graceful impala is the favorite prey of

lions and many other fierce predators. Luckily, it's also one of the most alert of the African creatures, with sharp senses of sight, hearing, and smell. And its association with baboons helps both animals. When a lion begins to creep up on the animals at a waterhole, the impala alert the baboons. And the baboons are large and fierce enough to drive off most predators—including lions.

Many ocean animals also team up for defense. One of these partnerships involves certain crabs and sponges. The crab—called, appropriately, the sponge crab—looks around until it finds the right kind of sponge. Then the crab uses its claws to snip off a piece of the sponge. It puts the sponge on top of its shell, holding it there with its hind legs. The sponge grows along with the crab, until it covers the crab's shell completely. This hides the crab from predators.

The sponge isn't just along for the ride. Sponges are filter feeders—that is, they filter tiny particles of food from the water. As the crab moves along the ocean floor, water currents pass through the sponge and provide a constant supply of food.

Other crabs team up with anemones. The pom-pom crab, for example, carries anemones in its claws. If an enemy approaches, the crab stretches out its claws and threatens the attacker with an anemone sting. The anemones benefit because the crab carries them to new, richer feeding grounds—on their own, anemones can move only very slowly. The anemones also may be able to pick up some scraps from the crab's meals—crabs are messy eaters.

Hermit crabs also make use of the poisonous sting of anemones. These crabs adopt the abandoned shells of other sea creatures as their homes, and it's not uncommon to see a hermit crab scuttling around in a shell that's coverered with anemones. There may be as many as eight anemones traveling with a single crab! With friends like these, the hermit crab is safe from most predators, and the anemones get a free ride to fresh feeding grounds.

Many ocean animals team up for defense. The sponge crab carries a sponge on top of its shell. The sponge hides the crab from predators, and it gets a constant supply of food in return.

Some crabs have partnerships with anemones for defense. The pom-pom crab above carries anemones in its claws. The hermit crab at right blankets itself with an abandoned shell covered with anemones. In both cases, the slow-moving anemones catch free rides to new feeding grounds.

SWEET TEAMWORK

Some animal partnerships are formed to satisfy a craving for something sweet to eat. The best known of these is probably the relationship between ants and aphids.

Aphids are tiny insects that excrete a sweet, sticky substance called honeydew. You can sometimes see dried honeydew on plant leaves, glistening in the sun. Aphids suck the juices from the plants that they live on, so gardeners consider them to be pests. But ants love aphids—because ants love honeydew.

Several kinds of ants have developed ways of keeping herds of aphids, much as people keep herds of cows. They collect aphids and bring them to a plant near their nest, so that honeydew will always be handy. Whenever an ant wants honeydew, it "milks" an aphid by tapping or stroking it. This prompts the aphid to release the sweet substance. In exchange, the ants protect the aphids.

Some ants go even further. The ants of one species build small mud shelters for their aphids and herd them inside at night, protecting them from predators and harsh weather. Those of other species take their aphids into their own nests for the night. In the morning, the aphids are taken back outside to feed on plant juices.

Some kinds of ants have also developed

partnerships with other insects. In Australia, ants called meat ants wait for the eggs of the imperial blue butterfly to hatch. When the butterfly larvae crawl out, the ants follow them around and protect them, using vicious bites to fight off predators. At first the ants receive nothing in return. But as the larvae grow into larger caterpillars, they begin to produce honeydew. Then the ants can milk them just as they milk aphids.

When the time comes for a caterpillar to change into a butterfly, it pupates and forms a chrysalis. During this dormant time, the ants guard it once again. But when it emerges as a full-grown butterfly, it must fly away quickly. At this stage the ants forget their partnership and will attack it.

The large blue butterfly of Europe and Asia has a similar partnership with ants. But the relationship is even closer. Red ants will take a blue butterfly caterpillar right into their nest. There they keep it supplied with food in exchange for honeydew. The ants will even feed their own newly hatched larvae to the hungry caterpillar.

The caterpillar pupates right in the nest, where it is safe. Scientists who have studied this partnership have discovered that large blue butterflies can't reproduce without the help of the red ants—the caterpillars don't seem to be able to pupate outside the ants' nest.

A fondness for sweet things is also the basis of a very different kind of animal partnership—the partnership between a bird called the black-throated honey guide and the honey badger, or ratel. Both these creatures live in Africa and parts of Asia.

The honey guide likes to eat the beeswax and larvae that are inside bees' nests, but the bird isn't strong enough to break a nest open. So when a honey guide finds a bees' nest, it looks around for a ratel. A ratel will eat almost anything, but these animals are especially fond of honey.

The bird guides the ratel to the nest, hopping around and calling to lead it on. Then the ratel uses its strong claws and teeth to break the nest open. In this way both animals get what they want.

What if the honey guide can't find a ratel? Then it will lead another creature to the nest. African people often follow honey guides to find a free supply of honey.

Ants and aphids have a relationship based on sweets. The ants protect the aphids so that they can get the sweet, sticky honeydew that the tiny insects secrete.

If you met up with one of these remarkably lifelike robotic dinosaurs, you might think you had been transported back to prehistoric times.

HERE COME THE DINOBOTS

Suddenly, right in front of you, you see it —a huge dinosaur. It turns to look at you with its beady eyes and opens its enormous jaws, revealing daggerlike teeth as long as your hands. A roar shatters the air. Can it really be *Tyrannosaurus* coming toward you?

Of course not. The last dinosaurs died out millions of years ago. But dinosaurs are on the move in museums, thanks to the work of a California company that makes lifelike robotic models of the long-extinct reptiles.

The company, Dinamation International, brings together scientists, artists, computer experts, and engineers. These people work as a team to produce dinosaur creations that are as accurate and realistic as possible.

The scientists help decide what each dinosaur should look like. This isn't easy— there's often little more to go on than a few fossilized bones and tracks. But from that scanty evidence, scientists can learn a great deal. Bones reveal the general size and shape of the beast, how its weight was distributed, and even how it moved. Tracks can show if the dinosaur lived in a herd or traveled alone. Marks on the teeth of a meat-eating dinosaur can show that it gnawed bones.

But there's a great deal that the fossil evidence won't reveal. What color was the dinosaur? What sort of sound did it make? People may never be able to answer these questions. So the team makes educated guesses, basing the answers on animals that are alive today.

Once the team has decided how the dinosaur should look, an artist makes detailed sketches and then a small clay model of the beast. When these are correct, a full-size clay model is built. The clay model is used as a mold to form the dinosaur's rubbery skin, which is made of flexible urethane foam. The model is also used to make light-weight plates that will lie under the skin and give the dinosaur its shape.

Meanwhile, engineers are working on the robot mechanisms that will bring the dinosaur to life. The dinosaur has a metal skeleton, with each joint designed to flex realistically. Compressed air, carried through tubes, is the force that moves the skeleton's parts. A computer controls the action, sending shots of air here and there to make the dinosaur raise its head, open its mouth, or roll its eyes. The computer also controls the sounds that the dinosaur will make.

When everything is ready, workers put the dinosaur robot together, fitting the plates and skin carefully over the metal skeleton. Then the computer program that controls the dinosaur is installed. Workers usually let the robot run for a couple of days, to fine-tune and adjust any parts.

Finally the dinosaur is sent off to be painted. Since the artists can't know what colors and patterns dinosaurs really had, they base the colors and patterns on what they know about animals that exist today. They may suppose, for example, that a *Stegosaurus* was bright green and yellow, to better attract a mate. Or they may give a dinosaur a pattern of stripes that would act as camouflage, hiding it from predators.

When the paint is dry, the dinosaur is ready to go on display. Groups of the robot dinosaurs are sent on loan or sometimes sold to museums. They are set up in scenes that mimic events that might have taken place millions of years ago. In one scene, for example, a meat-eating *Deinonychus* defends its prey from others of its kind. A vulturelike flying *Pteranodon* perches nearby, waiting for the leftovers.

The shows usually include some hands-on exhibits, too. For example, museum-goers might see a small robot of a *Dimetrodon*, an ancestor of the dinosaurs, with panels of skin stripped away. You can use a joystick to make the head, legs, and tail move and the mouth open and close.

The Dinamation shows have been highly successful. But the company isn't resting on its success. Besides dinosaurs, it has made robot models of ancient mammals—woolly mammoths, saber-toothed cats, and giant ground sloths. It has made imaginary mammals that don't yet exist but may evolve in the future. And its plans include exhibits of the endangered species of today—the animals that are in danger of dying out, just as the dinosaurs did millions of years ago.

The robot's metal skeleton is covered with rubbery "skin." Compressed air is shot through tubes to move the skeleton's joints. A computer controls all the action.

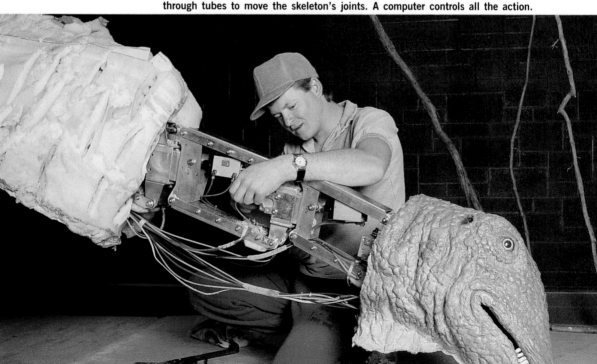

ANIMALS IN THE NEWS

"There's nothing new under the sun" is an old saying—but not necessarily a true one. In June, 1990, scientists in Brazil announced that they had discovered a new kind of monkey on an island off that country's coast. The squirrel-sized primate, a species of lion tamarin, has golden fur with a black face, forearms, and tail. Scientists named it *Leontopithecus caissara,* or **black-faced lion tamarin.** There are three other kinds of lion tamarins in Brazil. The black-faced monkeys, isolated on their island, had gradually developed different traits from those of their mainland relatives. Scientists said that the discovery showed the importance of finding new species before their habitats are destroyed by development.

A year after the worst North American oil spill ever—**the 1989 spill from the *Exxon Valdez*** in Prince William Sound in Alaska—scientists were still unsure of the long-term effects on wildlife. Right after the spill, many animals that were coated with oil, such as the sea otter below, died. (An $18.3 million effort to save oiled otters rescued just 225.) By 1990, the worst of the oil had been cleaned from the beaches, and populations of otters and other animals were recovering. But oil lingered along the rocky shore, and scientists feared that its poisonous effects would harm some wildlife for years.

All over the world, many kinds of animals are in danger of becoming extinct, or dying out. Some are threatened by hunters. Others are in danger because people are destroying their natural habitats. To call attention to the plight of these animals, the Zoological Society of San Diego sponsored its third annual art contest in the spring of 1990. Artists from kindergarten through adult competed in five different age categories, creating posters and paintings on the theme **"A Future in the Wild."** The picture above was painted by Jorge Huitron and was the first-place winner in the kindergarten through grade three division. It shows a contented cheetah in its African homeland. The winning artists were honored at an awards ceremony in August, and their artworks were displayed at the San Diego Wild Animal Park.

The **northern spotted owl** caused a furor in 1990. These owls live almost exclusively in the old-growth forests of the Pacific Northwest—stands of fir, cedar, redwood, and spruce that have stood for centuries. But most of these national forests have been cut for timber, and as a result today there are only about 2,000 known pairs of spotted owls left. In 1990, the U.S. government declared the spotted owl a threatened species. That meant that its habitat should be protected. But the timber industry objected, claiming that thousands of loggers would lose their jobs if timber cutting was reduced in the old-growth forests. After these objections, the government convened a special committee to balance the interests of the loggers and the owl.

The event shown above—a baby wood turtle hatching from its egg—is becoming more and more rare. In 1990, scientists estimated that about a third of the world's **turtle species** would need protection to survive. Some are hunted for meat, and many are threatened by development. For example, wood turtles, which live in the northeastern United States, are often killed crossing roads. In some areas, this has prevented adult turtles from reaching each other to breed.

Scientists announced in 1990 that they had rediscovered a tiny creature that many feared had died out. The animal, the **hairy-eared dwarf lemur,** was spotted deep in a rain forest in Madagascar, an island country off the eastern coast of Africa. Lemurs are primates—relatives of monkeys and humans—that evolved separately on this island. The hairy-eared dwarf lemur is the second smallest primate, just 5½ inches (14 centimeters) long. It was last seen in 1964.

SPIDER WEBS: STRONG AS STEEL

Covered with dew, a spider's web hangs from a branch like a jeweled necklace. The silk that forms the web is feather-light and looks fragile and delicate in the early morning rays of the sun. Yet this amazing material is actually stronger than steel and, at the same time, as elastic as a rubber band.

People have never been able to make a material with all the wonderful properties of natural spider silk. But now, using new techniques, researchers are trying to produce the silk commercially. If they succeed, spider silk may one day be used in everything from bullet-proof vests to stockings.

SILKEN NETS

Spiders are hunters that catch and eat insects. (Spiders themselves aren't insects.

They belong to a group called the arachnids, which also includes scorpions and ticks.) All spiders have special glands that produce spider silk, which is a protein. The silk is spun by being forced out as a liquid through tiny fingerlike organs called spinnerets. The liquid hardens into fine, tough threads after hitting the air.

Most spiders use their silk to build webs that will capture their prey. And there are almost as many different kinds of webs as there are different kinds of spiders. Some webs consist of just a strand or two of silk; others are a jumbled tangle of threads. Some spiders spin broad sheets that hang horizontally in bushes and trees. Still others construct tunnel-like traps of silk.

The master builders of the spider world

are the orb-weavers. "Orb" means "circle," and these spiders weave circular, wheel-like webs. Strong, dry threads, which act as spokes, run out from the center of the web and anchor it in place. The fine, sticky threads that spiral around the circle are coated with a sort of watery glue, to trap the spider's prey.

But web-building isn't the only use that spiders have for their silk—in fact, a few spiders don't build webs at all. Spiders can spin several different kinds of silk, each having a different purpose. All are made of the same basic protein, but they have different qualities.

After a spider catches an insect, for example, it wraps its prey in a special binding silk and stores it to eat later. Female spiders wrap their eggs in a soft, protective case made of another type of silk. When the baby spiders hatch, they spin long streamers of silk that catch the wind. The babies are lifted into the air and carried off, sometimes for many miles. Wherever they land, they make their homes.

All spiders also make a fine but extremely strong silk that they trail as a dragline—a sort of safety line. If you've ever startled a spider, you may have seen it drop to the ground and then, a moment later, scuttle back up its dragline to its web. Most of the cobwebs that people find in their homes are draglines that spiders have left behind.

SPIDER-SILK STOCKINGS

The remarkable properties of spider silk have long fascinated people. The silk is amazingly strong and flexible. When a spider web stops a flying insect, it's the equivalent of stopping an airliner with a rope net. The silk doesn't break because it's stronger than the best steel wire and can stretch to nearly twice its length before it snaps. And it's practically rot-proof.

Spider silk is so amazing that people would like to produce it commercially, in the same way that the silk of another creature—the silk moth—is used. Fibers produced by the silk moth caterpillar (or silkworm) are the basis of silk fabric. But raising spiders for their silk is a very different matter from raising silk moth caterpillars.

Unlike the caterpillars, which eat leaves, the spiders must have live insect food. Also, spiders attack each other as well as insects. And it would take many, many spiders to produce a useful amount of silk. By one estimate, 5,000 large spiders would have to spin day and night to make the silk for one dress. Thus in the past, spider silk has been used in only a few ways—to make cross hairs in gunsights, for example.

Now, however, some scientists think there may be a way to produce spider silk commercially. The technique involves genetic engineering (altering the material within cells that carries inherited traits). With genetic engineering, bacteria might be programmed to produce spider-silk protein.

The bacteria would be grown in big vats, and the protein would be extracted and spun into thread through mechanical spinnerets. If the plan works, spider-silk stockings may be the fashion craze of the future.

HUMMINGBIRDS: LITTLE FLYING JEWELS

In a burst of brilliant color, a tiny bird appears. It hovers for a second in front of a flower, its wings beating so fast that they are nothing but a blur. Then it zips away, vanishing as quickly as it appeared.

The bird could only be a hummingbird, one of nature's smallest and most charming creatures. Hummingbirds invite superlatives. Besides including the world's smallest birds, they are among the most colorful, with iridescent feathers in a range of jewel-like tones. They are easily the most acrobatic birds, performing astounding feats in flight. And without doubt, hummingbirds are among the most fascinating of all birds.

THE LONG AND THE SHORT OF IT

There are more than 300 different kinds, or species, of hummingbirds. All of them live only in the Western Hemisphere, but they are found in almost all parts of it.

The smallest hummingbird—and the smallest bird—is the rare and tiny bee hummingbird of Cuba. This bird really could be mistaken for a bee. It weighs about as much as a penny and is just 2½ inches (6.4 centimeters) long. And half that length is made up of its beak and its tail!

The largest hummingbird is the giant hummingbird, which lives in western South America from Ecuador to Chile. It weighs ten times as much as the bee hummingbird and is over 8 inches (21 centimeters) long, about the length of a common starling.

In between the bee and the giant are hummingbirds of all sorts and sizes. But most of the birds are small. And while not all hummingbirds are colorful, many are famous for their vivid tones—green, blue, ruby, violet, magenta. The brilliance of the birds' feathers has led people to call them "flying jewels."

This brilliance occurs because the feathers

of many hummingbirds are iridescent, so that they catch and reflect light. When sunlight strikes a hummingbird's feathers at the right angle, the color seems to explode in a burst of fiery glitter. Depending on where you stand and how the light strikes the bird, it may seem that there are several colors where in fact there is only one. When no light shines on the feathers, they appear black.

Males are often more colorful than females, although this isn't always so. In many species the colors are concentrated on the bird's crown or throat. Some hummingbirds also have special adornments—elaborate crests or long, streaming tail feathers—that add to their beauty. The streamertail, found in Jamaica, has a forked tail more than 6 inches (15 centimeters) long, far longer than its body.

Hummingbirds share certain other features. Most hummingbirds have long, slender bills that are ideal for sipping the birds' favorite food—the nectar of flowers. A hummingbird inserts its bill deep into a flower and then extends its long tongue to lap up the sugary nectar.

In South America, where there are many kinds of hummingbirds, scientists have noticed that each type has a bill of a certain length. The shortest are those of hummingbirds called thornbills and are just half an inch (1.25 centimeters) long. The longest bills are those of the swordbills—at five inches (over 12 centimeters), they are almost as long as the birds themselves.

In addition, some birds have straight bills, and some have curved bills. Each bill is ideal for feeding on the nectar of certain types of flowers. This allows many kinds of hummingbirds to live in the same area without competing for the same food sources.

TINY ACROBATS

Besides their tiny size and vivid colors, the most remarkable feature of hummingbirds is their ability to perform incredible feats in flight. A hummingbird will hover motionless in front of a flower to sip nectar and then actually fly backward to withdraw its bill from the bloom. It will dart a few inches to the side and hover again, perfectly positioned to sip from the next flower. Then it will suddenly dart away, reaching speeds of

Hummingbirds build their tiny nests of plant fibers, moss, and spider silk, and the nests can easily fit in a link of chain. Some of the brilliantly colored birds are so small, they can sit atop the eraser of a pencil.

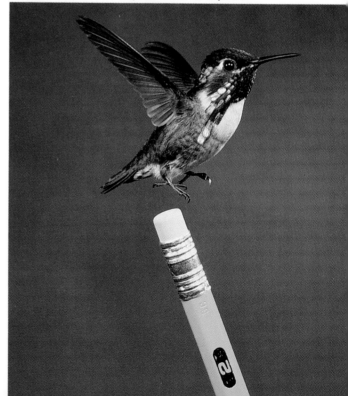

30 miles (48 kilometers) an hour almost immediately. Hummingbirds can even fly *upside down* for short distances. They are the only birds that can perform all these acrobatic feats.

Hummingbirds are such accomplished aerialists that they use their wings for everything—in fact, most appear unable to hop or walk. Mother hummingbirds have even been seen to shift position on their nests by rising on their wings, turning in the air, and settling down again like little helicopters.

A hummingbird's wings beat so fast—50 times a second in some species, as much as 80 times in others—that they are just blurs to the eye. (The rapid beating creates a humming sound, which has given the birds their name.) But by using slow-motion photography and by studying the way the birds' wings are put together, scientists have learned a lot about these incredible stunt flyers. When the tiny birds hover, for

example, their wings trace a figure-eight pattern in the air, moving forward and backward instead of up and down. The wings pivot so that each forward stroke and each backward stroke gives lift, helping the bird stay in the air. But the strokes cancel each other out, so the bird stays motionless.

HUMMINGBIRD HABITS

Most hummingbirds live in South America near the equator, where the climate is warm all year. But hummingbirds are found in almost all parts of the Western Hemisphere. The ruby-throated hummingbird breeds in much of the eastern United States and Canada but winters in Central America. The rufous hummingbird is found as far north as Alaska in the summer; it spends winters in Mexico. Other hummingbird species are found in the Caribbean and as far south as the tip of South America.

Even hummingbirds that don't migrate with the changing seasons travel over a wide area, constantly searching for food. For its size, a tiny hummingbird requires astounding amounts of food. It must consume half its

HUMMINGBIRDS IN YOUR GARDEN

Hummingbirds seem exotic—but they are surprisingly easy to attract to your backyard. All you have to do is provide a source of sugary nectar.

One way to do this is to plant some of the hummingbirds' favorite flowers. Try paintbrush, columbine, jewelweed, scarlet bugler, cardinal flower, bee balm, fuchsia, and trumpet honeysuckle. Hummingbirds find red flowers especially attractive.

You can also put out nectar feeders for the birds. You can buy one, or you can make one from a small bottle or vial. To make the feeder attractive, tape or glue an artificial plastic flower around the opening—preferably red. Hang the feeder in your garden, using thin wire or nylon fishing line.

Fill the feeder with a solution of one part sugar to four parts water. Every few days, change the solution and clean the feeder—but only with water, not soap.

Once hummingbirds discover your feeder, they will become frequent visitors to your garden.

Michele McLean

body weight in food each day—the equivalent of a full-grown man eating 300 hamburgers. To get what they need, hummingbirds feed throughout the day and often into dusk, when other birds have roosted for the night.

It was once thought that the birds lived entirely on flower nectar, but this isn't so. The sugary nectar provides a source of quick energy. That's essential for these active little birds, which burn up more energy than any other warm-blooded creature. But hummingbirds also need protein, and to get it they eat tiny insects and spiders. They lap up insects along with nectar or catch them in flight. They also pluck insects from leaves and spiders right from their webs, hovering in the air all the while.

Most kinds of hummingbirds raise several broods of young a year. The birds pair up briefly to mate, and the males leave the nest-building and child-raising chores to the females. For many hummingbird species, the nest is a tiny cup, no bigger than a walnut shell. Most are made of moss and plant fibers, bound together with strands of silk stolen from spider webs. The female lays two tiny eggs, and she raises her chicks on an insect diet. Hummingbirds will defend their nests with amazing courage, even driving off hawks many times their size.

Adult hummingbirds travel alone, rather than in flocks. And many are common visitors to gardens. When a bird finds a good feeding spot, with plenty of flowers, it will stake out a territory and guard it jealously, driving other hummingbirds away.

Hummingbirds can often be seen near water, enjoying frequent baths. Sometimes they almost seem to be playing as they splash about. Many are also uncommonly curious. They will fly up to explore anything, even a person's clothing, if it is brightly colored. The fact that they can speed away so quickly if danger threatens may account for their boldness. Hummingbirds do fall victim to predators, however. Other birds, frogs, and even predatory insects such as the praying mantis might eat them, perhaps mistaking the little birds for large insects.

The boldness and curiosity of hummingbirds only adds to their charm. When Spanish explorers arrived in the Caribbean, hummingbirds were among the wonders they

A hummingbird appears to hover motionless in front of a flower. Actually, its wings beat so fast that they are just a blur to the eye. This rapid beating creates a humming sound, which has given the birds their name.

reported. "The colors shine like those of the little birds artists paint to illuminate the margins of holy books," wrote one Spaniard. "They are hardy yet so little I would not dare tell of it if others had not seen them also."

Later, Europeans took a fancy to preserved hummingbirds, as ornaments on hats and other clothing. Thousands of the birds were killed. But today, people simply take delight in the beauty and charm of these fascinating and unique little birds. When a hummingbird visits the garden, it's always a welcome event.

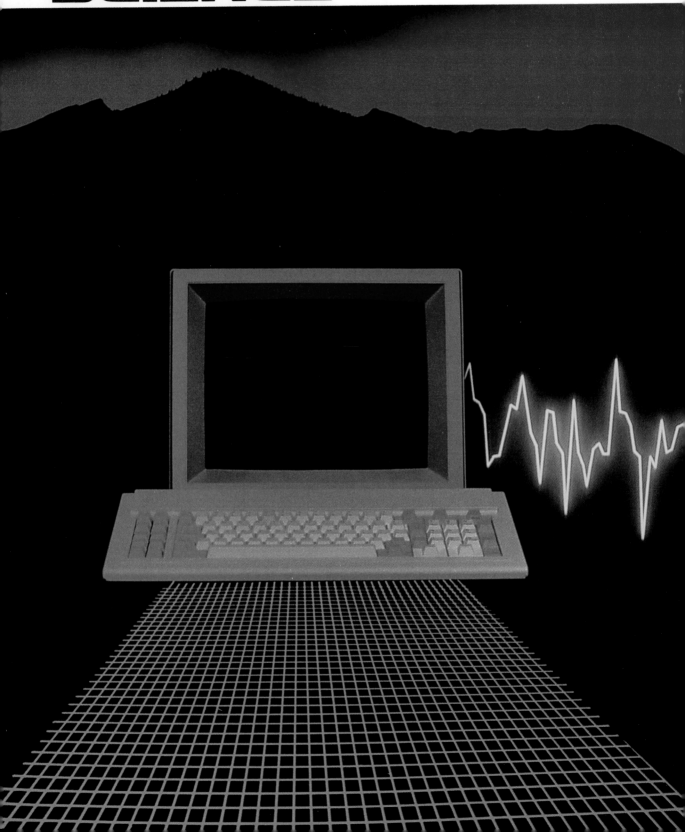

SCIENCE

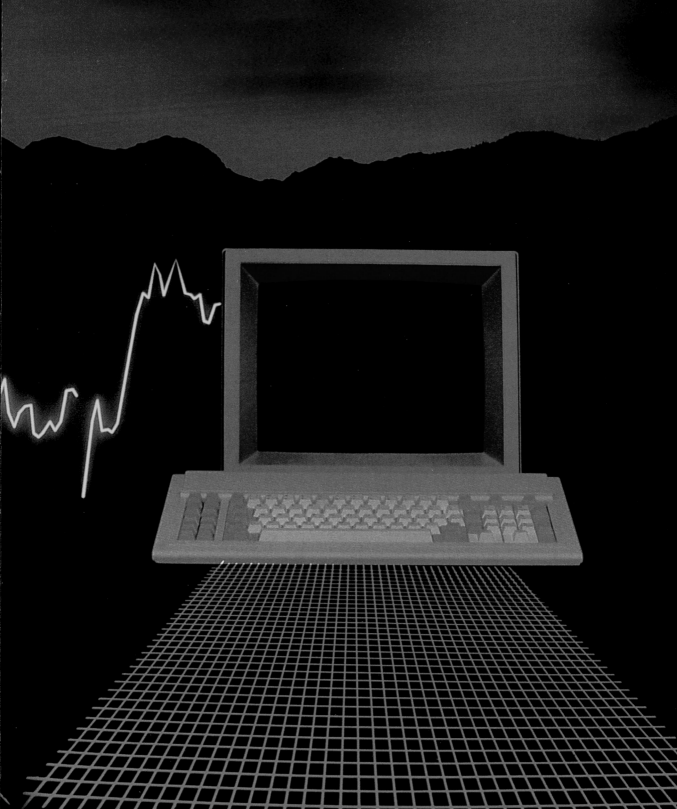

The 1990's are shaping up as the decade of the computer, as exciting developments give these machines new powers and new roles. Small personal computers are taking on jobs once reserved for much larger machines, while big computers are becoming ever more powerful and versatile.

COMPUTERS OF THE FUTURE

It's a Wednesday night in the year 2001, and you sit down at your computer to do your homework. "How may I help you?" the machine drawls in a soft Southern accent.

"I have to do a report on the Boston Tea Party," you say. "But I'd rather play a video game."

"I'm sorry, but games cannot be accessed until 8 p.m.," the computer replies. "I can provide the following material on the Boston Tea Party." The computer screen then flashes a list that includes four encyclopedia articles, a recent magazine piece, and a tele-vision documentary. You lightly touch the screen and choose the documentary.

As the TV show plays on the computer screen, you stop it from time to time to dictate notes to the computer. When the documentary ends, the computer speaks again.

"I have the information on baseball tickets that you requested this morning. Would you like to review it now?"

This scene isn't as far-fetched as it may seem. Today's computers are more powerful than ever—some can already speak and present recorded video material. The reason is that designers have vastly increased the memory of computers—and with it, their ability to store and process information.

One result is that the personal computer, or PC, has become the workhorse of the computer world. In recent years it has taken over jobs that only huge computers could do in the past. PC's range from desktop models to portables, some of which weigh as little as a pound. All are vastly smaller, less expensive, and faster than earlier computers.

At the same time, large computers have also increased their capabilities. Today's large computers are supercomputers, able to handle vast amounts of information and perform calculations with blazing speed.

Large and small, computers are being used in more ways than ever before. And the computers of tomorrow promise to have even more capabilities.

NEW IMAGES

Traditionally, computers have excelled in performing complicated mathematical calculations, keeping records, and handling written information. Now they are beginning to handle images in much the same way.

Improvements in computer graphics techniques allow the machines to create full-color pictures that are as realistic as photographs. Some systems can produce motion and the appearance of depth on the screen. And a technique called document imaging allows actual documents and photographs to be entered directly into a computer.

Most of these image-processing techniques aren't new, but in the past they required high-powered and expensive computer systems. Now, more and more of them can be performed by smaller and more affordable computers. At the same time, the quality of computer images has improved vastly. This has made them useful in many different fields.

Publishers can combine words with pictures and produce material entirely by computer. Manufacturers can use computer graphics to design new products and even new factories. And instead of being buried by mounds of paper, offices can set up "electronic filing cabinets" by scanning documents and storing them in computers.

Mapmakers are also turning to computers. Computerized mapmaking systems can combine images with a wealth of information from census reports and other sources— everything from the location of power lines to the number of houses on a street. The most complex mapmaking systems are being developed by governments. But businesses are using these methods to produce customized maps that help them calculate the best shipping routes and pinpoint the best locations for new facilities.

Computer graphics are especially helpful in scientific and technical fields because complex subjects can be quickly understood through pictures. And computers can produce pictures of things that would otherwise be difficult or impossible to see.

In hospitals, for example, surgeons can plan their operations by examining three-dimensional images of structures inside the human body. In research laboratories, chemists can use computer graphics to produce pictures of molecules that are far too small to be seen. And geologists can create three-dimensional models of rock formations hidden deep in the earth—to find, for example, a likely spot to drill for oil.

Sports scientists can use computer imaging to analyze an athlete's performance. First the performance is videotaped. A series of images showing the athlete at different points in the performance is transferred from the tape to the computer. On the computer, the scientist "marks" key spots on the athlete's body. And the computer uses these points to produce a stick figure that can be studied at every stage of movement.

By combining graphics with the power of a supercomputer, astronomers can produce pictures of events that otherwise could only be imagined, such as the birth of a galaxy or the death of a star. Many such events can't be observed—galaxies formed billions of years ago, and a star's life span is measured in millions of years. But a supercomputer can analyze these enormously complicated processes, compress the time scale, and produce full-color simulations of the events.

High-powered imaging and mapmaking systems are still very expensive. But some PC's already have many computer imaging capabilities. Computer designers say that in the near future, image processing will be a standard feature, even on home computers.

TALK TO ME

How about a computer that can carry on a conversation—talk to you, and understand what you say? Such machines may be commonplace in the not-too-distant future.

Computer designers have already made great strides in voice simulation, the ability of computers to reproduce the human voice. Early systems produced sounds that were more like electronic squawks than human speech. Now computers can produce pleasant voices and even duplicate regional accents and the speech of famous people.

Using sophisticated computer graphics, sports scientists can analyze an athlete's every leap, step, and vault.

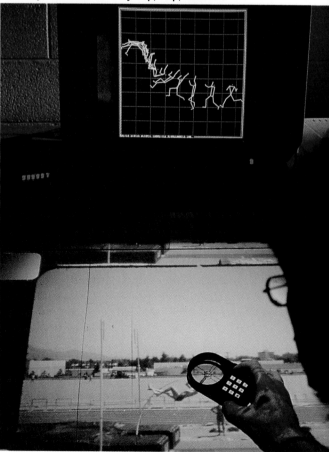

Astronomers can combine graphics with the power of a supercomputer and produce pictures of events that otherwise could only be imagined. Shown at the left is a simulation of the formation of Jupiter's Great Red Spot, an atmospheric storm.

Talking computers are expected to become important tools in teaching—especially in teaching foreign languages. Students will be able to type words on their computers and hear the computer "read" them with the correct pronunciation.

The ability of computers to reproduce sound will affect other areas. People will play, study, and compose music on computers. And when sound reproduction is combined with the latest computer graphics techniques, video games will rival feature films—with stereo sound tracks and realistic special effects.

Getting a computer to *understand* speech has proved more difficult than reproducing sound. The best speech-recognition systems can understand only about a thousand words. Partly, this is because the pronunciation of words varies depending on who is speaking. The computer may not recognize a word if there is even a slight variation in the way it is pronounced. But when a computer is "trained" to recognize just one person's voice, it can handle a larger vocabulary.

Computer experts expect these problems to be solved. And when they are, computers may be controlled entirely by voice commands. They will even take dictation.

COMPUTERS AND VIDEO

With their improved graphics and sound, computers are being linked with another new technology: the videodisc. And the combination has exciting possibilities.

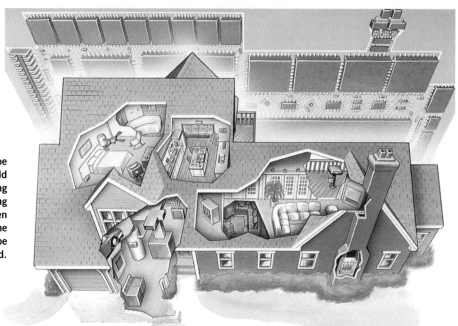

The house of the future may be run by computers that would do everything from turning on the lights to watering the lawn to telling you when your laundry was done. All the systems in the house would be completely remote-controlled.

Compact discs that hold written information have been used with computers for several years. With a special attachment, the computer can read the information on the disc and display it on the screen. An entire encyclopedia can fit on a single disc.

With videodiscs, however, the computer can display still pictures and full-motion video as well as words. A 12-inch disc holds tens of thousands of still pictures or well over an hour of full-motion video. You can tell the computer to call up any photo or any segment of the video. The screens in computer-videodisc systems produce pictures that are even sharper than those of standard television sets.

Computer-videodisc systems are being used in some schools, and some companies are using them to train employees. Teachers say that students learn faster with the systems—because the students are in control.

Suppose, for example, that you want to learn about cell division. A textbook can explain the process and show diagrams and photographs. A filmstrip or videotape can show actual cells dividing. A computer-videodisc system can do all that, too. And if you have a question or are confused at any point, you can stop the presentation to call up more information or to review what you've seen. The computer can also ask questions, to see if you've understood the material. If you give a wrong answer, it will give you more information in that area.

Someday the contents of entire libraries—not just books but pictures, recordings, and filmstrips—may be stored on videodiscs. People will use computers to get the information they want. To find out about a famous painting, for example, you might ask the computer to show you a high-quality reproduction of the picture, written material about it, and a video on the artist.

Computer-videodisc systems may eventually be found in homes, where they will be hooked up to television sets. At the touch of a button, people will be able to call up information to supplement what they see broadcast on television—background on a country that's featured on the evening news, or a full account of a historical event that's the subject of a miniseries.

NEW JOBS FOR COMPUTERS

As PC's become ever more powerful, they will be able to perform many jobs at once. While you are using your computer to type a letter or research a report, for example, the machine may also be tapping into a ticket reservation system to book seats for you and your friends at an upcoming rock concert.

Computers will take on new roles, too. The house of the future may be run by a computer that can do everything from turn on the lights to water the lawn.

An experimental home system like this has already been built. In it, a computer operates the home's electric, heating, and other

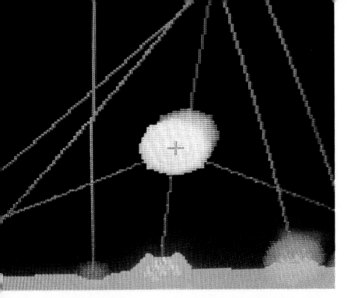

systems. All the lights and other equipment can be turned on and off from a central control panel, which features a touch-sensitive video screen. If you want to turn on the stereo, you just put your finger on the right spot on the screen.

Sensors keep track of temperature and automatically adjust the heat, report if someone is moving through a room, and indicate if the oven was left on. If an appliance breaks, the computer can even tell what went wrong. A voice-recognition system locks and unlocks doors at a spoken command. And moisture detectors buried in the ground outside turn on the sprinklers when the lawn is dry.

COMPUTING WITH LIGHT

The reason that computers have become more powerful even as they have grown smaller is that more and more of their electronic circuitry has been squeezed onto tiny silicon chips. Computer designers are working on even better chips. But sometime in the next century, the most powerful computers of all may have no electronic circuits and no silicon chips. Instead of electrical current, they will use pulses of light to do their work.

Experimental optical computers, as such devices are called, have already been built. They contain networks of lasers, mirrors, and lenses. As the machine makes its calculations, beams of laser light are focused and directed through the network by the lenses and mirrors. (Ordinary light contains light waves of many different lengths, which scatter in all directions. In laser light, the light waves are all the same length, and they travel together in a narrow beam.) The beams can be switched on and off as many as a billion times a second, which will give optical computers enormous speed.

Researchers say that when optical computers are perfected—perhaps sometime early in the 21st century—they will be a thousand times faster than the most powerful machines of today. They will be able to store vast amounts of information, and they may be able to perform millions of tasks at once. When that happens, you'll be able to finish your homework with the speed of light!

As computers have become more powerful, computer games have advanced. Early games (*top*) showed pictures that were simple and boxy-looking; more recent games (*center*) show more detailed pictures; some of today's games show images that have almost an artistic quality (*bottom*).

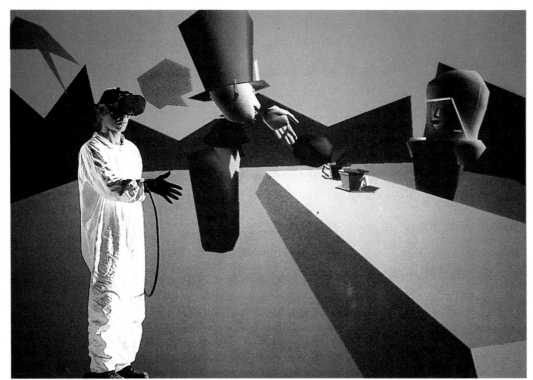

A computerized mask and glove allow you to enter the three-dimensional world of "virtual reality."

SUPER SIMULATIONS

Imagine playing a game of tennis right in your living room—or exploring Mars without leaving Earth. Both may be possible one day, through advanced computer simulations.

Computer simulations are already being used as training tools, mainly for airplane pilots. A flight simulator can mimic the sights, sounds, and sensations of flying a plane so realistically that it's hard to believe you're still on the ground.

From outside, the simulator is a big box on legs. Inside is a cockpit that is accurate down to the last gauge and switch. The windscreen shows a realistic view of ground and sky. And the whole box tilts and shifts as the simulator "flies." All the action is controlled by a computer. It responds to the pilot's actions. And it sets up emergency situations—a failed engine, for example—in order to test the pilot's reactions.

Another computer simulation puts medical students in the middle of a hectic emergency room. The student watches a computer-controlled video screen and has to make decisions on how to treat a patient with a gunshot wound. If the student makes the wrong decision, the patient "dies"—but fortunately, the patient is just an actor.

As realistic as these simulations are, they are crude compared to the systems that computer experts are now developing. New technology is able to create an environment called artificial or "virtual" reality. In one system, you need a computerized mask and glove. The mask has two tiny video screens, one in front of each eye. It is connected to a computer, which contains a special program. When you put the mask on, you're transported into a three-dimensional simulated world. And when you move your head up or down or sideways, the view changes.

The computerized glove allows you to interact with this artificial world. It contains sensors that report the position and movements of your hand. If you reach out to touch something in your artificial world, an image of a hand appears in front of your eyes and actually performs the action.

Researchers expect to develop ever more realistic video displays for these advanced simulations. Some are developing full body suits filled with sensors like those in the gloves. And virtual environments may one day be widely used, for recreation as well as training. People could explore exotic places and even distant planets, or even play a simulated game of tennis, right in their living rooms.

ALL IN A DREAM

You're late for math class, so you rush in and quickly take a seat. The teacher gives you a cold look and hands you a paper. It's a test—and you realize with a shock that you haven't studied. What's worse, the test makes no sense—the material is so unfamiliar that you can't answer a single question. You stare at the paper, fighting a rising sense of panic. Then, suddenly, the bell rings. Class is over, and you failed the test!

But what's this? That's not the class bell. It's your alarm clock. You're not in class; you're home in bed. And you didn't fail a test—you were only dreaming.

Dreams take the real world and turn it upside down. All sorts of unpredictable and impossible things can happen: You may meet old friends who have moved far away or relatives who passed on long ago. Your pet dog may talk. You may suddenly find the solution to a problem that's been troubling you for days. Your deepest wishes may be granted—or you may be chased by a bug-eyed monster. You may even fly.

Why do we dream? Do the events in dreams have meaning? People have been fascinated by these questions since ancient times. Long ago, some people thought that dreams might be messages from the gods. Others thought that dreams were predictions of future events.

Few people hold such beliefs today. In recent times scientists have studied dreams and learned much about them. Dreams, most experts believe, are messages from our subconscious. Buried feelings and fears are called up and interwoven with events that take place during the day. But in sleep, these messages are often disguised—and that's what makes dreams so fascinating.

STUDYING DREAMS

"To sleep: perchance to dream," says the prince in Shakespeare's play *Hamlet*. Scientists say there's no chance about it: everybody dreams! Even people who say they never dream actually do—they just don't remember their dreams.

How do scientists know? They have watched people dream in sleep laboratories.

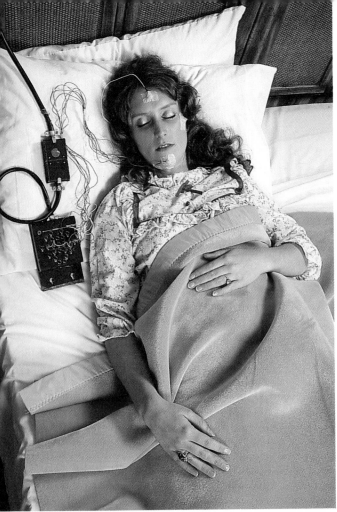

A volunteer is hooked up to electronic monitoring equipment at a sleep lab. By studying brain waves and other physical signs, scientists learn about sleep and dreams.

At a sleep laboratory, volunteers are hooked up to electronic monitoring equipment. An electroencephalograph, or EEG, records brain waves—the electrical impulses that are constantly given off by the brain. Other machines monitor eye movements and heart and breathing rates.

The volunteers' job is easy—they simply go to sleep. But all night long, scientists keep watch on the monitoring equipment. Brain waves vary with the brain's activity, so watching the EEG tells scientists what's going on while the volunteer is sleeping. Heart rate and other physical signs also vary through the night.

By studying sleeping volunteers, researchers have learned that there are different kinds of sleep. Every night, you go through a number of sleep cycles. Each cycle lasts about 90 minutes and is made up of a period of deep sleep and a period of light sleep. Near the end of the cycle comes a period of what scientists call *r*apid *e*ye *m*ovement, or REM, sleep.

During REM sleep, a person's eyes move back and forth as if he or she were watching something. Brain waves show patterns that resemble those seen in a person who is awake. The sleeper's heart and breathing rates may increase. And by waking volunteers during REM sleep, researchers have learned that this is when most dreams occur.

Over eight hours of sleep, most people have three to five dreams, each lasting five to fifty minutes. Usually, most of the dreams are forgotten by morning. But by waking volunteers in the middle of a dream and asking them about it, researchers have learned a lot about dreams.

For example, while many people think that they dream in black and white, dreams are almost always in color. Apparently the memory of the colors in our dreams fades even more quickly than the memory of the dreams themselves.

People usually hear as well as see in their dreams. Dreams may even involve the senses of smell and touch. Blind people dream as much as sighted people, but their dreams are made up of sounds, smells, and sensations. During REM sleep, their eyes don't move.

In many dreams, the dreamer simply watches the action. In others the dreamer plays a part. While sleeping, people seldom move or act out their dreams. That's because messages from the brain to the muscles are blocked during REM sleep.

Whether we watch the action or take part in it, many of our dreams involve people and places with which we're familiar. Often, dreams seem to be related to events that took place during the day and especially the hours just before sleep. But in dreams, people may behave strangely and familiar places may be oddly changed. Events often make no sense, although during the dream they may seem logical. Other dreams, however, are so realistic that on awakening, the dreamer can't believe that the events didn't really happen.

Knowing these facts about dreams doesn't explain what purpose dreams serve or why people dream what they do. But researchers have plenty of theories.

THE LANGUAGE OF DREAMS

One of the best-known theories of the meaning of dreams was developed by Austrian physician Sigmund Freud, in the 1890's. Freud originated psychoanalysis, a method of helping people with emotional problems. Part of Freud's complex dream theory stated that dreams are a way in which people fulfill subconscious wishes—wishes that they don't even know they have. The wish fulfillment happens indirectly, through symbols. That is, the images in dreams stand for ideas or things that are too stressful for the dreamer to picture directly and thus must be disguised.

More recently, some researchers have proposed theories that are almost the opposite of Freud's. According to one of these theories, dreams mean nothing at all. During sleep, the cerebral cortex (the part of the brain that's involved in thought) is stimulated randomly. Thus dreams are just meaningless images, called up by chance.

Another current theory states that dreams are a sort of housecleaning mechanism—a way in which the brain gets rid of incorrect associations and patterns of thought. (If this is so, it's best to forget your dreams.) And still other researchers think that dreams serve a vital biological purpose: By activating the brain during sleep, they keep it from drifting too deeply into unconsciousness.

Most people, however, believe that dreams have at least some meaning. And while many experts disagree with parts of Freud's dream theory, it is generally agreed that the mysterious images we see in sleep are symbols. If you dream about another person, for example, he or she may represent a character trait in yourself. Animals often stand for instincts and emotions. Colors may reflect your inner feelings—bright, sharp colors may indicate intense feelings, while black may indicate sadness.

Even the dream's setting is important. A house, for example, is supposed to be a symbol of the self. The basement stands for the unconscious, while the upper floors stand for the conscious mind. If you dream about a house with a lot of empty, unused rooms, your dream may be telling you that you're not using all your talents.

Everyone's dreams are unique. But certain experiences seem to occur in almost everybody's dreams at one time or another. And these experiences, too, may have symbolic meanings.

If you dream that you are falling, for example, your dream may show that you feel insecure. If you dream that you can't find something important, such as money or a set of keys, it may show that you don't want to accept grown-up responsibility. And a dream about failing an exam may show that you feel unprepared for life's demands.

But people who interpret dreams say that a dream's true meaning depends on the dreamer. Symbols are just a starting point in decoding a dream—you have to think about the dream and decide how it relates to your situation.

Many people spend a great deal of time and effort trying to understand and interpret their dreams. Some keep dream diaries or re-create their dreams in drawings. Some visit consultants who help decode the strange language of dreams. Other people find that simply telling a dream to a friend can help. In the course of talking about it, the meaning may become clear.

Sometimes dreams can help solve problems. Supposedly, the scientist Albert Einstein found the key to his famous theory of relativity in a dream. Thus some dream experts suggest that if you are troubled by a problem that you can't solve, you should focus on it just before you go to sleep. Try to state the problem as clearly as you can. Your dreams may provide the answer.

Even if your dreams don't solve your problems or reveal deep insights about yourself, thinking about them can be fun. But what if you're one of the many people who have trouble remembering dreams?

Dream experts say to try setting your alarm clock a half hour earlier than usual, so that you can "catch" a dream. Put a pad and pencil next to your bed and jot down the dream as soon as you wake up. And before you drift off to sleep at night, repeat to yourself, "I will remember my dream!"

BLENDING SCIENCE AND ART

Science and art often seem to have little in common. Science is concerned with facts and observations; art, with creativity and imagination. Yet these two very different fields blend beautifully in at least one area: botanical illustration. From a scientist's point of view, botanical illustrations are intended to show plants and flowers accurately, recording all the important details. But the best botanical illustrations are also works of art, reflecting all the delicacy and beauty of their subjects.

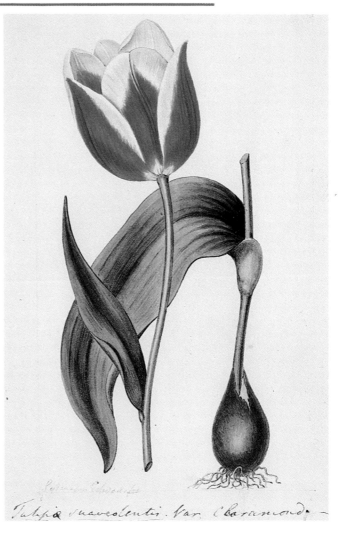

Tulipa suaveolentis. Var Charamond

The art of botanical illustration developed hand-in-hand with the science of botany, which deals with plants. Until the 1600's, artists generally depicted plants in one of two ways. Stylized pictures of plants and flowers had long been used as decorative designs and motifs. And pictures of plants also appeared in books called herbals, which told about the medicinal benefits that various plants were supposed to have. The drawings were included to help people identify plants that they might find in the wild. The artists who illustrated herbals generally copied from earlier works instead of drawing from actual plants. Thus the pictures—usually uncolored woodcuts—were often simplified and sometimes inaccurate.

In the late 1500's and the 1600's, several developments combined to change the way that plants were portrayed. One was the growth of interest in science in general and in botany in particular. People became much more interested in observing and understanding the world around them. In addition, there was more to observe and understand. The 1400's and 1500's had seen one of the world's greatest periods of exploration and discovery. Adventurers from Europe had sailed all over the world, and among the treasures they found on their travels were exotic new plants.

Together, these developments created a need for accurate, detailed illustrations of plants. And that need gave rise to a new sort of artist—one who could portray all the detail required in an accurate scientific record but still showcase the beauty of flowers and plants in a work of art.

Accuracy now required artists to draw from actual plants. Sometimes this was done with pressed specimens brought back from far-off lands. But soon artists began to ven-

109

Rosa centifolia Bullata.
Rosier à feuilles de Laitue.

ture into the field to sketch their subjects. Botanical artists were drawing and painting from nature long before this became an accepted practice for other artists, most of whom continued to work in their studios. Some botanical artists concentrated on the plants and flowers of fields and gardens close to home. But by the late 1600's, botanical artists were traveling to distant lands to record exotic plant species.

Demand for prints of botanical illustrations grew through the 1700's and 1800's, as collecting and cultivating exotic plants became a popular hobby. And advances in printing techniques—lithography and engraving—allowed artists to produce more delicate and detailed works than had been possible with the old woodcut method. Generally, an artist would create an illustration and then turn it over to a skilled engraver, who would produce a limited number of prints. The prints were in black and white;

usually they were carefully hand-colored by teams of colorists who worked under the engraver's supervision.

The styles of the artists varied. But because their illustrations were intended to serve as records and reference sources, many of the works followed a certain format. A botanical illustration often included more than one view of a plant, sometimes showing it at different seasons. Or details—flower parts, seed pods, roots—might be sketched alongside the main view.

Many artists became well known for their botanical works. One of the most famous of all time was Pierre Joseph Redouté, who began his career in the late 1700's as the drawing instructor of Queen Marie Antoinette of France. After the French Revolution and the rise of Napoleon Bonaparte, his work found favor with Napoleon's wife, Empress Josephine. Redouté's elegant watercolors of lilacs and roses from her gardens,

CALLA AETHIOPICA.

produced in the early 1800's, set a new standard for botanical art.

From the beginning, botanical illustration was a field in which women made a mark. Botany itself was considered a worthwhile subject for well-to-do women, and flower painting became a popular hobby. But many women became professional botanical illustrators. Among them was Maria Sibylla Merian, a Dutch artist who sailed for South America in 1698 and spent two years in the jungle, collecting and painting plants and insects. In the l730's, the British artist Elizabeth Blackwell produced *A Curious Herbal*, a collection of hand-colored engravings.

The publication that truly popularized the art of botanical illustration was *Curtis's Botanical Magazine*, founded by William Curtis of Britain in 1787. The magazine's goal was to provide information on the many plants that could be grown in English gardens and greenhouses, including the novel-

ties that were being imported from distant lands. The first issues—each consisting of three hand-colored engravings with text about the plants shown—sold quickly, and the magazine became a great success.

Although its circulation was never large, *Curtis's Botanical Magazine* had an important influence on English gardens, which are among the world's best loved. The magazine is still published, under the name *Kew Magazine* (after the British Royal Botanical Gardens at Kew). Its scope has broadened since Curtis's time, but it continues to include fine botanical illustrations. (An exhibit of works from this magazine completed a tour of six U.S. cities in 1990.)

Today botanical prints are enjoying a new popularity. They decorate the walls of many homes, and rare old prints are sought by collectors. It seems that there is wide appeal in the happy marriage of science and art represented by these beautiful illustrations.

The TGV, France's high-speed train, travels 186 miles (299 kilometers) per hour.

WHOOSH! IT'S A SUPERTRAIN!

This is the age of the jet and the automobile. For many people, travel means one or the other—you hop in your car for short trips or take a plane for longer ones. But if you had lived in the 1800's or in the first part of this century, your choices would have been different. For many trips, you would have taken a train.

Now this method of transportation is making a comeback. Railroads are getting ready to enter the 21st century with high-speed supertrains. These trains, which use the latest technology, are already becoming the preferred way to travel in several countries.

ALL ABOARD

The idea of using cars on tracks for transportation is an ancient one. But railroads really began in Britain in the early 1800's, first to carry coal from mines and, later, to carry passengers. From Britain, railroads spread over Europe and to North America.

The completion of the first transcontinental railway line, at Promontory, Utah, in 1869, was an important milestone in U.S. history. In a sense, railroads helped build and unify the country. By making it possible for people and goods to travel long distances, they helped open up new areas to farming, mining, and manufacturing. Towns sprang up along the railway lines, and train travel became part of everyday life.

But years ago, a long train trip meant hours of jolting, noisy travel. Train travel was also dirty—the powerful steam locomotives that pulled early trains burned coal, and they belched smoke and soot as they chugged along.

Over the years, improved trains and tracks made the ride smoother. Diesel and electric locomotives replaced steam ones. Dining cars and sleeping cars made long trips as comfortable as possible. All the same, when commercial air service began to expand in the years after World War II, most people were quick to choose planes over trains for their trips.

Now, however, that trend is starting to reverse. And supertrains are responsible for the change.

TRAINS FOR THE FUTURE

The new high-speed trains are a far cry from their ancestors. The ride is quiet and comfortable. And travel on the new supertrains has several advantages. It's cheaper than air travel. And while planes are faster, the trains depart from and arrive at city centers. There's no long, tiresome drive to the airport.

The first of these trains, the Japanese Bullet train, began operating in 1964. Today it streaks along at speeds as high as 142 miles (229 kilometers) an hour. And new models,

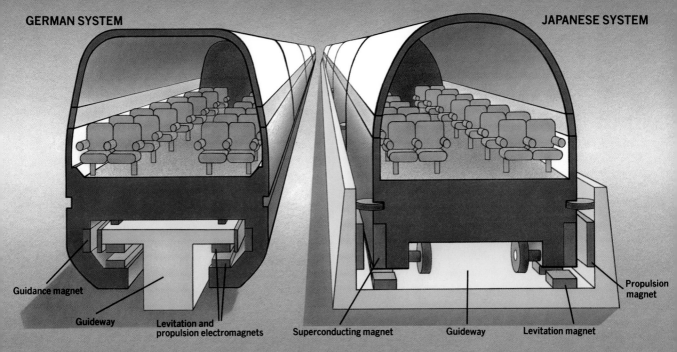

Guidance magnet

Guideway

Levitation and
propulsion electromagnets

Superconducting magnet

Guideway

Levitation magnet

Propulsion
magnet

Maglev (magnetically levitated) trains will run almost silently because there is no friction of wheel against rail.

The German maglev train makes use of the principle that magnets of opposite polarity attract each other. It uses conventional electromagnets. The train has winglike flaps that wrap around a T-shaped guideway. Both the guideway and the flaps contain electromagnets. Because of the magnetic attraction, the magnets in the guideway pull on the magnets in the wings, lifting the trains a fraction of an inch off the track.

The Japanese maglev train makes use of the principle that magnets of the same polarity repel each other. It uses magnets made with superconductors, which carry electrical current without resistance. The train rides in a troughlike guideway.   Super-conducting magnets in the guideway and in the sides of the train repel each other, lifting the train a few inches off the track.

scheduled to be introduced in 1992, will run as fast as 167 miles (269 kilometers) an hour.

Other trains are even faster. A French train known as the TGV, or *train à grande vitesse* (French for "high-speed train"), has been averaging 167 miles an hour since 1981. The newest model, introduced in 1989, travels at 186 miles (299 kilometers) an hour. In 1990, a TGV train set a speed record of 320 miles (515 kilometers) an hour, on a short section of track.

In addition, designers are developing new kinds of trains that can whiz along at about 300 miles (483 kilometers) an hour. What's more, they travel almost silently—all you hear is a *whoosh* as the train goes by.

The train is silent because it never actually touches its track—instead, it floats just above it. The technology that makes this possible is called magnetic levitation, or maglev for short. In maglev designs, powerful forces of magnetic attraction and repulsion lift the train off the track and move it along.

Germany and Japan are both developing maglev trains. The German train uses powerful electromagnets. Japan's train uses superconductors—materials that carry electricity with virtually no resistance—to create magnetic fields. Supertrains in the German design are closer to operation. And there are plans for a network of high-speed rail lines that will run throughout Europe.

So far there are no plans for a similar network in the United States. But maglev lines have been proposed for several intercity routes—between Los Angeles, California, and Las Vegas, Nevada; between Tampa, Orlando, and Miami, Florida; between New York City and Washington, D.C.—and for routes between cities and airports. Some people expect maglev trains to be operating in the United States by the year 2000. And U.S. firms are expected to join the Germans and Japanese in designing new maglev systems. If the new trend toward train travel continues, supertrains may bring about a revolution in transportation.

OUR FRAGILE EARTH—
It's the Only Home We Have

On April 22, 1990, some 200 million people in 140 countries joined in a common cause: to save the Earth. It was Earth Day 1990—an event that was a call for action to protect the fragile environment we live in.

There were street festivals, concerts, fairs, marches, and rallies. In France, people linked hands in a human chain that stretched 500 miles (805 kilometers). In Italy, 5,000 people lay down on a roadway to protest car exhaust. In Nepal, people climbed Mount Everest, picking up trash as they went. In Halifax, Nova Scotia, people gathered at sunrise and again at sunset to hear the singing of children's choirs and the chanting of a Micmac Indian medicine man.

In towns and cities across the United States, there were recycling demonstrations, tree planting ceremonies, and workshops on wildlife. In New York City, Washington, D.C., San Francisco, Boston, Chicago, and several other places, huge crowds gathered to hear concerts and speakers. At a Los Angeles high school, people sewed an Earth Day quilt. On the Maryland shore, they planted marsh grasses and set out nesting boxes for ducks.

At many of the events, the atmosphere was one of celebration—people were enjoying themselves on a beautiful spring day. But underlying the celebration was serious concern about the environment.

Concern about the environment isn't new. Twenty years earlier, on April 22, 1970, some 20 million Americans had called attention to threats to the environment in the first Earth Day. A few thousand people demonstrated in Washington, D.C. Elsewhere, people took part in local clean-ups and other activities that showed their concern.

While Earth Day 1970 had been much smaller than Earth Day 1990, it had helped make politicians aware that people were fed up with damage to the environment. New laws were passed to limit pollution, and the federal government set up the Environmental Protection Agency. But the effort petered out within a few years. The laws weren't enforced, and environmental damage continued to mount.

The 1980's saw a series of environmental disasters—including a nuclear power-plant accident in the Soviet Union that spewed radiation over much of Europe, and an oil spill off the coast of Alaska that was the worst oil spill ever in North American waters. At the same time, scientists began to warn of less visible but even more dangerous developments, including worldwide changes in the Earth's atmosphere and climate.

These events helped make people much more aware of the environment. They have begun to realize that life depends on a delicate balance of systems, and that the balance is in danger of being upset. They also realize that the environment is a global concern—no country and no person can ignore it.

That realization prompted Earth Day 1990, which was organized by a number of environmental groups. And it has also prompted new worldwide efforts to protect the fragile Earth. But solving the world's environmental problems won't be an easy task.

THREATENED WILDLIFE

There are more than 5 billion people in the world, and the number is growing so fast that the world's population is expected to double in less than 40 years. And as the population grows, people are taking over more and more wild areas and leaving less and less space for wildlife.

Tropical rain forests are home to the richest variety of plants and animals in the world—so rich that scientists haven't identified all the species that the forests hold. But these forests are being cut for timber and cleared to make room for farming at the rate of 40 to

Tropical rain forests are home to the richest variety of plants and animals in the world. But these forests are being destroyed to make room for agriculture at the rate of 40 to 50 million acres a year.

50 million acres a year. Forests in cooler climates are also being destroyed, by logging and development. Estimates released in 1990 show that the world has already lost 20 percent of its forests.

Forests aren't the only areas that are threatened. Great areas of grassland, such as the prairies of North America, have been plowed to grow crops or fenced as pasture for livestock. When grasslands are overgrazed or overcultivated, the soil washes or is blown away. The grasslands turn into wasteland, worthless as farmland or as a home for wild animals.

Wetlands—swamps, marshes, and bogs—are also threatened. These areas are home to many kinds of plants and animals, and coastal wetlands serve as nurseries for fish and other ocean creatures. But wetlands are being filled in for development. And in the ocean, the coral reefs that provide a rich habitat for thousands of animals are being buried in silt that runs off land that people have developed. The reefs are also mined for their coral and even dynamited by fishermen, to bring fish to the surface.

If these and other sensitive areas continue to be destroyed, the plants and animals that live in them will disappear. And even as people are destroying wildlife habitats, they are killing off animals directly.

Laws protect many endangered animals, but poachers continue to hunt them. Elephants are killed for their ivory. Pandas are killed for their skins. More killing results from carelessness. For example, commercial fishing nets scoop up rare turtles and marine mammals along with fish. Because these creatures need air, they drown when they are trapped in the nets.

Hundreds of plant and animal species have already disappeared, and every day more are in danger. In the United States alone, the number of species considered endangered or threatened rose from under 100 to more than 500 between 1970 and 1990. This is a great loss. Wild plants and animals are an important resource—they provide people with food, medicine, and other necessary substances. And the world will be a poorer place without the rich variety of life it now holds.

POLLUTION

In 1989 an oil spill off Alaska fouled hundreds of miles of shoreline and killed thousands of birds, fish, and other animals. It was a dramatic example of the damage pollution can do to wildlife. But pollution is damaging the environment every day, all over the world. And pollution harms people as well as wildlife.

Wetlands, streams, lakes, and ocean areas

Oil spills leave once-beautiful shorelines covered with globs of slime.

The Everglades, a wetland paradise in Florida, are being polluted by chemicals. This makes it difficult for its wildlife (such as this spoonbill) to survive.

are being contaminated by chemicals—toxic wastes produced by industry, and fertilizers and insecticides used in agriculture. The effects of this pollution can even be seen in the Everglades, a 10,000-square-mile (16,093-square-kilometer) swamp in Florida that is considered a U.S. national treasure.

In 1989, fish from the Everglades were declared unsafe to eat because of mercury contamination. And runoff from nearby farmlands, rich in fertilizers, has caused cattails and algae plants to multiply so fast that they have clogged waterways, making it impossible for fish, birds, and other animals to live. The environmental damage has also threatened the water supply of millions of people in south Florida, who obtain their water from the same system that feeds the swamp.

Air pollution is also having devastating effects. When people burn fossil fuels—coal, oil, and gasoline—the smoke and exhaust from the burning puts harmful chemicals such as ozone, sulfur dioxide, and nitrogen oxides in the air. These chemicals can build up in the air and can cause serious health problems. Cars that burn fuel more efficiently and produce cleaner exhaust have

been developed. But the air quality in many cities continues to worsen as their population grows.

Air pollution is also having harmful effects on the natural world. Some of the chemicals, in the form of sulfuric acid and nitric acid, are carried back to the ground in rain, fog, and snow. Precipitation that carries these pollutants is called *acid rain*. Acid rain is killing forests in North America and Europe. In the northeastern United States, it has made some lakes and streams so acid that life cannot survive in them.

Acid rain's effects on forests are complicated. Some trees are harmed directly. Acid rain damages the needles of the red spruce, for example, so that the trees can't turn sunlight into energy. In other cases, the effects are more subtle. The acid rain changes the chemistry of the soil, removing some elements that the trees need and producing others, such as aluminum, that can be toxic. Even if the trees don't die, they are weakened and are more likely to succumb to disease.

THE OZONE LAYER

Ozone in the air close to the ground is a dangerous pollutant; it's produced by car ex-

The air in many large cities is polluted by the fumes from burning fossil fuels (coal, oil, and gas). These harmful chemicals can cause serious health problems in people.

haust. But high in the atmosphere is a layer of ozone that performs an important job: It screens out much of the sun's harmful ultraviolet radiation. Without protection from the radiation, life on Earth couldn't survive. And the ozone layer is being destroyed by chemicals that people put in the air.

The ozone layer is thought to have formed billions of years ago, through the interaction of sunlight and oxygen. (The ozone produced by car exhaust doesn't rise to the upper atmosphere.) Because this interaction is still going on, the layer is constantly renewed. But since the 1970's, scientists have observed a thinning in the layer. The thinning is most serious over the Earth's poles— over Antarctica, the ozone level has dropped so much that scientists talk about a "hole" in the layer. But it's occurring worldwide.

Several pollutants are thought to be destroying the ozone. The most important are chlorofluorocarbons, or CFC's. CFC's are used as solvents, refrigerants, foaming agents in styrofoam and similar products, and propellants in aerosol sprays. When they are released into the air, they rise into the upper atmosphere and destroy the ozone.

The change in the ozone layer can't be seen or felt, but it could have serious results. Even a small increase in ultraviolet radiation can lead to higher rates of skin cancer and other health problems. The radiation can harm crops. And it can kill the tiny plants and animals that are at the bottom of the food chain. That might make survival impossible for larger animals.

Under an international treaty, 93 nations agreed in 1990 to phase out the use of CFC's, using other chemicals in their place. But some scientists fear that the chemicals used in place of CFC's will contribute to another problem: global warming.

GLOBAL WARMING

Air pollution and the thinning ozone are just the beginning of the problems that people have created in the atmosphere. Scientists have observed a worldwide warming trend that, they say, could be the beginning of a major change in the Earth's climate.

The problem is the *greenhouse effect*, caused by a buildup of carbon dioxide and other gases in the atmosphere. The gases are produced when fossil fuels are burned. And they act like the glass of a greenhouse to trap heat—they let sunlight pass through to warm the Earth, but they don't permit heat to escape back into space.

The destruction of natural areas such as the tropical rain forests contributes to the greenhouse effect. When the forests are cleared for agriculture, people often burn the cut timber, releasing huge amounts of carbon dioxide into the air. And because trees and other plants absorb carbon dioxide, cutting forests means that more carbon dioxide will remain in the atmosphere.

There is debate about how serious the greenhouse effect will be. Most scientists agree that even small changes in the world's average annual temperature could bring drought to fertile farmlands, dry up important inland waterways, and cause forests to die out. And some believe that the Earth will warm enough to melt the polar ice caps. That would raise sea levels, and coastal areas would be flooded.

The Earth has seen major climate changes in the past. But these changes took place over very long periods of time, and plants and animals were able to adjust to them. Now carbon dioxide and the other greenhouse gases are building up rapidly in the atmosphere as people burn more fossil fuels to run their cars and factories, heat their homes, and produce electricity. If the buildup continues, the Earth's climate may change too rapidly for life to adjust.

TRASH AND TOXIC WASTES

As the world's population has grown, disposing of household trash and the toxic wastes produced by industry has become a major problem. If trash and toxic wastes are burned, they pollute the air. If they are dumped at sea, they pollute the ocean. And if they are buried, pollution can seep through the ground, contaminating groundwater.

The huge amounts of trash that are discarded, especially in wealthy countries, are a symptom of another problem: the waste of the world's resources. The Earth has only so much ore to produce metal; only so much petroleum to produce fuel, fertilizer, and plastic; only so many trees to produce lumber and paper. People are rapidly using up these resources.

WHAT CAN BE DONE?

Alarm over the mounting damage to the environment has sparked new efforts to protect the fragile Earth. But scientists who have studied the problems warn that halting

Chemicals that pollute the air may be carried back to the ground in rain, fog, and snow. The pollutants formed when fossil fuels are burned create "acid rain"; this type of precipitation can kill trees. Other pollutants result from chemical pesticides and can cause twisted beaks in birds.

the damage to the environment will be a huge job, and that everyone must take part.

In many areas, there are new regulations to protect the environment. The United States passed a new clean air law in 1990. It requires car makers, power plants, and other polluters to meet tougher standards on pollution. California, where air pollution is a major problem, has passed rules that order strict auto-emisions controls and restrict the use of cars in crowded areas. Many towns and cities are starting to recycle some of their trash, so that paper, glass, metal, and plastic can be used again instead of just thrown away. And several countries have formed a group to study the greenhouse problem.

Individuals are also getting involved. As people become more aware of the dangers to the environment, they are trying to help. The steps are often simple—carpooling to work, recycling trash, turning off lights. These small steps make a difference when millions of people take them, saving thousands of acres of forest and preventing the release of millions of tons of pollutants into the air.

People are also speaking out about environmental issues, urging governments to protect wild areas and limit development. Membership in environmental and conservation groups is growing. And "green" political parties, which support conservation, have become important in many countries.

So far, however, these efforts have barely made a dent in the Earth's environmental problems. Many countries are reluctant to limit the use of fossil fuels—they are so important to modern life that doing so could hurt a country's economy. And CFC's and similar gases that have already been released into the atmosphere will continue to do harm for years to come.

Many people believe that the only way to lessen air pollution, damage to the ozone layer, and the greenhouse effect is to cut down on the use of fossil fuels and other activities that produce harmful gases. But the world's population continues to grow. Each year more people need food, energy, and living space.

Thus halting the damage to the environment will be a huge job. It may require some sacrifices by everyone. But many people believe that the job must be done if life on our fragile Earth is to survive. Their hope was that Earth Day 1990 would mark the start of a new chapter in the Earth's history, one in which people would become the caretakers, not the destroyers, of the natural world.

Disposing of household trash has become a major problem. And if plastic items are tossed in the ocean and wash up to shore, seals and other animals can get tangled up in the plastic and die.

Kids everywhere are joining together to protect the environment. Here, young people are taking part in a beach clean-up project in New Jersey.

WHAT YOU CAN DO

Young people all around the world are taking the lead in new efforts to protect the environment. Here are some of the things they're doing:

• In 1987, fifth graders in Closter, New Jersey, started a group called Kids Against Pollution to protest the use of polystyrene food containers. This foamy plastic, widely used by fast-food restaurants, doesn't break down and produces harmful fumes when it burns. Since then, the campaign has taken off—800 chapters of the group have formed across the United States and Europe.

• Several programs give schoolchildren a way to save the tropical rain forests. A Swedish program called the International Children's Rain Forest Program and another run by the Nature Conservancy, a U.S. group, use kids' donations to buy rain forest land. Kids often raise the money by collecting and selling recyclable trash.

• Children from all around the world designed posters in support of the environment in 1990. The posters were shown on a television special, "Earth '90," that was broadcast in June. Children's sing-

ing groups appeared along with rock and pop stars on the show.

• Third-grade students in Wisconsin cleaned up a trash-filled pond, planted trees and flowers around it, and created a wildlife refuge. Students in New Mexico, Utah, California, and other areas have done similar projects.

• Kids in many communities have led recycling and clean-up drives, picking up trash from beaches, parks, and roadsides.

What can *you* do to help save the environment? Plant a tree. Save water—just turning off the faucet while you brush your teeth can save as much as 10 gallons of water. Save energy—turn off lights and walk, bike, or use public transportation instead of the family car. Recycle newspapers and glass and metal containers instead of throwing them away. Use products that can be used again—don't buy throwaway dishes and utensils, and take your own shopping bag to the grocery store. And get involved with groups in your area that are working to save the environment.

KALEIDOSCOPES:
REFLECTIONS IN THE ROUND

A kaleidoscope is magical—it turns simple objects into images of fantastic beauty. And it's all done with mirrors. The mirrors—two of them—are inside the tube of the kaleidoscope, set up to form a V. Light reflected from objects at one end of the scope is bounced back and forth between them. When you look through the kaleidoscope's view hole, you see multiple images—the objects, their reflections in the mirrors, and reflections of the reflections.

The design in a kaleidoscope is always perfectly balanced, or symmetrical. In these designs, the most ordinary objects take on extraordinary beauty. Balloons, seashells, and flowers form delicate patterns. Common push pins explode in a colorful sunburst. And a bunch of items that might be found in your desk drawer—pencils, erasers, pennies, stamps—make up an intricate mosaic. Turning these common things into beautiful designs is the kaleidoscope's magic trick.

THE GREAT SHAPE UP!

Keeping fit has been a craze for twenty years. Everywhere you go, you see people walking, running, jogging, and cycling to improve their health. Health clubs and exercise classes have opened up in almost every town. Books and magazines explain the benefits of fitness and the ways to achieve it.

Until recently, however, one group sat out this rush to become physically fit: kids. All through the 1970's and 1980's, as adults became fitter and fitter, young people became flabbier and flabbier. But now that's changing. As parents and teachers have become more aware of the benefits of exercise, they have begun to encourage kids to join in.

FIT FOR LIFE

Why are so many people exercising? The reason is simple: exercise can help you feel better and live longer. Studies have shown that regular exercise reduces the risk of heart disease and other serious illnesses, helps people lose weight, and boosts their self-esteem.

Exercise seems to lower levels of cholesterol, a substance in blood that's associated with heart disease. There's also evidence that people who exercise regularly handle stress better and are less likely to die from a variety of other causes. And you don't have to work out like Superman to get these

perform poorly in basic fitness tests. Many can't run a mile in thirteen minutes —a speed that many fitness experts suggest adults *walk* to promote fitness. More children are overweight today than were overweight twenty years ago. And many have high blood levels of cholesterol and other warning signs of heart disease.

Why haven't kids jumped on the fitness bandwagon? One reason is that young people are generally healthy. Heart disease and many of the other problems that exercise helps prevent don't usually develop until later in life, even if the warning signs are present early. Thus many young people feel little need to exercise.

On top of that, parents and teachers often wrongly assume that because young people appear to be active, they are getting all the exercise they need. Thus parents often don't encourage children to exercise, and many schools require only an hour or less of gym a week.

But the amount and kind of exercise you get in an hour of gym or an afternoon of play with your friends isn't really enough to make you physically fit. And there's strong evidence that people who begin to exercise when they are young are healthier throughout their lives. Re-

Many schools are changing their physical education programs to include activities that promote fitness. Studies show that young people who exercise regularly are more confident and even perform better academically. Chinning and aerobic dancing are great exercises to help you stay healthy.

health benefits—even moderate exercise, such as a brisk daily walk, helps people live longer.

The link between fitness and health is so strong that U.S. corporations now spend about $300 million a year to encourage their employees to exercise. Some companies sponsor exercise classes; others have their own gyms, running tracks, and racquetball courts. They have found that these programs save money by reducing the cost of health care and ensuring that employees stay healthy and on the job.

While adults have been jogging and working out, however, kids have been busy at other activities—watching television and snacking. As a result, the majority of kids in the elementary through high school years

Vary your exercise program by including activities that are interesting and fun. Running, bicycling, and roller-blading all give your heart and lungs a good workout. So unglue yourself from the TV and shape up!

searchers have also discovered that fitness can have some immediate benefits for kids.

Some schools have found a link between fitness and academic performance. For example, a California school system began a program in which elementary-school students ran for twenty to forty minutes each morning. Teachers found that the children in the program did better on tests of basic academic skills. They also missed fewer school days because of illness.

A Canadian study compared students who had gym once a week to students who had gym every day and found similar results. The students who took gym daily spent less time in class but did better in reading and math. And other researchers think that being physically fit also makes children more confident socially.

All this has caused people to rethink the idea of fitness for young people. Many schools are now revising their physical education programs to include activities that promote overall fitness as well as teach sports skills. Some health clubs have begun to offer classes designed for kids, and there are even some clubs that are *just* for kids.

And parents are encouraging their children to join in when they exercise.

GET MOVING!

To turn a flabby body into a fit one—without injuring yourself in the process—you need both the right kind and the right amount of exercise.

The right kind of exercise consists of steady, sustained movement. This is known as aerobic exercise. ''Aerobic'' means ''with oxygen.'' Muscles use oxygen when they work; the oxygen is taken in by your lungs and carried to the muscles by your blood. In aerobic exercise your heart and lungs work harder to supply the muscles with the oxygen they need. But the muscles' demand for oxygen never exceeds the ability of the heart and lungs to supply it.

The heart is made of muscle, and like any other muscle it grows stronger with use. That's why this type of exercise helps strengthen the heart and prevent heart disease. Aerobic exercise also improves general muscle tone, makes you more flexible, and burns up calories, helping to control your weight.

A second type of exercise consists of short bursts of very strenuous activity, such as sprinting or lifting heavy weights. In these anaerobic (without oxygen) exercises, the muscles use oxygen faster than the heart and lungs can supply it. (You can actually feel this happening—you feel pain or a burning sensation in the muscles.) Thus you can't continue the activity very long. Anaerobic exercise builds up individual muscles, but it won't promote general fitness or burn up calories the way aerobic exercise does.

Many health clubs have classes in aerobic exercise, aerobic dancing (exercise done to music), and similar activities. But the really great thing about aerobic exercise is that there are many different ways to do it. Running, jogging, bicycling, swimming, rowing, and even roller skating all can give your heart and lungs a good workout. So can sports such as basketball, cross-country skiing, tennis, and racquetball.

This means that you can vary your exercise program and include a range of activities that are interesting and fun. If you do this, you'll be less likely to become a "fitness drop-out" and give up your workouts.

This approach is called cross-training, and it has another benefit: Varying your activities allows you to focus on different aspects of fitness. Aerobic dancing is great for increasing flexibility and coordination, for example. Rowing helps build upper-body strength, while swimming and cross-country skiing give all your muscles a workout.

The key in all these activities is to work hard enough to make your heart beat faster, but not so hard that you get really out of breath and your muscles start to hurt. To get the full benefit of aerobic exercise, you also have to keep the activity up for a period of time.

How long and how often you exercise depend a lot on how fit you are to begin with and how strenuous the activity you choose is. Fifteen or twenty minutes of brisk walking, three or four times a week, may be enough for someone who's badly out of shape. As your fitness improves, you can gradually lengthen your workouts and add more strenuous activities, such as running or jogging.

Whatever your fitness level, experts suggest taking some precautions to avoid injuries when you exercise:

• Begin your workout by warming up—doing easy activities that get the blood flowing to your muscles. Many people believe that stretching exercises are good warm-up activities. Or, if you're going to jog or run, you might start by walking briskly for three to five minutes.

• Finish your workout with a few minutes of easy activity, too—if you run, walk for a few minutes when you're done. As you walk, the action of your muscles helps push blood back to the heart, keeping your circulation flowing smoothly as your heart rate gradually returns to normal.

• Don't push yourself too hard when you exercise—do what's comfortable for you. Always increase your workload gradually, to give your muscles a chance to build strength for the increased work. And anytime you feel pain, stop what you're doing.

• Many experts add that children under 15 should avoid certain very strenuous activities, such as long-distance running. The reason is that their bones aren't fully developed and may be damaged by too much stress.

As long as you keep these precautions in mind, exercise can only do you good. So what are you waiting for? It's time to get off the couch, stop snacking, and shape up!

The Hubble Space Telescope, launched in April, was designed to give people their clearest view of the universe. But because of a flaw in the instrument's main mirror, some of the images weren't as clear as expected.

SPACE BRIEFS

Spectacular new views highlighted the 1990 space year, as spacecraft sent back data on distant planets and stars. The United States and the Soviet Union continued to lead the world in missions and research. But European and Asian countries were also active in space during the year.

THE HUBBLE SPACE TELESCOPE

The U.S. space shuttle *Discovery* went aloft on April 24, reaching an altitude of 381 miles (613 kilometers)—the highest ever attained by a shuttle. This mission was one of the year's highlights because in the shuttle's cargo bay was the Hubble Space Telescope, a $1.5 billion scientific observatory designed to give people the clearest view yet of the universe.

The telescope was the largest and most complex scientific instrument ever put in space. It was named for the American astronomer Edwin P. Hubble. In the 1920's, Hubble discovered that the universe is expanding. This discovery set the stage for the theory that the universe began in an explosion some 10 billion to 20 billion years ago.

Astronomers hoped that the Hubble telescope would be able to detect stars more than 14 billion light years away, thus providing information on what the universe was like shortly after its birth. (A light year is the distance light travels in one year—nearly 6 trillion miles, or 10 trillion kilometers. Light reaching the Hubble from an object 14 billion light years away would have left that object 14 billion years ago.) But on June 27, scientists reported that the telescope's main mirror was flawed. As a result, the telescope wasn't sharply focusing incoming light, and its images weren't as clear as expected.

In spite of its fuzzy focus, the Hubble was able to produce informative views of the heavens. It soon began sending back pictures that scientists said were better than those produced by ground-based telescopes. For example, pictures of the star cluster called 30 Doradus, in the constellation Dorado, showed at least 60 stars—not 27, as had previously been believed. And Hubble produced hundreds of pictures of an enormous storm in Saturn's dense atmosphere. The storm, more violent than any seen on Saturn in 60 years, was racing around the planet at 1,000 miles (1,600 kilometers) an hour.

Hubble also sent back evidence of what may be a black hole in outer space. (A black hole is an object that has such enormous gravitational pull that it prevents the escape of all matter and energy, even light.) Pictures showed that a distant galaxy called NGC 7457 has an extremely small center. Stars there are crowded together at least 30,000 times as densely as the stars in our galaxy, the Milky Way. Scientists were unable to explain the crowding. But some suggested that a black hole at the galaxy's center was the cause.

The National Aeronautics and Space Administration (NASA) plans to repair the Hubble on a 1993 shuttle mission. If the mission takes place, astronauts will link up with the telescope and install a new camera and other devices that will compensate for the flawed mirror, producing sharper pictures.

MORE SHUTTLE MISSIONS

The first space shuttle mission of 1990 occurred in January, when *Columbia* roared into space. During almost eleven days aloft —the longest mission in the history of the shuttle program—astronauts launched a communications satellite and retrieved the Long-Duration Exposure Facility (LDEF). The LDEF was a satellite that had been orbiting the Earth for almost six years. Aboard were 57 experiments. They included studies of the effects of space on various materials that are being considered for use in future spacecraft. There were also collecting devices that gathered gases and dust from outer space, including particles from comets.

OUT-OF-THIS-WORLD TOMATOES

About 4 million students from the United States took part in a giant experiment after *Columbia* retrieved the Long-Duration Exposure Facility (LDEF) satellite in early 1990. Aboard the LDEF were 12.5 million tomato seeds, sealed in airtight canisters. For almost six years, the seeds had been exposed to weightlessness, cosmic radiation, and other unworldly conditions.

Another 12.5 million tomato seeds had been stored in airtight containers on Earth for the same period of time. NASA divided the space seeds and the Earth seeds into groups of about 50 and placed each group in a foil container. The containers were mailed to 58,000 teachers around the country. Their students planted the seeds and reported back to NASA.

All the students were asked to record the seeds' germination rate, the plants' growth rate, the shape of the leaves, and changes in appearance that would indicate genetic mutations. High school and college students performed more advanced experiments, studying cell structures and what happened when the tomato plants were exposed to different kinds of fungi. Some even tried to interbreed the plants with other tomato strains.

The students' findings will be valuable as NASA plans long space missions and permanent bases on the moon or Mars, for which food may have to be produced in space. For example, if the space tomato plants show a high rate of mutations, then scientists will have to give seeds better protection, so that they can produce healthy tomatoes for future astronauts' dinners.

In late February, *Atlantis* was launched on a secret military mission. The astronauts reportedly deployed a spy satellite over the Soviet Union. After *Discovery*'s April Hubble mission, a series of mechanical problems caused a five-month interruption of shuttle flights.

Then, on October 6, *Discovery* returned to space carrying Ulysses, a spacecraft designed to survey the sun's polar regions. After Ulysses was deployed, its own rockets boosted it to a speed of more than 34,000 miles (55,000 kilometers) an hour. It headed toward Jupiter, where it will arrive in early 1992. Jupiter's powerful gravitational pull will act like a slingshot, swinging the spacecraft into an orbit around the sun. This orbit will bring Ulysses over the sun's southern

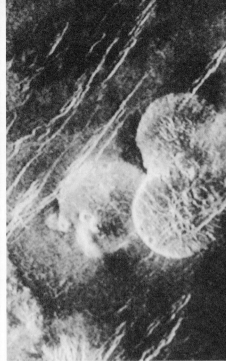

Magellan (*left*), a space probe bound for Venus, was deployed in 1989. In August, 1990, the probe went into orbit around that planet and began sending radar images back to Earth. One fascinating photo (*above*) showed seven huge pancake-shaped lava domes lined up in a row.

pole in mid-1994 and over its northern pole in early 1995. The Ulysses mission is a cooperative venture between the United States and the European Space Agency, which is sponsored by thirteen countries.

In November, *Atlantis* streaked into orbit on another secret military mission. According to reports, the goal was to launch a satellite to monitor the Persian Gulf region.

The year's final shuttle mission took place in December, when *Columbia* made its tenth mission. The seven astronauts spent much of the mission using Astro, an on-board observatory consisting of three ultraviolet telescopes and one X-ray telescope. Unfortunately, lint was found in the cooling systems of Astro's computers. This caused the computers to overheat, and only about half of the planned stars, galaxies, and other targets were observed.

MAGELLAN

In May, 1989, *Atlantis* had deployed Magellan, a space probe bound for Venus. Fifteen months later—in August, 1990—Magellan went into orbit around that planet. Radar aboard the craft "looked" through the thick clouds that cover Venus, producing detailed images of the surface that were sent back to Earth. By the time Magellan completes its mission, it is expected to map as much as 90 percent of the Venusian surface.

Right from the beginning, the images from Magellan fascinated scientists. The pictures showed ocean-size ancient lava flows, towering volcanic mountains, horseshoe-shaped dunes of dark sand, and deep impact craters formed by meteors. Seven enormous lava domes were lined up in one area of the planet's surface, looking like a row of giant pancakes. And there was something never seen on any other planet: an area as large as the state of Rhode Island marked with a crisscross pattern of lines. Scientists weren't certain what caused the strange pattern.

THE SOVIET SPACE PROGRAM

The Soviet's manned space program centers around Mir. This giant orbiting space station, launched in 1986, is visited by teams

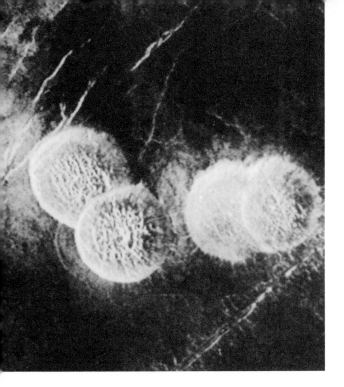

of cosmonauts for extended periods of time. On February 19, 1990, Alexander S. Viktorenko and Alexander A. Serebrov returned to Earth from a 22-week mission aboard Mir. While in space the men tested a "space motorcycle." This vehicle is designed for repair work outside the space station and for rescuing cosmonauts in distress.

About a week before Viktorenko and Serebrov ended their mission, they were joined by Anatoly Solovyev and Alexander Balandin, who had been launched into space on February 11. The new team remained in Mir until August 9. Their mission was marked by two space walks. The first, on July 17, was almost disastrous. Solovyev and Balandin had emerged from Mir to repair torn insulation. The work took much longer than expected, and the men's oxygen supply was running low. When they were finished, they discovered that the reentry hatch had been damaged upon opening and was unusable. They had to reenter Mir through an emergency porthole.

When Solovyev and Balandin returned to Earth, they brought back 23 pure crystals, estimated to be worth about $1 million each. The crystals were produced in the weightless space environment, which gave them a purity and quality that cannot be achieved on Earth. This makes them very valuable in producing computers and other electronic equipment.

On August 1, Gennady Manakov and Gennady Strekalov were launched. They docked their space capsule with Mir two days later. They weren't the only passengers aboard the capsule. Traveling with them were five Japanese quail, which were to be used in experiments during the following months.

On December 2, Viktor Afansev and Musa Manarov were aloft. With them was Toyohiro Akiyama of Japan—the first journalist ever sent into space. Once aboard Mir, Akiyama made a series of live radio and television broadcasts to Japan, describing the unpleasantness of weightlessness and space sickness; he commented that it felt as if his brain were "floating around in my head." Akiyama returned to Earth on December 10, with Manakov and Strekalov.

BRIEF BRIEFS

• On January 24, Japan launched two satellites on a mission to the moon. It was Japan's first lunar mission and the first such mission from any country since 1976. (Only the United States and the Soviet Union had previously sent spacecraft to the moon.) The larger of the two Japanese satellites, named Hiten, entered an elliptical orbit around the Earth. On March 19, as it neared the moon, Hiten deployed the smaller satellite, Hagoromo. Hagoromo, which is only 14 inches (35 centimeters) in diameter, entered an orbit around the moon.

• In April, China launched its first foreign satellite, an American telecommunications satellite called Asiasat. This satellite has an unusual history. It was first launched by the United States as Westar 6 in 1984. But it failed to attain orbit, and later that year it was recovered and brought back to Earth by astronauts aboard *Discovery*.

• In February, the U.S. spacecraft Voyager 1 sent back a "family snapshot" of the solar system taken from outer space. Voyager 1 and its sister craft, Voyager 2, were launched in 1977 on a grand tour of the outer solar system. This was the last picture to be transmitted by Voyager 1 as it headed out into interstellar space. But scientists who are analyzing the enormous amount of information these spacecraft provided are still making discoveries. For example, in 1990 a scientist studying a decade-old image taken by Voyager 2 found an eighteenth moon orbiting Saturn.

MAKE & DO

If you look up and see a huge butterfly fluttering over your head, don't be alarmed —it's not a giant insect. Chances are you're seeing a kite. The ancient sport of kite flying has always been popular with young people. Today it's enjoying a new wave of popularity. And elaborate, beautifully patterned kites, such as this Chinese butterfly, can often be seen floating in the air on breezy days.

GO FLY A KITE

Some people call it "painting the sky." Others say it's "dancing with the wind." But most people call it just plain "kite flying."

Today, millions of people all around the world are painting the sky with colorful kites. Kite flying is fun, and it's easy to do. Look up on a breezy spring afternoon and you're bound to see at least one diamond-shaped kite—probably the most familiar kite shape in North America. But you're also likely to see kites shaped like butterflies, eagles, flags, airplanes, flowers, masks—almost anything imaginable. For in recent years, the art of creating kites has become as popular as the sport of flying them.

MORE THAN AMUSEMENT

No one knows for sure who made the first kites, but it's believed that they were invented in China more than 2,000 years ago. According to one legend, a farmer got the idea when a gust of wind blew off his hat. The hat had a string that tied under the farmer's chin, so he didn't lose it. But the ability of the wind to carry his hat gave him an idea for a toy with which to amuse himself and his friends.

From early times, however, kites have been more than toys. They have had many practical uses. Some uses were military. About 500 A.D. one Chinese emperor used kites to signal his soldiers. The soldiers would work on nearby farms until they saw the kites flying above the emperor's palace. This was a signal that they should rush to the palace to help defend it against enemies seen approaching on the horizon.

During the American Civil War in the 1860's, the Union used kites to scatter leaflets over Confederate troops. The leaflets urged the Confederates to surrender, promising them amnesty if they would lay down their arms. During the Boer War in South Africa in the late 1890's, large kites were used to carry British soldiers over the fighting front to observe the enemy. During World Wars I and II, kites were used to disable enemy aircraft.

Kites have also been valuable scientific tools. The most famous experiment involving a kite was conducted by Benjamin Franklin during a thunderstorm in 1752. Flying a kite made of a silk handkerchief stretched on two cedar sticks, Franklin proved that lightning was the same as the electric current that flows through wires. (This was a very dangerous experiment; it could easily have killed Franklin!)

From the 1700's until the early 1900's, kites were used to collect weather data. Thermometers, anemometers, and other instruments used to measure weather factors were attached to kites and launched into the sky. Kites have also been used to tow boats and sleds and carry cameras into the atmosphere to take pictures of the Earth.

And kites are used to celebrate special occasions. In Japan, for example, people fly kites to welcome in the new year and to celebrate Children's Day on May 5. In China, the Festival of Ascending on High is actually a celebration of the practice of kite flying.

AN EXHILARATING PASTIME

Today most people fly kites simply for fun. Kites come in a wide variety of shapes, materials, and colors. There are diamonds, dragons, centipedes, birds, windsocks, and boxes. They're made of paper, plastic, nylon, satin. And they come in every color of the rainbow—usually, the more brilliant, the better.

Many kites are painted with fantastic designs. Some have appliquéd designs, with the part under the appliqué cut away so that all parts are equally filled with light. Still other kites are made of patchwork, with designs taken from classic quilt patterns. The result is often an item of great beauty. Many kites are so beautiful that people use them to decorate walls in their homes.

Despite the variety, all kites have three basic parts. The **wing surface** is designed to be lifted by the wind. The **flying line** is used to control the flight of the kite and keep it from being blown away. The **bridle** is the means by which the flying line is connected to the kite. It holds the face of the kite at an angle to the wind.

Traditional kites are flat and rigid. They usually need a tail to help keep the bottom of the kite down and the nose tilted up.

KITING TIPS

To have a truly unique kite, make and decorate your own! Kite-building materials are inexpensive and easy to obtain. Just choose the lightest materials possible: The heavier the material, the more it will pull the kite down.

The wing can be made from paper, cloth, nylon, or plastic. If you use paper, avoid the kinds that easily tear or crease. If you prefer cloth, select a fabric such as cotton sailcloth, which is lightweight yet tightly woven.

The wing's supporting frame is made of wood. Use wood that's light, strong, and flexible. Craft shops sell special kite dowels, but you can also use pieces of bamboo, spruce, or white pine.

Buy strong string for the flying line. You might consider using linen cord, fishing line, or braided nylon twine. The bridle may be made from ordinary string or a thin cord.

A word of caution: never use metal in any part of your kite. Don't use metal frames, metal-coated materials, wire, or tinsel. Metal conducts electricity, and you could get a shock.

Many books give directions for making various kite shapes. Start with something basic. The more elaborate the kite, the more complex the construction. But even a simple diamond-shaped kite can look spectacular. Choose colorful fabrics. Paint or appliqué wild designs on the wing.

Whatever kind of kite you build, keep in mind that for a kite to stay in the air it should be symmetrical—each side should be similar to the other.

Once you have your kite, you're ready to fly! Here are tips to help make your kite dance in the wind.

• Don't run with a kite to launch it. Stand with your back to the wind. Have a friend stand about 100 feet (30 meters) away, holding the kite pointing upward. As your friend lets go of the kite, pull in the line with a hand-over-hand motion. The kite will rise in the air.

• Pulling in on the kite line makes a kite rise. Letting the line out allows the wind to carry the kite away, but at the same time causes the kite to lose altitude. Combining the two—pulling, letting out line, and pulling again in a kind of pumping action—lets your kite fly high and far.

• Pulling on the line makes a kite move in the direction it is already headed. If your kite is diving or is otherwise out of control, don't pull. It only makes matters worse. Let your line go completely slack. When the kite rights itself, pull in on the line to make it rise into the air again.

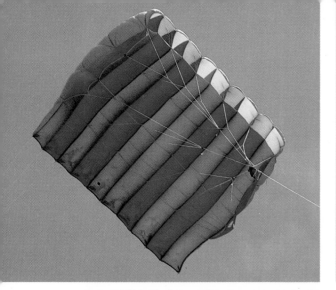

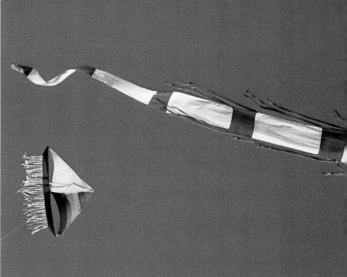

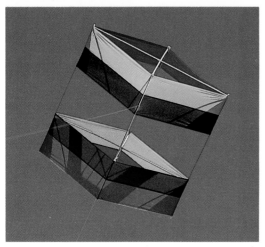

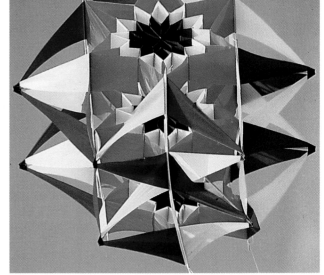

Bow kites look much like flat kites. But one or more of the sticks that form the frame are bent, giving the kite a curved form.

The box kite, which was invented in 1893, is a rigid kite consisting of two or more open-ended boxes. The boxes may be square, oblong, or triangular. Large box kites are powerful flyers. Those 6 feet (2 meters) or longer generally require two people to hold and maneuver the flying line.

The first nonrigid kite was the parawing, designed in the 1940's. (Hang-gliders are an adaptation of the parawing.) Sometimes called the flexiwing, the parawing has no central spine or other supporting sticks.

Another big step came in the 1960's, when a huge kite called the parafoil was designed. The parafoil resembles a parachute and has incredible lifting and gliding power. It's made entirely of fabric, with no supporting sticks.

Then there are the amazing kites from Asia: The caterpillar kite consists of a series of disks connected by lengths of string. The snake kite has a long tapering tail that ripples in the breeze. The butterfly kite, which flies best in light winds, has bowed wings. The Chinese lantern kite looks like a giant tube or can that is open at both ends.

Typically, a kite has a single flying line. If you add a second line, you can try stunt flying—creating loops, circles, hairpin turns, and other maneuvers. Expert fliers can even make their kites do somersaults and dance to music. And for even tighter control, some people use four flying lines, called quad lines.

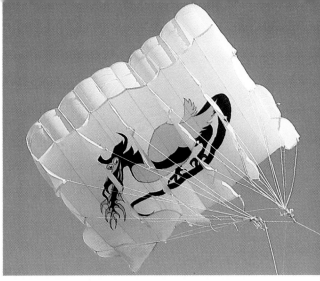

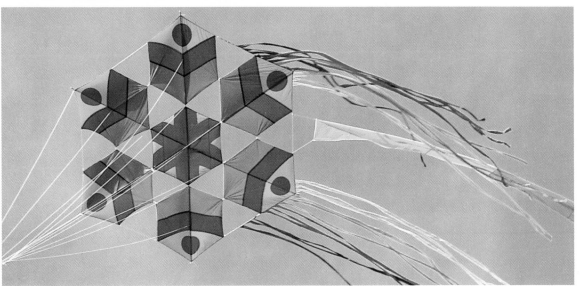

The largest kite ever built had an area of 6,000 square feet (557 square meters). When it was sent aloft, seventy people held onto it. But it was so powerful that it almost pulled those seventy people into the sky.

What is believed to have been the longest kite was called the Thai Snake. When fully stretched out across the sky, it had a length of almost half a mile (0.8 kilometer).

SHARING THE FUN

Sometimes it's fun to be all alone as you fly your kite. But at other times you may want to share your pleasure—perhaps with a few friends or perhaps with thousands of other kiting enthusiasts. One of the most popular group events is the annual Kite Festival, which takes place at the Smithsonian Institution in Washington, D.C. Participants can fly any kite they want. But if you wish to enter any of the festival contests, you must fly a homemade kite that is able to reach an altitude of 100 feet (33 meters) for a least one minute.

This is only one of the hundreds of kite festivals held in cities and towns in many countries. People compete for prizes, exchange kite-building secrets, and have a great time. Even those who don't fly kites enjoy these colorful events. Many people who come "just to watch" return the following year with kites of their own, for they have learned the joys of this fascinating pastime.

JENNY TESAR
Series Consultant
Wonders of Wildlife

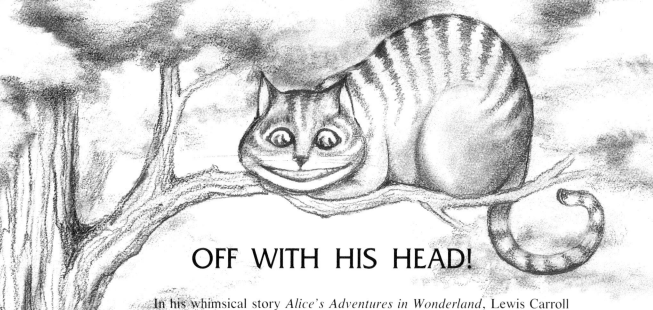

OFF WITH HIS HEAD!

In his whimsical story *Alice's Adventures in Wonderland*, Lewis Carroll describes a series of remarkable adventures that young Alice has after she falls down a well and enters a strange new world. At the home of the Duchess, she meets an odd creature called the Cheshire Cat. This cat, however, is not an ordinary one. It can grin from ear to ear. And it can disappear!

Someone wants to kill the Cheshire Cat. To learn the villain's name, you need a pencil and a sheet of lined paper. Carefully follow the directions given below. Hint: It will be easier if you rewrite the complete words at each step. The solution is on page 413.

1. Print the words CHESHIRE CAT.

2. Place an F at the end of the first word.

3. Find the fourth letter from the left. Move it to the end of the second word.

4. Find the letter that comes before J in the alphabet. Replace it with an E.

5. Put a T at the beginning of the first word.

6. Find the fifth consonant from the left. Move it between the A–T combination.

7. Put a space after the fourth letter of the first word.

8. Place an N after the first consonant of the second word.

9. Insert an O between the E-F combination.

10. Insert a Q between the E-O combination.

11. Find the first letter of the second word. Move it to the beginning of the third word.

12. Remove the second consonant from the left.

13. Place a U after the third vowel from the left.

14. Put a space before the sixth letter of the second word.

15. Remove the C. Replace it with an E.

16. Reverse the order of the letters in the second word.

The Cheshire Cat must have played his cards right, because he vanished before this heartless villain could strike!

THE GARDEN FENCE

This wall hanging brings the color and charm of a summer garden indoors, to brighten your home throughout the year. Made from small tree branches decorated with dried flowers, it looks just like a country fence in miniature.

Begin by gathering branches for the fence. These are easily found on forest floors and in parks, especially after a storm. The two horizontal fence pieces should be about the length of your forearm; the vertical pieces should be about half that length. All the pieces should be as straight as possible.

Using small nails, attach a sawtooth hanger to the back of the horizontal piece that will be the top of your fence. Then connect all the pieces. This is best done with a hot glue gun, although twine or tiny nails can be used.

Now you can give your fence some summer blooms. Start by gluing dried sphagnum moss and eucalyptus leaves along the bottom of the fence. A layer of fine wood shavings called excelsior can also be used. (These items are available in craft stores and garden shops.) Finally, add a colorful array of dried flowers.

Use your imagination to create variations on this basic design. You may wish to paint the fence white or another color. Construct a bower or a gate in the center of the fence. Add dried wheat and other grasses. Or perch a pair of tiny artificial birds among the flowers.

LEAF ART:
DON'T WASTE THEM, PASTE THEM!

Collect a variety of leaves to create insects, birds, fish, or any other type of animal—even imaginary creatures. First, dry the leaves by putting them between sheets of newspaper and placing them under a stack of heavy books for several days. Then make your design. Use glue or paste to hold each leaf in place.

STAMP COLLECTING

The year 1990 was a special one for stamp collectors—it marked the 150th anniversary of the world's first postage stamps, which were issued in Great Britain in May, 1840. The stamps, known as the Penny Black and the Two-Penny Blue, featured an identical design, a profile of young Queen Victoria. They were made possible by some ideas that we take for granted but were revolutionary back in the 1800's: that postage rates should be uniform and based on weight rather than distance, and that postage should be paid by the sender (rather than the receiver).

The anniversary was marked by an outpouring of commemorative designs from countries all over the world. Britain issued stamps in five denominations, some combining portraits of Queen Victoria and Queen Elizabeth II and some showing the Penny Black itself. Many other countries, from Norway to tiny Liechtenstein, also showed the Penny Black in their designs.

Meanwhile, the year saw a wealth of new issues on many other themes.

U.S. STAMPS

For only the second time in history, the United States and the Soviet Union released a joint stamp issue in 1990. The four stamps issued by each country were nearly identical in design, with the U.S. stamps carrying a denomination of 25 cents and the Soviet stamps 25 kopecks. They showed animals that are found in the oceans off both countries: the killer whale, the northern sea lion, the sea otter, and the common dolphin. (The first U.S.-Soviet joint issue had honored the 1975 Apollo-Soyuz space mission.)

Other 25-cent U.S. stamps covered a broad range of subjects. A popular group of five stamps, issued in booklets, showed historic lighthouses on the East and West coasts. This release was timed to mark the 200th anniversary of the U.S. Coast Guard, which was founded in 1790. Some of the lighthouses shown, such as the Cape Hatteras lighthouse in North Carolina, are threatened by coastal erosion today.

Classic films were commemorated in a block of four stamps. The designs depicted Judy Garland in *The Wizard of Oz*, Clark Gable and Vivien Leigh in *Gone With the Wind*, Gary Cooper in *Beau Geste*, and John Wayne in *Stagecoach*. And Olympic athletes of the past were honored in a booklet of five stamps. They included track and field stars Jesse Owens and Ray Ewry, swimmer Helene Madison, tennis player Hazel Wightman, and boxer Eddie Eagan.

The 1990 "Love" stamp bore a design of lovebirds over a heart and a garland. The stamp was based on a cut-paper design and resembled Pennsylvania folk art. The Postal Service also produced a group of stamps showing the elegant feathered headdresses of five Indian tribes: the Assiniboine, Cheyenne, Comanche, Flathead, and Shoshone.

A new 15-cent stamp—designed with vacation postcards in mind—showed a sunny beach scene with a beach umbrella. The year also saw the start of a new high-value series depicting American wildlife. The first of these $2 stamps showed a bobcat stretched out on a tree limb.

A new item of postal stationery was a stamped envelope bearing a hologram of professional football's Vince Lombardi Trophy. And the Post Office broke new ground with a plastic, self-adhesive, 25-cent stamp depicting the American flag. In a test program, this stamp was sold through automatic teller machines at banks in Washington State.

STAMPS AROUND THE WORLD

An increase in postal rates prompted a wide range of new stamp issues in Canada in 1990. Among the most charming were four 39-cent stamps showing dolls. Included were Indian and Eskimo (Inuit) dolls, the dolls of early European settlers, and commercial dolls of more recent times. A second group of 39-cent stamps showed work boats used by early European settlers. And Canada issued several different designs featuring its flag—one was released on June 29 to mark the flag's 25th anniversary.

Other Canadian issues focused on the natural world. A group of four 39-cent commemoratives celebrated the country's vast forests. And three stamps showed animals native to the country: the pronghorn (on a

$2 USA

**1990 STAMPS
FROM AROUND
THE WORLD**

125 Jahre Max und Moritz
100 +50
DEUTSCHE BUNDESPOST
FÜR DIE JUGEND 1990

VEREINTE NATIONEN
AIDS
s5
WELTWEITE AIDS-BEKÄMPFUNG

SCHÜTZT DIE NORDSEE
100
Deutsche Bundespost

20p
1840 · RSPCA · 1990

NAMIBIA 45¢
INDEPENDENCE 21 MARCH 1990
Theo Marais

NIPPON 1990
41 +4

NIPPON
62

150 JAHRE
1840 · BRIEFMARKE · 1990
POSTAGE
FUERSTENTUM   LIECHTENSTEIN
F ONE PENNY E
150

Plantes médicinales
Nations Unies
CINCHONA OFFICINALS

The WIZARD OF OZ
USA 25

ANTIGUA & BARBUDA   1¢
UPPER and LOWER
CASE
THE
PRINTING
PRESS

60P   EⁱⁱR
FARM ANIMALS
ST. HELENA

25 USA
CAPE HATTERAS, NORTH CAROLINA

39   CANADA

20
ALEXANDRA PALACE
STAMP WORLD EXHIBITION
LONDON 1990

37
TEMPLETON CARPET FACTORY
GLASGOW 1990
EUROPEAN CITY OF CULTURE

Boreal Forest   Forêt boréale
39   CANADA

L O V E
USA 25

USA 15

Australia 30c

palau

WEIHNACHTS MARKE 1979   60 +30   DEUTSCHE BUNDESPOST

CANADA   38

M-A. SUZOR-COTÉ
SEASON'S GREETINGS • MEILLEURS VŒUX

10P

GRENADA $1

GRENADA $1

GRENADA $1   GRENADA $1

9P

THE TWELVE DAYS OF CHRISTMAS

Christmas USA 20c

Fra Filippo Lippi, National Gallery

CHRISTMAS 1986

$1   CHRISTMAS ISLAND
INDIAN OCEAN

The Holly and the Ivy   15½P

I Saw Three Ships   19½P

We Three Kings   26P

Greetings USA 25

15P

ROBIN CALLANDER   ISLE of MAN

USA 22

GREETINGS

A TOPICAL
COLLECTION OF
CHRISTMAS STAMPS

45-cent stamp), the timber wolf (on a 61-cent stamp), and the beluga whale (on a 78-cent stamp). Canada also honored some creatures that never existed, in stamps that showed the sasquatch (bigfoot), werewolf, kraken, and Ogopogo (the last two are sea monsters). The four 39-cent stamps were the first in a series on Canadian folklore.

Four British stamps showed landmark buildings. Two were postal buildings—the British Philatelic Bureau in Edinburgh, Scotland, and the Alexandra Palace in London, site of the 1990 Stamp World Exhibition. The others showed landmarks in Glasgow, Scotland, which was honored as the 1990 European "city of culture" by the European Community.

The Royal Society for the Prevention of Cruelty to Animals (RSPCA) was honored with four stamps. Featured were a fluffy kitten, a puppy, a rabbit, and a duckling. Another group of four British stamps marked the 150th anniversary of the Royal Botanic Gardens at Kew, on the outskirts of London. These famous gardens include about 50,000 kinds of plants from all over the world.

The island of St. Helena, a British dependency, issued a group of stamps showing farm animals. Early European settlers introduced the animals to this remote island in the Atlantic Ocean.

Before the unification of Germany in October, 1990, West Germany issued a group of four stamps especially for children. The stamps showed the exploits of Max and Moritz, characters in a series of humorous illustrated poems that were popular in the late 1800's. Max and Moritz were forerunners of the comic strip *Katzenjammer Kids*, which was started around the turn of the century. Another West German issue promoted protection of the North Sea. It showed a collection of North Sea animals—birds, fish, a seal, and even an octopus.

The African country of Namibia, which finally gained independence in 1990, marked the event with three stamps. Against a background of a map of the country, one stamp showed a pair of hands with broken manacles, releasing a white dove. The second showed the country's flag and a portrait of its president, Sam Nujoma; the third showed the flag with a map of southern Africa.

Caribbean and South American countries produced a wealth of stamps during the year. Plants and animals were a favorite topic for many countries. Belize issued a series of definitives showing birds and butterflies, while Brazil showed flowers. The island country of Antigua and Barbuda showed Caribbean ocean life. Taking up another subject, Antigua and Barbuda showed the Disney character Goofy on a stamp that honored the invention of the printing press.

In Asia, Japan released a pair of stamps that marked the International Garden and Greenery Exposition held there in 1990. One showed two tiny fairies sitting in a flower, and the other showed a bicycle beneath a tree. China called attention to an endangered species with a stamp that showed the rare snow leopard. And China took part in its first joint issue ever, with Canada. Both countries issued stamps that honored Dr. Norman Bethune, a Canadian surgeon who worked in China in the late 1930's.

Among the stamps issued by the United Nations were six that supported the worldwide fight against AIDS (acquired immune deficiency syndrome). Another group of six U.N. stamps showed medicinal plants in designs that were based on old botanical prints. The United Nations is helping developing countries make use of their native plants to produce medicines.

A TOPICAL COLLECTION

Christmas cards are a tradition in many parts of the world. And with so many people mailing cards to wish their friends "Merry Christmas" or "Season's Greetings," it's not surprising that many countries issue special Christmas stamps every year.

These stamps would make an excellent topical collection—a collection built around a single theme. Christmas stamps include a wide range of designs. There are stamps that show scenes from the story of the first Christmas. Others depict Christmas celebrations and traditions, such as giving gifts and decorating the home. And still others are seasonal scenes of wintry, snow-covered landscapes. Even in summer, a collection of Christmas stamps can remind you of one of the happiest times of year.

CHARLESS HAHN
Stamp Editor
Chicago Sun-Times

BANGLES OF BEADS

Dazzle your friends with an armful of colorful bracelets—each made with safety pins that have been filled with beads.

Lay forty safety pins in a row, with the heads facing up. (Use more pins for a large wrist, fewer for a small wrist.) Open the pins and fill with beads. Follow one of the patterns shown, or create your own design. Close the pins, and securely fasten them.

Next, place forty empty pins in between the beaded pins. The heads of the empty pins should be facing down. (If you are using tiny beads, even *these* pins can be filled with beads.)

Use two strands of elastic thread to connect the pins. Be careful: As you connect the pins, make sure they all open outward, not toward your wrist! Pass one piece of elastic through the top holes in the row of pins—through the heads of the beaded pins and through the tails of the empty pins. Bring the ends together and knot. Repeat the process for the bottom of the row of pins. Place a drop of glue on the knots to prevent them from loosening.

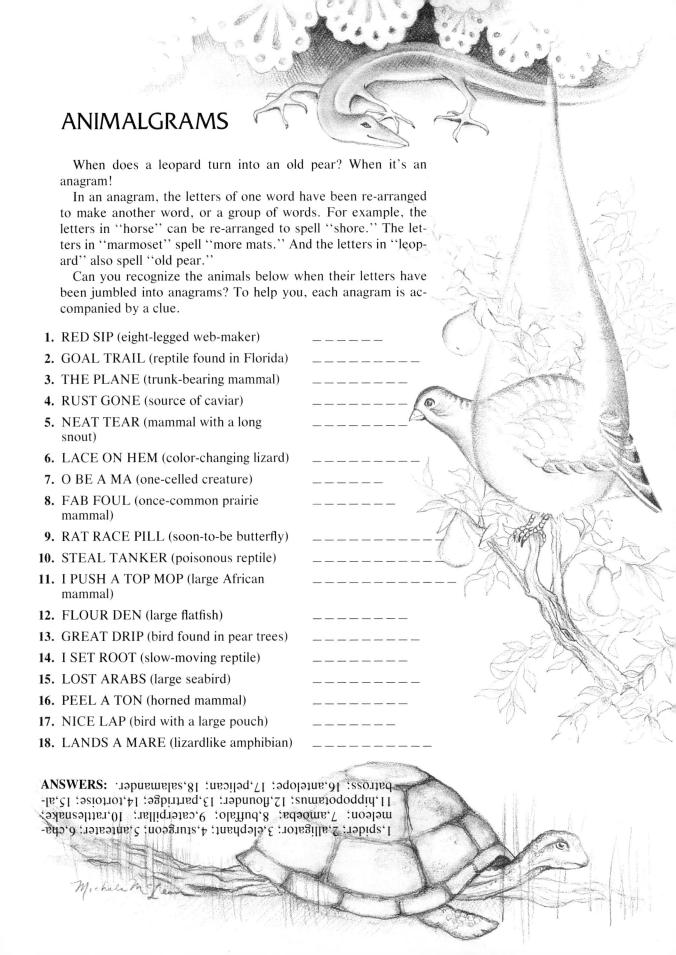

ANIMALGRAMS

When does a leopard turn into an old pear? When it's an anagram!

In an anagram, the letters of one word have been re-arranged to make another word, or a group of words. For example, the letters in "horse" can be re-arranged to spell "shore." The letters in "marmoset" spell "more mats." And the letters in "leopard" also spell "old pear."

Can you recognize the animals below when their letters have been jumbled into anagrams? To help you, each anagram is accompanied by a clue.

1. RED SIP (eight-legged web-maker) _ _ _ _ _ _

2. GOAL TRAIL (reptile found in Florida) _ _ _ _ _ _ _ _ _

3. THE PLANE (trunk-bearing mammal) _ _ _ _ _ _ _ _

4. RUST GONE (source of caviar) _ _ _ _ _ _ _ _

5. NEAT TEAR (mammal with a long snout) _ _ _ _ _ _ _ _

6. LACE ON HEM (color-changing lizard) _ _ _ _ _ _ _ _

7. O BE A MA (one-celled creature) _ _ _ _ _ _

8. FAB FOUL (once-common prairie mammal) _ _ _ _ _ _ _

9. RAT RACE PILL (soon-to-be butterfly) _ _ _ _ _ _ _ _ _ _ _

10. STEAL TANKER (poisonous reptile) _ _ _ _ _ _ _ _ _ _

11. I PUSH A TOP MOP (large African mammal) _ _ _ _ _ _ _ _ _ _ _

12. FLOUR DEN (large flatfish) _ _ _ _ _ _ _ _

13. GREAT DRIP (bird found in pear trees) _ _ _ _ _ _ _ _ _

14. I SET ROOT (slow-moving reptile) _ _ _ _ _ _ _ _

15. LOST ARABS (large seabird) _ _ _ _ _ _ _ _ _

16. PEEL A TON (horned mammal) _ _ _ _ _ _ _ _

17. NICE LAP (bird with a large pouch) _ _ _ _ _ _ _

18. LANDS A MARE (lizardlike amphibian) _ _ _ _ _ _ _ _ _ _

ANSWERS: 1.spider; 2.alligator; 3.elephant; 4.sturgeon; 5.anteater; 6.chameleon; 7.amoeba; 8.buffalo; 9.caterpillar; 10.rattlesnake; 11.hippopotamus; 12.flounder; 13.partridge; 14.tortoise; 15.albatross; 16.antelope; 17.pelican; 18.salamander.

SUMPTUOUS SACHETS

For hundreds of years people have used sachets—small bags of sweetly scented flowers, leaves, and herbs—to add a pleasant scent to their homes. Today, sachets are more popular than ever—and more creative than ever, too. They are made with every type of fabric imaginable, and in all shapes and sizes. Some don't even use dried potpourri plants, but depend on soaps and oils for fragrance.

One reason that sachets are so popular is that they can be used in any room of your home. They can even be used in cars and boats. Slip flat sachets among folded towels and sheets, under sofa pillows, and between books on your bookshelves. Tie ball sachets to bedposts and the arms of chairs, or cluster them in a glass bowl. Hang pouch sachets from closet rods, tuck them in dresser drawers, or put them in your stationery box. Display soap sachets in bathrooms, or hang them in linen closets. And don't forget your friends—sachets make wonderful gifts.

When making sachets, choose a potpourri that will be appropriate for the place where the sachets will be used. Sweet-smelling rose petals are ideal for feminine closets. Lavender or herb mixtures are good for bed linens. And fruity or spicy mixtures are appealing in kitchens.

There are two things you can do to help make the fragrance of sachets last a long time. Occasionally squeeze flat and pouch sachets, gently crushing the potpourri inside. Or add a few drops of special potpourri oils, which are called essence oils. They can be purchased in craft and flower shops. Use an oil that matches the scent of the sachet. For example, use a rose oil for a sachet filled with rose petals, a eucalyptus oil for one that contains eucalyptus leaves. If you can't open the sachet to add the oil directly to the dried plants, add the oil right through the fabric, at a point where any staining won't be visible.

Flat sachets. The basic parts of sachets like those on the opposite page are simply two identical pieces of fabric. Sew them partially together, to form a bag. Fill the bag

with potpourri, and then sew it closed. Endless variety is possible. The fabric can be embroidered; it can be pieced together from a combination of satins and laces; two lace handkerchiefs or heart-shaped doilies can be used. The sachets can be decorated with lace, ribbons, fabric roses, strings of tiny pearls, sequins, and beads.

Ball sachets. These sachets are "built" around a Styrofoam ball. The easiest kind to make is a fabric-covered ball. First add a few drops of essence oil to the ball itself, and then cover it with a pretty fabric. Use a matching ribbon to hold the fabric around the ball. Tie the ribbon into a big, floppy bow, and place a fabric rose or fancy button in the center. Trim the edges of the fabric with pinking shears. By choosing different fabric patterns, you can make ball sachets for every season of the year. How about a pumpkin-print fabric and cinnamon oil for Halloween?

You can make another type of ball sachet by covering the ball with a thin layer of white glue and then rolling it in lavender, crushed rose petals, or mixed potpourri. Gently wrap twine around the ball and add decorations to the top.

Or, begin by gluing satin ribbon onto the ball. Add layers of small eucalyptus leaves until the ball is completely covered. Top with ribbon bows, a hanging loop, and artificial berries.

Pouch sachets. These are made much like flat sachets. But after the bags are filled, the top is gathered and tied with ribbon or lace just above the potpourri. Embroidered flowers, dried flowers, or other decorations can be glued onto the ribbon. Or the gathered top of the sachet can be spread open, and a large fabric rose can be placed in its center. Fill some simple pouch bags with herbs and use them to scent your bath.

Soap sachets. Find some pretty, scented soaps and turn them into sachets by gluing on lace, embroidered flowers, strings of pearls, sequins, and other decorations. It's best to work with gathered lace, which can be purchased in craft and fabric stores. Circle the soap at least twice with the lace, to create a full, rich look.

A hanging soap sachet can be made from a length of wide ribbon. Turn under and sew closed the top of the ribbon, to make a hanging loop. Glue on heart-shaped soaps and various decorations. This makes a wonderful gift, particularly if you can color-coordinate it with the decor in your friend's home.

SITE-SEEING

When you visit a distant city, much of what you see may remind you of your home town. But other city sites are unique, and these are the things you don't want to miss: historical monuments, fairy tale palaces, beautiful parks.

Travelers will tell you that a trip to London isn't complete without watching the changing of the guard at Buckingham Palace. A trip to San Francisco must include a ride on one of the city's famous cable cars. And if you are going to Italy, ask someone to take your picture beside the Leaning Tower of Pisa.

The names of 25 famous sites are listed below (in the left column). Match each to its city and country (in the right column).

1. Alamo		a. Addis Ababa (Ethiopia)
2. Big Ben		b. Agra (India)
3. Brandenburg Gate		c. Athens (Greece)
4. Chapultepec Park		d. Beijing (China)
5. Chateau Frontenac		e. Berlin (Germany)
6. Colosseum		f. Copenhagen (Denmark)
7. Diamond Head		g. Honolulu (U.S.)
8. Eiffel Tower		h. Jerusalem (Israel)
9. EPCOT		i. Leningrad (U.S.S.R.)
10. Ginza		j. London (England)
11. Graceland		k. Madrid (Spain)
12. Hermitage		l. Mecca (Saudi Arabia)
13. Kaaba		m. Memphis (U.S.)
14. Kremlin		n. Mexico City (Mexico)
15. Lion Park		o. Moscow (U.S.S.R.)
16. Little Mermaid		p. New York City (U.S.)
17. Parthenon		q. Orlando (U.S.)
18. Prado		r. Paris (France)
19. SkyDome		s. Quebec (Canada)
20. Statue of Liberty		t. Rio de Janeiro (Brazil)
21. Sugar Loaf		u. Rome (Italy)
22. Taj Mahal		v. San Antonio (U.S.)
23. Tiananmen Square		w. Tokyo (Japan)
24. Wailing Wall		x. Toronto (Canada)
25. White House		y. Washington, D.C. (U.S.)

ANSWERS: 1,v; 2,j; 3,e; 4,n; 5,s; 6,u; 7,g; 8,r; 9,q; 10,w; 11,m; 12,i; 13,l; 14,o; 15,a; 16,f; 17,c; 18,k; 19,x; 20,p; 21,t; 22,b; 23,d; 24,h; 25,y.

Next, go on a hunt. The names of all 25 city sites are hidden in this search-a-word puzzle. Try to find them. Cover the puzzle with a sheet of tracing paper. Read forward, backward, up, down, and diagonally. Then draw a neat line through each place as you find it. One name has been shaded in for you.

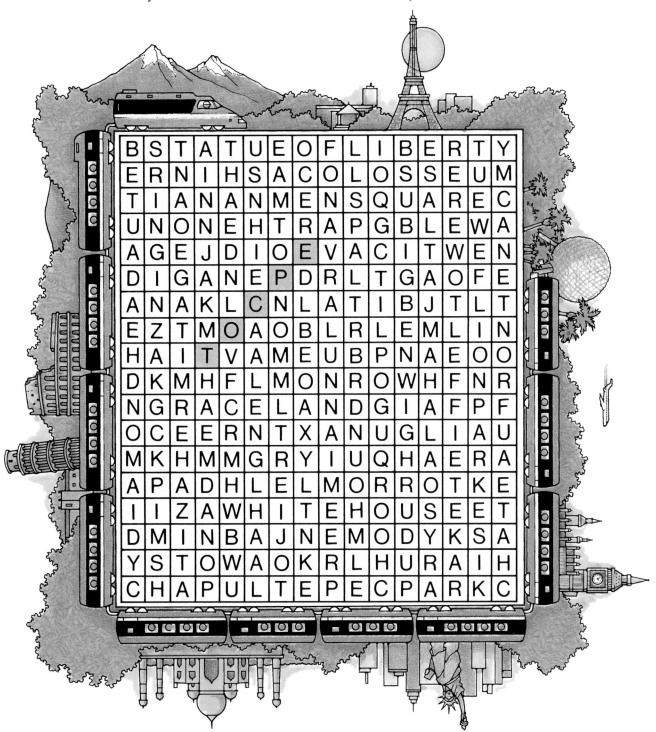

B	S	T	A	T	U	E	O	F	L	I	B	E	R	T	Y
E	R	N	I	H	S	A	C	O	L	O	S	S	E	U	M
T	I	A	N	A	N	M	E	N	S	Q	U	A	R	E	C
U	N	O	N	E	H	T	R	A	P	G	B	L	E	W	A
A	G	E	J	D	I	O	E	V	A	C	I	T	W	E	N
D	I	G	A	N	E	P	D	R	L	T	G	A	O	F	E
A	N	A	K	L	C	N	L	A	T	I	B	J	T	L	T
E	Z	T	M	O	A	O	B	L	R	L	E	M	L	I	N
H	A	I	T	V	A	M	E	U	B	P	N	A	E	O	O
D	K	M	H	F	L	M	O	N	R	O	W	H	F	N	R
N	G	R	A	C	E	L	A	N	D	G	I	A	F	P	F
O	C	E	E	R	N	T	X	A	N	U	G	L	I	A	U
M	K	H	M	M	G	R	Y	I	U	Q	H	A	E	R	A
A	P	A	D	H	L	E	L	M	O	R	R	O	T	K	E
I	I	Z	A	W	H	I	T	E	H	O	U	S	E	E	T
D	M	I	N	B	A	J	N	E	M	O	D	Y	K	S	A
Y	S	T	O	W	A	O	K	R	L	H	U	R	A	I	H
C	H	A	P	U	L	T	E	P	E	C	P	A	R	K	C

This imaginative collage is just bubbling over with glittery pearls—and other materials that give a 3-D effect.

POPULAR CRAFTS

Making something with your own hands is one of the most enjoyable and satisfying experiences. Whatever your level of skill—from beginner to expert—you'll find great pleasure in creating objects that are attractive and useful.

New crafts are constantly being introduced. But old favorites are popular, too. Here are four projects you'll want to try that combine new ideas and techniques with ones enjoyed by past generations.

PEARLY BUBBLES

Use your imagination and turn a pretty picture into a bubbly collage by adding pearls, beads, and other materials. The "Bubble Girl" picture above shows you how easy this can be. (This particular print can be ordered at a craft store.)

Glue the print onto a colored piece of mat board. Start adding items to create a 3-D effect. To add a rug, for example, outline the area to be covered on a piece of tracing paper. Then transfer this pattern to a sheet of typing paper. Glue strands of yarn to the paper. Cut out the rug and glue it onto the picture.

In a similar fashion, use pieces of printed fabrics to create a layered effect on the tub, the sponge, the scrub brush, and the cat. Add bows and lace ruffles as finishing touches. The fancy perfume bottles on the shelf over the bathtub are made with different shapes and colors of glass beads and gold-toned beads. Glue them one atop the other.

To make your picture burst with bubbles, apply lots and lots of small, medium, and large pearls around the tub. Dot the scrub brush with a few, and give the cat a couple to play with! The bubbles will seem extra soapy if you paint the pearls with iridescent glitter in glue.

Finally, place the finished collage in a shadowbox. Attach screw eyes and picture wire to the back of the box. You might want to hang your picture in the bathroom so you can see it while you relax in your own bubbly tub.

AN APPLE-ROSE WREATH

Turn an excelsior wreath into a lovely fall decoration by highlighting it with delicate roses made from dried apple slices.

Each rose is formed from six or seven apple slices. A bud requires three slices. Start by slicing unpeeled red Delicious apples into thin rounds. Dip them in lemon juice to prevent them from discoloring.

Place the slices on the wire rack in an oven and dry them for two and a half hours at 225°F (107°C), turning them every half hour. At the end of that time, the slices will be dry but pliable.

Roll a small slice to form the center of a rose. Continue adding slices, overlapping the edges, until you have formed an open flower or bud. Wrap floral wire around the bottom of the rose to hold the petals firmly in place.

Cover the excelsior wreath with lots of dried baby's breath, using hot glue or floral pins to hold the flowers in place. Put only a light amount of baby's breath on the areas where you plan to place the roses.

Arrange the roses on the wreath and glue them in place. Add additional baby's breath or other dried flowers and leaves around the roses. Weave a colorful ribbon among the roses, and end with a big bow and streaming tails.

This truly "delicious" creation will look great in your kitchen or dining room.

THIS CALENDAR IS FOREVER

Do you buy a new paper calendar every year? If you make this perpetual calendar, you'll never have to buy a paper one again.

The calendar's base is a rectangular plaque with a beveled edge. But even a wooden cutting board can be used. Sand the base lightly and wipe it clean with tack cloth. Paint or stain the beveled edge.

Use basswood stripping, available in hobby and craft shops, to make the tracks that hold the month and date blocks. You'll need two pieces of basswood for each track:

You can turn dried apple slices into delicate roses and create a "delicious" wreath for the fall season.

155

a narrow strip to be glued to the base and a wider strip to be glued on top of the narrow strip, thus forming a track in which to slide the blocks.

The month and date blocks are made from basswood, too. Cut 12 month blocks and 31 date blocks. Lightly sand the edges so the blocks are smooth. Then press black transfer letters and numbers onto the blocks to create the months and dates.

Now you have to use your math skills. Divide the plaque so that there are six evenly spaced horizontal sections. Each section should be just slightly higher than the blocks —you want the blocks to remain in the tracks, but you don't want the fit to be so snug that the blocks get stuck.

Glue the narrow basswood strips onto the plaque. After the glue has dried, set the wider strips on top, positioning them so that tracks are formed. Let dry.

Divide the space over the top strip into seven equal parts. Press black transfer letters for the days of the week in these spaces. As a final touch, decorate the plaque with stencils or stickers, perhaps with a country theme—apples, hearts, flowers.

At the beginning of each month, simply remove the prior month's blocks and put in the appropriate blocks for the current month. (Note: If a 31-day month starts on a Friday or Saturday, you'll need to begin your date blocks in the same section that's holding the month block.)

You now have something very special—a calendar that's perpetually accurate and perpetually beautiful.

GRANNY'S NOTE BOARD
Here's a perfect gift for a grandparent: A note board complete with pen and paper, and featuring a soft-sculpture Granny.

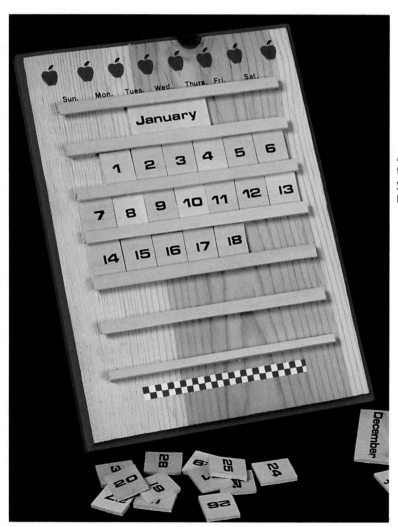

A perpetual calendar like this one lasts forever— you'll never have to buy a paper calendar again.

Begin with a base made from a piece of Styrofoam or thick cardboard. (You might ask your local fabric store for the cardboard insert from a fabric bolt.) Completely cover the base with natural colored burlap. Now cut two pieces of red checked fabric. Glue one piece to the top of the burlap, the other to the bottom. Glue strips of rickrack over the edges.

To make Granny's head, stuff the toe of a knee-high stocking with fiberfill. Try to get a flat, circular shape, with a diameter about half the width of the base. When you're satisfied with the shape, use needle and thread to tie off the stocking at the bottom of the head. Stitch the excess stocking to the back of the head.

Make Granny's nose by covering a marble-sized piece of fiberfill with a small piece of stocking. Sew the nose to the center of the face. Add two black beads for eyes and some stitches of red embroidery thread for a V-shaped mouth. Pink blush, applied with a make-up brush, will give Granny rosy cheeks.

Use gold-colored wire to shape Granny's glasses, and stitch them to the face at the bottom and sides. Granny's hair is fiberfill, fluffed up and lightly glued around the face. Sew red pindot fabric for her bonnet, edge it with white lace, and firmly stuff it with fiberfill. (The bonnet adds a lovely touch, but if your sewing skills are limited let Granny go bare-headed.) Glue the completed head to the top of the burlap.

Make a notepad holder from a strip of fabric or a double thickness of rickrack. Glue the two edges to the burlap, making certain there's enough room between the glued ends to slip a notepad over the strip.

Place a red marker upside down next to the notepad, and glue the cap section to the burlap. Stick a few push-pins on the base, to hold notes. Finally, sew two plastic curtain rings to the back of the base for hanging—and Granny's note board is ready to take messages.

You can, of course, replace the face with an appropriate one for other family members or friends. How about Mom's Shopping List?

NANCY TOSH
Editor
Crafts 'n Things magazine

This delightful note board just seems to be beckoning Granny to come over and jot down a few words.

COIN COLLECTING

Coin collectors, or numismatists, are always on the lookout for new and unusual coins. In 1990, they found much of interest, including a mistake from the U.S. Mint and a wide range of commemorative coins (coins that honor a person, place, or event).

U.S. COINS

Some lucky collectors received a big bonus from the U.S. Mint in the summer of 1990: special collector proof sets that contained an error and thus were far more valuable than the usual sets.

The Mint issues collector proof sets of U.S. coins each year. The sets contain one example of each coin, made with a special process that produces a bright, mirrorlike background and a brushed effect on the design of the coin. Normally, the coins in the sets carry an "S" mint mark—for the San Francisco Mint, where they are produced.

In 1990, a die (or stamp) from the Philadelphia Mint, which doesn't use a mint mark, was mistakenly used to produce cents for some of the proof sets. These coins thus bore no mint mark. The Mint sells proof sets for $11. But some happy collectors sold their error sets for as much as $1,400 after the mistake was discovered.

U.S. silver dollar commemorating the 100th anniversary of Dwight D. Eisenhower's birth

In other U.S. coin news, a commemorative silver dollar was issued by the U.S. Mint to mark the 100th anniversary of Dwight D. Eisenhower's birth. As an Army general in World War II, Eisenhower commanded U.S. forces in Europe and directed the Allied landing at Normandy in 1944. As a civilian after the war, he was president from 1953 to 1961. The obverse of the 1990 commemorative coin showed two profiles of Eisenhower, as a general and as president, to reflect his importance as both a military and political leader. The reverse showed the Eisenhower home in Gettysburg, Pennsylvania.

During the year plans were also being made to produce commemorative coins on a range of subjects in 1991 and 1992, including the 500th anniversary of the voyage of Christopher Columbus to the New World.

Canada's $200 gold coin honoring youth and flag, and its unusual $20 dollar bimetallic coin marking aviation

COINS AROUND THE WORLD

Canada regularly produces coins in silver and gold, and in 1990 the Royal Canadian Mint produced its first $200 gold coin. This commemorative honored both the youth of Canada and the 25th anniversary of the Canadian flag. The reverse design showed young people from several different cultural groups carrying the flag, with a map of Canada in the background.

A Canadian silver dollar marked the 300th anniversary of Henry Kelsey's explorations of the Canadian prairies. Kelsey, who was from England, was a governor of the Hudson's Bay Company and is thought to be the first European to see North American bison. The reverse of the coin showed Kelsey and several Indians overlooking a herd of bison. The obverse carried a new portrait of Queen Elizabeth II of Britain (who appears on all Canadian coins) by a Canadian artist, Dora dePedery-Hunt.

A Canadian $100 gold coin supported United Nations International Literacy Year. The reverse showed an Inuk native woman and two children. It also bore an inscription in Inuit (Eskimo) syllabics, a special alphabet for the Inuit language. Translated, the inscription read "literacy."

A pair of highly unusual $20 Canadian coins marked the start of a ten-coin series honoring aviation. Each of the silver coins depicted Canadian-built aircraft; inset into the design was a cameo portrait of a famous aviator in gold-plated silver. These were Canada's first bimetallic (two-metal) coins and were among only a few such coins to have been produced by any country at any time.

The Marshall Islands' $5 coin commemorating the 50th anniversary of the Battle of Britain

Aviation was also the theme of coins from several other countries in 1990. The year marked the 50th anniversary of the prolonged World War II air battle known as the Battle of Britain, in which Royal Air Force pilots defended their island country against the German Luftwaffe. The British Royal Mint produced silver and copper-nickel medals to mark the event, while the island of Jersey, just off the coast of England, issued a set of silver and gold coins. Even the Marshall Islands, in the central Pacific Ocean, produced Battle of Britain coins for 1990.

France unveiled the first four of a series of nineteen coins planned to honor the 1992 Winter Olympic Games, which it will host.

France's 500-franc gold coin celebrating the 1992 Winter Olympic Games, which it will host

On the obverse, the two coins minted in 1989 carried designs showing downhill skiing and figure skating; the two coins minted in 1990 showed bobsledding and speed skating. The reverse of all four showed a stylized image of the Olympic flame.

Bermuda's $2 silver coins of a cicada and a tree frog

Animals remained a popular theme for 1990 coins from several countries. Bermuda continued its series on exotic native animals with a pair of silver $2 coins, one showing cicadas and the other a tree frog. And Australia showed one of its most famous animals, the kangaroo, on a series of gold bullion coins. (Bullion coins are valued by the weight of the precious metal they contain rather than by their official denominations.) A silver bullion coin showed the kookaburra, an Australian bird with a distinctive "laughing" call.

Albania's award-winning 1988 "tunnel" coin

Awards for excellence and innovation were given to a 1988 silver coin produced by Albania to honor railroads. This coin's unique design showed a train entering a tunnel on one side, and leaving the tunnel on the other. The "tunnel" was an actual hole in the coin.

EARL A. SHOEMAKER
Numismatic News

MANY FRIENDS COOKING

OPEN-FACED SANDWICHES, from Denmark

What's an open-faced sandwich? It's a sandwich that is made of a single slice of lightly buttered bread, with the filling placed on top of it.

INGREDIENTS

- 1 can skinless and boneless sardines
- 1 celery rib
- ¼ cup mayonnaise
- 1 teaspoon lemon juice
- ½ teaspoon Worcestershire sauce
- 6 slices bread
- ¼ cup soft butter or margarine
- 6 lettuce leaves

EQUIPMENT

fork
mixing bowl
paring knife
measuring cup
measuring spoons
mixing spoon
butter knife

HOW TO MAKE

1. Drain the oil from the sardines and mash them with a fork.

2. Finely chop the celery. (Have an adult help you.)

3. Add the chopped celery, mayonnaise, lemon juice, and Worcestershire sauce to the sardines, and stir until well blended.

4. Butter each slice of bread and place a lettuce leaf on each. Top with the sardine-salad mixture.

This recipe serves 6 people.

SOUTHERN PECAN PIE, from the United States

"What's for dessert?" is a common question in the United States, a dessert-minded country. In the North, it might be apple pie. In the Southern states, especially Louisiana and Georgia, pecan pie is a favorite. Nearly every Southern cook has a recipe for pecan pie. Here is a classic version. Serve it with freshly made whipped cream.

INGREDIENTS

3 eggs
2 tablespoons sugar
2 tablespoons flour
2 cups dark corn syrup
1 teaspoon vanilla
¼ teaspoon salt
¼ cup pecans
1 9-inch pie shell

EQUIPMENT

mixing bowl
eggbeater
mixing spoon
measuring cups
measuring spoons
9-inch pie plate

HOW TO MAKE

1. Preheat the oven to 425°F.

2. In the mixing bowl, beat the eggs with the eggbeater until light and fluffy.

3. Add the sugar, flour, corn syrup, vanilla, and salt and beat well.

4. Break the pecans into small pieces and stir into the mixture.

5. Place the unbaked pie shell in a pie plate and pour in the filling.

6. Bake at 425°F for 10 minutes. Reduce heat to 325°F. Bake 40 minutes more. Cool and serve.

This recipe serves 6 to 8 people.

SPORTS

Like to skate? Weather too warm? "In-line" roller skating is the way to go. The wheels are in a straight line, rather than side by side, and the effect is a lot like ice skating. Also called "blading," the sport began when hockey players were looking for a way to practice during spring and summer. Now, hundreds of thousands of people enjoy blading just for the fun of it. It's also an excellent way to get in shape.

West Germany (white shirts) defeated Argentina, 1–0, in the final game to win the 1990 World Cup.

SOCCER: THE 1990 WORLD CUP

West Germans had much reason to rejoice in 1990. In the realm of politics, they looked forward to their reunification with East Germany. And in the realm of sports, they exulted in the victory of their team in World Cup soccer competition. Coached by the legendary Franz Beckenbauer—one of the greatest players in the world during the 1970s—the West Germans took the championship by defeating Argentina 1–0 in the final game, in Rome, Italy. Ironically, the contest was a rematch of the last World Cup final, held in 1986, which was won by Argentina.

Soccer is probably the world's most popular sport; it was estimated that one billion people all around the globe watched the final game on television. West Germany's triumph marked the end of a vast worldwide tournament that had actually begun two years earlier. Teams representing 113 nations had played qualifying matches to determine 22 of the 24 teams that participated in the final tournament. The defending champion, Argentina, and the host country, Italy, were automatically included.

In the finals, the 24 teams played 52 games in twelve Italian cities between June and July. Considering the size of the World Cup competition, it was inevitable that there were surprises; it was also perhaps inevitable that there was controversy.

The major surprises were provided by two small countries, Cameroon and Ireland, which performed remarkably well, both reaching the quarterfinals before they were eliminated. Another surprise was the presence of a United States team among the final 24 for the first time in 40 years; the team was, however, knocked out early, losing all three games it played.

Controversy developed over the fact that some very important matches were decided by penalty kicks and tie-breaking shootouts. The competition also suffered from some unstylish—even sloppy—play. The usual artistry of World Cup soccer was frequently missing. Further controversies involved violence among some fans.

But ultimately the tournament was as exciting as ever, especially in the final game, which pitted two of the world's great teams against each other. The Germans were the aggressors for much of the contest. Led by strikers Rudi Voeller and Juergen Klinsmann and fullback Andreas Brehme, they charged upfield again and again, but the Germans couldn't put the ball in the Argentine net. On defense, Guido Buchwald shadowed Diego Maradona, the star of Argentina's 1986 World Cup victory, denying him any chances for goals. Maradona was playing with injuries, and several of his key teammates were disallowed from playing in the final because of penalties they had incurred in previous games. So the weight of Argentina's hopes for victory lay almost entirely on the ailing Maradona. After the first 45-minute half, the score stood 0–0.

Play became especially ragged, and rough, in the second half. In the game's 64th minute, Argentina's Pedro Monzon was called for a particularly vicious foul, and the referee flashed a red card signaling elimination from the game. Monzon was the first player ever to be expelled from a World Cup final.

In the 84th minute, Rudi Voeller was fouled in the penalty area by Roberto Sensini of Argentina. For the infraction, West Germany was awarded a penalty kick. Andreas Brehme took the shot, his right foot slamming the ball just beyond the reach of Argentine goalie Sergio Goycochea. And that was the game. West Germany won, 1–0. Argentina's weak offense had managed only one shot on goal, compared with the victors' sixteen, in the entire 90 minutes.

The Early Rounds. The 24 teams in the final tournament had been divided into six groups, each of which played a round-robin schedule. It was in the first round that Cameroon stunned Argentina—and the world—by defeating the defending champions 1–0. Argentina bounced back, however, to become one of the 16 teams advancing to the second round. Cameroon ran out of luck in the quarterfinals, where it was topped by England, 3–2. The other ''little'' country, Ireland, also made it to the quarterfinals, losing 1–0 to Italy.

Argentina marched to the final by over-coming Brazil in the second round, 1–0; Yugoslavia in the quarterfinals, 3–2; and Italy in the semifinals, 5–4. West Germany knocked out the Netherlands, 2–1; Czechoslovakia, 1–0; and England, 5–4.

The semifinal losers, Italy and England, played a consolation game in Bari, Italy. The host country won, 2–1, on a penalty-kick goal by Salvatore Schillaci.

Looking to 1994. West Germany won its third World Cup championship in 1990; only Italy and Brazil have won as many. The 1994 tournament will be played in the United States. Looking ahead to that tournament, West Germany's coach Beckenbauer considered the notion of a united Germany—and the possibility of West and East Germans playing together on one team. ''In the future,'' he said, ''the Germans will be unbeatable.'' The world will have to wait four years to see if his prediction is correct.

Cameroon (green shirts) became the first African nation ever to reach the World Cup quarterfinals.

BASEBALL

Baseball had its share of surprises in 1990, not the least of which was the Cincinnati Reds' four-game sweep of the Oakland Athletics in the World Series.

Manager Lou Piniella's Reds held first place in the National League Western Division from opening day until the season ended, leading second-place Los Angeles by five games. Cincinnati then knocked off the Eastern Division champion Pittsburgh Pirates in six games in the National League Championship Series (NLCS).

Game 1 of the NLCS went to the Pirates, 4–3. But the Reds won Game 2, 2–1, on right fielder Paul O'Neill's two-run double and on the pitching of starter Tom Browning and relievers Rob Dibble and Randy Myers. Game 3 was also a Reds' victory, 6–3. Center fielder Billy Hatcher and second baseman Mariano Duncan contributed home runs. Danny Jackson was the winning pitcher. Rolling now, Cincinnati took Game 4, 5–3, on the pitching of Jose Rijo and homers by Paul O'Neill and third baseman Chris Sabo.

The Pirates won Game 5, 3–2. But Pittsburgh's season ended when the Reds triumphed in Game 6 by the score of 2–1. Starter Danny Jackson and relievers Norm Charlton and Randy Myers held the Pirates to just one hit. Myers and Rob Dibble were co-winners of the NLCS most valuable player (MVP) award.

In the American League, the powerful Oakland Athletics collected their third consecutive pennant. After topping the Western Division by nine games, the A's bludgeoned the Eastern Division champion Boston Red Sox in the ALCS in four straight. Oakland's pitching was superb. Dave Stewart, winning hurler in Games 1 and 4, was named MVP of the ALCS.

Following their sweep of Boston, the A's were heavily favored in the World Series. But the Reds brought their own "brooms" and swept the A's away.

In Game 1, the Reds jumped on Dave Stewart for four early runs, chasing him from the mound. Left fielder Eric Davis homered,

Pitcher Jose Rijo of Cincinnati was named most valuable player of the 1990 World Series for his two victories in the Reds' four-game sweep of the Oakland A's.

Billy Hatcher got three hits in three at-bats, and Jose Rijo pitched seven shutout innings. The final score was 7–0.

Game 2 was closer. The Reds won in the tenth inning, 5–4, when catcher Joe Oliver singled in the winning run. Billy Hatcher went four for four and thereby set a World Series record for his seven consecutive hits.

Tom Browning pitched six strong innings in Game 3, and Rob Dibble and Randy Myers finished up, as Cincinnati romped, 8–3. Chris Sabo homered twice and deftly handled ten chances in the field, tying a World Series record for third basemen.

In Game 4, Oakland's Stewart allowed only two runs, but Jose Rijo and Randy Myers gave up just one. The sweep was complete, and Rijo, for his two sparkling victories, was named World Series MVP.

The regular season was full of outstanding —and unusual—achievements. Nolan Ryan won the 300th game of his illustrious career and also pitched his sixth no-hitter, a record. It was one of nine no-hitters thrown in 1990; no other year in baseball had seen so many.

Willie McGee was traded from the St. Louis Cardinals to Oakland in August. But while with the Cards, he amassed enough plate appearances to win the NL batting title, hitting .335. Thus at the end of the season, an American Leaguer was the National League batting champ.

George Brett of Kansas City led the American League in hitting at .329. Also the AL's top hitter in 1976 and 1980, Brett is the first player to win batting titles in three different decades.

Ryne Sandberg of the Chicago Cubs hit 40 home runs and became the first second baseman to lead the NL in homers since the great Rogers Hornsby in 1925.

Cecil Fielder spent the 1989 season playing ball in Japan. He joined the Detroit Tigers in 1990 and proceeded to hit 51 home runs. The last time anyone surpassed the 50 mark was in 1977.

Despite Fielder's fine year, the MVP of the AL was Oakland's Rickey Henderson, who batted .325, hit 28 homers, and as usual led the league in stolen bases (65). Pittsburgh's Barry Bonds was the NL MVP; he batted .301, hit 33 homers, drove in 114 runs, and stole 52 bases.

The hitting and base-stealing of American League MVP Rickey Henderson led Oakland to the pennant.

Bonds's teammate Doug Drabek was the NL Cy Young Award winner for his 22–6 record and 2.76 earned run average (ERA). Oakland's Bob Welch, who won 27 games, received the Cy Young Award in the AL.

Honored as rookies of the year were Cleveland Indians catcher Sandy Alomar, Jr., who batted .290, and outfielder Dave Justice of the Atlanta Braves, who batted .282 with 28 homers.

1990 WORLD SERIES RESULTS

		R	H	E	Winning/Losing Pitcher
1	Oakland	0	9	1	Dave Stewart
	Cincinnati	7	10	0	Jose Rijo
2	Oakland	4	10	2	Dennis Eckersley
	Cincinnati	5	14	2	Rob Dibble
3	Cincinnati	8	14	1	Tom Browning
	Oakland	3	7	1	Mike Moore
4	Cincinnati	2	7	1	Jose Rijo
	Oakland	1	2	1	Dave Stewart

Visiting team listed first, home team second

MAJOR LEAGUE BASEBALL FINAL STANDINGS

AMERICAN LEAGUE

Eastern Division

	W	L	Pct.	GB
Boston	88	74	.543	—
Toronto	86	76	.531	2
Detroit	79	83	.488	9
Cleveland	77	85	.475	11
Baltimore	76	85	.472	11½
Milwaukee	74	88	.457	14
New York	67	95	.414	21

Western Division

	W	L	Pct.	GB
*Oakland	103	59	.636	—
Chicago	94	68	.580	9
Texas	83	79	.512	20
California	80	82	.494	23
Seattle	77	85	.475	26
Kansas City	75	86	.466	27½
Minnesota	74	88	.457	29

NATIONAL LEAGUE

Eastern Division

	W	L	Pct.	GB
Pittsburgh	95	67	.586	—
New York	91	71	.562	4
Montreal	85	77	.525	10
Chicago	77	85	.475	18
Philadelphia	77	85	.475	18
St. Louis	70	92	.432	25

Western Division

	W	L	Pct.	GB
*Cincinnati	91	71	.562	—
Los Angeles	86	76	.531	5
San Francisco	85	77	.525	6
Houston	75	87	.463	16
San Diego	75	87	.463	16
Atlanta	65	97	.401	26

*League Championship Series winners

MAJOR LEAGUE LEADERS

AMERICAN LEAGUE

Batting
(top 10 qualifiers)

	AB	H	Avg.
Brett, Kansas City	544	179	.329
Henderson, Oakland	489	159	.325
Palmeiro, Texas	598	191	.319
Trammell, Detroit	559	170	.304
Boggs, Boston	619	187	.302
Martinez, Seattle	487	147	.302
Griffey, Jr., Seattle	597	179	.300
McGriff, Toronto	557	167	.300
James, Cleveland	528	158	.299
Puckett, Minnesota	551	164	.298

NATIONAL LEAGUE

Batting
(top 10 qualifiers)

	AB	H	Avg.
McGee, St. Louis	501	168	.335
Murray, Los Angeles	558	184	.330
Magadan, New York	451	148	.328
Dykstra, Philadelphia	590	192	.325
Dawson, Chicago	529	164	.310
Roberts, San Diego	556	172	.309
Grace, Chicago	589	182	.309
Gwynn, San Diego	573	177	.309
Butler, San Francisco	622	192	.309
Sandberg, Chicago	615	188	.306

Home Runs

	HR
Fielder, Detroit	51
McGwire, Oakland	39
J. Canseco, Oakland	37
McGriff, Toronto	35
Gruber, Toronto	31

Home Runs

	HR
Sandberg, Chicago	40
Strawberry, New York	37
Mitchell, San Francisco	35
Bonds, Pittsburgh	33
Williams, San Francisco	33

Pitching
(top qualifiers, based on number of wins)

	W	L	ERA
Welch, Oakland	27	6	2.95
Stewart, Oakland	22	11	2.56
Clemons, Boston	21	6	1.93
Stieb, Toronto	18	6	2.93
Finley, California	18	9	2.40
Hanson, Seattle	18	9	3.24

Pitching
(top qualifiers, based on number of wins)

	W	L	ERA
Drabek, Pittsburgh	22	6	2.76
Martinez, Los Angeles	20	6	2.92
Viola, New York	20	12	2.67
Gooden, New York	19	7	3.83
Browning, Cincinnati	15	9	3.80
Maddux, Chicago	15	15	3.49

Little Leaguers from Taipei, Taiwan, won the 1990 World Series, their fourth title in five years.

LITTLE LEAGUE BASEBALL

When a baseball team from Taiwan arrived at Williamsport, Pennsylvania, for the 1990 Little League World Series, a 21-year tradition came with them. Previous teams from their country had won thirteen championships since 1969, including five during the 1980's. How would this new crop of Taiwanese youngsters fare? Very well, it turned out: They slugged their way to the title, scoring 43 runs in three games while holding their opponents to a combined total of 1.

Every year in late August, eight teams—four from the United States, and one each from Canada, Europe, the Far East, and Latin America—play in the Little League World Series, after winning their regional tournaments. The 1990 champions represented the San-Hua Little League from Taipei, the capital of Taiwan. Like all good baseball teams, whether in the big leagues or little, they won not only with hitting but also with excellent pitching and fine defense.

In the final contest, Taiwan overmatched the U.S. champions from Shippensburg, Pennsylvania, by the score of 9–0. Pitcher Sun Chao-Chi allowed only two hits and struck out the first eight batters he faced. He finished with sixteen strikeouts for the six-inning game. Sun also batted in his team's first run; he singled to right in the first inning,

sending home Liu Chien-Wen, who had doubled. The score stood at 1–0 until the fourth inning, when Taiwan added four more runs, and they finished off their victory with another four in the fifth.

Taiwan thus won its fourth Little League World Series in five years; in 1989, a Taiwan team was runner-up to the United States team from Trumbull, Connecticut.

Taiwan had reached the 1990 final with a 14–0 victory over a team from Ramstein Air Force Base, West Germany, in the first round, and a 20–1 shellacking of Trail, British Columbia, in the semifinal. Shippensburg's victims were Mobile, Alabama, 3–1, in the first round and Cypress, California, 5–4, in the semifinals. Also taking part in the Little League World Series tournament were teams from Matamoros, Mexico, and Brooklyn, Michigan.

One historical note: In the first round, Kelly Craig of the Canadian team became the first female starting pitcher in a Little League World Series game. Her opponents were the Mexican team. Unfortunately, she didn't get anyone out, and she was replaced after facing just three batters. Kelly switched over to first base, while her catcher, David Caron, moved to the mound, and he pitched the Canadians to victory.

BASKETBALL

The Detroit Pistons won their second consecutive National Basketball Association (NBA) championship in 1990, becoming only the third franchise in league history to take back-to-back titles. In the finals, they defeated the Portland Trail Blazers in five games, winning the last three on the Blazers' home court.

Coach Chuck Daly's Pistons had a regular-season record of 59–23, the best in the Eastern Conference. In the NBA as a whole, only the Los Angeles Lakers, at 63–19, were better; Portland, which finished second behind the Lakers in the Pacific Division of the Western Conference, also went 59–23.

Detroit swept the Indiana Pacers, 3 games

Playoff MVP Isiah Thomas (foreground) sparked the Detroit Pistons to their second consecutive NBA title.

to 0, in the first round of the playoffs, and then dropped the New York Knicks in five. In the Eastern Conference finals, they faced a tough Chicago Bulls team, led by the NBA's leading scorer, Michael Jordan. Detroit, with its gritty defensive style, prevailed, holding the Bulls to only 74 points in the seventh and deciding game.

Portland, meanwhile, reached the finals by overcoming the Phoenix Suns, 4 games to 2, in the Western Conference finals.

In Game 1 of the finals, played in Detroit, the Trail Blazers led most of the way. But Piston Guard Isiah Thomas tallied sixteen points in the fourth quarter, sparking his team to a 105–99 triumph.

Game 2 was an overtime thriller. Detroit center Bill Laimbeer hit six 3-point shots, including three in overtime, but Portland guard Clyde Drexler won the game by sinking two free throws with 2.1 seconds remaining. The final score was 106–105.

The next three games would be played in Portland, where the Pistons had lost 20 straight. But in Game 3, Detroit took a seven-point halftime lead and wound up winning 121–106, as guard Joe Dumars pumped in 33 points and Vinnie Johnson added 21.

Game 4 seesawed back and forth. Portland led early, but Detroit held a five-point margin at the half. The Pistons increased their lead in the third quarter, but the Blazers rallied late in the game to go up by a point. Finally, Isiah Thomas, who finished with 32 points, gave Detroit the lead for good on two free throws with 8.4 seconds remaining. At the buzzer, the score stood 112–109, and the Pistons had a 3-games-to-1 advantage.

Could Portland salvage at least one victory on its home court? In Game 5, they led 90–83 with only two minutes left. But the Pistons scored the final nine points, including seven by Vinnie Johnson, and the NBA title was Detroit's for the second year in a row. Thomas, who scored 29 points in the last game, was named the series' most valuable player (MVP).

During the regular season, Chicago's Jordan won his fourth straight scoring title, averaging 33.6 points per game. And for the third time in four years, Laker Earvin

NBA FINAL STANDINGS

EASTERN CONFERENCE

Atlantic Division

	W	L	Pct.
Philadelphia	53	29	.646
Boston	52	30	.634
New York	45	37	.549
Washington	31	51	.378
Miami	18	64	.220
New Jersey	17	65	.207

Central Division

	W	L	Pct.
Detroit	59	23	.720
Chicago	55	27	.671
Milwaukee	44	38	.537
Cleveland	42	40	.512
Indiana	42	40	.512
Atlanta	41	41	.500
Orlando	18	64	.220

WESTERN CONFERENCE

Midwest Division

	W	L	Pct.
San Antonio	56	26	.683
Utah	55	27	.671
Dallas	47	35	.573
Denver	43	39	.524
Houston	41	41	.500
Minnesota	22	60	.268
Charlotte	19	63	.232

Pacific Division

	W	L	Pct.
L.A. Lakers	63	19	.768
Portland	59	23	.720
Phoenix	54	28	.659
Seattle	41	41	.500
Golden State	37	45	.451
L.A. Clippers	30	52	.366
Sacramento	23	59	.280

NBA Championship: Detroit Pistons

COLLEGE BASKETBALL

Conference	Winner
Atlantic Coast	Clemson (regular season) Georgia Tech (tournament)
Big East	Connecticut, Syracuse (tied, regular season) Connecticut (tournament)
Big Eight	Missouri (regular season) Oklahoma (tournament)
Big Ten	Michigan State
Big West	Nevada-Las Vegas, New Mexico State (tied, regular season) Nevada-Las Vegas (tournament)
Ivy League	Princeton
Metro Athletic	Louisville (regular season and tournament)
Missouri Valley	Southern Illinois (regular season) Illinois State (tournament)
Pacific-10	Oregon State, Arizona (tied, regular season) Arizona (tournament)
Southeastern	Georgia (regular season) Alabama (tournament)
Southwest	Arkansas (regular season and tournament)
Western Athletic	Brigham Young, Colorado State (tied, regular season) Texas—El Paso (tournament)

NCAA, men: University of Nevada-Las Vegas
women: Stanford

NIT: Vanderbilt

(Magic) Johnson was regular-season MVP—he averaged 22.3 points and 11.5 assists. John Stockton of Utah led the league in assists, averaging 14.5 per game, and he set a record in the process—his total of 1,134 was the most ever in a season. Rookie of the year was San Antonio center David Robinson; the former U.S. Naval Academy star averaged 24.3 points and 12.0 rebounds per game. In the latter category, he was second only to Houston center Akeem Olajuwon, who averaged 14.0.

College Play. The Runnin' Rebels of the University of Nevada at Las Vegas (UNLV) won the National Collegiate Athletic Association (NCAA) men's championship, annihilating Duke in the final, 103–73. UNLV's Anderson Hunt led the way with 29 points, and Larry Johnson contributed 22 points and 11 rebounds. In winning their first national title, coach Jerry Tarkanian's Rebs became the first team to exceed 100 points in a championship game, and their 30-point margin of victory was also a final-game record. Hunt was named the game's MVP.

Ranked first in preseason polls, UNLV finished the regular season with a 29–5 record. They reached the NCAA finals by overcoming Georgia Tech, 90–81, in the semifinals. In the other semifinal, Duke eliminated Arkansas, 97–83.

The NCAA women's champion was Stanford, which sank eleven 3-point shots in beating Auburn, 88–81. Sonja Henning scored 21 points for the victorious Cardinals; Jennifer Azzi, player of the year in women's basketball, added 17 and was named MVP. It was Stanford's first NCAA title.

FOOTBALL

"Repeat" was the byword in football in 1990. In the National Football League (NFL), the San Francisco 49ers won Super Bowl XXIV and thus became the first team to win consecutive NFL championships in a decade. In the Canadian Football League, the Winnipeg Blue Bombers won their second Grey Cup since 1988. And in college football, a junior won the Heisman Trophy for the third year in a row.

In 1990, Jerry Rice of the San Francisco 49ers continued to excel as one of the NFL's finest receivers.

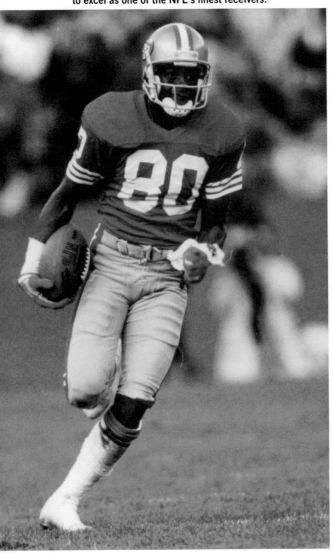

THE NFL PLAYOFFS AND SUPER BOWL XXIV

In 1989, the 49ers led the National Conference Western Division with a 14–2 record, tops in the NFL. The other National Conference playoff teams were the Eastern Division champion New York Giants, the Central Division champion Minnesota Vikings, and the two wild cards, the Los Angeles Rams and the Philadelphia Eagles.

In the wild-card game, a strong Los Angeles defense held the Eagles earthbound, and the Rams romped in an upset, 21–7. A week later, Los Angeles again overcame the odds, beating the Giants in overtime, 19–13. Meanwhile, San Francisco drubbed Minnesota, 41–13, gaining 403 yards against the NFL's best defense.

The National Conference title game thus pitted two California teams against each other—but it wasn't much of a contest: 49er quarterback Joe Montana passed for 262 yards and two touchdowns, and the defense stifled L.A. The final score was 30–3.

In the American Conference, only the Western Division champion Denver Broncos won more than ten regular-season games in 1989; thus it was fitting that they ultimately reached the Super Bowl. The Buffalo Bills topped the Eastern Division, the Cleveland Browns led the Central Division, and the wild-card teams were the Houston Oilers and the Pittsburgh Steelers.

Pittsburgh had to go to overtime to eliminate Houston in the wild-card game, 26–23. The Steelers' bubble burst, however, the following week: Ahead for most of the game, Pittsburgh couldn't halt a fourth-quarter Denver drive, and the Broncos won, 24–23. Cleveland, meanwhile, survived a late rally by Buffalo and won 34–30.

In the American Conference title game, Bronco quarterback John Elway supplied the heroics, completing 20 passes for 385 yards and three touchdowns. The final tally was Denver 37, Cleveland 21.

Super Bowl XXIV matched the best teams in each conference, but long before it was over, no doubt remained as to which was the best team in the NFL. Played on January 28, 1990, in the Superdome in New Orleans, Louisiana, it was the most one-sided Super Bowl ever. The 49ers led 13–3 at the quarter, 27–3 at the half, 41–10 after three quarters, and 55–10 at the final whistle. Joe Montana completed 22 of 29 passes for 297 yards, including five for touchdowns. His primary target, Jerry Rice, made seven catches for 148 yards and three touchdowns, and the 49er defense intercepted Elway twice.

San Francisco thus joined the Pittsburgh Steelers as the only teams to win four Super Bowls. The 49ers were also the first team to win two straight since the Steelers in 1979 and 1980. Joe Montana was named the game's most valuable player, and he and his talented teammates looked ahead to attempting to win their third consecutive Super Bowl in 1991.

THE 1990 NFL REGULAR SEASON

Unrelenting in their excellence, the 49ers posted the best regular-season record in 1990, winning fourteen games while losing only two. The other National Conference division titlists were the New York Giants and the Chicago Bears; wild-card berths went to Philadelphia, the New Orleans Saints, and the Washington Redskins. (A new playoff format allowed for three wild-card teams in each conference.)

Buffalo, the Cincinnati Bengals, and the Los Angeles Raiders were division champs in the American Conference; the wild-card teams were Houston, the Kansas City Chiefs, and the Miami Dolphins.

Houston quarterback Warren Moon became the first player to pass for more than 20,000 yards in both the NFL and the Canadian Football League. Among the year's top running backs were Barry Sanders of Detroit and Thurman Thomas of Buffalo. Buffalo's Bruce Smith established himself as one of the top defensive players.

THE CANADIAN FOOTBALL LEAGUE

The Grey Cup game, played on November 25, 1990, at B.C. Place in Vancouver, British Columbia, was as much of a rout as the Super Bowl. The Eastern Division champion Winnipeg Blue Bombers crushed the Edmonton Eskimos, playoff winners in the West, by 50–11. Leading by only 10–4 at the half, the Bombers blew the stadium apart in the third quarter, scoring 28 points. Winnipeg quarterback Tom Burgess was the game's most valuable offensive player, completing 18 passes for 286 yards and three touchdowns.

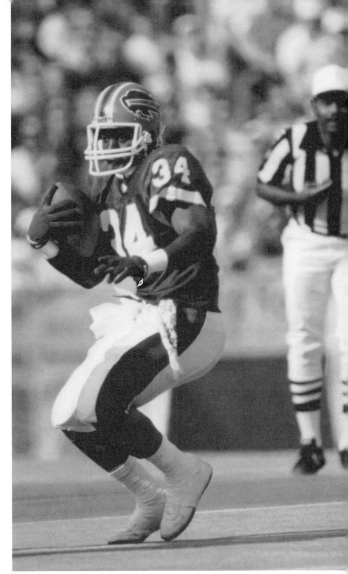

The highly successful running game of the Buffalo Bills was built around Thurman Thomas.

COLLEGE FOOTBALL

The University of Colorado, 10–1–1 during the regular season, was ranked number one in one poll; Colorado topped Notre Dame (9–2) in the Orange Bowl. Georgia Tech (10–0–1), ranked number one in another poll, defeated Nebraska (9–2) in the Citrus Bowl. Miami (9–2) trounced Texas (10–1) in the Cotton Bowl; Tennessee (8–2–2) dropped Virginia (8–3) in the Sugar Bowl; and Washington (9–2) bested Iowa (8–3) in the Rose Bowl.

For the third straight year, a junior won the Heisman Trophy. Quarterback Ty Detmer of Brigham Young University passed for 4,869 yards, eclipsing the record of 4,699 set by Andre Ware, the Heisman winner in 1989.

Brigham Young University quarterback Ty Detmer won the 1990 Heisman Trophy as the best college player.

1990 NFL FINAL STANDINGS

AMERICAN CONFERENCE

Eastern Division

	W	L	T	Pct.	PF	PA
Buffalo	13	3	0	.813	428	263
Miami	12	4	0	.750	336	242
Indianapolis	7	9	0	.438	281	353
N.Y. Jets	6	10	0	.375	295	345
New England	1	15	0	.063	181	446

Central Division

	W	L	T	Pct.	PF	PA
Cincinnati	9	7	0	.563	360	352
Houston	9	7	0	.563	405	307
Pittsburgh	9	7	0	.563	292	240
Cleveland	3	13	0	.188	228	462

Western Division

	W	L	T	Pct.	PF	PA
L.A. Raiders	12	4	0	.750	337	268
Kansas City	11	5	0	.688	369	257
Seattle	9	7	0	.563	306	286
San Diego	6	10	0	.375	315	281
Denver	5	11	0	.313	331	374

NATIONAL CONFERENCE

Eastern Division

	W	L	T	Pct.	PF	PA
N.Y. Giants	13	3	0	.813	335	211
Philadelphia	10	6	0	.625	396	299
Washington	10	6	0	.625	381	301
Dallas	7	9	0	.438	244	308
Phoenix	5	11	0	.313	258	396

Central Division

	W	L	T	Pct.	PF	PA
Chicago	11	5	0	.688	348	280
Tampa Bay	6	10	0	.375	264	367
Green Bay	6	10	0	.375	271	347
Detroit	6	10	0	.375	373	413
Minnesota	6	10	0	.375	351	326

Western Division

	W	L	T	Pct.	PF	PA
San Francisco	14	2	0	.875	353	239
New Orleans	8	8	0	.500	274	275
L.A. Rams	5	11	0	.313	345	412
Atlanta	5	11	0	.313	348	365

COLLEGE FOOTBALL

Conference	Winner
Atlantic Coast	Georgia Tech
Big Eight	Colorado
Big Ten	Illinois, Iowa, Michigan, Michigan State (tied)
Big West	San Jose State
Pacific-10	Washington
Southeastern	Tennessee
Southwest	Texas
Western Athletic	Brigham Young

Citrus Bowl: Georgia Tech 45, Nebraska 21
Cotton Bowl: Miami 46, Texas 3
Orange Bowl: Colorado 10, Notre Dame 9
Rose Bowl: Washington 46, Iowa 34
Sugar Bowl: Tennessee 23, Virginia 22

Heisman Trophy: Ty Detmer

In 1990, Beth Daniel won the Ladies PGA. And Nick Faldo won both the Masters and the British Open.

GOLF

PROFESSIONAL		AMATEUR	
	Individual		**Individual**
Masters	Nick Faldo	**U.S. Amateur**	Phil Mickelson
U.S. Open	Hale Irwin	**U.S. Women's Amateur**	Pat Hurst
Canadian Open	Wayne Levi	**British Amateur**	Rolf Muntz
British Open	Nick Faldo	**British Ladies Amateur**	Julie Hall
PGA	Wayne Grady	**Canadian Amateur**	Warren Sye
World Series of Golf	Jose-Maria Olazabal	**Canadian Ladies Amateur**	Sarah Lebrun Ingrim
U.S. Women's Open	Betsy King		
Ladies PGA	Beth Daniel		**Team**
		Curtis Cup	United States

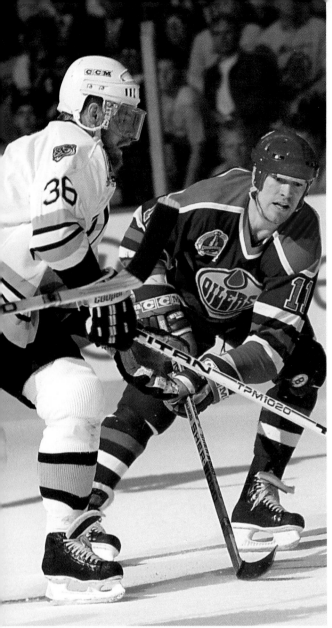

In 1990, the Edmonton Oilers won their fifth Stanley Cup in seven years. Oiler Mark Messier (*right*) was the National Hockey League's MVP.

HOCKEY

In the five seasons between 1984 and 1988, the Edmonton Oilers won four Stanley Cups. And then they traded away the "Great One," Wayne Gretzky. But in 1990, the Oilers won the National Hockey League (NHL) championship yet again—defeating the Boston Bruins, 4 games to 1, in the Stanley Cup finals. Even without Gretzky, possibly the best player of the last ten years, the Oilers continued their dynasty. And they could well claim that they were one of the finest teams in the history of the sport.

But the Oilers didn't get to the top without a fight. The end of the regular season found the Oilers only in second place in the Smythe Division. Their 90 points—on a record of 38 victories, 28 defeats, and 14 ties—left them nine points behind the Calgary Flames (42–23–15), the defending Stanley Cup champions. In fact, three other teams, all in the Adams Division, also had better regular-season records than the Oilers: the Boston Bruins, with 101 points; the Buffalo Sabres, with 98; and the Montreal Canadiens, with 93.

Everyone starts off even when the playoffs begin, but almost immediately Edmonton was knocked into a hole: In the opening round, the Winnipeg Jets beat them in three of the first four games. A bleak memory arose—in 1989, the Oilers had been eliminated in the first round by the Los Angeles Kings, Gretzky's new team. Now facing the same fate, the Oilers didn't succumb; they rallied to defeat the Jets in the next three contests. The momentum they gained from this turnaround carried them through the rest of the playoffs.

In the second round, playing for the Smythe Division title, Edmonton took on Los Angeles, wiping them out in four straight games. Then, in the Campbell Conference finals against the Chicago Black Hawks, they won four out of six.

In the Wales Conference, the Boston Bruins showed why they had the best regular-season record: They outskated the Hartford Whalers, 4 games to 3, in the first round; they trounced the Montreal Canadiens, 4 games to 1, in the Adams Division finals; and they swept the Washington Capitals in four straight in the conference finals.

Game 1 of the Stanley Cup finals, played in Boston, was an epic contest—it lasted 115 minutes, 13 seconds, the longest game ever played in NHL finals. Tied 2–2 after regulation time, the teams battled late into the third overtime before Edmonton's Petr Klima took a fine pass from Jari Kurri and wristed the puck into the net past Bruin goalie Andy

NHL FINAL STANDINGS

WALES CONFERENCE

Adams Division

	W	L	T	Pts.
Boston	46	25	9	101
Buffalo	45	27	8	98
Montreal	41	28	11	93
Hartford	38	33	9	85
Quebec	12	61	7	31

Patrick Division

	W	L	T	Pts.
N.Y. Rangers	36	31	13	85
New Jersey	37	34	9	83
Washington	36	38	6	78
N.Y. Islanders	31	38	11	73
Pittsburgh	32	40	8	72
Philadelphia	30	39	11	71

CAMPBELL CONFERENCE

Norris Division

	W	L	T	Pts.
Chicago	41	33	6	88
St. Louis	37	34	9	83
Toronto	38	38	4	80
Minnesota	36	40	4	76
Detroit	28	38	14	70

Smythe Division

	W	L	T	Pts.
Calgary	42	23	15	99
Edmonton	38	28	14	90
Winnipeg	37	32	11	85
Los Angeles	34	39	7	75
Vancouver	25	41	14	64

Stanley Cup: Edmonton Oilers

OUTSTANDING PLAYERS

Hart Trophy (most valuable player)	Mark Messier, Edmonton
Ross Trophy (scorer)	Wayne Gretzky, Los Angeles
Vezina Trophy (goalie)	Patrick Roy, Montreal
Norris Trophy (defenseman)	Ray Bourque, Boston
Selke Trophy (defensive forward)	Rick Meagher, St. Louis
Calder Trophy (rookie)	Sergei Makarov, Calgary
Lady Byng Trophy (sportsmanship)	Brett Hull, St. Louis
Conn Smythe Trophy (Stanley Cup play)	Bill Ranford, Edmonton

Moog. Oiler goalie Bill Ranford contributed 50 saves to the sudden-death victory.

In Game 2, Ranford shone again and Kurri notched a hat trick (three goals) as the Oilers won, 7–2. They thus returned home leading two games to none. But the Bruins bounced back in the third game, 2–1, hanging on to win after first-period goals by John Byce and Greg Johnston.

Undeterred, Edmonton slammed Boston in Game 4 by the score of 5–1. Glenn Anderson and Craig Simpson each tallied two goals and two assists, and Mark Messier added three assists. And back in Boston for Game 5, Edmonton finished off the Bruins by the score of 4–1, as Anderson and Simpson each scored again, and Ranford blocked 29 of Boston's 30 shots.

So the Stanley Cup once again belonged to Edmonton, for the fifth time in the team's brief eleven-year existence—a remarkable record. Ranford won the Conn Smythe Trophy as the playoffs' most valuable player (MVP). He tied the NHL record of sixteen playoff victories in one year. The entire Oiler defense, in fact, was sterling throughout Stanley Cup play. It prevented two of Boston's top scorers, Cam Neely and Craig Janney, from scoring any goals.

Ranford's teammate Mark Messier was the winner of the Hart Trophy, as MVP of the regular season. Second in scoring, he totaled 129 points on 45 goals and 84 assists. Ironically, the NHL scoring leader was ex-Oiler Gretzky (142 points, 40 goals, 102 assists). Pittsburgh's Mario Lemieux, usually the top scorer, wound up with 123 points, but he missed the last six weeks of the season because of an injury.

Also during the regular season, Gretzky surpassed Gordie Howe as the NHL's all-time leading scorer. Howe had compiled 1,850 points, on 801 goals and 1,049 assists, in 26 seasons. Gretzky's 1,851st point came in only his eleventh season. Dramatically, Gretzky scored the record-setter, his 641st career goal, against the Oilers in Edmonton.

And Brett Hull of the St. Louis Blues, son of Hall of Famer Bobby Hull, became only the sixth player in history to score 70 or more goals in one season. Known, like his father, for a ringing slap shot, the young Hull finished up with 72.

In 1990, Swiss skier Pirmin Zurbriggen (*above*) won the World Cup championship. Jill Trenary of the United States (*right*) captured the women's figure-skating title in both the world championships and U.S. championships.

ICE SKATING

FIGURE SKATING

World Championships

Men	Kurt Browning, Canada
Women	Jill Trenary, U.S.
Pairs	Ekaterina Gordeyeva/Sergei Grinkov, U.S.S.R.
Dance	Marina Klimova/Sergei Ponomarenko, U.S.S.R.

United States Championships

Men	Todd Eldredge
Women	Jill Trenary
Pairs	Kristi Yamaguchi/Rudi Galindo
Dance	Susan Wynne/Joseph Druar

SPEED SKATING

World Championships

Men	Johann Olav Koss, Norway
Women	Jacqueline Boerner, East Germany

SKIING

WORLD CUP CHAMPIONSHIPS

Men	Pirmin Zurbriggen, Switzerland
Women	Petra Kronberger, Austria

U.S. ALPINE CHAMPIONSHIPS

Men

Downhill	Skip Merrick
Slalom	Felix McGrath
Giant Slalom	Tommy Moe
Super Giant Slalom	A. J. Kitt
Combined	Kyle Wieche

Women

Downhill	Lucie Laroche
Slalom	Monique Pelletier
Giant Slalom	Kristi Terzian
Super Giant Slalom	Krista Schmidinger
Combined	Julie Parisien

SWIMMING

Only two world records were set in swimming in 1990, both by Americans. Tom Jager (*above*) reduced the men's 50-meter freestyle mark to 21.38 seconds. And Mike Barrowman (*right*) set a new standard in the men's 200-meter breaststroke—2 minutes, 11.53 seconds.

Nineteen-year-old Californian Pete Sampras became the youngest men's singles champ in U.S. Open history.

TENNIS

Steffi Graf entered 1990 ranked number one in women's tennis, and Ivan Lendl was listed first among the men. By the end of the year, Lendl had been bumped from the top spot by Stefan Edberg. And although Graf was still in front, she had some tough competition close on her heels. The 21-year-old West German led the women for the fourth year in a row, but she wasn't as totally dominating as she had been in 1988 and 1989. She didn't seem to be slowing down; the others seemed to be catching up.

As the year began, both Lendl and Graf garnered victories in the Australian Open. The Czechoslovakian-born Lendl, 30, defeated Edberg in the finals in unusual circumstances. Edberg had won the first set, 6–4. Lendl took the second, 7–6, and was leading in the third, 5–2, when Edberg pulled an abdominal muscle. Unable to continue, the 24-year-old Swede had to drop out, conceding the match.

Graf's victory in the finals was more conventional, but it wasn't easy. She beat Mary Joe Fernandez in straight sets, 6–3, 6–4. But the 18-year-old Floridian aggressively attacked Graf's backhand and was even leading, 4–1, in the second set before Graf rebounded to win. It was Graf's third consecutive triumph in the Australian Open.

It would also be Graf's last victory in a Grand Slam event during the year. Although she would come close, the other three major titles would elude her.

TOURNAMENT TENNIS

	Australian Open	French Open	Wimbledon	U.S. Open
Men's Singles	Ivan Lendl, Czechoslovakia	Andres Gomez, Ecuador	Stefan Edberg, Sweden	Pete Sampras, U.S.
Women's Singles	Steffi Graf, West Germany	Monica Seles, Yugoslavia	Martina Navratilova, U.S.	Gabriela Sabatini, Argentina
Men's Doubles	Pieter Aldrich, South Africa/ Danie Visser, South Africa	Emilio Sanchez, Spain/ Sergio Casal, Spain	Rick Leach, U.S./ Jim Pugh, U.S.	Pieter Aldrich, South Africa/ Danie Visser, South Africa
Women's Doubles	Jana Novotna, Czechoslovakia/ Helena Sukova, Czechoslovakia	Jana Novotna, Czechoslovakia/ Helena Sukova, Czechoslovakia	Jana Novotna, Czechoslovakia/ Helena Sukova, Czechoslovakia	Gigi Fernandez, U.S./ Martina Navratilova, U.S.

Davis Cup Winner: United States

In the French Open, Graf reached the finals, where she was confronted by Monica Seles of Yugoslavia. Only 16, Seles, known for her unrelenting competitiveness, whipped Graf by 7–6 and 6–4. She thus became the youngest woman ever to win the French Open. The previous youngest, Arantxa Sanchez Vicario of Spain, was 17 when she took the title the year before—her finals opponent had also been Steffi Graf.

On the men's side, age rather than youth prevailed. Andres Gomez of Ecuador, 30, won the first Grand Slam event of his career by defeating Andre Agassi, a 20-year-old from Nevada, by 6–3, 2–6, 6–4, and 6–4.

At Wimbledon, Edberg staked his claim to the men's number-one ranking. Frustrated at having been forced to withdraw from the Australian Open finals, he outlasted West German Boris Becker 6–2, 6–2, 3–6, 3–6, and 6–4. It was Edberg's first major title since Wimbledon in 1988; Becker had won the same event in 1989.

Much of the excitement at Wimbledon centered around Martina Navratilova, who for many years was the world's best woman player. The 33-year-old Navratilova, a Czechoslovakian-born American, made tennis history by winning her ninth Wimbledon singles title. She beat Zina Garrison of Texas, 26, playing in her first Grand Slam finals. The scores were 6–4 and 6–1. As for Steffi Graf, she lost to Garrison in the semifinals.

Graf reached the finals of the U.S. Open, but she was stopped in her quest for her third straight triumph there by Gabriela Sabatini. Working with a new coach, the 20-year-old Argentinian altered her game to excellent effect: Beating Graf 6–2 and 7–6, she won her first Grand Slam title.

The men's champion at the U.S. Open was a surprising young Californian named Pete Sampras. A slender six-footer with a shotgun serve, he ripped Andre Agassi, 6–4, 6–3, and 6–2. He had eliminated Ivan Lendl in the quarterfinals and John McEnroe, in the midst of a comeback attempt, in the semis. At 19, Sampras became the youngest men's singles champ in U.S. Open history. And, seeded 12th at the beginning of the tournament, he was also the lowest seed to win the tournament since 1966. Sampras's future looked bright.

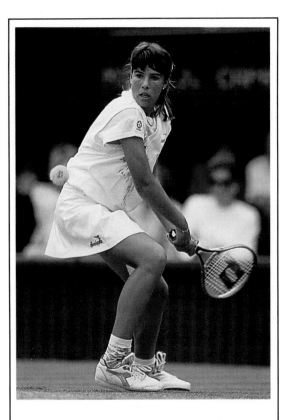

JEN-NI-FER!

She's touted as the game's next superstar: She seems to have all the tools. And she's young, even for a sport where stardom frequently comes early. Her name is Jennifer Capriati, and she became a professional tennis player in 1990 upon reaching the age of 14.

What's she got? For one thing, a 95-mile-per-hour serve. For another, a powerful ground stroke. A solid backhand. And she attacks the net like a pit bull in battle. Tennis stadiums echo with her huge grunts each time she hits the ball. The fans respond with cries of "Jen-ni-fer!"

Off the court, Jennifer Capriati reveals the engaging personality of the charming teenager that she is. Add a winning smile, and it's easy to understand why the 5-foot 7-inch young woman from Wesley Chapel, Florida, has become so popular.

The important question is, of course, will she succeed? In her rookie year, Capriati did pretty well, winning her first singles title at the Mount Cranmore International in July. At Wimbledon, she became the youngest player to ever win a main-draw match (past the qualifying rounds). At this and the other Grand Slam events, she earned respect for her play.

Barring injuries, and if she maintains her zest for the game, Jennifer Capriati is expected to rise quickly to tennis fame.

TRACK AND FIELD

World records were set in 1990 in the men's javelin throw and in the men's shot put. In July, Steve Backley (*left*) of Britain, hurled the javelin 293 feet, 11 inches, surpassing the previous mark of 292 feet, 4 inches set by Patrik Boden of Sweden in March. American Randy Barnes (*below*) put the shot 75 feet, 10¼ inches in May, breaking the former record by 2¼ inches. (Barnes was suspended for steroid use after a later meet; he denied the charges.)

A new winter sport called snowboarding has been giving people a lift. And as these two teenagers demonstrate, it rivals downhill skiing for thrills.

SPORTS BRIEFS

Some unusual sports grabbed attention in 1990: roller-blading, snowboarding, and an auto race that didn't consume a single drop of gasoline. In chess, the most intellectual of games, two great players locked horns with the world championship at stake. And on a larger scale, thousands of athletes competed in dozens of sports in the Asian Games and the Goodwill Games.

TOPSY-TURVY SEASONS

Imagine going ice skating in the summer and surfing when the snow flies. Sound ridiculous? But you can do just this with a couple of new sports that were the rage in 1990.

Well, maybe roller-blading isn't exactly ice skating—but it's a lot like it, and you can go roller-blading when the weather is warm. And maybe a snowboard isn't exactly a surfboard and you won't find waves on a hill or a mountain—but who's complaining when you're having plenty of winter fun?

It's all very simple. In roller-blading, which is also called "in-line" roller skating, you slide along on wheels that are positioned in a straight line—similar to the blades on ice skates. The sport got its start when hockey players were looking for a way to practice and keep in shape during the off-season. The in-line roller skate was developed, and people quickly discovered that besides the benefits of exercise, roller-blading offered a good deal of fast-moving fun. Now, hundreds of thousands of people have taken up the sport. One caution: you can go pretty fast, so it's a good idea to wear knee pads and hand guards. Helmets, too. And if you're worried about a bumpy ride, just stay on the smooth pavement.

Now suppose you're a surfer who lives in

the high latitudes. How do you keep up with your favorite sport when the temperature nudges below freezing? Try out a snowboard, or ''stick,'' the word snowboarding enthusiasts prefer to use. A ''stick'' may be anywhere from three to six feet long and ten inches wide; it's like a surfboard, and also like a skateboard. Zipping back and forth down a slope is called ''shredding,'' a term borrowed from surfing.

Between roller-blading and snowboarding, you can make January seem like July, and vice versa!

SILENT STRUGGLE

The two men could hardly be more different. One was brooding, emotional, and physically imposing. The other was cool, reserved, and physically slight. The first attacked his opponent's position ferociously. The other carefully and slowly maintained a solid defense. And the two men couldn't conceal their dislike for each other. But they had something very important in common—brooding, emotional Gary Kasparov and cool, reserved Anatoly Karpov were without question the best chess players in the world. In late 1990, like two great boxers, Kasparov and Karpov slugged it out in a 24-game world championship chess match. To chess fans,

the event was like a heavyweight title bout, the World Series, and the Super Bowl all rolled into one.

Kasparov, a 27-year-old from the Soviet Republic of Azerbaijan, began the match as world champion. He had won the title from Karpov, 39, also from the Soviet Union, in 1985. Right from the start of their latest encounter, the match looked to all the experts like one that would make history.

The first twelve games of this 24-game match were played in New York City, and the second twelve were played in Lyons, France. A victory was worth one point, and a draw a half point. The first contestant to score 12½ points would win the title. In case of a 12–12 tie, Kasparov would retain his crown. The stakes were high: Besides the right to call himself the champion, the winner would pocket about $1.7 million; the loser's share would be about $1.3 million.

And so, sitting just a few feet apart, their heads bent in concentration, Kasparov and Karpov engaged in a silent, though intense, struggle. The first game was a draw. But in the second game, Kasparov, playing white, launched some crucial, innovative moves that seemed to leave him at a disadvantage. The audience, consisting of chess fans and numerous grandmasters (chess experts) from

A study in black and white: With the world chess title at stake, Gary Kasparov and Anatoly Karpov went head to head in a 24-game match. Kasparov won.

Sunrayce USA was a race for solar cars that traveled through eight states from Florida to Michigan. The winner was *Sunrunner* (above), built by students from the University of Michigan.

around the world, was dumbfounded at first. But slowly it began to dawn on the observers that Kasparov's tactic was brilliant, and in fact he had written a new chapter in the annals of chess. Kasparov won the contest, taking a 1½ to ½ lead in the games.

The loss in the second game didn't ruin Karpov; he was too good a player for that. After four straight draws, Karpov won the seventh contest. Five more draws followed, and by the time the opponents finished the first half of the match, each had 6 points. When the battle continued in France in November, Kasparov began to dominate. After five draws, he won game 18; game 19 was a draw, and Kaparov won game 20. When the match was all over, the champion retained his title, 12½ points to 11½.

NO RAIN, PLEASE

As automobile races go, this one was pretty slow. But it just may offer part of the solution to the problem of higher and higher gasoline prices. That's because the cars in this race didn't use any gasoline at all—instead, they ran on energy from the sun. They were solar-powered.

In the summer of 1990, the General Motors Corporation sponsored Sunrayce USA, a competition in which solar cars raced across 1,641 miles (2,641 kilometers) from Florida to Michigan. Solar cars bear little resemblance to the family automobile. Nor do they look much like the powerful machines that run in such races as the Indianapolis 500. Solar cars are built to be extremely light and aerodynamic, and their bodies are covered with thousands of tiny solar cells that can change sunlight into electricity in order to power the car's engine. (On cloudy days, solar cars get their "fuel" from batteries.)

The GM Sunrayce USA attracted 32 college teams. The winner was the *Sunrunner,* built by engineering students at the University of Michigan. Over the eleven days of the race, *Sunrunner* averaged no more than 30 miles (48 kilometers) per hour, and reached a top speed of about 50 miles (80 kilometers).

In November, at the approach of summer in the Southern Hemisphere, a similar race took place in Australia. The World Solar Challenge covered about 1,850 miles (3,000 kilometers), north to south, beginning in Darwin and ending near Adelaide. The winner was the Swiss entry, *Spirit of Biel,* which averaged 40 miles (65 kilometers) per hour. The University of Michigan's *Sunrunner* finished third.

Chinese gymnasts warm up in preparation for competition in the 1990 Asian Games—the Asian Olympics—which attracted 7,000 athletes to Beijing, China. The host country won the majority of the gold medals.

Few people suggest that solar cars will quickly become common on the roads and highways of the world. But what is learned in these races may help us overcome our great dependence on oil-based fuels.

A SHOWCASE FOR CHINA ... AND THE U.S.

China, the most populous country on Earth, hadn't looked good in the eyes of the world in recent years. In June, 1989, responding to pro-democracy rallies in the capital city of Beijing, the Communist government had called in troops who killed hundreds of student demonstrators. Barely fifteen months later, seeking to improve its image, the Chinese government called for a massive cleanup job in the capital in anticipation of the Asian Games—the Olympics of Asia.

Beijing has long been filled with statues and posters bearing the likeness of Mao Zedong, the late leader of China and the founder of the Chinese Communist Party. But in 1990, the face and figure of a more sprightly fellow was seen around the city: Pan-Pan the panda, the official mascot of the 11th Asiad, as the Games are also called. A successful Asiad, the government hoped, would place China in contention as a site for the Olympics in the year 2000.

After the city's millions of residents cleaned up, Chinese athletes "cleaned up" too, winning 183 of a possible 308 gold medals in 29 sports. South Korea, which had hosted the previous Asiad in 1986, was second with 54 golds, and Japan was third, with 38.

In men's swimming, China's Shen Jianqiang won five gold medals, more than any of the other 7,000 athletes who took part in the Games. Chinese divers also excelled, as they were expected to. So did the country's cyclists and weight lifters. But China also did well in sports in which it had little experience. Boxing, for example, had been banned in China until 1987; but Chinese boxers had evidently learned enough in the few years since then to win one gold and five silver medals.

Half a world away, in Seattle, Washington, another set of Games took place in July. The Goodwill Games featured participants from around the globe. As in the Asian Games, the host country fared quite well. Women swimmers from the United States, in particular, were dominant. They won eight of ten possible gold medals, successfully competing with long-time powerhouse East Germany in numerous races. Janet Evans of the United States, who won three gold medals in the 1988 Olympics, collected three golds and two silvers at the Goodwill Games. Her teammate, 17-year-old Summer Sanders, won two golds, one of them at the expense of Evans in the 400-meter individual medley.

Both the Asian Games and the Goodwill Games were viewed by many of the participants as "tuneups" for the 1992 Olympics in Barcelona, Spain.

BRIEF BRIEFS

• Gymnastics is a sport whose stars, especially the women, are often young teenagers. Add to the list of young champions the name of Kim Zmeskal of Houston, Texas. In June, 1990, at the age of 14, she won the United States senior women's all-around title. Barely four and a half feet tall and weighing just 70 pounds, Kim unexpectedly beat the previous year's winner, Brandy Johnson, 17, of Altamonte Springs, Florida, who placed third. Second was Betty Okino of Elmhurst, Illinois. Kim's coach was the legendary Bela Karolyi, who also was the mentor of past Olympic champions Nadia Comaneci and Mary Lou Retton.

• The ancient Olympics were born thousands of years ago in Athens, Greece. In tribute, the first of the modern Olympics were held in Athens, in 1896. For the 100th anniversary of those first modern Games, Athens again sought to be the host city. But the Greek capital was turned down by the International Olympic Committee. Instead, the site chosen for the 1996 Summer Olympics was Atlanta, Georgia.

• For the second year in a row, and the third time since 1986, Greg LeMond won the Tour de France, cycling's most prestigious race. After 21 days and 2,112 miles (3,400 kilometers), *le maillot jaune*—"the yellow jersey," symbolic of leadership in the Tour —belonged once again to the 29-year-old from Wayzata, Minnesota. When he crossed the finish line in Paris in July, LeMond had defeated his nearest rival, Claudio Chiappuci of Italy, by 2 minutes and 16 seconds in total elapsed time.

• Some people race on bicycles. Others race on dogsleds. Susan Butcher, 35, went one better than Greg LeMond: In March, 1990, she won her fourth Iditarod Trail Sled Dog Race in five years. On the way, she set a new record for the grueling 1,158-mile (1,864-kilometer) run from Anchorage to Nome, Alaska—11 days, 1 hour, 53 minutes, and 23 seconds.

• Lisa Leslie of Morningside High School in Los Angeles, California, scored 101 points in a basketball game in February, all in the first half! But the 6-foot, 5-inch center couldn't break the U.S. record of 105 points because the opposing team refused to play the second half. The final score was 102–24.

In June, 14-year-old Kim Zmeskal of Houston, Texas, won the U.S. senior women's all-around gymnastics title. She hoped to win a berth on the U.S. Olympic team that will compete in 1992 in Barcelona, Spain.

Since a half in high school basketball is sixteen minutes long, Lisa averaged more than six points per minute.

• Mike Tyson, the 24-year-old heavyweight boxing champion, seemed unbeatable. He had 33 knockouts and no defeats in 37 bouts. But in February, 1990, the sports world was shocked when James "Buster" Douglas knocked Tyson out in the tenth round of a title fight. Douglas's reign lasted barely eight months. In October, overweight and out of shape, Douglas lost his championship when he was decked by Evander Holyfield in round three. Tyson, who said he had regained his form, was set to fight Holyfield in 1991.

187

The year 1990 marked the 125th anniversary of the end of the U.S. Civil War, a tragic chapter in American history. The Battle of Antietam (below) was fought on September 17, 1862, near Sharpsburg, Maryland. The Southern forces, which had invaded Northern territory for the first time in the war, were turned back by Union troops. But more than two years would pass before the two sides made peace in the spring of 1865.

THE COUNTING OF AMERICA

On April 1, 1990, the United States sat for a national family portrait. It was census day —the day on which the U.S. government attempts to count every man, woman, and child in the country.

The 1990 census was the twenty-first such head count undertaken in the United States. It was also the largest ever—the government tried to reach some 250 million people. What did the government want to know? Beyond mere numbers, the 1990 census was designed to provide a detailed picture of the United States—who its people are, where they're from, and where and how they live.

THE REASONS FOR THE COUNT

The original purpose of the U.S. census was to ensure that everyone is properly represented in the House of Representatives, and this is still a main goal. Every state is guaranteed at least one seat in the House. The rest of the 435 seats are divided up among the states on the basis of their populations, using census figures that are taken decennially (every ten years). After each census, the seats are re-apportioned, or divided up again, to reflect changes in population.

Census figures are also used to draw the boundaries of Congressional voting districts, so that each district will have roughly the same number of people. This helps ensure that everyone is represented equally in Congress. And state and local governments use the census figures to redraw the boundaries of their own legislative districts.

Census information also helps determine how billions of dollars in federal funds will be used each year. Federal programs that provide aid for everything from highway construction to school lunches use census figures to find out which areas are most in need of funds.

Towns, civic groups, businesses, and individuals use the figures, too. For example, census figures showing the number of pre-school children in your town could help the town decide if a new school will be needed. And census figures help businesses know where to build new stores for potential shoppers and which locations will be able to provide workers for new manufacturing plants.

HOW THE CENSUS WAS TAKEN

Although April 1 was the official census day, the actual count began earlier in the year and went on for many months after that date. In late March, the Census Bureau (the government agency in charge of the census) mailed questionnaires to 88 million homes. Census workers delivered the forms in person to another 18 million households in remote areas, such as parts of the Deep South and the western mountains. To locate all the households and keep track of the millions of addresses, the bureau used some 500 powerful minicomputers. For the first time, computers also generated about 7 million maps for use in taking the census.

Most households received a short questionnaire that took about fifteen minutes to fill out. But about one of every six households received a longer form that asked detailed questions about housing, income, education, disabilities, and so on. Most people were instructed to mail the forms back to the Census Bureau by June 1, the official deadline. In some cases, census workers went to homes and retrieved the forms.

The bureau also made special efforts to count groups of people who had often been overlooked in past censuses. On the night of March 20–21, for example, 15,000 census workers fanned out across the country to find homeless people. They called at shelters for the homeless and also checked parks, subway stations, all-night movie theaters, and other places where homeless people often camp.

Almost immediately, however, it was clear that the 1990 census was running into problems. Some 4.8 million forms were returned by the Postal Service, marked "undeliverable." The bureau's mailing list also left out entire city blocks, several zip-code areas, and even two whole towns (Ross, California, and Raymond, Mississippi). By many estimates, only a fraction of the homeless were reached. And by late April, the bureau had received only 63 percent of the forms back, far fewer than it expected. It appeared that many people weren't responding to the count.

Even though people were required by law to complete and return the forms, they had many reasons for not doing so. Many tossed out the form by mistake, thinking it was a piece of junk mail. Others couldn't read the form because they couldn't speak English. Some people found the form, especially the long form, too confusing or too time-consuming to fill out. Still others felt that the questions on the form invaded their privacy.

Americans were required by law to complete and return their census forms. But, for various reasons, many did not. In fact, by late April, there were so many people who hadn't responded that the Census Bureau hired thousands of extra workers to track down the missing households.

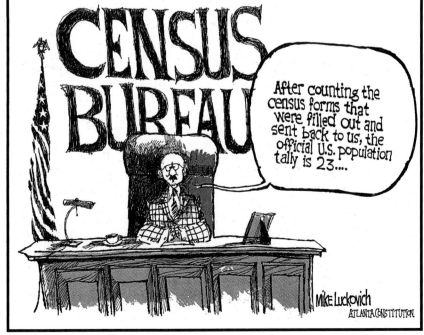

The Census Bureau tried especially hard to find and count groups of people who had been overlooked in past censuses, such as the homeless.

They worried that the information they gave might be used against them in some way, even though census information is supposed to be kept confidential.

Because the census count is supposed to be as complete as possible, the Census Bureau tried to track down people who didn't return forms. It hired thousands of extra workers who combed city streets to find missed households and knocked on doors, hoping to get people to answer in person the questions they had failed to answer by mail. Even so, it was clear that the count couldn't be really complete.

The response was especially low among minority groups, poor people living in cities, and illegal aliens (foreign citizens living in the United States without official permission). This raised concern that the final results wouldn't reflect the U.S. population accurately. Similar concerns had been raised by the 1980 census—by some estimates, that count had reached more than 99 percent of whites but only about 94 percent of blacks.

Large cities claimed to have lost millions of dollars in federal aid, as well as political representation, as a result of undercounting

in 1980. They expected to lose even more as a result of the problems with the 1990 census. Thus some people argued that the Census Bureau should adjust its figures, using statistical methods to estimate the number of people it had missed. But others argued that this would just lead to more errors.

In response to criticism, the Census Bureau conducted spot checks in August and October, recounting some 20 million housing units in all. The bureau also defended the accuracy of the census. While the country's fifteen largest cities claimed that their population had been undercounted by more than a million, census officials expected the spot checks to turn up no more than 200,000 missed people nationwide.

ADDING IT UP

While the debate on undercounting continued, census workers rushed to complete their work. Computers whirred around the clock to sort and add the information from the forms. By December 31, the Census Bureau was to present President George Bush with a state-by-state population report.

Long before then, however, the Census

Bureau was predicting some of the results. The predictions were based on early tabulations of census results and on surveys that the bureau takes every month. The surveys cover thousands of households, and they give the government a sort of crystal ball with which to keep abreast of changes in housing and population.

Here are some of the trends that the 1990 census was expected to show:

• Preliminary figures had put the population at about 246 million. But the final official count was 249.6 million. This was an increase of about 10 percent from 1980, the slowest rate of growth in any decade since the 1930's.

• The average size of a U.S. household would be 2.6 people, the smallest ever.

• The population of the Northeast was expected to fall behind the population of the West. States in the South and West were expected to gain seats in Congress, while those in the Northeast would lose seats.

• The early figures also showed that California would keep its place as the country's most populous state. In fact, the figures showed that California's population had grown 24 percent since 1980, accounting for nearly a quarter of the country's entire population growth.

• Much of California's growth—and much of the population growth nationally—came from immigration.

• Asian and Hispanic Americans would form two of the fastest-growing ethnic groups. The number of Asian Americans was expected to be up 70 percent, and the number of Hispanic Americans up 50 percent, from 1980.

• Rural areas were losing population faster than expected; metropolitan areas on both the East and West coasts were gaining.

• New York City would remain the largest city—a position it has held since the very first census, in 1790. But the Los Angeles region would be the fastest-growing of the country's major metropolitan areas, and Los Angeles would pass Chicago to become the second-largest city.

Would these predictions prove correct? The answer will come in 1991, as thousands of pages of detailed census reports are released. Together, the reports will provide a portrait of the United States.

WHICH STATES ARE GROWING THE FASTEST?
(Estimated percentage change in population, 1980–1990)

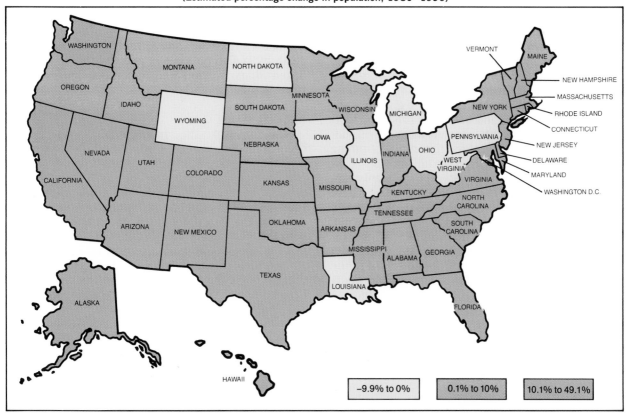

| −9.9% to 0% | 0.1% to 10% | 10.1% to 49.1% |

THE BATTLE OF WOUNDED KNEE

In December of 1890, the American Indian Wars came to a bloody climax on the banks of Wounded Knee Creek in South Dakota. On a chill winter morning, just four days after Christmas, U.S. Cavalrymen and Sioux Indians fought a brief but vicious battle that left more than 200 Indians dead, including many women and children.

The year 1990 marked the 100th anniversary of the Battle of Wounded Knee, as the army called it—or the Wounded Knee Massacre, as Indians remember it. This was the last tragic act in a violent saga that lasted for more than 100 years and pitted white settlers on the western frontier against Native Americans. For decades, the Indians had angrily watched as white settlers grabbed their lands and even tore up their sacred burial grounds searching for gold.

As one Sioux Indian remarked, "They (the white people) made us many promises, more than I can remember, but they never kept but one; they promised to take our land and they took it."

THE GHOST DANCE RELIGION

By the 1880's, most of the Indian tribes had been forced onto reservations by the U.S. government. On the reservations the old tribal ways began to die out. No longer was the young Indian supposed to be a warrior and hunter roaming the land freely. Now Indians were told to live on the reservation and become farmers. Well-meaning missionaries told them that they must give up their Indian religion and become Christians. Corrupt Indian agents cheated them by providing only part of the food rations and clothing supplied by the U.S. government.

Into this bleak landscape suddenly appeared a ray of hope. In 1889, a young Paiute Indian prophet named Wovoka began preaching a new religion of salvation for the Indians. According to Wovoka, if the Indians followed his teachings, the white man would disappear and life would return to the way it had been before. The buffalo herds would come back; the spirits of dead Indians would rise up and rejoin the living; and there would be a new world of peace.

To make this come about, said Wovoka, the Indians must dance the Ghost Dance and sing Ghost Dance songs, which Wovoka taught his followers. Soon the Ghost Dance religion spread across the plains to most of the western tribes. Among those who joined in were many of the Sioux Indians living on the Pine Ridge and Standing Rock reservations in the Dakotas.

At the Standing Rock Reservation lived the great Sioux chief and medicine man Sitting Bull. Fourteen years earlier, in 1876, Sitting Bull had been one of the Indian leaders who had defeated General George Custer and the 7th Cavalry at the Battle of the Little Big Horn—better known as "Custer's Last Stand." Although Sitting Bull had lived peacefully on the reservation for many years, he was still feared by many of the local white settlers.

Army officers and reservation officials watched nervously as Sitting Bull's Sioux Indians joined in the Ghost Dance frenzy. Many whites feared that Sitting Bull was using the Ghost Dance to stir up an Indian uprising. Troops were rushed into the area and General Nelson Miles, the commanding officer, ordered Sitting Bull's arrest.

On December 15, the Indian reservation police, backed by troops, tried to arrest the old chief. When his followers protested, a gun battle broke out. Sitting Bull was shot to death by Indian policemen, and more than a dozen Sioux warriors and Indian policemen were also killed.

THE LAST MAJOR CLASH

Now it was the Indians who were frightened. Fearing that the troops might attack them, many fled the reservation. Army officers persuaded most to return, but one band of Miniconjou Sioux under Chief Big Foot fled into the Badlands. General Miles believed that Big Foot intended to link up with the Sioux at the Pine Ridge reservation, and that this would spark a general uprising.

More than 3,000 troops were deployed to capture Big Foot's band. On December 28, a detachment of the 7th Cavalry corralled the fleeing Indians and marched them to the regiment's main camp on Wounded Knee Creek. By now the Indians were hungry, ex-

This painting shows Sioux Indians performing the Ghost Dance. The Indians believed that if they followed the Ghost Dance religion, life would return to the way it had been before the white man came.

hausted, and suffering from the cold. Big Foot was so sick with pneumonia that he had to be carried in an army wagon.

During the night, the troops surrounded the Indian band, which consisted of 120 warriors and 230 women and children. The 7th Cavalry was the same regiment that had been whipped by the Sioux fourteen years earlier at the Battle of the Little Big Horn. Some of the soldiers were spoiling for a fight, and there was talk of avenging Custer.

At daybreak on the morning of December 29, Colonel James Forsyth, commander of the 7th, ordered his troopers to ring the Indian camp. Then he ordered the Sioux to turn in their guns. There were scuffles as soldiers roughly seized rifles from Indians unwilling to give them up.

Suddenly a shot rang out, probably fired by an Indian. In response, the soldiers unleashed a volley of carbine fire directly into the mass of Indians. Men, women, and children were shot down, many as they tried to run away. Indian warriors rushed at the sol-

diers—believing that their ghost shirts would stop the soldiers' bullets—and there was vicious hand-to-hand fighting.

When the shooting finally stopped, more than 150 Indians were dead—half of them women and children. Many others later died of their wounds, and the final death toll was probably over 200. Twenty-five soldiers were also killed and 39 were wounded— many, it is believed, by the crossfire of their fellow soldiers. The fight at Wounded Knee was the last major clash between Indians and the army on the western frontier. After that, the Plains Indians resigned themselves to reservation life.

Some historians have called Wounded Knee a tragic blunder rather than a deliberate massacre. But most people regard Wounded Knee as a symbol of the harsh and unjust treatment suffered by Native Americans during the settlement of the western frontier.

HENRY I. KURTZ
Author, *The Art of the Toy Soldier*

THE THRILL OF THE RIDE

Slowly, the car lurches higher and higher. It's above the treetops now, supported only by a spindly wooden frame. Your heart is beating faster, and your palms begin to sweat —something dreadful is about to happen.

Suddenly, the car swings around a bend and takes you over the top, plunging down toward the ground at 60 miles an hour. The wind whips your hair back and brings tears to your eyes. Your stomach is in your throat and your heart is in your knees. Your mouth is wide open, and you're screaming for all you're worth.

And you love every minute of it!

For sheer thrills and terrifying chills, nothing beats a roller coaster. Variations of this exciting amusement-park ride have been around for about three hundred years. And while roller coasters have had their ups and downs over the years, today they are more popular than at any time since the 1920's. New coasters—ever higher and faster, with steeper drops and more devilish twists and turns—are opening all the time. People spend hours in line, waiting for a ride that lasts a couple of minutes. And when the ride is over, they rush back to the line to wait again.

SLIPPERY BEGINNINGS

It was the Russians who came up with the basic idea behind the roller coaster. The first

coal from mines at the top of Mt. Pisgah to Mauch Chunk, at the foot of the mountain. As a passenger ride, it carried people to the top of the mountain and then sent them down again. Traveling at just 5 miles (8 kilometers) an hour, the Mauch Chunk Railway was tame by the standards of today's coasters. But the scenery was beautiful, and the ride was an instant success.

Soon artificial coasting courses were being built. In these rides, the slides were made up of fat rollers placed one after another, conveyor-belt style. The coasting-course fad didn't last long—but the name "roller coaster" survived.

Like the earlier Russian Mountains, these roller coasters carried people straight down —there were no stomach-flipping ups and downs. The first ride that resembled a modern coaster, with artificial hills and valleys, appeared in 1884. It was the Switchback Gravity Pleasure Railway, built by La-Marcus A. Thompson at Coney Island in Brooklyn, New York. In it, riders boarded a ten-person wheeled car and were carried down an undulating (up-and-down) track at six miles (10 kilometers) an hour.

People lined up to take a five-cent ride on

The 1884 Coney Island coaster. Riders paid only a nickel for the thrill of being terrified. Today's coasters are a lot more sophisticated, and the rides are more expensive, but people still find them to be a scream!

coasters were actually ice slides built in St. Petersburg (now Leningrad) in the 1600's. The slides, supported by wooden frames and angled at about 50 degrees, provided a slick, fast surface for sleds. Riders climbed to a platform at the top and then shot straight down the slide at thrilling speeds.

The French adopted the concept but redesigned the rides. They added tiny wheels to the sleds, so that ice wasn't needed and the slides could be enjoyed year-round. The first of the French slides, which were called Russian Mountains, was introduced in Paris in the early 1800's.

A half century later, the popular rides spread to the United States. The first U.S. coaster, which began operating in 1870, was actually a converted railway in Pennsylvania. It originally had been designed to carry

THE SCIENCE OF THRILLS

A day at an amusement park doesn't seem like an educational activity. But at many parks, it's not uncommon to see science students scurrying from ride to ride with notebooks. That's because the rides—and especially the big roller coasters—demonstrate some basic principles of physics.

Once the cars in a roller coaster reach the top of the first hill, for example, gravity (which pulls downward) is the only force that sends them speeding along the tracks. That means that the speed of a coaster ride is closely related to the height of the first hill—the bigger the drop, the more speed the cars pick up as they plunge down. This is why taller coasters (and the tallest is as high as a 20-story building) provide more thrills.

Speed also makes it possible for the cars to flip upside-down through corkscrews and loops. As long as the cars are traveling fast enough, centrifugal force (which pushes outward) will keep you glued to your seat, even when the car is at the top of the loop.

The big loops on coasters aren't perfect circles. They are teardrop shapes called *clothoid loops*. In a perfect circle, the cars would slow down too much at the top of the loop. Then the force of gravity might be stronger than the centrifugal force, causing passengers to fall out of their seats. The elongated shape of the clothoid loop keeps the cars moving faster at the top, increasing the centrifugal force.

Centrifugal force also acts on the cars when they whip around curves. That's why roller coaster tracks are banked, or angled, on curves—if the tracks were level, centrifugal force might send the cars flying off.

Designers calculate these forces carefully when they build a new coaster. They know just how fast the cars will be traveling at each point and how much each turn must be banked. That, combined with rider harnesses and rigorous operating and inspection standards, makes roller coasters far safer than they look.

the new invention, and Thompson soon was taking in about $700 a day. It was clear that lots of people were willing to pay money to be scared. Soon other amusement park owners were clamoring for similar rides, and a roller-coaster boom began.

By 1920, most amusement parks had some kind of roller coaster. The designers of these coasters made many improvements on Thompson's first design. For example, the Switchback Railway track followed a straight course (rather than the circular course used by today's coasters), and the cars had no power. That meant that the cars had to be pushed to the top of the track after each ride. Circular tracks and power lifts were among the first refinements made in roller-coaster design.

Then designers concentrated on making each new coaster bigger, steeper, faster—in other words, more terrifying—than the one before. The scarier a coaster was, it seemed, the more people it drew. An especially terrifying roller coaster was the Coney Island Cyclone, perhaps the most well-known coaster of all time. World-famous aviator Charles Lindbergh declared it to be "a greater thrill than flying an airplane at top speed."

Another heart-stopper was built at Playland, in Rye, New York. It was 90 feet (27 meters) high, and at one point the cars plunged underground—adding an extra thrill to the ride and making this the first coaster to go underground.

But in the 1930's, the roller-coaster boom came to an end. An economic depression settled in, and many people were out of work. Fewer people went to amusement

On King Cobra (Kings Island, Ohio), riders wear cushioned harnesses and remain standing up during the entire looping ride.

Magnum XL-200 (Cedar Point Park, Sandusky, Ohio) is billed as the tallest, non-looping steel coaster, with a 20-story plunge.

parks—they just didn't have the money for rides. As park attendance dropped, roller coasters stood idle. Many were torn down.

After the Depression and World War II, however, the situation began to change. A new kind of amusement park—the theme park—appeared. Disneyland, which opened in Anaheim, California, in 1955, was the first of these parks. Disneyland introduced its first roller coaster, the Matterhorn Bobsleds, in 1958, and the ride was instantly popular.

Soon other theme parks were being built. And more often than not, roller coasters were the centerpieces of these parks. Just as in the 1920's, people wanted the thrills and excitement that only a roller coaster could provide.

TERRIFYING TWISTS

Like amusement parks of the past, parks of today are constantly competing to have the biggest, tallest, fastest, and scariest roller coaster. And today's roller coasters provide thrills that riders of the 1890's could never have imagined. For one thing, they travel at up to ten times the speed of the early coasters.

Today's roller coasters don't just send riders around curves and up and down a few hills, either. The cars hurtle through corkscrews and spirals, turn upside-down in complete loops, and plunge riders into total darkness. And some coasters are even designed to carry riders standing up.

Many of these hair-raising designs were

made possible by the development of tubular steel tracks in the late 1950's. These tracks make coaster rides faster, smoother, and quieter. Because the wheels of the cars grip the tubular tracks from top to bottom, rather than riding on top as they do on flat rails, the new tracks also allow designers to throw in a whole series of inverted loops and corkscrews. And they make possible some other terrifying twists. In the Iron Dragon, at Cedar Point in Sandusky, Ohio, the cars are suspended from an overhead steel track. They swing out around turns and skim over water and treetops—with nothing between riders and the ground.

But for some roller-coaster enthusiasts, there's nothing like an old-fashioned wooden coaster, or "woodie." Loops and corkscrews are fine, but the jolts, shakes, and roar of a woodie add extra thrills to the ride. Thus woodies are still being built. Many are new designs. The Texas Giant, at Six Flags Over Texas in Arlington, is typical of these. It takes riders 40 stories into the air on the first hill—and there are 20 more plunges still to come.

There's also great interest in restoring old coasters and in re-creating some of the best old designs. The Coney Island Cyclone, famous in the late 1920's, is still running and has been named a national landmark. The Raging Wolf Bobs, in Aurora, Ohio, is a replica of a famous coaster built in Chicago's Riverview Park in the 1920's. There are even plans for a "park of the past"—Electric Park, near Indianapolis, Indiana. Set to open in 1991, it will feature several designs from famous amusement parks of the 1920's.

Old or new, it seems that roller coasters have a special appeal. What heart-stopping twist will coaster designers think up next? Whatever it is, one thing is certain: People will line up for a chance to experience the thrill of the ride.

The Texas Giant (Six Flags Over Texas, Arlington) opened in 1990. A "woodie," it's high, fast, and wild.

THE CIVIL WAR
An Anniversary Album

In all of American history, perhaps no chapter is darker than that of the Civil War, the bitter conflict between the North and the South. The war broke out in 1861, after a number of Southern states seceded, or withdrew, from the Union. It ended four years later, in April, 1865, when Southern forces surrendered to the North. The year 1990 marked the 125th anniversary of the end of the war, which had caused enormous pain on both sides. (Above: Large areas of Georgia were left devastated by a Northern army under General William Tecumseh Sherman, which cut a swath of destruction from Atlanta to the sea in 1864.)

The issues that tore the country in two in 1861 were slavery and states' rights. These issues had been simmering for a long time. Since Colonial times, the Southern economy had been based on large plantations that were worked by slaves. In the North, farms were smaller, so there was little need for slave labor. The North also developed manufacturing and other industries earlier than the South. By the early 1800's, slavery had been outlawed in most of the North.

Many Northerners believed that slavery was immoral and shouldn't be allowed in the western territories that were then seeking statehood. Some thought that it should be abolished completely. But in the South, most people felt that each state should decide the question of slavery for itself. And they believed that slavery was essential to their way of life. Southerners disagreed with Northerners on other issues, too. But slavery was the issue that provoked the most passionate disagreement.

In the mid-1850's, the divisions between the North and the South grew deeper. The question of whether the territory of Kansas should enter the Union as a slave or free state led to bitter debates in Congress— and bloodshed between pro- and anti-slavery groups in the territory. Meanwhile, abolitionists—people who wanted to abolish, or end, slavery—were gaining support in the North. Harriet Beecher Stowe's novel *Uncle Tom's Cabin* (advertised in the poster at right), published in 1852, presented a picture of suffering slaves that won many people to the abolitionist cause. In 1859, the abolitionist John Brown tried to start a slave rebellion. The attempt failed and Brown was hanged. But the incident increased the split between Northerners, who saw Brown as a hero, and Southerners, who saw him as a dangerous criminal.

By 1860 there were about 4 million slaves, making up nearly a third of the South's population. Originally, slaves that worked the Southern plantations were imported from Africa. As public feeling against slavery grew, the United States banned the importation of slaves in 1808. However, slaves were still bought and sold within the country, often at slave auctions such as the one shown below.

In 1858, the issue of slavery was taken up by two candidates in a race for a U.S. Senate seat in Illinois. They were Senator Stephen Douglas and Abraham Lincoln, a lawyer and former congressman. In seven debates around the state, Douglas presented the case for each state's right to decide the issue. Lincoln called slavery an evil that was harming blacks, whites, and the entire country.

The Lincoln-Douglas debates drew national attention. Lincoln lost the senatorial election, but his name became well known all over the country. In 1860, the Republican Party, which opposed slavery, chose him as its presidential candidate. The Democratic Party split, with Northern Democrats choosing Stephen Douglas as their candidate and Southern Democrats supporting John C. Breckinridge. Lincoln, who had been born in a log cabin in Kentucky, had wide appeal in the North. The Republicans presented him as Honest Abe, a homespun man of the people. On November 6, Lincoln won the election, sweeping the Northern states.

Many Southerners were outraged by Lincoln's election. Although he hadn't proposed banning slavery, they believed he would do so. In December, 1860, South Carolina became the first state to secede from the Union. It was quickly followed by Alabama, Mississippi, Florida, Georgia, and Louisiana. These states formed a separate nation: the Confederate States of America. Jefferson Davis (*right*) was named president. (Five more states—Texas, Virginia, North Carolina, Tennessee, and Arkansas—later joined the Confederacy.) Feelings were so strong that Lincoln received death threats and had to travel in secrecy to Washington, D.C., for his inauguration on March 4, 1861.

Lincoln hoped that war could be avoided. But matters came to a crisis within two weeks of his inauguration. Fort Sumter, at the entrance to Charleston harbor in South Carolina, was still under Union control but was running out of supplies. When a supply fleet sent by Lincoln approached the fort on April 12, 1861, Confederate forces opened fire. Fort Sumter fell to the South within two days, and the Civil War was under way. (Below: The Confederate flag flies over Fort Sumter.)

Recruits, like the young Georgia soldier at left, flocked to the banners of both sides. At first, the South had several victories. One of the most important was the first Battle of Bull Run (or Manassas), in which Confederate forces routed Northern soldiers just a few miles from Washington, D.C., in July, 1861. Defeats such as this made people in the North realize that the war would be long and hard. President Lincoln began to assemble the largest fighting force that the country had ever seen. In all, throughout the four years of the war, more than 2 million men took up arms—more than 1.5 million for the North and 900,000 for the South.

Among the soldiers who fought for the North were nearly 200,000 blacks. Many were former slaves who had escaped through a system of hiding places called the Underground Railroad. Although they were often discriminated against, in pay and other ways, they fought courageously. (Below: Black and white soldiers on the field at the Battle of Olustee, Florida, 1864.)

There was fighting at sea, too. Northern ships blockaded Southern ports, disrupting shipping and weakening the South economically. One of the most famous naval battles of the Civil War took place on March 9, 1862, between the USS *Monitor* and the CSS *Virginia* (formerly the *Merrimack*). Neither was a clear winner, but the battle was the first between ironclads—ships with metal-covered hulls.

Between battles, soldiers like those shown below relaxed in camp. Army life involved many hardships, including pests such as lice and fleas and, above all, disease. In the Union armies, disease accounted for seven of every ten deaths; the number was even higher in the South. As the war continued, Confederate soldiers also had more and more difficulty obtaining supplies.

By the President of the
United States of America
A Proclamation

I Abraham Lincoln, President of the United States of America, and commander-in-chief of the Army and Navy thereof, do hereby proclaim and declare that hereafter, as heretofore, the war will be prosecuted for the object of practically restoring the constitutional relations between the United States, and each of the states, and the people thereof, in which states that relation is, or may be suspended, or disturbed.

That it is my purpose, upon the next meeting of Congress to again recommend the adoption of a practical measure tendering pecuniary aid to

In the fall of 1862, Lincoln took an important step: He issued the Emancipation Proclamation, which freed slaves in the Confederate states and took effect in January, 1863. Because the North didn't control the South, not many slaves were freed immediately. But the proclamation strengthened the Northern cause, and it established an important principle. The Thirteenth Amendment to the Constitution, which became law just after the war, outlawed slavery forever throughout the United States. (Left: A draft of the Emancipation Proclamation in Lincoln's handwriting.)

The long, bitter war came to an end in 1865. Union armies had driven deep into the South. In early April, they captured Richmond, Virginia, the Confederate capital. Southern forces tried to retreat but were surrounded by Union troops. On April 9, the Confederate forces surrendered to the North at Appomattox Court House, Virginia. (Right: The surrender was made by one of the South's greatest military leaders, General Robert E. Lee, shown standing on the left in this picture. It was accepted by the famous Northern General Ulysses S. Grant, shown on the right.)

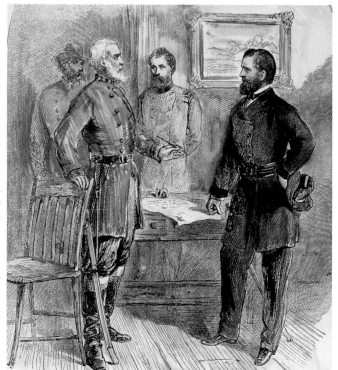

Just five days after the surrender at Appomattox, tragedy struck the nation. On the evening of April 14, President Lincoln went to Ford's Theatre in Washington to see a play. Suddenly a shadowy figure entered the president's booth, pulled a gun, and shot Lincoln in the head. The president died just after dawn the next morning. His assassin was John Wilkes Booth, an actor who had been a strong supporter of the South.

The president's death caused an outpouring of grief. Lincoln had just been elected to a second term, and many people had counted on his leadership in healing the deep national wounds caused by the war. The Civil War had established the supremacy of the federal government over the states, and it had freed the slaves. But the cost had been enormous—by some estimates, 620,000 Americans died in the war, more than in World War I and World War II and Vietnam combined. Even when the fighting stopped, much remained to be done. The economy of the South had been shattered by the war, and the old Southern way of life was gone. And while blacks were freed from slavery, they were only beginning what would prove to be a long, difficult struggle for civil rights and equality.

Still, the Union had been preserved. And in the years that followed, the country was able to put the bitterness of the Civil War behind it and begin one of its greatest periods of growth and expansion.

AMERICA'S ROYAL PALACE

Set on spacious grounds in the center of downtown Honolulu, Hawaii, is the only building in the United States ever to serve as an official royal residence. The building is stately Iolani Palace, where monarchs once ruled the kingdom of Hawaii. The palace, built in the late 1800's, was the seat of royalty for just a little more than ten years. Today it's a museum that offers a fascinating glimpse of the last days of the Hawaiian kings and queens.

The Hawaiian monarchy was founded by Kamehameha I in 1796. By 1810, after having fought a series of wars, he unified the islands. He was followed on the throne by a succession of relatives. But in 1872, King Kamehameha V died and left no heir. And so William Charles Lunalilo became the first elected king of Hawaii. In just thirteen months, however, he too died without an heir. Another election was held, and in 1874 David Kalakaua was chosen king.

Kalakaua wanted to help the economy of the islands grow, and one of his first acts was to travel to the United States to establish a trade agreement. He left instructions that the royal residence, an aging building, should be spruced up while he was away. But workers soon discovered that termites had destroyed so much of the building that it wasn't worth saving. When Kalakaua returned, he found that his palace had been torn down!

It took Kalakaua several years to convince the Hawaiian legislature to appropriate money for a new palace. But in 1879, work on the new Iolani Palace finally began.

Kalakaua wanted the palace to be large and modern, to befit the king of an important island country. Architects from Australia and the United States had a hand in the design, and most of the materials were imported—cedar from Oregon, etched glass from California, slate roof tiles from Pennsylvania. The king saw to it that the building had the latest modern gadgets—toilets, sinks with running water, telephones.

Kalakaua and his wife, Queen Kapiolani, moved into the new palace in 1882. The building quickly became the center of Hawaii's political and social life. Kalakaua loved parties, big dinners, and other social events. Among the people he entertained were European princes and famous writers such as Robert Louis Stevenson. The king also continued to improve the palace with the latest modern inventions. Electric lights were installed in 1887—Iolani Palace had electricity before the White House did.

When Kalakaua died in 1891, his sister, Liliuokalani, came to the throne. It was a time of turmoil in the islands. The influence of the United States was growing stronger, and business interests attempted to dominate government policies. Liliuokalani tried to limit these influences. But in 1893 she was forced to turn over the government to a group of businessmen who wanted the United States to annex Hawaii. They formed a provisional (temporary) republic. The queen moved out of the palace, and it was converted into a government office building.

Two years later Liliuokalani returned to her palace—but not to rule. In 1895, a group of her supporters staged an uprising, hoping to restore the monarchy. The attempt failed, and Liliuokalani was arrested and convicted of having known about the plot. For almost eight months she was confined to a room in Iolani Palace.

It was a lonely life. During the day she was permitted to have just one of her ladies with her. She wasn't allowed to have newspapers or books. But she could enjoy her favorite pastime—music. The queen played several instruments and was also a songwriter. She had earlier written one of Hawaii's most famous songs, *Aloha Oe* ("Farewell to Thee"). And in her prison room she composed the words and music of the "Queen's Prayer," which speaks of her sorrow.

After Liliuokalani was released, Iolani Palace continued to serve as a government building while the islands became first a U.S. territory and then a state. Kalakaua's bedroom and library were the governor's office. Legislators met in the dining and throne rooms.

It wasn't until 1969, after a new state cap-

The new Iolani Palace was built during King Kalakaua's reign, and he and Queen Kapiolani moved in in 1882.

itol was built next to the palace grounds, that government officials moved out. Then a careful restoration of Iolani Palace began. Once again, termites had damaged the structure. Steel supports were added, and workers created exact reproductions of the original woodwork and plaster decorations. Original furnishings were found and returned to the palace. In all, the program cost more than $7 million—twenty times what it had cost to build the palace in the 1880's.

Today Iolani Palace is restored to its original grandeur. Visitors tour the building and stroll through the parklike grounds, which are filled with stately palms and brilliant tropical flowers. As they do, they catch a glimpse of a colorful and important chapter in Hawaii's history.

JENNY TESAR
Series Consultant
Wonders of Wildlife

CALL IT A DAY!

Did you ever wonder why a week has seven days, or how the days got their names? The answers lie far back in history, in the times when people first developed calendars to keep track of the days as the year passed.

Many ancient calendars were very different from ours. The Chinese, for example, developed a calendar with sixty-day months and ten-day weeks. The Mayan Indians of Central America had thirteen-day weeks. But in ancient Mesopotamia, the Babylonians used a seven-day week. Their calendar was based on observations of the night sky, and they named each day for a different heavenly body. The ancient Hebrews also chose the seven-day week. For them, it mirrored the biblical story of creation, which says that the world was created in six days and that the seventh day was a day of rest.

The calendar of the Romans, who conquered much of the ancient world, originally had months but no weeks. But the Romans eventually adopted the seven-day week, and this custom gradually spread through their empire. The Romans named the days for the sun, the moon, and the gods that they associated with the five planets that can be seen with the naked eye.

Since our calendar is based on the Roman one, the seven-day week is still with us. There have been a few attempts to change it—during the French Revolution, for example, French authorities tried to switch to a ten-day week. But the change didn't take hold. And perhaps because the seven-day week is so old, each day has a tale of its own.

Sunday

In the Roman calendar, Sunday was *dies solis*—the day of the sun. As the Romans expanded their rule into Europe, they conquered tribes who spoke Germanic languages. These tribes adopted the Roman calendar, but they changed the names of the days to follow their own language. *Dies solis* became *Sunnandag* (sun's day). And over many years, that name developed into the modern English Sunday.

In the Christian tradition, Sunday is the Sabbath —a day of rest and worship. And as Christianity spread throughout the Roman Empire, the Romans changed the name of the first day of the week to *dies dominicus*, or day of the Lord. Thus languages that trace their roots to Latin, such as French and Spanish, have different names for Sunday: *dimanche* in French, *domingo* in Spanish.

Today Sunday is a day of relaxation in most places—schools and most businesses are closed, and people spend the day as they please. But in the past, observance of the Sabbath was often strictly enforced. The Puritan colonists who settled in New England, for example, had rigid rules: There could be no work and no play. People spent the day at the meeting house, praying and listening to sermons, and even simple activities such as cooking, running, kissing, and cutting hair were banned.

Monday

The Romans called the second day of the week *dies lunae*, or day of the moon. Modern languages that come from Latin have similar names—*lundi* in French, and *lunes* in Spanish. But the groups that spoke Germanic languages substituted their own word for the moon and came up with *Monandag*, which developed into the modern English Monday.

In ancient times, Monday was considered an unlucky day. This may have been because there were many superstitions about the moon. Some people even thought that gazing at the moon could drive a person insane. (In fact, the word "lunacy" comes from the Latin word for moon.) Monday was unpopular for another reason in days gone by. It was washday—and washing all a family's clothes by hand was a lot of work.

Even today, Monday is an unpopular day. This has less to do with superstition than with the fact that Monday marks the end of the weekend. After two days off, most people have to wake up early and head back to school or work. But some Mondays are better—in the United States and a number of other countries, many holidays fall on Mondays. And that gives everyone a three-day weekend.

Tuesday

The Romans named the third day of the week *dies Martis*, for Mars, the god of war. It is still known as *mardi* in French and as *martes* in Spanish. The Germanic people used the name of their own war god, Tiu—giving us the name Tuesday.

A few Tuesdays have special importance. The Tuesday after the first Monday in November is Election Day in the United States. People go to the polls to choose the officials who will run the government.

In the Christian calendar, Shrove Tuesday comes right before Lent, the 40-day period of prayer and fasting that leads up to Easter. It's the last chance for people to eat, drink, and make merry. In days gone by, people tried to use up all the butter and other fats they had on this day because they would have to give up fats during Lent. Rich, buttery foods became a Shrove Tuesday tradition. So this day is also known as Pancake Tuesday, and as Fat Tuesday (or *Mardi Gras*, in French).

Today some cities still hold Mardi Gras parades and festivals. The Mardi Gras celebration in New Orleans is one of the most famous. But most Tuesdays are just ordinary days. And Tuesdays of the past were pretty dull: Just as Monday was washday, Tuesday was ironing day.

Wednesday

The ancient Romans named the fourth day of the week after Mercury, the messenger of the gods and guardian of the spiritual life. Their *dies Mercurii* became *mercredi* in modern French and *miercoles* in Spanish.

The Germanic people chose a different god to honor on this day: Woden (or Odin), the chief of their gods and, like Mercury, the ruler of the spiritual life. In English, Woden's day became Wednesday—the name that's used today. But Wednesday goes by still another name in modern German: *Mittwoch*, or midweek. As the fourth of the seven days, Wednesday marks the midpoint of the week.

In some places, Wednesday was traditionally a market day. Farm families went to town to sell their produce and to buy the supplies they needed. Since they traveled by horse and wagon, the trip usually took all day.

Thursday

In ancient Rome, Jupiter (or Jove) was honored on *dies Jovis*, the fifth day of the week. Thus this day is called *jeudi* in French and *jueves* in Spanish. Jove was the Roman god of thunder and lightning, so Germanic tribes named the day after their own god of thunder—Thor. That gave us the modern English Thursday.

In Muslim countries, Thursday is the traditional day for weddings. Because Friday is the Muslim sabbath, everyone will have the day following the wedding off.

Friday

Venus, the goddess of love and beauty, was honored by the Romans on the sixth day of the week. Their *dies Veneris* became *vendredi* in French and *viernes* in Spanish. Germanic people chose another goddess: Frigga, the wife of Woden. That gave us Friday, the English name for this day.

In the past, Friday was considered an unlucky day. Perhaps this was because Friday was hang-

One of the most important U.S. holidays falls on the fourth Thursday in November: Thanksgiving. The first Thanksgiving feast was held by the Pilgrim settlers of New England in 1621. It lasted three days. After that, Thanksgiving gradually became a traditional way to celebrate the harvest. But every town chose its own day until 1863, when the feast was declared a national holiday.

In those days, a Thursday holiday was a welcome break from routine. Thursday was sweeping day in many homes. Furniture was dusted, floors were swept, and rugs were dragged outdoors and beaten to knock the dirt out. Before the days of vacuum cleaners, cleaning the house was a lot more work.

Saturday

The Romans named the last day of the week for Saturn, a god they associated with farming. And because the Germanic tribes had no god to substitute for Saturn, many of them kept the Roman name. Thus the Roman *dies Saturni* developed into the English name Saturday.

The French name *samedi* may also be a reference to the god of farming. It probably developed from *semer*, the French word for sowing. But the names used in some languages have a different origin. Saturday is the Jewish day of worship, and in the Bible the seventh day of the week is referred to simply as "sabbath." Thus Saturday is *sabado* in Spanish and *lordag* (Lord's day) in Swedish.

Traditionally, Saturday was bath day. Before homes had indoor plumbing, bath water had to be drawn from a well, carried indoors, and heated over a fire. Once a week was considered quite enough for this work, so every Saturday people cleaned up and got ready to begin a new week.

man's day—the day when public executions were held. And because the number thirteen was also considered unlucky, any Friday that was also the thirteenth day of the month was thought to be especially bad. Even today, some people are superstitious about Friday the Thirteenth.

For most people, however, Friday is one of the best days of the week. In Western countries, it's the last day of work and school—people look forward to the weekend. And in the Islamic religion, Friday is a day of worship. Thus schools, shops, and offices in Muslim countries are closed on this day.

THE BATTLE OF WATERLOO

As darkness descended on the evening of June 18, 1815, a few battered battalions of French troops formed a last line of defense against attacking British and allied soldiers. The French troops were part of Emperor Napoleon Bonaparte's elite "Old Guard." Weary from a full day of fighting near the Belgian town of Waterloo, the guardsmen managed hoarse shouts of "Long Live the Emperor" as they fixed bayonets and stood firm.

A British officer called upon the French troops to surrender. They refused with defiant curses. In a matter of minutes the French soldiers were overwhelmed by superior numbers. But their heroic defense enabled Napoleon, the greatest military genius of his day, to escape from the battlefield.

Exactly 175 years later, on June 18, 1990, French and British re-enactors (people who re-enact historical events) donned period costumes and refought the Battle of Waterloo—one of the many special events that marked this turning point in world history.

A GREAT MILITARY LEADER

Just who was Napoleon—and why did France and its European neighbors fight a war that lasted nearly 25 years?

Most historians consider Napoleon one of the great military leaders of all time. Under him, French armies carried the ideas of the French Revolution—of liberty and equality—throughout Europe. They also carved out a great empire for France. By 1812, that empire extended from Spain and Italy in the south to Denmark and Norway in the north—and all the way to the borders of Russia in the east.

Napoleon's rise to power was swift. Born in 1769, he was a young and ambitious army officer at the time of the French Revolution (1789). When the revolutionaries toppled the French monarchy and executed King Louis XVI, other European kingdoms—including Austria, Britain, and Prussia—attacked France.

Napoleon cast his lot with the revolutionaries and was given important military assignments. In time, he won a string of brilliant victories over France's enemies. By 1799 he was so popular that he was able to overthrow the existing French government and make himself first consul of France.

Napoleon reorganized the French government and created new, more liberal codes of laws. One of these codes still exists today, serving as the basis of French civil law. But Napoleon was also a ruthless dictator, driven by a desire to conquer all of Europe.

In 1804, Napoleon had himself crowned emperor of France. More military victories and conquests followed—over Austria in 1805 and Prussia in 1806. His three brothers were made kings of Holland, Spain, and the German kingdom of Westphalia.

Soon, however, cracks appeared in the empire. Spanish patriots revolted against French rule in 1808. British troops under the Duke of Wellington were sent to aid the Spanish rebels. Eventually, the French were driven out of Spain.

Hoping to gain new territory in the east, Napoleon gathered an army of 600,000 men and invaded Russia. The fierce resistance of the Russians and the frigid Russian winter combined to defeat the French. Napoleon's army retreated, leaving behind half a million French soldiers killed or captured.

Napoleon now found himself under attack by the combined armies of Austria, Prussia, and Russia. In 1814 the allies captured Paris, and Napoleon was forced to abdicate (give up) his throne. He was sent to live in exile on the island of Elba.

But Napoleon wasn't finished. In March, 1815, he escaped from Elba and returned to Paris. His old soldiers quickly rallied to his banner. A new king, Louis XVIII, had been put on the French throne, but he fled when Napoleon arrived.

THE FINAL BATTLE

Once again Napoleon was ruler of France. But this time his reign would be a short one—known as the "Hundred Days." The European powers opposed to him quickly assembled an army led by Britain's Duke of Wellington.

In June, Napoleon led a newly organized French army of 125,000 men into Belgium. His aim was to drive a wedge between Wel-

Napoleon—one of the great military leaders of all time. The Battle of Waterloo was the final battle of the Napoleonic Wars, and it led to the fall of this famous French leader.

lington's mixed force of British, Dutch, and Belgian troops and a Prussian army under General Gebhard von Blücher.

On June 16, Napoleon slammed into Blücher's Prussians and routed them. Wellington quickly dug in with his own army of 64,000 men on Mont St. Jean, a hill just south of Waterloo. Napoleon held Wellington and the British army in low regard. "This whole affair will not be more serious than swallowing one's breakfast," he told his generals on the eve of the Battle of Waterloo.

At 11:30 a.m. on the morning of June 18, Napoleon launched his first attack, striking at several fortified farms below the crest of Mont St. Jean. British troops defending the farms beat off the attackers. A second French assault in the early afternoon reached the crest of the hill and nearly broke through the British lines on the ridge. But a British cavalry counterattack drove the French troops back. Next came an attack by an entire corps of French cavalry. British infantrymen quickly formed defensive squares. The French cavalry crashed against these bayonet-ringed squares, and this attack also failed.

Finally, as light began to fade, Napoleon brought up his battle-hardened Imperial Guard, which he always held in reserve. Six thousand strong, these elite troops swarmed up the hill in three waves. Wellington was ready for them, having taken up a position near his own Foot Guards regiments. As Napoleon's infantry came within musket range, Wellington waved his cocked hat and shouted, "Stand up Guards. Make ready. Fire!" Muskets crackled and the volley tore wide gaps in the French lines.

Now Wellington ordered his army to attack with the bayonet, and the French were driven back down the hill. At this crucial moment, General Blücher—who had re-grouped his Prussian troops—arrived on the field. The Prussians hit Napoleon's exposed right flank and the entire French army fled in disorder.

Some 44,000 soldiers on both sides were killed or wounded at Waterloo, prompting Wellington to observe, "Nothing except a battle lost can be half so melancholy as a battle won."

Napoleon fled to Paris where he tried again to rally his supporters. But the end had finally come for the French leader and his empire. On June 22, he abdicated for a second, and final time. He was exiled to the island of St. Helena, where he died a few years later, in 1821.

In 1840, Napoleon's remains were brought to Paris and placed in a great marble tomb at the Hôtel des Invalides, the Home for Disabled Soldiers. A glorious but bloody chapter in French history had come to an end.

HENRY I. KURTZ
Author, *The Art of the Toy Soldier*

A friend . . . a bicycle . . . a beautiful sunset to mark the end of a perfect day. Friendship and good times are part of what being young is all about.

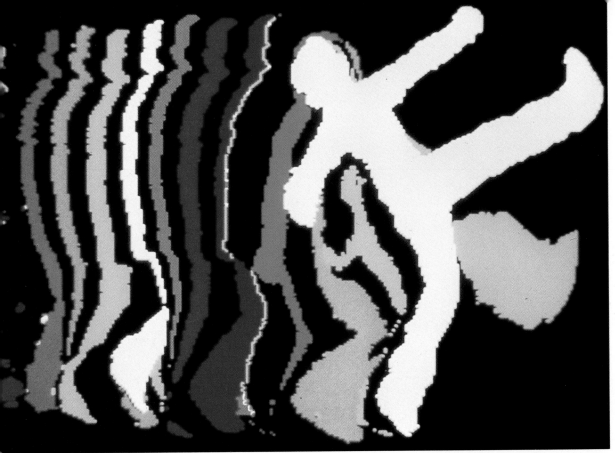

San Francisco's Exploratorium teaches scientific principles in an exciting way. At the Recollections exhibit, a computer and video projector can transform your "shadow" into a moving, multicolored work of art.

THE EXPLORATORIUM

It's fun. It's fascinating. It's exciting. That's how visitors, young and old alike, describe the Exploratorium, an unusual science museum in San Francisco, California.

The Exploratorium lives up to its name. It was planned to help people understand the world around them. The museum was the idea of a well-known scientist named Frank Oppenheimer. Oppenheimer had seen that visitors often came away from conventional museums with very little new information. And he believed that the glass-enclosed displays, rules, and "Please Do Not Touch" signs in many museums discouraged visitors from learning much of anything.

Oppenheimer's idea was to create a completely new kind of museum, one where people could learn about scientific principles by participating in scientific experiments. He also wanted his museum to be a community institution where people of all ages—from kindergarten children to senior citizens—could listen, touch, pound, and do scores of fascinating experiments.

The idea was revolutionary when the Exploratorium first opened in 1969. At that time the museum had just three exhibits. But the Exploratorium proved almost instantly popular. Today there are some 650 exhibits—all meant to be manipulated, not just looked at. Each year half a million people visit the museum, which is housed in San Francisco's Palace of Fine Arts, a landmark structure built for the Panama-Pacific Exposition of 1915. The museum also sends its exhibits on tour. And museums all over the world have imitated the Exploratorium by creating similar hands-on exhibits of their own.

The words "science museum" don't describe the Exploratorium well. It's more like a large-scale science workshop than a museum. And it involves visitors in ways that

Left: Visitors are amazed by a swirling column of artificial fog, created by air currents. Below: Are the people really shrinking and growing in this "Alice in Wonderland" room? You'll have to visit the museum to figure out the illusion.

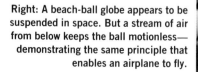

Right: A beach-ball globe appears to be suspended in space. But a stream of air from below keeps the ball motionless—demonstrating the same principle that enables an airplane to fly.

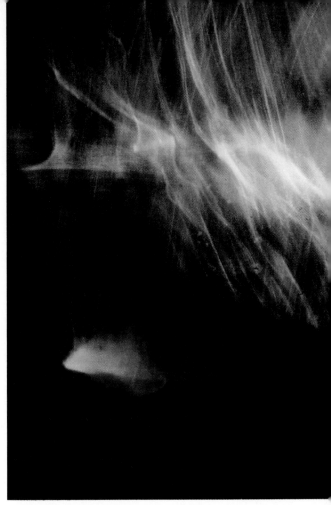

One of the most beautiful exhibits at the museum is Sun Painting, which is a huge screen covered with swirls of color. It's all done with prisms, mirrors, and sunlight.

help them understand not just *what* they see but also *how* they see it. All the exhibits demonstrate aspects of human perception and the natural world. They are based on light, sound, and motion; on waves, temperature, and heat; on animal behavior; on the senses of hearing, sight, and touch. They let visitors investigate basic scientific principles, such as the principles of electricity and magnetism, as well as the ways in which people perceive the world around them.

Some of the exhibits are meant to trick the senses. In a room that could be straight from *Alice's Adventures in Wonderland*, people seem to grow and shrink, depending on where in the room they stand. It's really the room that's cockeyed; it has been carefully set up to create an optical illusion.

Other exhibits play tricks with mirrors. In one of these, two people sit on opposite sides of a window. But this isn't an ordinary window—it's a mirror, too. And by adjusting the level of various lights, the two people can make their faces blend together into one.

As you wander through the museum, you will come upon a beach-ball globe suspended in midair—with seemingly no support. In reality, a stream of air from below keeps the ball motionless. The air rushing over the curved surface of the ball demonstrates the same effect that creates lift on the wings of an airplane and allows the plane to fly.

The Exploratorium also has its very own tornado—a swirling column of artificial fog created by air currents. In another exhibit, you rely on your sense of touch to guide you through a pitch-dark maze of small chambers, each lined with a different texture. And a soap-film exhibit lets you blow huge soap bubbles, far larger than any you could make at home. It's fun, and it demonstrates how soap makes water molecules cling together to form the thin surface of a bubble.

The Exploratorium's exhibits go beyond traditional science to include art and music. In fact, each year the museum invites visual and performing artists to create new works that it then showcases.

But the art in the Exploratorium isn't the sort that usually hangs on museum walls.

One of the most beautiful exhibits is called Sun Painting. It's a huge screen covered with swirls of color. Behind the screen is an array of prisms, which break white light into all the colors of the rainbow. Sunlight captured by collectors on the building's roof passes through the prisms and bounces off mirrors, creating the brilliant, colorful splashes on the screen. And by interfering with the light as they approach the screen, visitors can make the colors move, shift, and change.

At an exhibit called Recollections, your "shadow" seems to be transformed into a moving, multicolored work of art. The image you see isn't really your shadow, however. When you enter and move around this exhibit, a video camera takes your picture. The picture is fed through a computer processor and a color video projector. And your form appears on the wall as a colorful kaleidoscope of images—breaking up, reforming, and leaving echoes of itself as you walk around or change position.

Still other art exhibits play with your senses, converting one into another. A tree hung with tiny lights converts sound into sight—the lights twinkle and blink with every sound you make. At an exhibit called Light Strokes, you can do finger painting without making a mess. You run your fingers over a pressure-sensitive plate, and a computer converts your touch into a picture on a screen in front of you. The computer will even let you select any of more than 4,000 colors for your work of art.

A short walk from the museum is Wave Organ, an exhibit that's part park, part sculpture, part musical instrument, and part science. Built of blocks of granite along the edge of San Francisco Bay, it is a memorial to Frank Oppenheimer, who died in 1985. Visitors can stroll through the memorial, stopping to rest and view the harbor from stone benches. As they do, the air is filled with a strange music: the music of the bay itself. Waves in the bay set up vibrations in a series of air-filled plastic pipes that rise from sea level to open among the stones of the memorial. The sounds the pipes produce —gurgles, moans, and sighs—vary with the winds, tides, and weather.

These are just a few of the fascinating exhibits at the Exploratorium. And the museum is continually coming up with new exhibits that encourage people to get involved with science in new ways. (Some of the new exhibits are even being built in a workshop that's open to public view.) Teenage guides are on hand to explain how the exhibits work, as well as the principles behind them. They help visitors operate lenses, test balance sticks, peer through prisms, and play musical instruments.

All through the museum, visitors are encouraged to push, pull, poke, talk, listen, and play. There are no guards and no "Please Do Not Touch" signs. In fact, the Exploratorium has only one rule: no bicycling on the museum floor.

They may be the most unlikely heroes ever to march onto a TV or movie screen: a band of turtles. But these aren't ordinary turtles. They are the size of humans and experts in the martial arts, and their favorite food is pizza. They are, of course, the **Teenage Mutant Ninja Turtles**, whose live-action movie was one of the biggest hits of 1990. The turtles were originally the idea of cartoonists Peter Laird and Kevin Eastman, who created them for comic books in 1983. Each turtle is named for a Renaissance artist: Raphael, Michelangelo, Donatello, and Leonardo. As the story goes, the turtles were accidentally dropped into a pool of radioactive goo in a New York City sewer, and it was this that caused them to develop their special characteristics. They were trained in the martial arts by a wise old rat named Splinter. The turtles were already featured on Saturday morning cartoons (*above*) when their live-action film was released in 1990. For the film, actors portraying the turtles wore high-tech suits in which the facial expressions were changed by remote control. Young fans clearly liked the movie—in its first weekend, it took in $25.4 million, making it the second biggest film premiere in history (after *Batman*). And sales of turtle-related merchandise—from comic books to pajamas—were expected to reach $600 million for the year.

Ready, set, go! The runners below are competing in **Junior Bloomsday**, one of the few road races just for kids. The event, held each April in Spokane, Washington, was started in 1986 as a companion to Spokane's adult race, the Lilac Bloomsday Run. Kids 4 to 12 years old race over a course ½ to 2 miles (0.8 to 3.2 kilometers) long, depending on their age. Before the event, many of the entrants take part in an eight- to ten-week training program, earning a patch and certificates that show how far they've run. And they're all winners—because they have fun and improve their fitness.

One of the most popular new television shows of 1990 was *Doogie Howser, M.D.*—the adventures of a 16-year-old who (incredibly) is already a fully qualified physician. **Neil Patrick Harris**, the star of the show, was also 16. Harris had been acting since fourth grade, when he played the part of the dog Toto in a school production of *The Wizard of Oz*. His first professional role came in the 1988 film *Clara's Heart*, and he landed parts in several TV films before his 1990 success in *Doogie Howser*. Despite a busy schedule, Harris managed to keep up with his high-school courses. He also found time for some favorite hobbies—performing magic tricks and filming home-video spoofs of horror films.

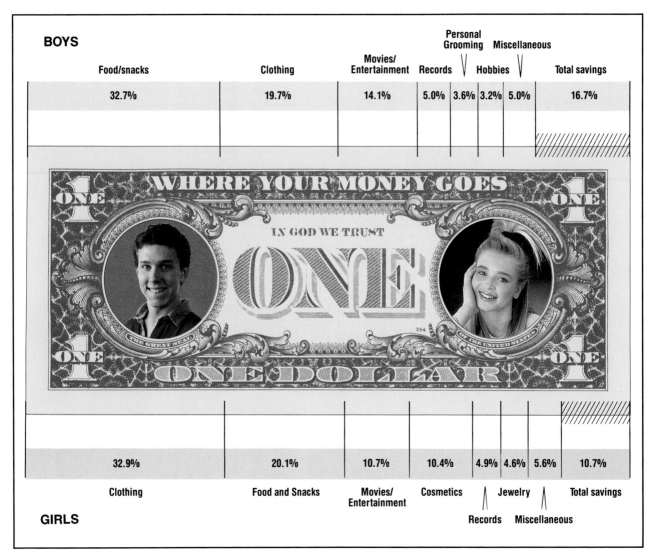

BOYS

Food/snacks	Clothing	Movies/Entertainment	Records	Personal Grooming	Hobbies	Miscellaneous	Total savings
32.7%	19.7%	14.1%	5.0%	3.6%	3.2%	5.0%	16.7%

WHERE YOUR MONEY GOES

Clothing	Food and Snacks	Movies/Entertainment	Cosmetics	Records	Jewelry	Miscellaneous	Total savings
32.9%	20.1%	10.7%	10.4%	4.9%	4.6%	5.6%	10.7%

GIRLS

Does money burn a hole in your pocket? Do you find you've spent it almost before you can count it? **Where does your money go?** If you're like many teens today, the answer is probably clothing and food. A recent survey of kids age 13 to 15 showed that these are the two biggest spending categories, together accounting for more than half their money. While boys spend a third of their cash on food and about 20 percent on clothes, those percentages are reversed for girls at this age. Movies and entertainment take the next biggest budget bite for both groups, followed by records for boys and cosmetics for girls. (Younger children are more apt to spend in another category: toys and games.) Both groups also manage to save some of their money—boys save more than 16 percent, and girls save more than 10 percent. And this money isn't just nickels and dimes. The survey showed that kids in the 13-to-15 age group receive an average of just under $34 a week in earnings and allowances. Researchers believe that, altogether, young people between the ages of 6 and 15 have more than $6 billion in spending money each year. That means that kids are big business.

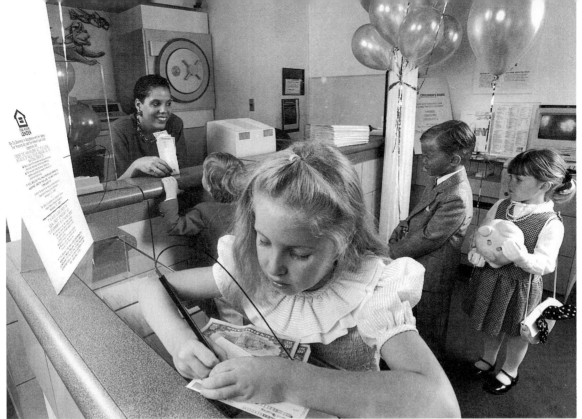

Instead of spending your money, why not put it in a bank? Maybe you could put it in a bank that's just for kids. The First Children's Bank (*above*) is one of several **kids-only banks** that have opened in recent years. It's located in a corner of F.A.O. Schwarz, the famous toy store in New York City. Customers must be under 18—but over 6—to open a checking account.

For 15-year-old **Tyler Kepner** of Gwynedd Valley, Pennsylvania, baseball is a passion. And he has turned his passion into a business—publishing a baseball magazine, *KP Baseball Monthly*. Each 25-page issue, with articles on everything from baseball cards to player salaries, goes to about 200 subscribers.

Four plays by young writers were presented on the Broadway stage in 1990 at the ninth annual **Young Playwrights Festival**. The festival is sponsored by the Foundation of the Dramatists Guild as a way of encouraging young authors to write for the stage. Each year writers under age 19 are invited to submit their plays. All receive detailed evaluations of their work, and the best plays are given professional productions in New York City. In 1990, the plays chosen were by authors ranging from 15 to 18 years old. *Mutterschaft* (below), by Gregory Clayman, 18, was a comedy about a teenager and her mother who get involved with the same man. *Believing*, by Allison Birch, 17, was set in Trinidad and dealt with abuse of women and children. *Psychoneurotic Phantasies*, by Gilbert Feke, 15, brought Sigmund Freud and other psychoanalysts into a farce about teenagers looking for the perfect date. And *Hey Little Walter*, by Carla Alleyne, 17, was about a high-school student who sells drugs to support his family—and brings them hardship as a result.

Matthew Peter Headrick, 17, won the 1990 Westinghouse Science Talent Search, the prestigious competition for high-school science students in the United States. Matthew, who is from Chicago, submitted a project concerning molecular genetics. It was judged the best of the 1,431 entries, and it won him a $20,000 scholarship.

Walt Disney's *Fantasia* has been a favorite with young and old alike ever since it premiered in 1940. For the film's 50th anniversary in 1990, Disney Studios released a restored version of the animated classic. The two-hour film has no dialogue. It matches eight well-known orchestral works to segments that range from comic (Mickey Mouse in Paul Dukas's *The Sorcerer's Apprentice*) to scary (a demon in Mussorgsky's *Night on Bald Mountain*).

The actors and actresses who star in *Full House* are just some of the many people who work together to create the popular TV series. Video and film productions offer exciting career paths. They bring together people with many different skills, from costume designers to sound technicians.

CAREERS IN FILM AND VIDEO

What would it be like to star in a network television drama or direct a major motion picture? To cover sports and news events as a professional video camera operator? To produce the fantastic special effects you see in films? These are just some of the careers that are possible in film and video—two of the most exciting career fields there are.

Film and video are closely related. The major differences between them lie in technical areas. Film images are recorded on photographic film; video images are recorded on magnetic tape or broadcast live on television. Thus people who make films need some knowledge and skills that are different from those that are needed in video production. But many steps in production are the same (or nearly so) in film and in video. And so are many of the careers.

Film and video have something else in common: they are highly competitive fields. Most feature films are produced by a handful of big motion picture studios. Television networks are the major video producers, although there are independent studios too. And there are many candidates for jobs at the major film and TV studios. Many people in film and video work free-lance—they are hired for a specific project and then move on to another project at another studio.

People who want to break into these fields can take several routes. Some work for small documentary or educational filmmakers. Some make training films and videos for corporations. Some produce material for cable television or for the home video market. And some work in advertising, creating the commercials you see on television. It's common for people to gain experience in one of these areas before doing work for a major studio.

Some film and video careers—especially acting and directing—require special talents and are very hard to break into. But acting and directing are just the tip of the iceberg where possible careers are concerned. Film and video bring together people with many different skills and abilities, from costume designers to sound technicians. A sampling of film and video careers follows. Each has its own requirements and rewards—but all will give you a chance to be "in pictures."

ACTORS AND ACTRESSES

For many people, acting is the film and video career that comes to mind first—after all, the people we see in films (and most of the people we see on television) are **actors** and **actresses**.

Most actors and actresses study their craft in college and drama school, and many continue their training throughout their careers. And most performers spend many years breaking into their profession. They try out for bit parts that pay very little (and sometimes nothing at all). Some start with small theater groups; others in commercials.

Even so, acting is so competitive that many actors and actresses can't find enough work to make a living. It's common for them to hold full-time jobs in other fields. And when they do find acting work, they work hard. At film and video studios they often arrive early in the morning and put in long hours. The same scene may be shot over and over again, until everyone is satisfied that it's right. But for those who succeed in this profession, all the training and hard work are worth it.

Several film and video careers are closely related to acting. **Television announcers** and **news readers** don't need acting skill, but they do need good speaking voices and poise in front of the camera. Some people concentrate on "voice-overs"—they don't appear on camera, but their voices are heard speaking parts in cartoons, narrating documentaries, and selling products in commercials.

When you see the hero in a feature film jumping from a moving train or falling off a horse, chances are you're watching a **stunt person** who has taken the performer's place for the dangerous scene. On film, you won't see the wires and other devices that are used to make the stunt less risky. But stunt work is dangerous—it requires strength, coordination, skill, and training.

DIRECTORS

Directors are important in both film and video productions. But often the work they do differs in the two fields.

In motion pictures, the director is the guiding artistic force. He or she is in charge of the set and crew. And it's the director's vision that makes the finished film what it is. Often the director is involved at all stages, from the first script through the final steps in production.

A video director may do many of these things. But in broadcast video, the director is under a lot of time pressure. Productions must be put together quickly, to meet tight deadlines. And live broadcasts create even more pressure. The director has to supervise the action of as many as four cameras and make on-the-spot decisions about which images will be broadcast at any moment.

Assistant directors and associate directors help the director with this work. In films, they may prepare shooting schedules and make sure that last-minute script changes are distributed to the cast. In broadcast video, one of the assistant director's most important jobs is to make sure that every segment of a production fits its allotted time period.

Successful directors have usually studied filmmaking in school and have worked their

Director Woody Allen. In motion pictures, the director is the guiding artistic force. It's the director's vision that makes the finished film what it is.

way up through the ranks. Many start out directing commercials or low-budget films.

PRODUCERS

The **producer** is the head of a film or video production and the one who carries it through every stage, from the initial idea through the distribution of a movie or the broadcast of a television show. The producer may develop an idea, buy a script or have one written, and choose a director. Or a director may come to a producer with an idea.

One of the most important parts of the producer's job is to develop a budget for the production and obtain financial backing—and some productions cost millions of dollars. The producer may also hire other people who will be involved in the production, such as performers and technical experts. Assistant producers help in the work, taking over a lot of the details and paperwork.

Some film producers have a say in the artistic and technical aspects of making the movie, but many leave this part of the work to the director. In video, the producer tends to be more closely involved. In either field, though, the producer must know all aspects of production. Most producers have years of experience and, like directors, have worked their way up through the ranks.

DESIGN

In any film or video production, there's a lot of work to do before shooting can begin. Much of it involves design.

Scenic (or **set**) **designers** plan the sets that will serve as a backdrop for the action. They begin with sketches and scale models; then they supervise the construction of the sets. A set may be simple—a desk and a backdrop for a TV news show, for example. But a feature production may require many sets.

Scenic artists do much of the actual work on scale models. They also put the finishing touches—including painting, plastering, and lettering—on the sets, which are built by studio carpenters. But not all productions are shot in studios. **Location specialists** find any outside settings that may be required—a rugged mountain landscape or a quaint New England town, for example.

Property buyers work with the designers to obtain all the necessary props. **Costume designers** are in charge of obtaining all the costumes and accessories. **Makeup artists** may be involved at this stage, too. The script

Makeup artists can perform magic—as can be seen in this transformation of mild-looking Robert Englund into horror-film king Freddy Krueger.

SPECIAL EFFECTS

An alien spaceship hovering over a crowd of people . . . Superman soaring into the air . . . Indiana Jones leaping across a vast chasm. You may have seen all these scenes in movies—but none really happened. They were the work of experts in special effects.

Special effects (or EFX) specialists combine the skills of filmmakers and magicians. And they use everything from modeling clay to explosives to computer animation in their work. If the script calls for fog, they have machines to produce it. If a car is to explode, they set up the shot.

Some special effects are produced using miniature sets and models. To create the image of a spaceship hovering over a house, for example, filmmakers might build the entire scene in miniature. The scene would be filmed close up, so that it would fill the screen and seem real.

Many movie monsters and other imaginary characters also begin as models. They're made of flexible material, and they may be operated by puppeteers or by computers. Or they may be brought to life with stop-motion animation: A camera operator shoots just a second of film, the EFX experts change the figure's position just slightly, and the camera shoots again. In this way, bit by bit, an entire scene is shot. And when all the separate shots are run together, the figure's movement seems real.

Other special effects rely on a little wizardry in film processing. Indiana Jones doesn't really jump across a chasm—he jumps in front of a "blue screen" in the studio. When the film is processed, the blue background disappears. Then the image of the leaping character is combined with film of the terrifying chasm.

As a career, special effects work requires a lot of technical knowledge and skill. And most EFX experts have years of training, gained by working in the film industry alongside experts in the field.

---

for a feature production may call for an actor to age 30 years or turn into a werewolf. Makeup artists figure out how the change can be made convincing on camera.

For feature films and major video productions, all this design work may be coordinated by an **art director**. The art director must approve everything from locations to costumes, and he or she makes sure that all the design elements blend smoothly.

The requirements for these careers are similar to those for other design careers: a good eye and knowledge of a specific area, such as clothing or interior design. In addition, designers who work in film and video need to know about the technical end of production, so that they understand its requirements and limitations.

ON THE SET

The set is ready, the actors are in place, and production is about to begin. And on hand are dozens of technical experts, each with a special job.

Among the most important are the people who will actually record the images. The camera angle, the way a shot is framed, and the kind of lighting, lens, and camera used are critical to the final look of the production. Especially in films, the chief camera person (called the **cinematographer** or **director of photography**) may have an important effect on the overall mood and look of the production.

Camera work in both film and video requires a great deal of technical expertise and a good eye for composition. **Camera opera-**

tors and assistants do much of the actual filming and taping. They must be able to handle a wide range of video and film equipment. Some have specialties, such as operating underwater cameras. Camera operators for TV news shows must be ready to travel to far off places at a moment's notice, to capture events as they happen.

Audio engineers are responsible for sound recording. They select and position the microphones that pick up the sound—a job that can be especially challenging when the production is being shot on location. In a television studio, audio engineers work in a booth filled with electronic equipment, mixing and adjusting the sound from microphones on the set.

The credits for film and video productions usually list two positions with odd-sounding titles: **gaffers** and **grips**. Gaffers are lighting experts. They work closely with the camera people and the director, determining how various lights, filters, and reflectors should be placed. Grips help set up and move lights, sets, and other equipment used in production —camera dollies, rigging, sandbags, mats.

Many other specialists are on hand when a film or video production is being shot. They include **carpenters**, who make repairs and last-minute changes to the set, and **engineers** who are experts in electronic equipment. Props are kept ready by the **property master**, who also keeps on hand odds and ends ranging from glue to picture hangers.

Many large productions use a **still photographer**, who takes publicity pictures and any shots that are needed during production. If work on a scene is to continue on another day, for example, the photographer may take still photographs of the set and the actors so that the props, costumes, and makeup can be exactly the same when shooting resumes.

Two important people on any large production are the **script supervisor** and the **production manager,** or **PM**. In feature productions, scenes generally aren't shot in order. The script supervisor's job is to keep track of the shooting schedule and make sure that nothing is left out. He or she may also prompt performers who forget their lines.

The job of the production manager may cover everything from hiring technicians to making sure that morning coffee is waiting when the actors and crew arrive on the set. The production manager ensures that the right performers and equipment are on hand for the scenes that will be shot on any given day and obtains any permits needed for shooting on location. It's an enormous job, and the PM usually has several production assistants who help carry out the details.

POST-PRODUCTION

In films and most recorded video produc-

On the set of *M*A*S*H*. Camera work requires a great deal of technical expertise and a good eye for composition. The cinematographer and camera operators are critical to the final look of the production.

Film and video editors put the scenes in order, decide on which "takes" to use, and determine how long a scene should run. Video editors (*right*) work by copying segments of tape onto a master tape.

tions, there's still a lot of work to do after shooting is complete. And this post-production work includes many important jobs.

The finished film or video is put together by **editors**. They put the scenes in order, but there's much more to this job. Which of the many "takes" of a scene should be used? How long should the scene run? Often scenes that are planned and shot are completely eliminated in editing—perhaps the production is too long, or perhaps the scene just didn't work out. Editing is painstaking work, but it's very important to the look and pace of the finished production. A good editor has the eye of a cinematographer and the instincts of a director.

Video editors work by copying segments of tape onto a master tape. Film, however, is spliced together, usually by a worker known as a **conformer**, who follows the editor's instructions and makes sure that the splices are invisible. Processing is also important in filmmaking—the lab that processes the film can use special techniques that change the texture of images, turn day into night, and produce special effects.

The soundtrack for a film or video also goes through post-production changes. **Sound mixers** add background music, voice-overs, and sound effects, such as the boom of an explosion or the squeal of automobile tires. In many video productions, the editor does this job as well.

OTHER CAREERS

Film and video offer many other possibilities for careers. Scriptwriters prepare the scripts for the productions. Composers and arrangers prepare the background music. Other people are concerned with marketing, publicity, and the business aspects of production. They aren't directly involved in productions—but they get to share the excitement of this glamorous field.

GETTING STARTED

Many colleges and universities, and even some high schools, offer courses in film and video. They provide a good way to learn about the field. There are also internship programs that give students a chance to work on professional productions.

For more information on film and video careers, contact the following organizations:

American Film and Video Association—920 S. Barnsdale Road, La Grange Park, IL 60525

National Film Board of Canada—P.O. Box 6100, Montreal, Quebec H3C 3H5

National Academy of Television Arts and Sciences—110 West 57th Street, New York, NY 10019

Canadian Alliance of Video Professionals—407, boul. St-Laurent, Montreal, Quebec H2Y 2Y5

Actors' Equity Association—165 West 46th Street, New York, NY 10036

Canadian Actors Equity Association—260 Richmond Street East, Toronto, Ont. M5A 1P4

Directors Guild of America—7950 Sunset Blvd., Hollywood, CA 90046

Directors Guild of Canada—3 Church Street, Toronto, Ont. M5E 1M2

Alliance of Motion Picture and Television Producers—14144 Ventura Blvd., Sherman Oaks, CA 91423

Canadian Association of Motion Picture Producers—663 Yonge Street, Toronto, Ont. M4Y 2A4

American Society of Cinematographers—1782 North Orange Drive, Hollywood, CA 90028

YOUNG PHOTOGRAPHERS

Photography is a way of capturing a passing moment. But it can be much more, as the young people who took the pictures on these pages clearly know. They won prizes in the 1990 Scholastic Art Awards competition, which includes divisions in drawing and many other forms of art as well as photography. The contest is open to U.S. and Canadian students in grades 7 through 12.

These photographs reflect an enormous range of expression—stark patterns of driftwood on sand, artfully arranged scenes and multiple exposures, pictures brought to life with careful hand tinting. And for some shots, of course, the photographer was on hand, with camera ready, to capture the perfect moment.

Driftwood,
**by Jennifer Geer, 18,
Kingsport, Tennessee**

Experimental,
**by Felicia Zimmerman, 14,
Rush, New York**

Model with Fan—White, by Andrea Lane, 14, Dodge City, Kansas

Flowered Awakening,
by Ava Berlin, 17,
Lakewood, Colorado

Symmetry,
by Alison Kloepper, 17,
St. Paul, Minnesota

Country Hearth,
by Nathan Cooke, 14,
Gillett, Pennsylvania

Blowin' in the Wind,
by Amy Beeman, 16,
Rockford, Illinois

REATIVITY

In folk paintings, self-taught artists often showed people engaged in everyday pursuits. This scene, painted by an anonymous artist in 1800, shows a family at home. The mother holds a baby on her lap, while one of the daughters plays with a pet dog. Even the family's caged birds are included. Today many museums have collections of folk art, and the works are valued for their freshness and charm.

This 1837 painting shows the simple charm of folk art. Folk art is an appealing blend of art and craftsmanship, and it provides a fascinating record of days gone by.

THE CHARM OF FOLK ART

Works of art by great masters of the past are on display in museums all over the world. They are admired, studied, and analyzed by scholars. But art of quite another kind has become increasingly popular in recent years. This is folk art—painting, sculpture, and everyday decorated objects made by people who were self-taught and often knew little about formal artistic techniques or the works of great masters.

Folk art is a blend of art and craftsmanship. It appeals because of its freshness and simple charm, and it provides a fascinating record of life in the past. Today many museums have collections of folk art alongside their collections of formal art. And there are some museums devoted exclusively to it.

Throughout history, each culture has produced its own varieties of folk art. In Amer-

ica, the tradition of folk art began in colonial times and continued at least to the early 1900's. Some of the self-taught artists became well known. More often, their works were unsigned, and their names have been lost. But examples of their work remain.

PAINTING

Many American folk art painters—and they included children as well as adults—were amateurs who made pictures for their families and friends. Drawing and painting were popular hobbies, and many people assembled their works in sketchbooks.

There were also self-taught professionals, who used their skills to earn a living. Among the most common of these were portrait painters. Before photography became popular in the late 1800's, people were eager to have painters make portraits of family members. Thus many painters traveled from town to town, offering their services to people in each place they stopped.

Some of these paintings were quickly (and sometimes poorly) done. But many of the self-taught portrait painters showed high levels of skill and talent. The portraits generally followed a standard format. They showed people in stiff poses—seated or standing, often holding a book or some other object. Children were shown in these formal poses, too, holding their favorite toys or pets.

In most folk art portraits, the greatest attention was given to the face, to capture a likeness of the subject. The rest of the figure and the background often had a flat, simplified look. Still, the paintings provide a fascinating record of the clothes and furnishings of the past.

The large portraits painted by traveling artists were hung in the parlors of many homes, where visitors would see them. As a hobby, many people also made small watercolor portraits of friends and family members. Silhouettes cut from paper were another popular way of capturing a likeness.

Folk art painters also produced landscapes, seascapes, and other scenes. Seascapes generally showed famous ships or naval battles, while most landscapes were peaceful views of homes, farms, and towns.

Before the age of photography, people often asked artists to paint pictures of their homes for the same reason they had portraits painted—to record a likeness. Thus the main goal was to show the houses accurately. But the artists generally cleaned up the scene as they put it on canvas. Piles of junk, peeling paint, and other unattractive elements were left out, and everything was made to look neat and trim. These pictures show the homes of the past in an idealized way—as they might have been, not necessarily as they really were.

Historic events and scenes from the Bible were also favorite subjects for folk painters, both amateur and professional. So were still-life scenes, featuring flowers, fruit, and everyday objects. And in the 1800's another kind of painting became popular: the memorial. These works were made to mark the death of a family member. In somber tones, they generally showed family members gath-

Portraits of children, often shown holding something, were very popular in colonial times. While many were skillfully done, they showed the subjects in stiff poses.

Landscapes produced by folk artists showed peaceful views of homes, farms, and towns.

ered around the tombstone of the departed one—or perhaps draped across the stone, sobbing with grief.

Births, marriages, and other important life events were often recorded on documents that used a style of folk art called fraktur. A fraktur combined decorative lettering with elaborate and colorful watercolor designs—hearts, flowers, animals, and human figures. Fraktur birth and marriage certificates hung on the walls of many homes. Fraktur techniques were also used to illustrate Bible stories and other favorite legends and tales.

In many fraktur pieces, the writing is as pretty as the

Baskets of fruit were also a favorite subject.

design. In fact, before the days of typewriters and computers, penmanship was an art form. Schoolchildren were drilled in penmanship techniques, and there were even professional penmanship masters. People who had mastered those techniques often showed off their skills by creating gifts or presentation pieces for friends. In these works, the words take second place to the elaborate pictures and designs formed entirely by the free-flowing pen strokes.

SCULPTURE

Just like painting, folk art sculpture covers an enormous range. Artists used the materials that were at hand, such

244

as metal and pottery, to create their works. Aboard whaling ships, sailors whiled away the hours at sea by carving delicate designs

There were many kinds of folk art sculpture, but not all were designed with a specific use in mind. Many pieces were meant to simply delight the eye. This whirligig, or wind toy, sat on fences or posts outside many homes, its broad paddle-arms twirling in the breeze.

in the teeth and bones of whales, a technique called scrimshaw. Some of these pieces were purely decorative, but others were made for a specific purpose—perhaps kitchen utensils or yarn winders.

Many other folk art carvings were made of wood. And like the scrimshaw objects, many of these woodcarvings were designed to be used as well as admired. Among the most striking examples are the free-standing fig-

ures that were used in the 1800's to advertise cigars. Large figures (some even life-size) were placed in front of tobacconists' shops or in shop windows; smaller ones were set on counter tops. They included a wide range of characters—Indians, soldiers, pot-bellied politicians, and Cuban and Turkish figures advertising cigars from those countries.

Births, baptisms, and other important life events were recorded on documents that used a style of folk art called fraktur—which combined decorative lettering with colorful and detailed watercolor designs.

Certificate of Birth and Baptism

Other shopkeepers, from shoemakers to grocers, also used carved figures as advertisements. And carved poles with brightly painted stripes were used to mark barbershops, a tradition that began in England and spread to North America. In each case, the carvings made the shops easy to identify. They also reflected the skill and creativity of their makers.

Weathervanes also combined beauty with a purpose. They helped people predict the weather, since certain kinds of weather tend to come with winds from certain directions. But, perched on the rooftops of all sorts of buildings, weathervanes were also decorative sculpture. Some were carved from wood. But many were made from metal—silhouettes cut from sheets of tin, or molded shapes of copper or zinc.

The design of a weathervane often indicated the use of the building it adorned. There were fish vanes on fish markets, for example, while sheep and cows sat atop barns. But butterflies, eagles, Indians, and other fanciful designs were also used.

Later weathervanes were mass-produced from molds, but the early ones were made individually by hand. And before the days of factories and mass production, children's toys were also made by hand. Many were carved of wood. Animal figures, often set on wooden wheels, were especially popular. Relatively few of these hand-carved wooden toys survive today—evidence that they were loved and used by their owners.

Not all folk art sculpture was designed with a specific use in mind, however. Many pieces were meant simply to delight the eye. Figures of people and animals—dogs, cats, eagles, lions, and even some imaginary beasts—decorated many 19th-century rooms. Some were carved from pine and brightly painted. Others were ceramic, made by potters as gifts for family and friends. Many of these figures show their subjects in comical poses. Because of this, and because they had no use, these sculptures became known as "whimsies."

Somewhere between whimsies and toys were the whirligigs, or wind toys, that sat on posts or fences outside many homes in the 1800's. These were carved figures that, in place of arms, had broad paddles that twirled in the breeze. Often the whirligig makers chose military officers and policemen as subjects, poking fun at their serious expressions and stiff posture.

EVERYDAY ART

Some of the most interesting folk art includes the hundreds of hand-made everyday objects that filled homes in the 1700's and 1800's. Butter molds, pastry boards, and walking sticks all provided an outlet for the woodcarver's artistic expression. Pieces of furniture, especially chests and chairs, were carved and sometimes painted with colorful designs or with false woodgrain patterns. Geometric and floral patterns were stenciled on walls and worked into floor coverings.

Some of the most interesting pieces of folk art are the hand-made everyday objects that filled homes in the 1700's and 1800's. Pieces of furniture, for example, were often elaborately carved and colorfully painted.

246

Hand-made quilts are among the best-known examples of folk art in fabric. Many were exquisitely crafted in classic patterns of flowers and geometric shapes. Others featured unique designs from the quilt maker's imagination.

Potters produced decorated crocks and jugs in whimsical shapes. Tinsmiths made metal pots and boxes that were painted with bright floral designs. And designs were pierced into tin lanterns, so that the lanterns would cast patterned shadows.

Fabric provided another outlet for artistic expression. Decorative patterns were used to make everything from embroidered table covers to bed linens. Hand-made quilts are perhaps the best-known examples of folk art in fabric. Some were made in classic patterns of flowers and geometric shapes. Others featured unique designs dreamed up by the maker. And some were album quilts—designed and made by a group, with each person contributing a square to the design.

By the early 1900's, factories were mass producing most of the everyday objects that had once been made by hand. Mail-order catalogs and improved transportation made these manufactured items available even in remote rural areas. Meanwhile, ideas about art were being spread widely by newspapers and magazines. It became difficult for an individual artist *not* to be influenced by the latest trends and developments in the world of formal art.

Thus many people feel that true folk art died out in North America. But others think that the tradition lives on, and that folk art is being produced even today—by artists who are self-taught and steer their own creative course.

Dan Aykroyd, Jessica Tandy (best actress), and Morgan Freeman in *Driving Miss Daisy* (best motion picture).

1990 ACADEMY AWARDS

CATEGORY	WINNER
Motion Picture	*Driving Miss Daisy*
Actor	Daniel Day-Lewis (*My Left Foot*)
Actress	Jessica Tandy (*Driving Miss Daisy*)
Supporting Actor	Denzel Washington (*Glory*)
Supporting Actress	Brenda Fricker (*My Left Foot*)
Director	Oliver Stone (*Born on the Fourth of July*)
Cinematography	Freddie Francis (*Glory*)
Song	"Under the Sea" (*The Little Mermaid*)
Foreign-Language Film	*Cinema Paradiso* (Italy)
Documentary Feature	*Common Threads: Stories From the Quilt*
Documentary Short	*The Johnstown Flood*

Jihmi Kennedy, Denzel
Washington (best supporting
actor), and Morgan Freeman
in *Glory*.

Daniel Day-Lewis (best actor)
and Ruth McCabe in *My Left Foot*.

Birds make their homes in this simple "gourd" house. But far more elaborate structures—both antique and contemporary—have also been created for birds. The fanciful birdcages and birdhouses on these pages reflect some of the architectural designs of the time in which they were made.

STRICTLY FOR THE BIRDS

People have always loved birds for their beauty, their song, and their soaring flight. So it's not surprising that in all cultures, people have created homes for birds—cages, in which to keep birds captive, and birdhouses, in which wild birds can build their nests.

What is surprising is the fantastic range and beauty of these bird homes. Birdcages and birdhouses may be simple, useful structures. But many are elaborate expressions of creativity that reflect the architectural trends of the time in which they were made.

BIRDCAGES

Caged birds have been kept since ancient times. The ancient Romans were particularly fond of parrots and other talking birds: The Roman emperor Augustus had a raven that called out *Ave, Caesar!*—"Hail, Caesar!" And many wealthy Romans kept orioles, doves, and smaller birds in wicker cages.

In terms of design, however, birdcages may have reached their peak in the 1800's, during the Victorian era. Among the most elaborate was one made around 1880 for King Ludwig II of Bavaria, who practically bankrupted his treasury building the luxurious castle of Neuschwanstein. In Ludwig's Neuschwanstein bedroom was a huge birdcage made of mirrors, glass, and fruitwood and mahogany, carved to mimic the ruler's richly decorated four-poster bed.

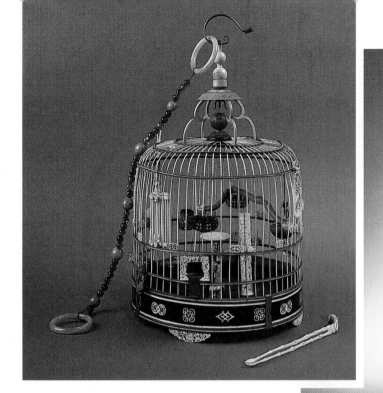

Many other birdcages of this time (shown on this page) were also "bird palaces." Luxurious materials—ivory, porcelain, painted glass, rich woods, semiprecious stones—were used in their construction. Some birdcages rose in tiers, or levels. Others sported turrets and towers that reflected Renaissance architecture, or spires and pointed arches that reflected the Gothic style.

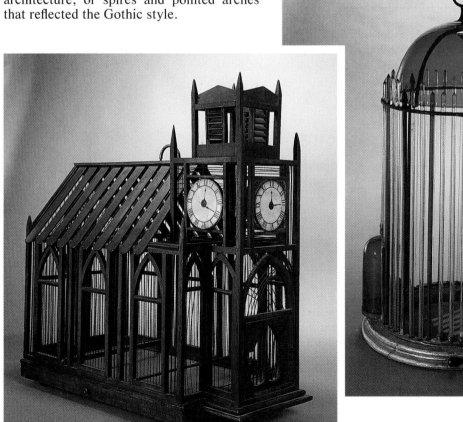

When trade between China and Europe and North America increased during the 1800's, this influenced styles in the West. Bamboo and Oriental designs became popular in home furnishings, and many fancy metal and bamboo birdcages were made in China for export to the West. At the same time, growing industrialization and new manufacturing processes made other materials, such as machine-stamped metal grillwork, widely available. Such materials, too, found their way into birdcage design. Thus elaborate birdcages became less expensive to produce and could be owned by almost everyone.

Today's birdcages are usually far simpler than the Victorian ones. They are practical, well-planned homes for the birds that live in them. The elaborate birdcages of earlier times are still popular for their beauty—but birds are rarely kept in them. Antique birdcages are valued as collector's items, and many people use antique cages or reproductions as decorative accents in their homes.

BIRDHOUSES

Caged birds have always been symbols of captivity. As a result, there's something a bit sad about a birdcage—even if the bird inside is content. But wild birds are symbols of freedom, and that's another reason why people have always loved them and enjoyed having them around. And one way to attract wild birds is to provide them with birdhouses in which they can build their nests and raise their young.

A basic birdhouse is a simple box, with a sloped roof to shed rain and the right sized entrance hole for a certain kind of bird. Unlike birdcages, birdhouses must stand up to

the weather outside; so they are usually built of sturdy materials. Most are designed for one nesting pair of birds. But perhaps the most striking birdhouses are those designed for purple martins (opposite page, below).

Martins, which are a type of swallow, nest in colonies. So a purple martin house is really an apartment building for birds, with separate cubbyholes for each martin family. The first and simplest martin houses were nothing more than hollowed out gourds hung out by Indians to attract the birds. But martin houses have been built of everything from old wooden boxes to plastic pipe and aluminum. Some are designed for just a few nesting pairs. Some are true skyscrapers, designed to house as many as 600 pairs.

Both martin houses and birdhouses that are meant for single pairs of birds have been produced in a staggering array of styles. They have been made to look like cottages and castles, churches and barns. Like birdcages, they have been seen as decorative accents—for gardens rather than for living rooms. And also like birdcages, many birdhouses have reflected the architectural styles of their time. In fact, leading architects and landscape designers of the past often included birdhouses in their plans.

This trend is still strong today. In the late 1980's, for example, a group of architects was commissioned to design birdhouses for a museum show in Long Island, New York. Their work reflected the latest trends in contemporary architecture—as well as some wonderful flights of fancy (opposite page, top, and this page).

Birdhouses like these, like the birdhouses and birdcages of the past, are much more than simple homes for birds. They are expressions of their makers' creativity.

Agatha Christie, the world-famous mystery writer.

AGATHA CHRISTIE: THE QUEEN OF CRIME

For fans of mystery novels, 1990 was a special year. It marked the 100th anniversary of the birth of one of the world's most famous mystery writers—Agatha Christie. Christie was the creator of two of the best-known detectives in fiction, Miss Jane Marple and Hercule Poirot. She was also one of the best-selling authors of all time.

The anniversary was marked with a festival at Christie's birthplace in England. Several of her books were reissued, and tributes to the writer appeared in newspapers and magazines. Altogether, the events offered mystery fans a chance to look back over the life of the woman who became known as the Queen of Crime and the Duchess of Death. That life itself had touches of mystery and adventure.

Christie's childhood was as ordinary as it could have been. She was born Agatha Mary Clarissa Miller on September 15, 1890, in Torquay, a seaside resort on the southwestern coast of England. Her mother was English; her father, American. The family was well off, and, like many girls of her time, Agatha didn't go to school. Instead, she was tutored at home until she reached her teens. She and her older sister Madge often wrote stories for amusement.

Agatha dreamed of becoming a concert pianist but was too shy to perform in public. Then, when she was 24, she married Archie Christie, a pilot in the Royal Air Force. World War I had just broken out, and he served in France. Agatha worked as a hospital nurse, first tending the wounded and later in the hospital dispensary (pharmacy).

It was in the dispensary—where she was surrounded by poisons as well as medicines—that Christie was inspired to write her first mystery novel. The plot hinged, of course, on a poisoning. And it featured a short, dapper, and meticulous Belgian detective: Hercule Poirot. The book, *The Mysterious Affair at Styles,* was rejected by several publishers before it appeared in 1920.

By this time the war was over. Christie continued to write mysteries, and she had her first major success with *The Murder of Roger Ackroyd* in 1926. The book was controversial because of its surprise ending—some readers felt that the author hadn't provided enough clues for them to solve the puzzle.

While the book made Christie's name known to mystery fans, it was an incident in her personal life that helped make her famous. On December 3, 1926, she left her home and disappeared. Her car was found abandoned the next day, and with great publicity a nationwide search was launched. She was found ten days later in a hotel in northern England, registered under another name.

Doctors announced that she had been upset about troubles in her marriage and had suffered an attack of amnesia, or loss of memory. But, whether she couldn't remember or simply chose to be silent, she never explained her mysterious disappearance.

She divorced her husband two years after the incident and later married Max Mallowan, an archeologist she had met on a trip to Iraq. Meanwhile, she had begun to earn a living as a writer of mysteries. Besides Hercule Poirot and other detectives, her novels began to feature Miss Marple, an elderly, gossipy woman from a typical English village who was a relentless sleuth. Christie's detectives soon rivaled Sherlock Holmes in fame and popularity.

In a typical Christie mystery, a murder (never a gory one) takes place in an upper-class British setting—a country home, for example. Often even the murderer behaves with impeccable manners. The detective uses sheer intelligence to puzzle out the clues, and the motives for the crimes are basic ones—jealousy, greed, and ambition. Above all, Christie's books are known for their clever plots.

Throughout most of her career, Christie produced a book each year. She would do most of the writing on winter mornings and evenings, finishing the book in the spring. It would be published the following December, and a "Christie for Christmas" became a gift-giving tradition.

Besides a total of 78 mysteries, Christie wrote 6 romantic novels (under the name Mary Westmacott), 4 nonfiction books (including her autobiography), and 19 plays. Her play *The Mousetrap* opened in London in 1952 and was still running 38 years later in 1990, the longest running English-language show ever.

There have been more than 20 films of Christie novels, including *Witness for the Prosecution* (1957), *And Then There Were None* (filmed several times), *Murder She Said* (1961), *Murder on the Orient Express* (1974), and *Death on the Nile* (1978). Christie rarely approved of the screen portrayals of her detectives, but the films were enormously popular. Television productions have also been made of many of the books.

In recognition of her work, Christie was named a Dame Commander of the British Empire in 1971. But she was modest about her accomplishments. She once described herself as a "perfect sausage machine," grinding out books, and said that she had simply been lucky.

At the time of her death in 1976, Agatha Christie was one of the best-known authors in the world. And her books have continued to sell. In fact, they have been so popular that more than 2 billion copies have been sold, in English and more than 40 other languages. The only book to have sold more copies is the Bible.

Agatha Christie created two of the best-known detectives in fiction. They have been portrayed by various actors and actresses in a number of enormously popular films. Here, Peter Ustinov stars as the dapper Hercule Poirot in *Evil Under the Sun*, and Margaret Rutherford plays the gossipy Miss Jane Marple in *Murder at the Gallop*.

PEOPLE, PLACES, EVENTS

Television situation comedies have long presented an idealized view of the American family. But in 1990, a very different sort of family ruled the airwaves: **The Simpsons.** As cartoon stars of a prime-time show of the same name, the Simpsons present a view of the family that is . . . well, twisted. Homer Simpson, the father, works as a safety inspector at a nuclear power plant, where his boss routinely refers to him as "bonehead." Marge Simpson, the mother, sports a blue beehive hairstyle and buzzes back and forth between her home and the local mall. And then there's spike-haired, smart-mouthed, 10-year-old Bart Simpson, who carries obnoxiousness to new heights. Rounding out the family are Bart's younger sisters Lisa (whose ability to butter up adults leads her brother to call her a "sniveling toad") and infant Maggie (whose only role is to suck constantly on a pacifier). The Simpsons were created by cartoonist Matt Groening and first appeared on short segments of *The Tracey Ullman Show*. Late in 1989 they began their own half-hour show on the Fox network and promptly took the country by storm. And by mid-1990, Bart Simpson was well on the way to becoming a pop hero—T-shirts featuring the character were selling out everywhere. Fox felt enough confidence in the show to move it to Thursday evenings, where it would compete with *The Cosby Show*, one of the most popular traditional situation comedies of all time.

In 1990, 28-year-old **Tom Cruise** was one of the movies' biggest box-office draws. He had his first hit film in 1983 with *Risky Business*. This was followed by starring roles in *Top Gun, The Color of Money, Rain Man,* and other movies, which showed his growing range as an actor. He won several awards, and in 1990 he was nominated for an Academy Award—for his role in *Born on the Fourth of July,* a story of a disabled veteran who opposes the Vietnam War.

On April 28, 1990, the longest running show in the history of Broadway closed. It was **A Chorus Line**, which portrayed the experiences of a group of seventeen dancers who compete for roles in a fictional Broadway musical. The show opened in 1975, and in 1976 it won nine Tony Awards (including the award for best musical) and the Pulitzer Prize for drama. By the time the curtain came down on the 6,137th and final performance, some 510 different performers had appeared in the show.

Claude Monet was among the best-known of the French Impressionist painters, who revolutionized the art world in the late 1800's. In 1990, museums in Boston, Chicago, and London hosted a special traveling exhibit that was called **"Monet in the '90s: The Series Paintings."** Monet's works, considered shocking at first, had been widely accepted by the 1890's. But, instead of resting on his success, he then began to create some of his most famous paintings. Traveling all through France, he would paint a series of canvases of the same scene. Each would show the effects of different light and weather conditions—the clear light of dawn, midday sun, the glow of evening, a soft mist—on the subject. These paintings demonstrated the Impressionist view that art should capture nature's fleeting moments and reflect their moods as the artist perceives them. (At left and below are two paintings from Monet's *Poplars* series.)

A sweeping, modern building is the home of Canada's newest and largest museum, the **Canadian Museum of Civilization.** The museum is set on a hill in Hull, Quebec, across the Ottawa River from the Canadian Parliament buildings in Ottawa. It showcases the full range of Canadian history and cultural heritage in spectacular exhibits, many using computers, videos, and other high-tech electronics. In the History Hall, there are re-creations of an early whaling ship, a town square in 18th-century New France, and a Victorian street. In the Grand Hall, which is larger than a football field, visitors can see a collection of West Coast Indian totem poles and reproductions of Indian houses. The Cultural Traditions Hall (*right*) is devoted to the Chinese-Canadian community. In parts of the museum, costumed performers and artisans portray people from the past. And a special children's section gives youngsters a chance to dress up in costumes and take part in craft workshops. The museum, which officially opened in mid-1989, was designed by Canadian architect Douglas Cardinal.

The 1990 Academy Award for best actress went to **Jessica Tandy** for her starring role in the film *Driving Miss Daisy*. Tandy, 80, had long been one of the most famous stage actresses. Many of her most acclaimed roles were in plays in which she co-starred with her husband, actor Hume Cronyn. They were married in 1942 and worked together in plays such as *The Fourposter* (1951) and *The Gin Game* (1977).

The year 1990 marked the 50th anniversary of one of the greatest discoveries in the field of prehistoric art—the **Lascaux cave paintings**. In 1940, a group of teenage boys exploring caves in Lascaux, France, stumbled upon a huge cavern covered with ancient paintings of animals. The paintings had been made during the Ice Age, some 17,000 years earlier, by Cro-Magnon people. After the discovery, so many people flocked to see the paintings that, to prevent damage to the art, the cavern was closed to the public in 1963. Tourists visiting the caves now view replicas.

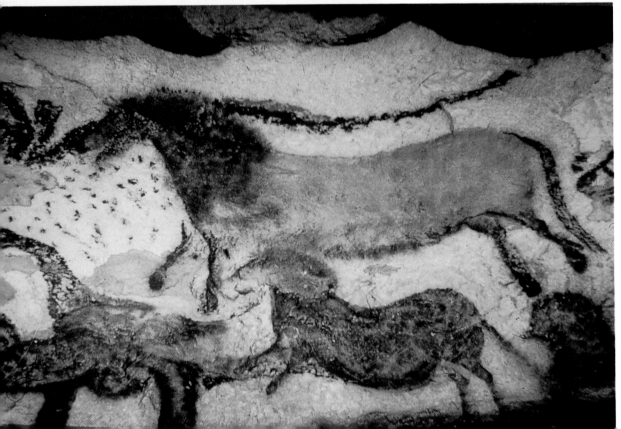

The hottest movie of the summer of 1990 was **Dick Tracy**, based on the adventures of the comic-strip detective of that name. The square-jawed detective was played by Warren Beatty (left, speaking into his two-way wrist radio), who also produced and directed the film. The film used painted backdrops to simulate a city of the 1930's and bright colors to convey a comic-strip feeling. And characters inspired by the comic strip, which was created by Chester Gould in the 1930's, were featured in the film. They included Tess Trueheart, Tracy's girlfriend (played by Glenne Headly), and villains such as Mumbles (Dustin Hoffman) and Big Boy Caprice (Al Pacino).

The rock group **New Kids on the Block** drew some two million fans on their 63-day tour in the summer of 1990. Especially popular with younger teens, the Kids began as a local group in Boston. By 1990 they had several million-selling albums out. And New Kids products—everything from posters to sleeping bags—were bringing in about $400 million for the year. All this made some people compare the Kids' popularity to that of the Beatles in the 1960's. (Clockwise from upper left are Joseph McIntyre, Danny Wood, Donnie Wahlberg, Jordan Knight, and Jonathan Knight.)

HAPPY BIRTHDAY, BUGS BUNNY

What 50-year-old Hollywood celebrity has starred in more than 160 short films, five feature films, nineteen primetime television specials, and television shows that have run—continuously—for thirty years? None other than Bugs Bunny, the carrot-chomping, wisecracking animated rabbit.

Bugs Bunny marked his 50th birthday in 1990. And his creators, Warner Bros. Inc., lined up an array of special events in celebration. Among them were birthday parties at the seven Six Flags amusement parks, located at various cities in the United States, and the televising of 65 classic Bugs Bunny cartoons. A commemorative short, featuring the best moments of Bugs's career, was released to movie theaters, and the first new Bugs Bunny cartoon to be shown in theaters

in 26 years premiered in the fall. Pictures of Bugs, grinning a buck-toothed grin and munching a carrot, appeared on products that ranged from watches to thermal underwear. And there was a special TV tribute that traced the history of the cocky, quick-witted hare.

"WHAT'S UP, DOC?"

Bugs Bunny has been a favorite with cartoon audiences since 1940, when his character first appeared in an animated short called *A Wild Hare*. But his origins go back even farther than that.

His beginnings can be traced to a 1938 short, *Porky's Hare Hunt*, in which Porky Pig is outwitted by a rabbit. The rabbit of that film wasn't Bugs—he was white instead of gray, and nuttier than the Bugs of later films. But he had many of Bugs's traits. He chomped a carrot calmly in the face of danger, drank "hare remover" to become invisible, and uttered a typically Bugs-ian line: "Of course you realize, this means war!"

Over the next few years, several versions of the rabbit character appeared. Gradually, he took on recognizable features—gray top fur, bent legs, buck teeth. And he took on the name Bugs—largely by accident. At that time, Warner's animated shorts were directed by Ben Hardaway, whose nickname was Bugs. People working at the studio began to label the rabbit drawings "Bugs' Bunny," and the name stuck.

By 1940, when *A Wild Hare* was released, Bugs was recognizably Bugs—perfectly cool, always in control, incredibly cocky, and most of all smart. Credit for this version of Bugs is generally given to Fred Avery, Warner's animation director at the time. The short film was nominated for an Academy Award.

In *A Wild Hare*, Bugs met his hunter—Elmer Fudd, who would be his opponent in many cartoons to come—with the line that became his trademark: "What's up, Doc?" And he spoke the line in the voice that would be his from then on. It was supplied by Mel Blanc, who also did the voice of Porky Pig and many other cartoon characters. For Bugs, Blanc chose a voice that had overtones of Brooklyn and the Bronx but a special twist all its own—the voice of a wiseguy with long ears.

Blanc also provided the sound of the carrot-chomping that was as much Bugs Bunny's trademark as any of his lines. He found this harder than the voice: It was difficult to chomp, chew, swallow, and be ready for the next line—and he hated carrots! So he did the chomping separately, and engineers patched it into the soundtrack.

During World War II, Bugs's mixture of brashness, coolness, toughness, and intelligence made him a favorite emblem of America's fight against Nazi Germany. And during and after the war, his films kept theater audiences laughing.

The classic hunter-and-hare plot quickly gave way to an endless variety of situations. Bugs slipped in and out of costumes and roles like a true quick-change artist. In *Hare Conditioned* (1945), he appeared as a female shoe buyer, driving a salesclerk wild. In *Baseball Bugs* (1946), he played all the positions on a major league baseball team—including pitcher and catcher at the same time. In *Racketeer Rabbit* (1946), he acted out a showdown between a policeman and a gangster. In *Bully for Bugs* (1953), he accidentally burrowed into a Mexican bullring—and faced the bull as a matador.

No matter what the plot or situation, however, Bugs Bunny's cartoons generally had one thing in common: The rabbit won.

STAR STATUS

As his fame and popularity grew, Bugs Bunny also began to appear in cartoons as himself—that is, as a Hollywood star. In several of these shorts, he sported a smoking jacket, ascot, and dark glasses. He was shown at home at his fabulous Beverly Hills estate, which featured a swimming pool, formal gardens, and his home—a rabbit hole.

Along the path to stardom, Bugs was featured in his own comic book and newspaper comic strip. He made several recordings and cameo appearances in two films. In 1958, Bugs appeared as King Arthur's court jester in the animated film *Knighty Knight Bugs*. Outfitted in armor, he attempted to rescue the legendary singing sword from the Black Knight, who was played by another Warner character, Yosemite Sam. The film won an Academy Award for best animation.

Two years later, Bugs Bunny cartoons began to appear on television. The "wascally wabbit" proved to be as big a favorite with TV audiences as he had been with moviegoers. The cartoons remained popular, too—in 1990, the top-rated Saturday morning TV show was *The Bugs Bunny and Tweety Show*. Meanwhile, nineteen Bugs Bunny specials have appeared in prime time. In fact, with reruns of his various cartoons and shows, Bugs has been on television every day for the last thirty years.

With professional credits like that, it's not surprising that Bugs has been admired by the Hollywood filmmaking community. In 1985, he was awarded a star in the "Walk of Fame" on Hollywood Boulevard. He was only the second cartoon character in history —and without question the first rabbit—to be so honored. And the 1990 celebrations for his 50th birthday were right in keeping with the wisecracking rabbit's star status.

THE MUSIC SCENE

An ear-pleasing array of musical sounds was heard during 1990, as established stars checked in with solid offerings and talented newcomers made their voices known. Much of the musical year moved to a dance beat: Not only were many performers singing danceable tunes, they were also showing off fancy footwork in dance-oriented concerts and videos.

IN STEP

In 1990, it seemed, you couldn't be a pop star if you didn't dance. It was no longer enough to have a great singing style; to succeed in this era of music videos, you also had to have great moves. Dancing became so important to stage shows that, when it was impossible to sing and dance at the same time, many performers gave up live vocals. Instead, they lip-synced to prerecorded tapes, the better to perform acrobatic dance steps. Some music critics felt that this practice defeated the purpose of seeing a "live" performance, but most concert-goers seemed to enjoy the total package.

A leader in this trend was Madonna, whose videos and concert tours had long emphasized dancing. For her 1990 "Blonde Ambition" tour, Madonna had changed her look again, but her dance routines were more tightly choreographed than ever. She even had a hit single, "Vogue," that was inspired by a dance craze in which participants strike poses like fashion models. ("Vogue" could be found on *I'm Breathless,* an album of music "from and inspired by" the movie *Dick Tracy,* in which Madonna had a feature role.)

Janet Jackson's 1990 concerts featured rhythmic dance routines performed in high-tech settings. She toured to promote her 1989 album, *Janet Jackson's Rhythm Nation 1814,* which remained on the charts into 1990. By year's end the album had sold some five million copies, and six of its singles had reached the top five on Billboard's pop-sin-

Madonna was as popular as ever in 1990. And her dance routines reflected the fancy footwork trend so popular during the year.

gles chart. Only one other pop album in history—George Michael's *Faith*—had ever generated six top-five singles.

Choreographer-turned-singer Paula Abdul had shown off her abilities on the 1988 album *Forever Your Girl* and its videos. In 1990 she was busy choreographing a film biography of 1960's rock star Jim Morrison. In the meantime, her fans had to be content with *Shut Up and Dance,* an album of songs taken from the *Forever* album.

Male performers, too, donned their dancing shoes. One of the most phenomenal successes was the teen group New Kids on the Block. Their album *Step by Step* hit the number-one spot on the charts and sold more than three million copies. The New Kids' sold-out concert tour attracted tens of thousands of fans, who responded ecstatically to their singing, rapping, and dancing.

NEW AND NOTEWORTHY

A chorus of new voices was heard during the year as some singers debuted with hit albums, and others scored the first popular successes of their careers.

With her shorn head and waif-like appearance, Irish singer-songwriter Sinéad O'Connor seemed an unlikely candidate for pop celebrity. Yet she became the decade's first new pop superstar. Her recording of "Nothing Compares 2 U," a song by Prince, flew to the top of the pop singles chart in just six weeks. Her album *I Do Not Want What I Haven't Got* rose even more rapidly, reaching the number-two position on the album chart in just three weeks. The video of "Nothing Compares 2 U" won three MTV video music awards, including best video of the year.

The most successful debut album of 1990 belonged to Wilson Phillips. The California-based trio united the offspring of two of the most famous pop groups of the 1960's. Its members were Carnie and Wendy Wilson, daughters of Brian Wilson of the Beach Boys, and Chynna Phillips, the daughter of John and Michelle Phillips of the Mamas and the Papas. True to their family heritage, the trios emphasized soaring vocal harmonies on their album *Wilson Phillips*.

Another group, Nelson, could also claim solid musical roots. Matthew and Gunnar Nelson, twin sons of the late pop star Rick Nelson, released *After the Rain*. The recording made the album charts and generated a hit single, "(Can't Live Without Your) Love and Affection."

A promising debut album was released by Mariah Carey, a 20-year-old whose powerful voice impressed critics. A number of other women vocalists made strong impressions with hit singles. Lisa Stansfield's disco-inspired soul hit "All Around the World" shared the top of the charts with Jane Child's synthesized funk number "Don't Wanna Fall in Love" and Alannah Myles's rocking "Black Velvet."

A new group, Bell Biv DeVoe, scored with *Poison*, an album of rap-flavored dance music that quickly reached Billboard's top-ten album list. The three members of the group were alumni of the bubble-gum soul group New Edition. (Another former New Edition member, Bobby Brown, had scored as a solo artist in 1989.)

The MTV video music award for best new artist went to Michael Penn for the video of his song "No Myth," a catchy folk-pop tune with a Beatles-like flavor. Penn (brother of actor Sean Penn) also received praise for his major-label album debut, *March*. The music of another singer-songwriter, Karl Wallinger of World Party, also showed the influence of the Beatles. *Goodby Jumbo*, the group's second album and first popular success, combined psychedelic sounds of the 1960's with many other musical elements, including soul, funk, and country.

Sinéad O'Connor was the decade's first new pop superstar. She had a hit single and a hit album, and she won three video music awards.

M. C. Hammer was the year's most successful rap artist.

RAP ON THE RISE

Rap, with its pounding beat and spoken rhymes, continued to make its presence known on the music scene. Rap had come a long way since its beginnings as a form of urban street music. Rappers were raising their technique to a high art, performing nimble vocal acrobatics as they delivered increasingly complex raps. And, using a process called digital sampling, rappers were able to "borrow" snatches of music from a wide variety of sources. These innovations helped make rap more popular; by 1990, it was becoming big business.

By far the most successful rap artist of the year was M. C. Hammer. His album *Please Hammer Don't Hurt 'Em* reached number one on both Pop and Black album charts, with some five million copies sold. A single from the album, "U Can't Touch This," was made into a video that won several MTV video music awards. Its popularity helped spur album sales. Hammer's videos and live concerts featured a squad of energetic dancers and backup singers, as well as his own high-speed dance moves. The singer capped his year's successes by forming his own record label and embarking on a national tour. Hammer's opening act, rapper Vanilla Ice, scored with the song "Ice Ice Baby," which hit number one on the pop-singles chart.

Another sign of rap's increasing popularity was a new television series, *Fresh Prince of Bel Air*, that starred rapper Will Smith, the "Fresh Prince," of the duo D. J. Jazzy Jeff and the Fresh Prince. However, even as some rappers reached for mainstream acceptance, others sparked controversy. The Miami-based rap group 2 Live Crew was heavily criticized for its crude and graphic lyrics. In June, the Crew's album *As Nasty as They Wanna Be* became the first recording to be declared obscene by a Federal court. Despite—or perhaps because of—the controversy, the album sold nearly two million copies.

FAMILIAR VOICES

The year was a productive one for many established musicians. Rock and roll legends continued to win new fans, while younger performers followed up recent successes with ambitious new efforts.

Billy Joel's 14th album, *Storm Front*, included the musical history lesson "We Didn't Start the Fire," which became the singer's 28th hit single. Phil Collins' album . . . *But Seriously* reached Billboard's top-five lists, as did "Cradle of Love," a single from Billy Idol's album *Charmed Life*. Soulful ballad writer Michael Bolton had a hit with *Soul Provider*. Paul Simon's *The Rhythm of the Saints*, like his 1986 release *Graceland*, featured sounds from other cultures. British guitar hero Eric Clapton checked in with *Journeyman*, an album of blues tunes old and new.

Two legendary folk-rock performers released new albums. Bob Dylan's latest effort was *Under the Red Sky*. Neil Young joined forces with his former collaborators, the band Crazy Horse, to record *Ragged Glory*. Both albums emphasized the singers' rough but distinctive vocal styles.

The B-52's, a favorite party band of the late 1970's, staged a comeback in 1990. The band's eccentric but highly danceable sound struck a chord with a new generation of listeners. Their album *Cosmic Thing* went to number one, spurred by the popular single "Love Shack." Heart, led by sisters Ann and Nancy Wilson, released *Brigade*, its first album in three years. Fleetwood Mac retained its well-known sound on *Behind the Mask*, despite the addition of two new guitarists-composers.

Prince released *Graffiti Bridge*, a soundtrack album for his latest movie. The album's inventive arrangements and engaging pop-funk sound promised that Prince would continue to be one of pop music's most creative—and most imitated—figures. The Time, a band sponsored by Prince, was featured on *Graffiti Bridge* and also released an album of its own, *Pandemonium*.

Harlem-born soul singer Keith Sweat's album *I'll Give All My Love to You* climbed the charts and was cited as an outstanding example of "new jack swing," a fusion of rap, pop, and soul. British pop-soul singer George Michael followed his twelve-million-selling solo debut, *Faith*, with *Listen Without Prejudice, Vol. 1*, an album of mostly acoustic songs (not using electronic instruments). Pop-soul duo Hall and Oates departed from their usual dance-oriented sound on *Change of Seasons*, a mostly acoustic album with no dance tracks.

A Night on the Town was the third album by Bruce Hornsby and the Range. Most songs featured Hornsby's piano playing but also added more heft to the band's gentle sound. Australian band Midnight Oil followed up its big 1988 hit *Diesel and Dust* with *Blue Sky Mining*.

Superstar record producer Quincy Jones produced *Back on the Block*, an all-star album celebrating the talent of black musicians. Among the artists appearing on the album were music legends Ray Charles, Ella Fitzgerald, Sarah Vaughan, and Miles Davis; *a cappella* vocalists Bobby McFerrin, Take 6, and Al Jarreau; and rappers Al B. Sure! and Melle Mel.

SOUND ALTERNATIVES

Hard rock and heavy metal music continued to win enthusiastic listeners. Living Colour followed up an impressive 1989 debut with *Time's Up*, which again showcased the talents of the group's guitarist Vernon Reid

The B-52's, a popular '70's band, made a comeback.

and vocalist Corey Glover. Jon Bon Jovi's album, *Blaze of Glory/Young Guns II*, produced a hit single, "Blaze of Glory." "Unskinny Bop," a single from Poison's album *Flesh and Blood*, also reached the top five. Newcomers Faith No More had a winner with *The Real Thing*, which went gold. Other successful metal/hard rock albums included releases by the groups Winger, Ratt, Stryper, and Warrant.

Several releases in 1990 brought classic blues sounds to a wider audience. Guitarist Robert Cray had a winner with *Midnight Stroll*, his first album in a few years. Veteran blues vocalist Etta James showed off her soulful style in *Stickin' to My Guns*. Three talented musicians, the late jazz drummer Art Blakey, New Orleans pianist Dr. John, and saxophonist David "Fathead" Newman, joined forces on *Bluesiana Triangle*, an album of blues-based tunes. Just before his tragic death in a helicopter crash in August, virtuoso blues guitarist Stevie Ray

Living Colour impressed rock music fans with their 1990 album, *Time's Up.*

Vaughan had completed an album with his brother, guitarist Jimmie Vaughan. *Family Style* was released in October. It featured the brothers' blues guitar playing, as well as Cajun-, soul-, and gospel-flavored songs.

The down-home strains of country music continued to be heard, with well-received new releases by the Nitty Gritty Dirt Band, Johnny Cash, Emmylou Harris, Carlene Carter, and George Strait.

ROCK WITH A CONSCIENCE

The trend toward social activism continued in 1990, as musicians donated time and performances to aid their favorite charities and social causes.

The wives of the former Beatles spearheaded a project to help orphans left in poverty by the political turmoil in Rumania. The four wives—Olivia Harrison, Barbara Bach, Yoko Ono, and Linda McCartney—organized the recording of *Nobody's Child*, featuring performances by George Harrison, Elton John, Stevie Wonder, and other famous artists. All profits from the album benefited the Rumanian Angel Appeal.

M. C. Hammer, Tone-Lōc, and other leading West Coast rappers all joined forces to record "We're All in the Same Gang," a rapped plea for an end to the gang violence plaguing the California cities of Los Angeles and Oakland.

In June a number of British rock stars gathered at Knebworth, England, for a concert to benefit London's Nordoff-Robbin Music Therapy Centre. Performers included Paul McCartney, George Michael, Phil Collins, Mark Knopfler, Eric Clapton, and Tears for Fears. The Centre is a favorite charity of the musicians because it uses music to help disabled children.

In July, East Germany's Berlin Wall was the scene of an $8 million production of *The Wall*, an epic rock suite by British musician Roger Waters. The event was staged to benefit the Memorial Fund for Disaster Relief, a charity to aid victims of natural disasters. The large cast of performers included Sinéad O'Connor, Joni Mitchell, Van Morrison, and Cyndi Lauper. A 60-foot-high, 600-foot-long Styrofoam wall was erected, and then toppled, during the course of the show.

1990 GRAMMY AWARDS

Record of the Year	"Wind Beneath My Wings"	Bette Midler, artist
Album of the Year	*Nick of Time*	Bonnie Raitt, artist
Song of the Year	"Wind Beneath My Wings"	Larry Henley, Jeff Silbar, songwriters
New Artist of the Year		Milli Vanilli (award revoked)
Pop Vocal Performance—female	"Nick of Time"	Bonnie Raitt, artist
Pop Vocal Performance—male	"How Am I Supposed to Live Without You"	Michael Bolton, artist
Pop Vocal Performance—group	"Don't Know Much"	Linda Ronstadt, Aaron Neville, artists
Rock Vocal Performance—female	*Nick of Time*	Bonnie Raitt, artist
Rock Vocal Performance—male	*The End of the Innocence*	Don Henley, artist
Rock Vocal Performance—group	*Traveling Wilburys, Volume One*	Traveling Wilburys, artists
Country Vocal Performance—female	*Absolute Torch and Twang*	k. d. lang, artist
Country Vocal Performance—male	*Lyle Lovett and His Large Band*	Lyle Lovett, artist
Country Vocal Performance—group	*Will the Circle Be Unbroken, Volume Two*	The Nitty Gritty Dirt Band, artists
Rhythm and Blues Vocal Performance—female	"Giving You the Best That I Got"	Anita Baker, artist
Rhythm and Blues Vocal Performance—male	"Every Little Step"	Bobby Brown, artist
Rhythm and Blues Vocal Performance—group	"Back to Life"	Soul II Soul, artists
Music Video Performance	"Leave Me Alone"	Michael Jackson, artist
Score for a Motion Picture	*The Fabulous Baker Boys*	Dave Grusin, composer
Cast Show Album	*Jerome Robbins' Broadway*	Jay David Saks, producer
Classical Album	*Bartok: 6 String Quartets*	Emerson String Quartet, artists

MUSIC NOTES

The fifth annual Rock and Roll Hall of Fame Awards were held in January. Performers inducted were the Kinks, the Who, Simon and Garfunkel, the Platters, the Four Tops, the Four Seasons, Hank Ballard, and Bobby Darin. Also inducted were the songwriting teams of Gerry Goffin and Carole King; and Brian Holland, Lamont Dozier, and Eddie Holland. Louis Armstrong, Charlie Christian, and Ma Rainey were honored as early influences on rock and roll.

The 90th anniversary of a song that has become a symbol of black pride was celebrated during the year. "Lift Every Voice and Sing" was written in 1900 by black author and educator James Weldon Johnson. A new recording of the song was made by singer Melba Moore, with profits to benefit the National Association for the Advancement of Colored People (NAACP), the United Negro College Fund, and the National Association for Sickle Cell Disease.

Milli Vanilli won the 1990 Grammy Award as best new artist. But the duo didn't do the singing on their debut album, it was discovered at year's end, and their Grammy was taken back.

Ted Danson (best actor, comedy series), Kirstie Alley, and Woody Harrelson in *Cheers*.

1990 EMMY AWARDS

CATEGORY	WINNER
Comedy Series	*Murphy Brown*
Actor—comedy series	Ted Danson (*Cheers*)
Actress—comedy series	Candice Bergen (*Murphy Brown*)
Supporting Actor—comedy series	Alex Rocco (*The Famous Teddy Z*)
Supporting Actress—comedy series	Bebe Neuwirth (*Cheers*)
Drama Series	*L.A. Law*
Actor—drama series	Peter Falk (*Columbo*)
Actress—drama series	Patricia Wettig (*thirtysomething*)
Supporting Actor—drama series	Jimmy Smits (*L.A. Law*)
Supporting Actress—drama series	Marg Helgenberger (*China Beach*)
Miniseries	*Drug Wars: The Camarena Story*
Comedy or Drama Special	*Caroline?* and *The Incident* (tied)
Variety, Music, or Comedy Program	*In Living Color*

Jimmy Smits (best supporting actor, drama series) and Larry Drake in *L.A. Law* (best drama series).

Peter Falk (best actor, drama series) in *Columbo*.

SCULPTURES IN THE SAND

If you've ever been to the beach, you've probably tried your hand at building a simple fort or a castle in the sand. You may even have discovered that with a little water and a few simple tools, sand can be used to create all sorts of fanciful sculptures. Sculpting in sand is challenging and fun—so much so that sand sculpture contests have become popular events in many seaside areas. In fact, sand sculpture has become "big"—in more ways than one.

Imagine, for example, a sand castle nearly the height of a four-story building, stretching 198 feet (60 meters) along the beach. Such a castle was built at Treasure Island, Florida, a few years ago. About 1,400 volunteers worked for almost two weeks to pile and carve the 20,000 tons of wet sand that formed the castle. They worked under the direction of—believe it or not—professional sand-castle builders. The finished work, called Bluebeard's Castle, was one of the largest sand castles ever built, and it drew some 400,000 spectators.

Although the evidence has long since washed away, people have probably been modeling sand since ancient times. But as far as anyone knows, enormous and elaborate creations like Bluebeard's Castle are something new. Some are designed and built by professionals for films and promotional events. Others are built for the sand sculpture contests that are held in beachfront resorts everywhere—from Virginia Beach, Virginia, to Imperial Beach, California, to White Rock, British Columbia.

The contests are a way of drawing crowds to the resorts, and they often offer prize money to the best entries. Both amateurs and professionals compete in various categories, often working in teams. What do the sculptors build? Besides castles, nautical subjects—from sea serpents to sunken ships—are the most popular. But just about any subject might appear in the sand: telephones, televisions, and cars alongside pigs, dogs, dragons, and other real and fanciful animals. At one contest, a team led by a dentist

Sand sculpture contests are very popular today. Many of the creations are quite elaborate and detailed, and they involve careful planning. The whimsical pig, fanciful automobile, and four-story-tall Bluebeard's Castle shown on this page drew thousands of spectators—before the sculptures were washed away by the tides.

carved a set of teeth accompanied by a toothbrush and a tube of toothpaste.

Sand is easy to shape and carve, but creating a large or elaborate sand structure can be tricky. First comes careful planning and design work—most sand sculptures are wider than they are tall, so that they won't tumble down too easily. Then wet sand must be piled in the rough shape of the sculpture, which is hard work if the sculpture is very large. Sometimes the sand is piled and compacted into wooden forms, which are later removed.

Finally, the sand artists carefully carve the final shape, using tools that range from putty knives to melon-ball scoops. Meanwhile, to keep the sand from drying out and crumbling away, the sculpture is dampened with a spray of water from time to time.

All this must be done quickly—because all sand sculptures have short lives. Sooner or later, the tide will come in and wash the creation away.

FUN TO READ

Tony dreams of becoming the most famous baker in all of northern Italy. His daughter, Serafina, also has a dream: to marry. And both their dreams suddenly seem likely to come true when Angelo, a young nobleman, passes through their village. Their story is told in *Tony's Bread*, written and illustrated by Tomie dePaola. And, along the way, this colorful folktale explains why the rich Italian bread called *panettone* is shaped like a flowerpot.

Alice's Adventures in Wonderland *is one of the most famous children's books of all time. And 1990 marked a birthday for the book— the 125th anniversary of its first publication, in 1865. Since that time, this enchanting and humorous tale has been translated into some thirty languages and loved by generations of young people around the world.*

Alice's Adventures in Wonderland *was written by Charles Lutwidge Dodgson, who used the pen name Lewis Carroll. Dodgson, a British professor of mathematics, had a stammer that made him shy among adults. But he got along wonderfully with young people. Although he had no children of his own, he often spent time with the children of his friends. And among them were three young girls—Alice, Lorina, and Edith Liddell—who became the inspiration for the first* Alice *story.*

One day, after a boating party on a river near the girls' home, Dodgson entertained them with a tale about a little girl named Alice who falls asleep and dreams a series of wild adventures. Following a white rabbit down a hole, she finds herself in a strange fantasy world where animals talk and simple objects like playing cards come to life. She meets a collection of comical characters—among them the Mad Hatter and the March Hare, who preside over a riotous tea party; the Queen of Hearts, who is constantly ordering her subjects beheaded; and the Cheshire Cat, who can appear and disappear at will.

Later Dodgson wrote the tale down and illustrated it with sketches. He gave it the title Alice's Adventures Underground *and presented it to Alice Liddell in 1863. The world might never have known about the story if a friend of the Liddells hadn't seen it in their home. He was so charmed by the tale that he told them it should be published. And the Liddells then managed to convince Dodgson to send it to a publisher.*

The book appeared in 1865 with new illustrations by Sir John Tenniel, a famous political cartoonist of the day. It was an instant success. A few years later a second Alice *book,* Through the Looking-Glass, *appeared. It, too, became a classic. Children have loved the books because they are filled with fantasy and nonsense rhymes. But the books also poke fun at many adult situations, and that has made them popular with grown-ups, too.*

An excerpt from Alice's Adventures in Wonderland *follows. In it, Alice plays croquet with the Queen of Hearts and the royal court, the members of which are actually playing cards. This is a very strange croquet game indeed—the "balls" are hedgehogs, and the "mallets" are flamingos!*

The Queen's Croquet-Ground

A large rose tree stood near the entrance of the garden. The roses growing on it were white, but there were three gardeners at it, busily painting them red. Alice thought this a very curious thing, and she went nearer to watch them, and, just as she came up to them she heard one of them say, "Look out now, Five! Don't go splashing paint over me like that!"

"I couldn't help it," said Five, in a sulky tone. "Seven jogged my elbow."

On which Seven looked up and said, "That's right, Five! Always lay the blame on others!"

"*You'd* better not talk!" said Five. "I heard the Queen say only yesterday you deserved to be beheaded."

"What for?" said the one who had spoken first.

"That's none of *your* business, Two!" said Seven.

"Yes, it *is* his business!" said Five. "And I'll tell him—it was for bringing the cook tulip-roots instead of onions."

Seven flung down his brush, and had just begun "Well, of all the unjust things—" when his eye chanced to fall upon Alice, as she stood watching them, and he checked himself suddenly. The others looked around also, and all of them bowed low.

"Would you tell me, please," said Alice, a little timidly, "why you are painting those roses?"

Five and Seven said nothing, but looked at Two. Two began in a low voice, "Why, the fact is, you see, Miss, this here ought to have been a *red* rose tree, and we put a white one in by mistake. And, if the Queen was to find it out, we should all have our heads cut off, you know. So you see, Miss, we're doing our best, afore she comes, to—" At this moment, Five, who had been anxiously looking across the garden, called out "The Queen! The Queen!" and the three gardeners instantly threw themselves flat upon their faces. There was a sound of many footsteps, and Alice looked around, eager to see the Queen.

First came ten soldiers carrying clubs. These were all shaped like the three gardeners, oblong and flat, with their hands and feet at the corners. Next the ten courtiers; these were ornamented all over with diamonds, and walked two and two, as the soldiers did. After these came the royal children. There were ten of them, and the little dears came jumping merrily along hand in hand, in couples; they were all ornamented with hearts. Next came the guests, mostly Kings and Queens, and among them Alice recognized the White Rabbit. It was talking in a hurried nervous manner, smiling at everything that was said, and went by without noticing her. Then followed the Knave of Hearts, carrying the King's crown on a crimson velvet cushion; and, last of all in this grand procession, came THE KING AND QUEEN OF HEARTS.

Alice was rather doubtful whether she ought not to lie down on her face like the three gardeners, but she could not remember ever having heard of such a rule at processions. "And besides, what would be the use of a procession," thought she, "if people had all to lie down on their faces, so that they couldn't see it?" So she stood where she was, and waited.

When the procession came opposite to Alice, they all stopped and looked at her,   and the Queen said, severely, "Who is this?" She said it to the Knave of Hearts, who only bowed and smiled in reply.

"Idiot!" said the Queen, tossing her head impatiently. And, turning to Alice, she went on, "What's your name, child?"

"My name is Alice, so please your Majesty," said Alice very politely. But she added, to herself, "Why they're only a pack of cards, after all. I needn't be afraid of them!"

"And who are *these?*" said the Queen, pointing to the three gardeners who were lying around the rose tree. For, you see, as they were lying on their faces, and the pattern on their backs was the same as the rest of the pack, she could not tell whether they were gardeners, or soldiers, or courtiers, or three of her own children.

"How should *I* know?" said Alice, surprised at her own courage. "It's no business of *mine*."

The Queen turned crimson with fury, and after glaring at her for a moment like a wild beast, began screaming "Off with her head! Off with—"

"Nonsense!" said Alice, very loudly and decidedly, and the Queen was silent.

The King laid his hand upon her arm, and timidly said, "Consider, my dear, she is only a child!"

The Queen turned angrily away from him, and said to the Knave, "Turn them over!"

The Knave did so, very carefully, with one foot.

"Get up!" said the Queen in a shrill, loud voice, and the three gardeners instantly jumped up,

and began bowing to the King, the Queen, the royal children, and everybody else.

"Leave off that!" screamed the Queen. "You make me giddy." And then, turning to the rose tree, she went on, "What *have* you been doing here?"

"May it please your Majesty," said Two, in a very humble tone, going down on one knee as he spoke, "we were trying—"

"*I* see!" said the Queen, who had meanwhile been examining the roses. "Off with their heads!" and the procession moved on, three of the soldiers remaining behind to execute the unfortunate gardeners, who ran to Alice for protection.

"You shan't be beheaded!" said Alice, and she put them into a large flower pot that stood near. The three soldiers wandered about for a minute or two, looking for them, and then quietly marched off after the others.

"Are their heads off?" shouted the Queen.

"Their heads are gone, if it please your Majesty!" the soldiers shouted in reply.

"That's right!" shouted the Queen. "Can you play croquet?"

The soldiers were silent, and looked at Alice, as the question was evidently meant for her.

"Yes!" shouted Alice.

"Come on, then!" roared the Queen, and Alice joined the procession, wondering very much what would happen next.

"It's—it's a very fine day!" said a timid voice at her side. She was walking by the White Rabbit, who was peeping anxiously into her face.

"Very," said Alice. "Where's the Duchess?"

"Hush! Hush!" said the Rabbit in a low, hurried tone. He looked anxiously over his shoulder as he spoke, and then raised himself upon tiptoe, put his mouth close to her ear, and whispered "She's under sentence of execution."

"What for?" said Alice.

"Did you say 'What a pity!'?" the Rabbit asked.

"No, I didn't," said Alice. "I don't think it's at all a pity. I said 'What for?'"

"She boxed the Queen's ears—" the Rabbit began. Alice gave a little scream of laughter. "Oh, hush!" the Rabbit whispered in a frightened tone. "The Queen will hear you! You see she came rather late, and the Queen said—"

"Get to your places!" shouted the Queen in a voice of thunder, and people began running about in all directions, tumbling up against each other. However, they got settled down in a minute or two, and the game began.

Alice thought she had never seen such a curious croquet-ground in her life. It was all ridges and furrows; the croquet balls were live hedgehogs, and the mallets live flamingos, and the soldiers had to double themselves up and stand on their hands and feet, to make the arches.

The chief difficulty Alice found at first was in managing her flamingo. She succeeded in getting its body tucked away, comfortably enough, under her arm, with its legs hanging down, but generally, just as she had got its neck nicely straightened out, and was going to give the hedgehog a blow with its head, it *would* twist itself around and look up into her face, with such a puzzled expression that she could not help bursting out laughing. And, when she had got its head down, and was going to begin again, it was very provoking to find that the hedgehog had unrolled itself, and was in the act of crawling away. Besides all this, there was generally a ridge or a furrow in the way wherever she wanted to send the hedgehog to, and, as the doubled-up soldiers were always getting up and walking off to other parts of the ground, Alice soon came to the conclusion that it was a very difficult game indeed.

The players all played at once without waiting for turns, quarreling all the while, and fighting for the hedgehogs. And in a very short time the Queen was in a furious passion, and went stamping about, and shouting ''Off with his head!'' or ''Off with her head!'' about once in a minute.

Alice began to feel very uneasy. To be sure, she had not as yet had any dispute with the Queen, but she knew that it might happen any minute, "and then," thought she, "what would become of me? They're dreadfully fond of beheading people here. The great wonder is, that there's any one left alive!"

She was looking about for some way of escape, when she noticed a curious appearance in the air. It puzzled her very much at first, but after watching it a minute or two she made it out to be a grin, and she said to herself, "It's the Cheshire Cat. Now I shall have somebody to talk to."

"How are you getting on?" said the Cat, as soon as there was mouth enough for it to speak with.

Alice waited till the eyes appeared, and then nodded. "It's no use speaking to it," she thought, "till its ears have come, or at least one of them." In another minute the whole head appeared, and then Alice put down her flamingo, and began an account of the game, feeling very glad she had someone to listen to her. The Cat seemed to think that there was enough of it now in sight, and no more of it appeared.

"I don't think they play at all fairly," Alice began, in rather a complaining tone, "and they all quarrel so dreadfully one can't hear oneself speak—and they don't seem to have any rules in particular. At least, if there are, nobody attends to them—and you've no idea how confusing it is all the things being alive. For instance, there's the arch I've got to go through next walking about at the other end of the ground —and I should have croqueted the Queen's hedgehog just now, only it ran away when it saw mine coming!"

"How do you like the Queen?" said the Cat in a low voice.

"Not at all," said Alice. "She's so extremely—" Just then she noticed that the Queen was close behind her, listening. So she went on "—likely to win, that it's hardly worthwhile finishing the game."

The Queen smiled and passed on.

"Who *are* you talking to?" said the King, coming up to Alice, and looking at the Cat's head with great curiosity.

"It's a friend of mine—a Cheshire Cat," said Alice. "Allow me to introduce it."

"I don't like the look of it at all," said the King. "However, it may kiss my hand, if it likes."

"I'd rather not," the Cat remarked.

"Don't be impertinent," said the King, "and don't look at me like that!" He got behind Alice as he spoke.

"A cat may look at a king," said Alice. "I've read that in some book, but I don't remember where."

"Well, it must be removed," said the King very decidedly. And he called to the Queen, who was passing at the moment, "My dear! I wish you would have this cat removed!"

The Queen had only one way of settling all difficulties, great or small. "Off with his head!" she said without even looking around.

"I'll fetch the executioner myself," said the King eagerly, and he hurried off.

Alice thought she might as well go back and see how the game was going on, as she heard the Queen's voice in the distance, screaming with passion. She had already heard her sentence three of the players to be executed for having missed their turns, and she did not like the look of things at all, as the game was in such confusion that she never knew whether it was her turn or not. So she went off in search of her hedgehog.

The hedgehog was engaged in a fight with another hedgehog, which seemed to Alice an excellent opportunity for croqueting one of them with the other. The only difficulty was, that her flamingo was gone across to the other side of the garden, where Alice could see it trying in a helpless sort of way to fly up into a tree.

By the time she had caught the flamingo and brought it back, the fight was over, and both the hedgehogs were out of sight. ''But it doesn't matter much,'' thought Alice, ''as all the arches are gone from this side of the ground.'' So she tucked it away under her arm, that it might not escape again, and went back to have a little more conversation with her friend.

When she got back to the Cheshire Cat, she was surprised to find quite a large crowd collected around it. There was a dispute going on between the executioner, the King, and the Queen, who were all talking at once, while the rest were silent, and looked very uncomfortable.

The moment Alice appeared, she was appealed to by all three to settle the question, and they repeated their arguments to her, though, as they all spoke at once, she found it very hard to make out exactly what they said.

The executioner's argument was, that you couldn't cut off a head unless there was a body to cut it off from; that he had never had to do such a thing before, and he wasn't going to begin at *his* time of life.

The King's argument was that anything that had a head could be beheaded, and that you weren't to talk nonsense.

The Queen's argument was that, if something wasn't done about it in less than no time, she'd have everybody executed, all around. (It was this last remark that had made the whole party look so anxious.)

Alice could think of nothing else to say but ''It belongs to the Duchess. You'd better ask *her* about it.''

''She's in prison,'' the Queen said to the executioner. ''Fetch her here.'' And the executioner went off like an arrow.

The Cat's head began fading away the moment he was gone, and, by the time he had come back with the Duchess, it had entirely disappeared. So the King and the executioner ran wildly up and down, looking for it, while the rest of the party went back to the game.

LOOKING AT BOOKS

HERE COMES THE CAT! / СЮДА ИДЕТ КОТ!

Here Comes the Cat! is a first—the first jointly produced U.S.-Soviet book for children. Frank Asch, an American artist, and Vladimir Vagin, a Soviet illustrator, pooled their talents to create this colorful picture book, in which words are shown in both English and Russian. The story is simple: A mouse travels throughout the land to warn other mice that a cat is coming. The surprise comes when the ferocious feline finally appears—but turns out to be just a sweet pussycat carting a huge wheel of cheese for the mice to share.

Time Out

It's 1887 in London, and Tweeny and her parents—Wilks, a butler, and Ethel, a parlour maid—set off on a very unusual trip. With the help of a book of spells, the family travels to the year 1987. Their exciting adventures in the future begin in their own sitting room—now a young boy's playroom. *Time Out* was written by Helen Cresswell and illustrated by Peter Elwell.

The Magic Paintbrush

What would it be like to make your drawings come to life? Nib, an orphan who wants to be an artist, finds out when he receives a magic paintbrush that has this power. But he soon learns that the power is a very mixed blessing. *The Magic Paintbrush*, which is based on an old Chinese tale, was written and illustrated by Robin Muller. In 1990 the book won the Canadian Governor General's Children's Literature Award for illustration.

BEST WITCHES

What do witches like on pizza? Poison ivy, according to one of the verses in *Best Witches*. This collection of poems by Jane Yolen, illustrated by Elise Primavera, is all about witches, ghosts, and similar creepy creatures. You'll be quizzed on the witch's TV show, bump into a warlock's cat, and dine at the Ritz with a modern witch. The book includes some rhymes that are spooky and some that are silly, mixing giggles with Halloween chills.

Lon Po Po

A RED-RIDING HOOD STORY FROM CHINA

Lon Po Po is an old Chinese tale, translated and illustrated by Ed Young. Western readers will find that the story has a familiar ring—it's very like the European folktale of Little Red Riding Hood. In this story, three clever little girls outwit a hungry wolf who masquerades as their grandmother. The book won the 1990 Randolph Caldecott Medal as the best American picture book for children.

THE LADY WHO PUT SALT IN HER COFFEE

In the 1800's, Lucretia Peabody Hale wrote a series of stories about the Peterkin family that became great favorites with children. *The Lady Who Put Salt in Her Coffee* is one of those stories, with new illustrations by Amy Schwartz. In this tale, the family is thrown into confusion when Mrs. Peterkin mistakenly puts salt instead of sugar in her coffee and, of course, cannot drink it. So they rush off to consult a chemist, an herb expert, and a sensible lady from Philadelphia in the hope of setting things right.

NUMBER THE STARS

During World War II, Nazi Germany took control of most of Europe and systematically began to kill the Jewish population. *Number the Stars*, set in Denmark at the time of the Nazi occupation, tells what happened to two young friends—Ellen, who is Jewish, and Annemarie, who is not—during that dark chapter in history. It's a story of ordinary people who show extraordinary courage in the face of danger. This book, written by Lois Lowry, won the 1990 John Newbery Medal, the highest American award for a book for young people.

Princess Furball

This old folktale begins when a king betroths his only daughter to an ogre. Not surprisingly, the princess has other ideas—and she promptly runs off to make her own life. She finds work as a kitchen maid in the royal palace of a neighboring kingdom. There, with the help of her own cleverness and a little magic, she soon catches the eye of the handsome king. *Princess Furball* is a variation of the Cinderella story, retold by Charlotte Huck and illustrated by Anita Lobel.

Robert Louis Stevenson's Treasure Island *is one of the most famous adventure stories of all time—a rousing tale of a boy who gets involved with pirates and a hunt for buried treasure. It has been delighting readers for more than 100 years.*

As a boy, Stevenson himself loved adventure and the sea. But poor health often kept him home, and thus his adventures were limited to reading and imagination. Poor health continued to plague Stevenson for most of his life. But even as an adult, he loved adventure—and he conveyed that love in the stories that he wrote.

Treasure Island *was Stevenson's first novel. It was begun in 1881, while the writer and his family were staying in Scotland. It rained every day, and Stevenson passed some of the time drawing and painting with his young stepson, Lloyd Osbourne. One day Stevenson drew a watercolor map of an imaginary island, complete with places named after pirates and clues to buried treasure. He then began to make up a story to go along with the map. Each morning Stevenson wrote; after lunch, he read what he had written to the family.*

A friend who came to visit heard the tale and urged Stevenson to publish it. The author later finished the story on a visit to Switzerland, and it was published in serial form in Young Folks, *a magazine for young people. In 1883, it appeared in book form.* Treasure Island *soon became a classic. It has been translated into many languages and filmed several times.*

The hero and narrator of Treasure Island *is Jim Hawkins, the son of an innkeeper. His adventure begins when Billy Bones, a pirate, comes to stay at the inn and dies in frightening circumstances. Jim and his mother search the pirate's chest for money that he owed them and find a map—a treasure map, showing the burial place of the treasure of the notorious pirate Captain Flint. Jim narrowly escapes a group of Flint's men who are after the map, and he takes it to the leading men of the district, Squire Trelawney and Dr. Livesey. They decide to seek the treasure. They charter the schooner* Hispaniola, *and Jim is to go along as cabin boy. The excerpt that follows begins as the* Hispaniola *is about to set sail. The ship's captain has doubts about some of the crew—with good reason, as it turns out. But no one suspects the jovial, peg-legged ship's cook, Long John Silver. (If you come across terms you don't know, check the glossary on the last page.)*

TREASURE ISLAND

The Voyage of the *Hispaniola*

All night we were in a great bustle getting things stowed in their place, and boatfuls of the squire's friends came to wish him a good voyage and a safe return.

We never had a night at the "Admiral Benbow Inn" when I had half the work; and I was dog-tired when, a little before dawn, the boatswain sounded his pipe, and the crew began to man the capstan-bars. I might have been twice as weary, yet I could not have left the deck; all was so new and interesting to me—the brief commands, the shrill note of the whistle, the men bustling to their places in the glimmer of the ship's lanterns.

Long John, who was standing by, with his crutch under his arm, at once broke out in the air and words I knew so well:

"Fifteen men on the Dead Man's Chest—"

And then the whole crew bore chorus:

"Yo-ho-ho, and a bottle of rum!"

Even at that exciting moment it carried me back to the old "Admiral Benbow" in a second; and I seemed to hear the voice of the captain piping in the chorus. But soon the anchor was short up; soon it was hanging dripping at the bows; soon the sails began to draw, and the land and shipping to flit by on either side. And before I could lie down to snatch an hour of slumber the *Hispaniola* had begun her voyage to the Isle of Treasure.

I am not going to relate that voyage in detail. It was fairly prosperous. The ship proved to be a good ship, the crew were capable seamen, and the captain thoroughly understood his business. But before we came the length of Treasure Island, two or three things had happened which require to be known.

Mr. Arrow, the mate, turned out even worse than the captain had feared. He had no command among the men, and people did what they pleased with him. But that was by no means the worst of it; for after a day or two at sea he began to appear on deck with hazy eye, red cheeks, stuttering tongue, and other marks of drunkenness. Time after time he was ordered below in disgrace. Sometimes he fell and cut himself; sometimes he lay all day long in his little bunk at one side of the companion; sometimes for a day or two he could be almost sober and attend to his work at least passably.

In the meantime we could never make out where he got the drink. That was the ship's mystery. Watch him as we pleased, we could do nothing to solve it; and when we asked him to his face, he would only laugh, if he were drunk, and if he were sober, deny solemnly that he ever tasted anything but water.

He was not only useless as an officer and a bad influence amongst the men, but it was plain at this rate he would soon kill himself outright; so nobody was much surprised, nor very sorry, when one dark night, with a head sea, he disappeared entirely and was seen no more.

"Overboard!" said the captain. "Well, gentlemen, that saves the trouble of putting him in irons."

But there we were, without a mate; and it was necessary, of course, to advance one of the men. The boatswain, Job Anderson, was the likeliest man aboard, and, though he kept his old title, he served in a way as mate. Mr. Trelawney had followed the sea, and his knowledge made him very useful, for he often took a watch himself in easy weather. And the coxswain, Israel Hands, was a careful, wily, old, experienced seaman who could be trusted at a pinch with almost anything.

He was a great confidant of Long John Silver, and so the mention of his name leads me on to speak of our ship's cook, Barbecue, as the men called him.

Aboard ship he carried his crutch by a lanyard round his neck, to have both hands as free as possible. It was something to see him wedge the foot of the crutch against a bulkhead, and, propped against it, yielding to every movement of the ship, get on with his cooking like some one safe ashore. Still more strange was it to see him in the heaviest of weather cross the deck. He had a line or two rigged up to help him across the widest spaces—Long John's earrings, they were called; and he would hand himself from one place to another, now using the crutch, now trailing it alongside by the lanyard, as quickly as another man could walk. Yet some of the men who had sailed with him before expressed their pity to see him so reduced.

"He's no common man, Barbecue," said the coxswain to me. "He had good schooling in his young days and can speak like a book when so minded; and brave—a lion's nothing alongside of Long John! I seen him grapple four, and knock their heads together—him unarmed."

All the crew respected and even obeyed him. He had a way of talking to each, and doing everybody some particular service. To me he was unweariedly kind; and always glad to see me in the galley, which he kept as clean as a new pin; the dishes hanging up burnished, and his parrot in a cage in one corner.

294

"Come away, Hawkins," he would say, "come and have a yarn with John. Nobody more welcome than yourself, my son. Sit you down and hear the news. Here's Cap'n Flint—I calls my parrot Cap'n Flint, after the famous buccaneer—here's Cap'n Flint predicting success to our voyage. Wasn't you, Cap'n?"

And the parrot would say, with great rapidity, "Pieces of eight! pieces of eight! pieces of eight!" till you wondered that it was not out of breath, or till John threw his handkerchief over the cage.

"Now, that bird," he would say, "is maybe two hundred years old, Hawkins—they lives forever mostly; and if anybody's seen more wickedness it must be the devil himself. She's sailed with great Cap'n England, the pirate. She's been at Madagascar, and at Malabar, and Surinam, and Providence, and Portobello. She was at the fishing up of the wrecked plate ships. It's there she learned 'Pieces of eight,' and little wonder; three hundred and fifty thousand of 'em, Hawkins! She was at the boarding of the *Viceroy of the Indies* out of Goa, she was; and to look at her you would think she was a babby. But you smelt powder—didn't you, Cap'n?"

"Stand by to go about," the parrot would scream. "Ah, she's a handsome craft, she is," the cook would say, and give her sugar from his pocket, and then the bird would peck at the bars and swear straight on, passing belief for wickedness. "There," John would add, "you can't touch pitch and not be mucked, lad. Here's this poor old innocent bird o' mine swearing blue fire, and none the wiser, you may lay to that. She would swear the same, in a manner of speaking, before chaplain.'' And John would touch his forelock with a solemn way he had, that made me think he was the best of men.

In the meantime, the squire and Captain Smollett were still on pretty distant terms with one another. The squire made no bones about the matter; he despised the captain. The captain, on his part, never spoke but when he was spoken to, and then sharp and short and dry, and not a word wasted. He owned, when driven into a corner, that he seemed to have been wrong about the crew, that some of them were as brisk as he wanted to see, and all had behaved fairly well. As for the ship, he had taken a downright fancy to her. ''She'll lie a point nearer the wind than a man has a right to expect of his own married wife, sir. But,'' he would add, ''all I say is we're not home again, and I don't like the cruise.''

The squire, at this, would turn away and march up and down the deck, chin in air.

''A trifle more of that man,'' he would say, ''and I shall explode.''

We had some heavy weather, which only proved the qualities of the *Hispaniola*. Every man on board seemed well content, and they must have been hard to please if they had been otherwise; for it was my belief there was never a ship's company so spoiled since Noah put to sea. Double grog was going on the least excuse; there was duff on odd days, as, for instance, if the squire heard it was any man's birthday; and always a barrel of apples for any one to help himself that had a fancy.

''Never knew good come of it yet,'' the captain said to Dr. Livesey. ''Spoil fo'c'sle hands, make devils. That's my belief.''

But good did come of the apple barrel, as you shall hear; for if it had not been for that, we should have had no note of warning, and might all have perished by the hand of treachery.

This was how it came about:

We had run up the trades to get the wind of the island we were after —I am not allowed to be more plain—and now we were running down for it with a bright lookout day and night. It was about the last day of our outward voyage, by the largest computation. Some time that night, or, at latest, before noon of the morrow, we should sight the Treasure Island. We were heading S.S.W., and had a steady breeze abeam and a quiet sea. The *Hispaniola* rolled steadily, dipping her bowsprit now and then with a whiff of spray. All was drawing alow and aloft; everyone was in the bravest spirits, because we were now so near an end of the first part of our adventure.

Now, just after sundown, when all my work was over and I was on my way to my berth, it occurred to me that I should like an apple. I ran on deck. The watch was all forward looking out for the island. The man at the helm was watching the luff of the sail, and whistling away gently to himself; and that was the only sound excepting the swish of the sea against the bows and around the sides of the ship.

I got bodily into the apple barrel, and found there was scarce an apple left; but, sitting down there in the dark, what with the sound of the waters and the rocking movement of the ship, I had either fallen asleep, or was on the point of doing so when a heavy man sat down with rather a clash close by. The barrel shook as he leaned his shoulders against it, and I was about to jump up when the man began to speak. It was Silver's voice, and, before I had heard a dozen words, I would not have shown myself for all the world, but lay there, trembling and listening, in the extreme of fear and curiosity; for from these dozen words I understood that the lives of all the honest men aboard depended upon me alone.

What I Heard in the Apple Barrel

"No, not I," said Silver. "Flint was cap'n; I was quartermaster, along of my timber leg. The same broadside I lost my leg, old Pew lost his deadlights. It was a master surgeon, him that ampytated me—out of college and all—Latin by the bucket, and what not; but he was hanged like a dog, and sun-dried like the rest, at Corso Castle. That was Robert's men, that was, and comed of changing names to their ships—*Royal Fortune* and so on. Now, what a ship was christened, so let her stay, I says. So it was with the *Cassandra*, as brought us all safe home from Malabar, after England took the *Viceroy of the Indies;* so it was with the old *Walrus*, Flint's old ship, as I've seen-a-muck with the red blood and fit to sink with gold."

"Ah!" cried another voice, that of the youngest hand on board, and evidently full of admiration, "for he was the flower of the flock, was Flint!"

"Davis was a man, too, by all accounts," said Silver. "I never sailed along of him; first with England, then with Flint, that's my story; and now here on my own account, in a manner of speaking. I laid by nine hundred safe from England, and two thousand after Flint. That ain't bad for a man before the mast—all safe in bank. 'Tain't earning now, it's saving does it, you may lay to that. Where's all England's men now? I dunno. Where's Flint's? Why, most on 'em aboard here. Old Pew, as has lost his sight, spends twelve hundred pound in a year, like a lord in Parliament. Where is he now? Well, he's dead now and under hatches; but for two years before that, shiver my timbers! the man was starving. He begged, and he stole, and he cut throats, and starved at that, by the powers!"

"Well, it ain't much use, after all," said the young seaman.

" 'Tain't much use for fools, you may lay to it—that, nor nothing," cried Silver. "But now, you look here; you're young you are, but you're as smart as paint. I see that when I set my eyes on you, and I'll talk to you like a man."

You may imagine how I felt when I heard this abominable old rogue

addressing another in the very same words of flattery as he had used to myself. I think, if I had been able, that I would have killed him through the barrel. Meantime, he ran on, little supposing he was overheard.

"Here it is about gentlemen of fortune. They lives rough, and they risk swinging, but they eat and drink like fighting-cocks, and when a cruise is done, why it's hundreds of pounds instead of hundreds of farthings in their pockets. Now, the most goes for rum and a good fling, and to sea again in their shirts. But that's not the course I lay. I puts it all away, some here, some there, and none too much anywheres, by reason of suspicion. I'm fifty, mark you; once back from this cruise I set up gentleman in earnest. Time enough, too, says you. Ah, but I've lived easy in the meantime; never denied myself o' nothing heart desires, and slep' soft and ate dainty all my days, but when at sea. And how did I begin? Before the mast, like you!"

"Well," said the other, "but all the other money's gone now, ain't it? You daren't show face in Bristol after this."

"Why, where might you suppose it was?" asked Silver, derisively.

"At Bristol, in banks and places," answered his companion.

"It were," said the cook; "it were when we weighed anchor. But my old missis has it all by now. I would tell you where, for I trust you; but it 'u'd make jealousy among the mates.''

"And can you trust your missis?" asked the other.

"Gentlemen of fortune," returned the cook, "usually trusts little among themselves, and right they are, you may lay to it. But I have a way with me, I have. When a mate brings a slip on his cable—one as knows me, I mean—it won't be in the same world with Old John. There was some that was feared of Pew, and some that was feared of Flint; but Flint his own self was feared of me. Feared he was, and proud. They was the roughest crew afloat, was Flint's; the devil himself would have been feared to go to sea with them. Well, now, I tell you, I'm not a boasting man, and you seen yourself how easy I keep company; but when I was quartermaster, *lambs* wasn't the word for Flint's old buccaneers. Ah, you may be sure of yourself in old John's ship.''

"Well, I tell you now," replied the lad, "I didn't half a quarter like the job till I had this talk with you, John; but there's my hand on it now.''

"And a brave lad you are, and smart, too," answered Silver shaking hands so heartily that the barrel shook, "and a finer figurehead for a gentleman of fortune I never clapped my eyes on.''

By this time I had begun to understand the meaning of their terms. By a "gentleman of fortune" they plainly meant neither more nor less than a common pirate, and the little scene that I had overheard was the last act in the corruption of one of the honest hands—perhaps of the last one left aboard. But on this point I was soon to be relieved, for, Silver giving a little whistle, a third man strolled up and sat down by the party.

"Dick's square," said Silver.

"Oh, I know'd Dick was square," returned the voice of the coxswain, Israel Hands. "He's no fool, is Dick." And he turned his

quid and spat. "But look here," he went on, "here's what I want to know, Barbecue: how long are we a-going to stand off and on? I've had a'most enough o' Cap'n Smollett; he's hazed me long enough, by thunder! I want to go into that cabin, I do. I want their pickles and wines, and that."

"Israel," said Silver, "your head ain't much account, nor ever was. But you're able to hear, I reckon; leastways, your ears is big enough. Now, here's what I say: you'll berth forward, and you'll live hard, and you'll speak soft, and you'll keep sober, till I give the word; and you may lay to that, my son."

"Well, I don't say no, do I?" growled the coxswain. "What I say is, when? That's all I say."

"When! by the powers!" cried Silver. "Well, now if you want to know, I'll tell you when. The last moment I can manage; and that's when. Here's a first-rate seaman, Cap'n Smollett, sails the blessed ship for us. Here's this squire and doctor with a map and such—I don't know where it is, do I? No more do you, says you. Well then, I mean this squire and doctor shall find the stuff, and help us to get it aboard, by the powers! Then we'll see. If I was sure of you all, sons of double Dutchmen, I'd have Cap'n Smollett navigate us half-way back again before I struck."

"Why, we're all seamen aboard here, I should think!" said the lad Dick.

"We're all fo'c'sle hands, you mean," snapped Silver. "We can steer a course, but who's to set one? That's what all you gentlemen split on, first and last. If I had my way I'd have Cap'n Smollett work us back into the trades at least; then we'd have no blessed miscalculations and a spoonful of water a day. But I know the sort you are. I'll finish with 'em at the island, as soon's the blunt's on board, and a pity it is. But you're never happy till you're drunk. Slit my sides, I've a sick heart to sail with the likes of you!"

"Easy all, Long John," cried Israel. "Who's a-crossin' of you?"

"Why, how many tall ships, think ye, have I seen laid aboard? and how many brisk lads drying in the sun at Execution Dock?" cried Silver, "and all for this same hurry and hurry and hurry. You hear me? I seen a thing or two at sea, I have. If you would on'y lay your course, and a p'int to windward, you would ride in carriages, you would. But not you! I know you. You'll have your mouthful of rum tomorrow, and go hang."

"Everybody know'd you was a kind of chapling, John; but there's others as could hand and steer as well as you," said Israel. "They liked a bit o' fun, they did. They wasn't so high and dry, nohow, but took their fling, like jolly companions every one."

"So?" says Silver. "Well, and where are they now? Pew was that sort, and he died a beggar-man. Flint was, and he died of rum at Savannah. Ah, they was a sweet crew, they was! on'y where are they?"

"But," asked Dick, "when we do lay 'em athwart, what are we to do with 'em, anyhow?"

"There's the man for me!" cried the cook, admiringly. "That's what I call business. Well, what would you think? Put 'em ashore like maroons? Or cut 'em down like that much pork?"

"Billy Bones was the man for that," said Israel. " 'Dead men don't bite,' says he. Well he's dead now hisself; he know the long and short on it now; and if ever a rough hand come to port, it was Billy."

"Right you are," said Silver, "rough and ready. But mark you here: I'm an easy man—I'm quite the gentleman, says you; but this time it's serious. Dooty is dooty, mates. I give my vote—death. When I'm in Parlyment, and riding in my coach, I don't want none of these sea-lawyers in the cabin a-coming home, unlooked for, like the devil at prayers. Wait is what I say; but when the time comes, why, let her rip!"

"John," cries the coxswain, "you're a man!"

"You'll say so, Israel, when you see," said Silver. "Only one thing I claim—I claim Trelawney. I'll wring his calf's head off his body with these hands. Dick!" he added, breaking off, "you just jump up, like a sweet lad, and get me an apple, to wet my pipe like."

You may fancy the terror I was in! I should have leaped out and run for it, if I had found the strength; but my limbs and heart alike misgave me. I heard Dick begin to rise, and then some one seemingly stopped him, and the voice of Hands exclaimed:

"Oh, stow that! Don't you get sucking of that bilge, John. Let's have a go of the rum."

"Dick," said Silver, "I trust you. I've a gauge on the keg, mind. There's the key; you fill a pannikin and bring it up."

Terrified as I was, I could not help thinking to myself that this must have been how Mr. Arrow got the strong waters that destroyed him.

Dick was gone but a little while, and during his absence Israel spoke in the cook's ear. It was but a word or two that I could catch, and yet I gathered some important news, for, besides other scraps that tended to the same purpose, this whole clause was audible: "Not another man of them 'll jine." Hence there were still faithful men on board.

When Dick returned, one after another of the trio took the pannikin and drank—one "To luck"; another with a "Here's to old Flint"; and Silver himself saying, in a kind of song, "Here's to ourselves!"

Just then a sort of brightness fell upon me in the barrel and, looking up, I found the moon had risen, and was silvering the mizzen-top and shining white on the luff of the foresail; and almost at the same time the voice of the lookout shouted, "Land ho!"

Council of War

There was a great rush of feet across the deck. I could hear people tumbling up from the cabin and the fo'c'sle; and, slipping in an instant outside my barrel, I dived behind the foresail, made a double toward the stern, and came out upon the open deck in time to join Hunter and Dr. Livesey in the rush for the weather bow.

There all hands were already congregated. A belt of fog had lifted almost simultaneously with the appearance of the moon. Away to the southwest of us we saw two low hills, about a couple of miles apart, and rising behind one of them a third and higher hill, whose peak was still buried in the fog. All three seemed sharp and conical in figure.

So much I saw, almost in a dream, for I had not yet recovered from my horrid fear of a minute or two before, and then I heard the voice of Captain Smollett issuing orders. The *Hispaniola* was laid a couple of points nearer the wind, and now sailed a course that would just clear the island on the east.

"And now, men," said the captain, when all was sheeted home, "has any one of you ever seen that land ahead?"

"I have, sir," said Silver. "I've watered there with a trader I was cook in."

"The anchorage is on the south, behind an islet, I fancy?" asked the captain.

"Yes, sir; Skeleton Island they calls it. It were a main place for pirates once, and a hand we had on board knowed all their names for it. That hill to the nor'ard they calls the Fore-mast Hill; there are three hills in a row running south'ard— fore, main, and mizzen, sir. But the main—that's the big 'un with the cloud on it—they usually calls the Spy-glass, by reason of a lookout they kept when they was in the anchorage cleaning; for it's there they cleaned their ships, sir, asking your pardon."

"I have a chart here," says Captain Smollett. "See if that's the place."

Long John's eyes burned in his head as he took the chart; but, by the fresh look of the paper, I knew he was doomed to disappointment. This was not the map we had found in Billy Bones's chest, but an accurate copy, complete in all things—names and heights and soundings—with the single exception of the red crosses and the written notes. Sharp as must have been his annoyance, Silver had the strength of mind to hide it.

"Yes sir," said he, "this is the spot, to be sure; and very prettily drawn out. Who might have done that, I wonder? The pirates were too ignorant, I reckon. Ay, here it is: 'Capt. Kidd's Anchorage'—just the name my shipmate called it. There's a strong current runs along the south, and then away nor'ard up the west coast. Right you was, sir," says he, "to haul your wind and keep the weather of the island. Leastways, if such was your intention as to enter and careen, and there ain't no better place for that in these waters."

"Thank you, my man," says Captain Smollett. "I'll ask you, later on, to give us a help. You may go."

I was surprised at the coolness with which John avowed his knowledge of the island; and I own I was half frightened when I saw him drawing nearer to myself. He did not know, to be sure, that I had overheard his council from the apple barrel, and yet I had, by this time, taken such a horror of his cruelty, duplicity, and power, that I could scarce conceal a shudder when he laid his hand upon my arm.

"Ah," says he, "this here is a sweet spot, this island—a sweet spot for a lad to get ashore on. You'll bathe, and you'll climb trees, and you'll hunt goats, you will; and you'll get aloft on them hills like a goat yourself. Why, it makes me young again. I was going to forget my timber leg, I was. It's a pleasant thing to be young, and have ten toes, and you may lay to that. When you want to go a bit of exploring, you just ask old John, and he'll put up a snack for you to take along."

And clapping me in the friendliest way upon the shoulder, he hobbled off forward, and went below.

Captain Smollett, the squire, and Dr. Livesey were talking together on the quarter-deck, and, anxious as I was to tell them my story, I dared not interrupt them openly. While I was still casting about in my thoughts to find some probable excuse, Dr. Livesey called me to his side. He had left his pipe below, and being a slave to tobacco, had meant that I should fetch it; but as soon as I was near enough to speak and not be overheard, I broke out immediately:—"Doctor, let me speak. Get the captain and squire down to the cabin, and then make some pretense to send for me. I have terrible news."

The doctor changed countenance a little, but next moment he was master of himself.

"Thank you, Jim," said he, quite loudly, "that was all I wanted to know," as if he had asked me a question.

And with that he turned on his heel and rejoined the other two. They spoke together for a little, and though none of them started, or raised his voice, or so much as whistled, it was plain enough that Dr. Livesey had communicated my request; for the next thing that I heard was the captain giving an order to Job Anderson, and all hands were piped on deck.

"My lads," said Captain Smollett, "I've a word to say to you. This land that we have sighted is the place we have been sailing for. Mr. Trelawney, being a very open-handed gentleman, as we all know, has just asked me a word or two, and as I was able to tell him that every man on board had done his duty, alow and aloft, as I never ask to see it done better, why, he and I and the doctor are going below to the cabin to drink *your* health and luck, and you'll have grog served out for you to drink *our* health and luck. I'll tell you what I think of this: I think it handsome. And if you think as I do, you'll give a good sea cheer for the gentleman that does it.''

The cheer followed—that was a matter of course; but it rang out so full and hearty that I confess I could hardly believe these same men were plotting for our blood.

''One more cheer for Cap'n Smollett,'' cried Long John, when the first had subsided.

And this also was given with a will.

On the top of that the three gentlemen went below, and not long after, word was sent forward that Jim Hawkins was wanted in the cabin.

I found them all three seated round the table, the doctor smoking away, with his wig on his lap, and that I knew was a sign that he was agitated. The stern window was open, for it was a warm night, and you could see the moon shining behind on the ship's wake.

''Now, Hawkins,'' said the squire, ''you have something to say. Speak up.''

I did as I was bid, and as short as I could make it, told the whole details of Silver's conversation. Nobody interrupted me till I was done, nor did any one of the three of them make so much as a movement, but they kept their eyes on my face from first to last.

''Jim,'' said Dr. Livesey, ''take a seat.'' And they made me sit down at the table beside them, and all three, one after the other, and each with a bow, drank to my good health, and their service to me, for my luck and courage.

''Now, captain,'' said the squire, ''you were right, and I was wrong. I own myself an ass, and I await your orders.''

''No more an ass than I, sir,'' returned the captain. ''I never heard of a crew that meant to mutiny but what showed signs before, for any man that had an eye in his head to see the mischief and take steps according. But this crew,'' he added, ''beats me.''

''Captain,'' said the doctor, ''with your permission, that's Silver. A very remarkable man.''

''He'd look remarkably well from a yard-arm sir,'' returned the captain. ''But this is talk; this don't lead to anything. I see three or four points, and with Mr. Trelawney's permission, I'll name them.''

''You, sir, are the captain. It is for you to speak,'' says Mr. Trelawney, grandly.

''First point,'' began Mr. Smollett. ''We must go on, because we can't turn back. If I gave the word to go about, they would rise at once. Second point, we have time before us—at least, until this treasure's found. Third point, there are faithful hands. Now sir, it's got to come to blows sooner or later; and what I propose is, to take time by the forelocks, as the saying is, and come to blows some fine day when they least expect it.''

"Jim, here,'' said the doctor,''can help us more than anyone. The men are not shy with him, and Jim is a noticing lad.''

"Hawkins, I put prodigious faith in you,'' added the squire.

I began to feel pretty desperate at this, for I felt altogether helpless; and yet, by an odd train of circumstances, it was indeed through me that safety came. In the meantime, talk as we pleased, there were only seven out of the twenty-six on whom we knew we could rely; and out of these seven one was a boy, so that the grown men on our side were six to their nineteen.

You will have to read the rest of the book to find out what happens!

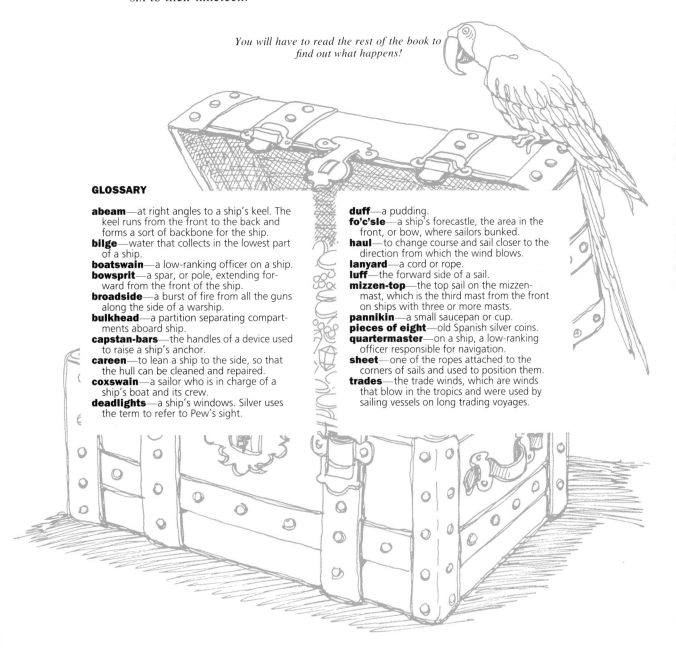

GLOSSARY

abeam—at right angles to a ship's keel. The keel runs from the front to the back and forms a sort of backbone for the ship.

bilge—water that collects in the lowest part of a ship.

boatswain—a low-ranking officer on a ship.

bowsprit—a spar, or pole, extending forward from the front of the ship.

broadside—a burst of fire from all the guns along the side of a warship.

bulkhead—a partition separating compartments aboard ship.

capstan-bars—the handles of a device used to raise a ship's anchor.

careen—to lean a ship to the side, so that the hull can be cleaned and repaired.

coxswain—a sailor who is in charge of a ship's boat and its crew.

deadlights—a ship's windows. Silver uses the term to refer to Pew's sight.

duff—a pudding.

fo'c'sle—a ship's forecastle, the area in the front, or bow, where sailors bunked.

haul—to change course and sail closer to the direction from which the wind blows.

lanyard—a cord or rope.

luff—the forward side of a sail.

mizzen-top—the top sail on the mizzenmast, which is the third mast from the front on ships with three or more masts.

pannikin—a small saucepan or cup.

pieces of eight—old Spanish silver coins.

quartermaster—on a ship, a low-ranking officer responsible for navigation.

sheet—one of the ropes attached to the corners of sails and used to position them.

trades—the trade winds, which are winds that blow in the tropics and were used by sailing vessels on long trading voyages.

POETRY

THE DAFFODILS

I wandered lonely as a cloud
   That floats on high o'er vales and hills,
When all at once I saw a crowd,
   A host of golden daffodils;
Beside the lake, beneath the trees,
Fluttering and dancing in the breeze.

Continuous as the stars that shine
   And twinkle on the milky way,
They stretched in never-ending line
   Along the margin of a bay:
Ten thousand saw I at a glance,
Tossing their heads in sprightly dance.

The waves beside them danced, but they
   Outdid the sparkling waves in glee:
A poet could not but be gay,
   In such a jocund company:
I gazed—and gazed—but little thought
What wealth the show to me had brought:

For oft when on my couch I lie
   In vacant or in pensive mood,
They flash upon that inward eye
   Which is the bliss of solitude,
And then my heart with pleasure fills
And dances with the daffodils.

WILLIAM WORDSWORTH (1770–1850)

THE GRASSHOPPER AND THE CRICKET

The poetry of earth is never dead:
When all the birds are faint with the hot sun,
And hide in cooling trees, a voice will run
From hedge to hedge about the new-mown mead;
That is the Grasshopper's—he takes the lead
In summer luxury,—he has never done
With his delights; for when tired out with fun
He rests at ease beneath some pleasant weed.

The poetry of earth is ceasing never:
On a lone winter evening, when the frost
Has wrought a silence, from the stove there shrills
The Cricket's song, in warmth increasing ever,
And seems to one in drowsiness half lost,
The Grasshopper's among some grassy hills.

JOHN KEATS (1795–1821)

THE SECRETS OF OUR GARDEN

You think it's only a garden,
   With roses along the wall;
I'll tell you the truth about it—
   It isn't a garden at all!

It's really Robin Hood's forest,
   And over by that big tree
Is the very place where fat Friar Tuck
   Fought with the Miller of Dee.

And back of the barn is the cavern
   Where Rob Roy really hid;
On the other side is a treasure-chest
   That belonged to Captain Kidd.

That isn't the pond you see there,
   It's an ocean deep and wide,
Where six-masted ships are waiting
   To sail on the rising tide.

Of course it looks like a garden,
   It's all so sunny and clear—
You'd be surprised if you really knew
   The things that have happened here!

RUPERT SARGENT HOLLAND (1878–1952)

A GENTLE WIND

A gentle wind fans the calm night:
A bright moon shines on the high tower.
A voice whispers, but no one answers when I call:
A shadow stirs, but no one comes when I beckon,
The kitchen-man brings in a dish of lentils:
Wine is there, but I do not fill my cup.
Contentment with poverty is Fortune's best gift:
Riches and Honor are the handmaids of Disaster.
Though gold and gems by the world are sought and prized,
To me they seem no more than weeds or chaff.

FU HSÜAN (3RD CENTURY)

THE CAMEL'S COMPLAINT

Canary-birds feed on sugar and seed,
　Parrots have crackers to crunch;
And as for the poodles, they tell me the noodles
　Have chicken and cream for their lunch.
　　But there's never a question
　　About *my* digestion—
　　　Anything does for me.

Cats, you're aware, can repose in a chair,
　Chickens can roost upon rails;
Puppies are able to sleep in a stable,
　And oysters can slumber in pails.
　　But no one supposes
　　A poor camel dozes—
　　　Any place does for me.

Lambs are enclosed where it's never exposed,
　Coops are constructed for hens;
Kittens are treated to houses well heated,
　And pigs are protected by pens.
　　But a camel comes handy
　　Wherever it's sandy—
　　　Anywhere does for me.

People would laugh if you rode a giraffe,
　Or mounted the back of an ox;
It's nobody's habit to ride on a rabbit,
　Or try to bestraddle a fox.
　　But as for a camel, he's
　　Ridden by families—
　　　Any load does for me.

A snake is as round as a hole in the ground,
　And weasels are wavy and sleek;
And no alligator could ever be straighter
　Than lizards that live in a creek.
　　But a camel's all lumpy
　　And bumpy and humpy—
　　　Any shape does for me.

CHARLES E. CARRYL (1841—1920)

A LANE

From house to house he goes
A messenger small and slight;
And whether it rains or snows
He sleeps outside in the night.

UNKNOWN

MONDAY'S CHILD IS FAIR OF FACE

Monday's child is fair of face,
Tuesday's child is full of grace,
Wednesday's child is full of woe,
Thursday's child has far to go,
Friday's child is loving and giving,
Saturday's child works hard for its living,
And a child that is born on the Sabbath day
Is fair and wise and good and gay.

UNKNOWN

little wildrose

There once lived an old man and an old woman. Now they had been very happy all their years together, but they would have been happier still if they had had children. Often they would sit beside the fire and talk of how they would have brought up their children if only some had come to bless their house.

One day the old man seemed more thoughtful than usual, and at last he said to his wife, "Listen to me, old woman! I am going on a long journey—all around the world—to see if I can find a child. For my heart aches to think that when we die, our house will fall into the hands of a stranger." Then he filled a bag with food and money and bade his wife farewell.

The old man wandered and wandered and wandered, but no child did he see. One morning his wanderings led him to a forest that was so thick with trees that no light could pass through the branches. The old man stopped when he saw this dreadful place, but summoning up all his courage he plunged boldly in.

After walking a long distance, he at last came to the mouth of a cave where the darkness seemed a hundred times darker than even the woods. And with a pounding heart he entered.

For some minutes the silence and darkness so overwhelmed him that he stood where he was, not daring to move even one step. Then he made a great effort and went on a few paces, and suddenly, far before him, he saw a glimmer of light. He walked straight toward the faint rays until he could just barely see an old hermit with a long white beard. He cautiously approached him and said, "Good morning, wise father!"

"My son," whispered the hermit, in a voice that echoed through the cavern, "what brings you to this dark and dismal place? Hundreds of years have passed since my eyes have looked on the face of a man, and I did not think to ever look on one again."

"My misery has brought me here," replied the old man. "I have no child, and all our lives my wife and I have longed for one. So I left my home and went out into the world, hoping that somewhere I might find what I am seeking."

Then the hermit picked up an apple from the ground and gave it to him, saying, "Eat half of this apple and give the rest to your wife, and cease wandering throughout the world."

The old man joyously thanked the hermit and left the cave. He made his way through the forest as fast as he could and finally arrived in fields filled with flowers, which dazzled him with their brightness. Suddenly he was seized with a desperate thirst. He looked for a stream, but none was to be seen, and his tongue grew more parched every moment.

At last his eyes fell on the apple, which all this while he had been holding in his hand, and in his thirst he forgot what the hermit had told him. So instead of eating merely his own half, he ate the half that was to have been for his wife. And after that he fell asleep.

When he awoke, he saw something strange lying on a bank a little way off, in the middle of long trails of pink roses, and he went to see what it was. To his surprise and joy, it proved to be a little girl about two years old, with skin as pink and white as the roses above her. He took her gently in his arms, but she did not seem at all frightened and cooed with delight. The old man wrapped his cloak around her and set off for home as fast as his legs would carry him.

When they were close to the cottage where he lived, he placed the child in a basket that was sitting near the door and ran into the house crying, ''Come quickly, wife, for I have brought you a daughter, with hair of gold and eyes like stars!''

At this wonderful news the old woman flew downstairs, almost tumbling down in her eagerness to see the treasure. But when her husband led her to the basket, it was completely empty! The old man was nearly beside himself with horror, while his wife sat down and sobbed with grief and disappointment.

They searched everywhere, thinking that somehow the child might have gotten out of the basket and was hiding. But the little girl was nowhere to be found.

"Oh, where can she be?" moaned the old man in despair. "Why did I ever leave her, even for a moment? Have the fairies taken her or has some wild beast carried her off?"

And they began their search all over again, but neither fairies nor wild beasts did they meet. So with sore hearts they gave up and turned sadly into their cottage.

And what had become of the baby? Well, finding herself left alone in a strange place she began to cry with fright, and an eagle hovering above heard her and went to see what the sound was. When he beheld the fat pink and white creature he thought of his hungry little ones at home, and swooping down he caught her up in his claws and was soon flying with her over the tops of the trees. In a few minutes he reached the one in which he had built his nest, and laying little Wildrose (for so the old man had named her) among his downy young eaglets, he flew away.

The eaglets naturally were rather surprised at this strange animal, so unexpectedly dropped down in their midst. But instead of eating her, as their father had thought, they nestled up close to her and spread out their tiny wings to shield her from the sun.

Now, in the depths of the forest where the eagle had built his nest, there ran a stream whose waters were poisonous. And on the banks of this stream there lived a horrible serpent with two heads. The serpent had often watched the eagle flying overhead, carrying food to his young ones. And he carefully awaited the moment when the eaglets would begin to try their wings and fly away from the nest.

Of course, if the eagle himself were there to protect them, even the serpent, big and strong as he was, knew he could do nothing. But when the eagle was absent, any little eaglets that ventured too near the ground would be sure to disappear down the monster's throat.

That very day, the serpent was so hungry that he could not wait any longer for his supper, and he came out of the stream with a rushing noise and made straight for the tree. Four eyes of flame came creeping nearer and nearer, and two fiery tongues were stretching out closer and closer to the little birds who were trembling in the farthest corner of the nest. But just as the tongues had almost reached them, the serpent gave a fearful cry and turned and fell backward.

Then came the sound of battle from the ground below, and there were such roars and snarls that the eaglets were more frightened than ever and thought their last hour had come. Only Wildrose was undisturbed and slept sweetly through it all.

When the eagle returned, he saw traces of the fight below the tree. He hastened to his nest and asked happily, "Who has slain the serpent?" The eaglets answered that they did not know, only that they had been in danger of their lives and at the last moment had been saved. Then a sunbeam struggled through the thick branches of the tree and caught Wildrose's golden hair as she lay curled up in the corner. And as the eagle looked, he wondered whether the little girl had brought him luck and if it was her magic that had killed his enemy.

From that day, Wildrose lived like a little princess. The eagle flew about the wood and collected the softest, greenest moss he could find to make her a bed. And he picked all the brightest and prettiest flowers in the fields to decorate it. And when the eaglets were able to fly from their nest, he taught them where to look for the fruits and berries that she loved.

So the time passed by. With each year Wildrose grew taller and lovelier, and she lived happily in her nest and never wanted to leave. She was content to just stand at the edge of the treetops in the sunset, looking upon the beautiful world. For company she had all the birds in the forest, who came and talked to her. For playthings she had all the strange flowers that the birds brought her from afar, and the butterflies that danced with her. And so the days slipped away and she was sixteen years old.

One morning the king's son went out to hunt, and he had not ridden far before a deer darted out from under a grove of trees and ran before him. The prince instantly gave chase, and where the stag led he followed until at length he found himself in the depths of the forest.

The trees were so thick and the woods so dark that he paused for a moment and listened, straining to catch some sound to break the silence. But there was nothing. He stood still, wondering if he should go on, when he noticed a beam of light flowing through the top of a tall tree. In its rays he could see the nest with the young eaglets, who were watching him over the side.

The prince fitted an arrow into his bow and took aim, but before he could let fly, another ray of light dazzled him. So brilliant was it that his bow dropped and he covered his face with his hands. When at last he ventured to peek, Wildrose, with her golden hair flowing around her, was looking at him. This was the first time that she had ever seen a man.

"Tell me how I can reach you," he cried. But Wildrose smiled and shook her head, and sat down quietly.

The prince saw that it was no use, and he turned and made his way out of the forest. But so strong was his longing for Wildrose that he twice returned to the forest in the hope of finding her. But fortune failed him and he went home as sad as ever.

At length the king sent for his son and asked him what was causing his unhappiness. The prince confessed that the image of Wildrose filled his soul and that he would never be happy without her. At first the king felt rather distressed. He doubted whether a girl from a treetop would make a good queen. But he loved his son so much that he promised to do all he could to find her.

So the next morning heralds were sent forth throughout the whole kingdom to inquire if anyone knew where a maiden could be found who lived in a forest on top of a tree. Great riches were promised to anyone who should find her. But nobody knew.

All the girls in the kingdom had their homes on the ground and laughed at the notion of being brought up in a tree. "A nice kind of queen she would make," they said, as the king had done.

The heralds were almost in despair, when an old woman stepped out of the crowd and spoke to them. "I can show you the maiden who lives in the treetops," she said.

But the heralds only laughed and said, "Go away, old witch! You will bring us bad luck." But the old woman stood firm and declared that she alone knew where to find the maiden.

At last the eldest of the heralds said, "The king's orders are clear: whoever knows anything of the maiden is to come at once to court. Put her in the coach and take her with us."

So in this fashion the old woman was brought to court.

"You have declared that you can bring hither the maiden from the wood?" asked the king, who was seated on his throne.

"Yes, Your Majesty, and I will keep my word," said she.

"Then bring her at once," said the king.

"Give me first a kettle and a tripod," said the old woman, and the king ordered them brought instantly. The old woman tucked them under her arm and went on her way. A little distance behind followed the prince and the royal huntsmen. But when they reached the forest, the old woman bade them all wait outside and entered the dark woods by herself.

She stopped underneath the tree where the maiden dwelt, and, gathering some dry sticks, started a fire. Next, she placed the tripod over it and the kettle on top. But something was the matter with the kettle. As fast as the old woman put it where it was to stand, that kettle was sure to roll off. It really seemed bewitched, and no one knows what might have happened if Wildrose, who had been all the time peeking out of her nest, had not lost patience and cried out:

"The tripod won't stand on that hill; you must move it!"

"But where am I to move it to, my child?" asked the old woman, looking up to the nest, and at the same time trying to steady the kettle

with one hand and the tripod with the other.

"Didn't I tell you that it was no good doing that?" said Wildrose, more impatiently than before. "Make a fire near a tree and hang the kettle from one of the branches."

The old woman took the kettle and hung it on a little twig, which immediately broke, and the kettle fell to the ground.

"If you would only show me how to do it, perhaps I should understand," she said.

Quick as a wink, the maiden slid down the smooth trunk of the tree and stood beside the old woman, to teach her how things ought to be done. But in an instant the old woman caught the girl up and swung her over her shoulder. And she ran as fast as she could to the edge of the forest where she had left the prince, who rushed eagerly to meet them.

When Wildrose saw the handsome prince, and came to know how kind and tender he was, she was overjoyed at her new life. She missed her friends in the forest very much, but she visited them often. And one day, not too long after, a wondrous wedding was celebrated in the kingdom. Dressed all in gold, with pearls and diamonds twined in her hair, Wildrose became the wife of the gentle prince. And everyone who saw the bride declared that a perfect queen could only be found on top of a tree!

the end

THE NEW BOOK OF KNOWLEDGE
1991

The following articles are from the 1991 edition of
The New Book of Knowledge. They are included
here to help you keep your encyclopedia up to date.

INCAS

The Incas, an American Indian people, were originally a small tribe in the southern highlands of Peru. In less than a century, during the 1400's, they built one of the largest, most tightly controlled empires the world has ever known. Their skill in government was matched by their feats of engineering. Roads, walls, and irrigation works constructed by the Incas are still in use today.

Spanish conquerors captured the Inca emperor in 1532 and began to break up the empire. But the Indian people of Peru never forgot their Inca heritage. Many, even now, believe that a new Inca emperor will someday arise to restore the glory of their ancestors.

► SOCIAL ORDER

To fully appreciate the Inca achievement, it helps to visualize the difficult terrain of western South America. Along the coast are some of the world's driest deserts. Next to these flat coastal lands rise the jagged peaks of the Andes, whose eastern slopes are covered with rain forests. The native people of this varied region all lived under the rule of a single man, the emperor, addressed as "Chief Inca," "Son of the Sun," and "Lover of the Poor."

The Empire

The basic unit of Inca society was the village, or neighborhood, in which the residents thought of each other as at least distantly related. Marriage was within the neighborhood. Villages, as well as towns with two or more neighborhood units, were grouped into provinces. The empire as a whole was divided into four quarters, with the capital, Cuzco, at the center.

The Emperor. As a supposed descendant of the sun, the "Chief Inca" ruled by divine right. He ate from gold and silver dishes and never wore the same clothes twice. When messengers came before him, he remained hidden behind a screen. Like the pharaohs of Egypt, he took his own sister as his queen.

Established custom guaranteed that the emperor behave responsibly. He attended to the needs of his subjects and, to a limited extent, took part in public activities. When it was time for planting, the emperor himself broke the first clod of earth with his golden spade.

Nobles. The noble class came from Cuzco, home of the original Inca tribe. But as the empire grew, there were not enough nobles to fill all the offices. Men of ability, therefore, were chosen to form a second class of nobles. All men who were nobles, whether of the first

The remains of terraced hillsides and stone walls built by the Incas at Machu Picchu high in the Andes Mountains in southern Peru.

or second class, wore ear ornaments to set them apart from commoners.

The four nobles who governed the four quarters of the empire served as the emperor's council.

Labor Service. Instead of paying taxes, the Inca people performed regularly assigned labor on government lands. The produce of this labor was stored in warehouses and was used by the government, or by the people themselves in time of need.

The Quipu. The Incas kept precise records of what was in each warehouse. They also kept census records, in order to know how much labor service each community could give. Yet they had no writing, not even picture books as did the Aztecs. The Inca records were kept by means of knotted strings, called *quipus* (KEE-poos).

The typical *quipu* had several strings attached to a main string. The group of knots farthest from the main string recorded units; the next group, tens; the next, hundreds; and so forth.

Language. Many different languages were spoken in ancient Peru. The Incas of Cuzco spoke Quechua (KETCH-wah). To unify the empire, they spread the language, and as a result Quechua became, and still is, the most widely spoken Indian language in the Americas.

Colonists and Armies. Another means of strengthening the empire was to make entire communities settle in new locations. Loyal to the emperor, these colonists could keep watch over any newly conquered communities.

Conquest itself was accomplished by imperial troops, armed with stones that were hurled either singly by twirling a sling, or in groups attached to a system of connected strings. A weapon of stones connected in this manner is called a *bola*.

Almost all men, including the emperor, served in the army at one time or another. To be a warrior was every man's ideal.

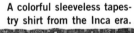

A colorful sleeveless tapestry shirt from the Inca era.

Way of Life

There are many gaps in our knowledge of Inca life. But we do have written accounts from several explorers and missionaries, as well as from two Incas: Garcilaso de la Vega and Waman Puma (Falcon Lion).

From these we know that most Incas lived in villages. Even Cuzco, the capital, was not a large city. Workers who supplied its needs lived in small settlements in the surrounding countryside.

Dress. When Inca people got up in the morning, they did not have to get dressed. They slept in their clothes. Women wore long gowns with a sash at the waist. Men wore loincloths and sleeveless shirts that hung almost to the knees. Both sexes wore sandals and long capes.

Food. The first meal of the day was at eight or nine in the morning. Most dishes were soups or stews. Beans, peppers, tomatoes, peanuts, and sweet manioc were used. But the more important foods were maize (corn) and potatoes. So-called Irish and Idaho potatoes actually originated in ancient Peru. Almost the only meat regularly used was guinea pig.

Work. Men, if they were not on military duty, worked in the fields. Women did spinning and weaving and took care of the home. Often, however, wives helped their husbands with the farming. Since there was no regular schooling (except for the children of nobles), most young people learned adult chores by watching their parents and other adults.

Some workers tended flocks of llamas. The llama, a relative of the camel, provided coarse wool for spinning and was used as a beast of burden. There were no wheeled vehicles, but a llama could carry 100 pounds (45 kilograms).

Shelter. The average house was a one-room structure of stone or mud brick, roofed with thatch. At night the whole family slept together on the floor. There were no mattresses (not even for the emperor). People doubled a huge blanket and crawled inside.

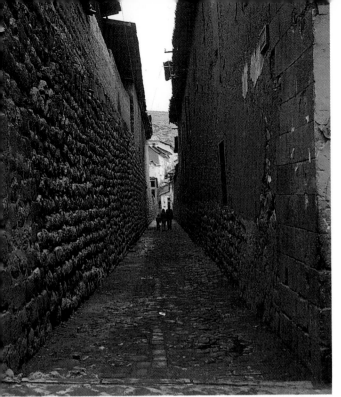

An ancient narrow street in Cuzco, Peru. Note the Inca stone wall on the left.

Religion

The most sacred shrine in Peru was the Temple of the Sun, in Cuzco. There was also a temple dedicated to the god of creation, Viracocha (wee-rah-KOH-chah). Other important deities were the Earth Mother and the spirit called Thunder, or God of the Weather.

People everywhere worshiped their ancestors. Each neighborhood kept a mummy, supposedly of the ancestor from whom all the living were descended. Mummies of the emperors were kept in palaces in Cuzco.

Feasts and the Calendar. The Incas developed an accurate calendar by observing the movements of the sun. By observing the moon, they divided the year into twelve months and planned their major religious feasts accordingly.

A feast celebrating the harvest was held in the month corresponding to May. June marked the great feast of the Sun. Rituals of planting were held in August. Sacrifices of guinea pigs and llamas were required on such occasions. Sometimes human beings were sacrificed.

Crafts and Engineering

The Incas were competent artists, but their works are valued less for beauty than for technical perfection. They are known not so much for sculpture and painting as for weaving, road and bridge construction, and stone masonry.

Textiles. Inca weaving rivaled the best work done in Europe. The finest cloth was a kind of tapestry, finished on both sides, with intricate, colorful designs. This was a woman's craft. Most others were done by men.

Metalwork. The science of metallurgy was more advanced in Peru than anywhere else in the Americas. Deep mining was practiced, as well as a kind of smelting to remove metal from raw ore. Copper and tin were combined to produce bronze, which made stronger weapons and tools. Metalworkers also knew about casting, soldering, and riveting.

Masonry. Stone walls built by Incas were so perfectly fitted that even today a knife blade cannot be inserted in the joints. Stone buildings in Cuzco rose to heights of two and three stories.

Waterworks. Streams were rechanneled to bring in fresh water and carry off sewage. To irrigate fields in the highlands, hillsides were terraced, like the rice paddies of China.

Roads. Roads connected all towns and villages with Cuzco. In the mountains the roads were built with retaining walls, switchbacks, culverts, and tunnels. Swift streams were crossed by suspension bridges.

Along the roads there were post houses, where runners waited to relay messages. Messengers carrying a *quipu* or a small package could travel 150 miles (240 kilometers) a day. It is said that in this way the emperor in Cuzco, high in the mountains, received fresh fish from the sea.

▶ HISTORY

The record of civilization in western South America begins long before the Incas. About A.D. 500 there were great cultures flourishing along the seacoast and in the Andes. On the south coast of Peru the Nazca people produced textiles and colored pottery of much refinement. On the north coast the Moche crafted pottery that portrayed animals, plants, and human faces with a realism never equaled by the later cultures of Peru.

About A.D. 900 a civilization known as Chimu emerged on the north coast. The Chimu, who built a large walled city called Chan Chan, were one of the many peoples conquered by the Inca army in the 1400's.

Rise of the Incas

According to legend, Cuzco was founded by a god-man called Manco Capac, whose father, the Sun, had sent him to civilize the world. From Manco descended a line of rulers known to later generations as emperors. It is doubtful, however, that the first six or seven could have been more than local chiefs.

Under the eighth chief, called Viracocha Inca, the rule of Cuzco was perhaps extended a few miles beyond its home valley. The history of the empire really begins with Viracocha Inca's son, called Pachacuti.

Pachacuti. During the reign of this great leader, the Incas added territory from the present border of Bolivia all the way north to central Ecuador. It was Pachacuti who began many of the imperial policies described above. Under Pachacuti's son, Tupa Inca Yupanqui, the empire was extended southward to central Chile, so that it then spanned a distance of more than 2,500 miles (4,000 kilometers). The eleventh ruler, Huayna Capac, added only small territories in Ecuador and eastern Peru.

Spanish Conquest

When the conqueror Francisco Pizarro arrived in 1532, the Inca Empire was torn by a civil war. Huayna Capac's son Huáscar had been installed as emperor in Cuzco. But another son, Atahualpa, also claimed the throne and marched on Cuzco with his own army.

Taking advantage of the confusion, Pizarro captured Atahualpa. On Atahualpa's orders, Huáscar was murdered. Hoping to free himself, Atahualpa then offered to fill his prison cell with gold. Pizarro agreed, and llama trains began arriving with loads of gold objects. The incredible ransom was paid. But Pizarro had Atahualpa executed nevertheless.

Tupac Amaru. Although the Spaniards seized control of Peru, they could not extinguish the spirit of rebellion. A leader known as Tupac Amaru, last of the royal Incas, established a shadow empire in the eastern mountains and was not conquered until 1572. Two hundred years later another Tupac Amaru led a revolt in the southern highlands. Tupac Amaru II was caught and executed in 1781.

Inca Heritage

Quechua, the language of the Incas, is still widely spoken in Ecuador, Bolivia, and north-

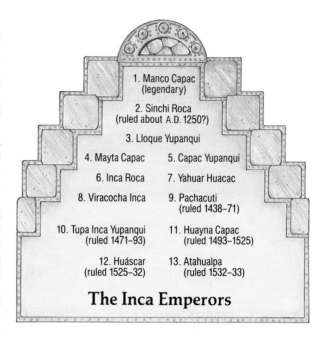

1. Manco Capac (legendary)
2. Sinchi Roca (ruled about A.D. 1250?)
3. Lloque Yupanqui
4. Mayta Capac   5. Capac Yupanqui
6. Inca Roca   7. Yahuar Huacac
8. Viracocha Inca   9. Pachacuti (ruled 1438–71)
10. Tupa Inca Yupanqui (ruled 1471–93)   11. Huayna Capac (ruled 1493–1525)
12. Huáscar (ruled 1525–32)   13. Atahualpa (ruled 1532–33)

The Inca Emperors

west Argentina. In Peru it is the native language of approximately half the population. Most of the Quechua people of Peru live in the highlands. However, in recent years many have migrated to Lima and other coastal cities, where they live in crowded neighborhoods.

Inkarrí. The memory of the Incas remains alive. Modern legends say that an Inca ruler will yet return, bringing a better life for the Quechua. Sometimes this hero is called Amaru (from Tupac Amaru), more often Inkarrí (from Inca and the Spanish word *rey*, meaning king).

In the 1960's and 1970's the Peruvian government took steps to improve conditions for the Quechua people and to give the Inca heritage more prominence in national life. Quechua was made an official language of Peru, together with Spanish. The portrait of Tupac Amaru II appeared on Peruvian paper money. And government officials made speeches to Quechua audiences, proclaiming, "Inkarrí is here!"

At the same time, schoolchildren in Peru were being taught to recite the names of the Inca emperors—the way young people everywhere learn multiplication tables and the alphabet. Some Peruvians can recite all 13 names in a single breath.

JOHN BIERHORST
Author, *The Mythology of South America*

The Road Runner always gets the better of Wile E. Coyote, his hapless pursuer, in a popular series of animated cartoons. Through the technique of animation, imaginary creatures appear to live and move.

ANIMATION

The word "animate" comes from the Latin word *anima*, or soul, and literally means "to give life to." In filmmaking, animation is a technique that makes inanimate (lifeless) drawings or objects appear to live and move. Animation is most often used to make cartoon movies and television shows. It can also be used in television commercials or in educational films. Animation is sometimes used in combination with live action in movies.

Unlike live-action films, which record the movements of living actors, animated films create an illusion of motion. Bugs Bunny never really dove down his rabbit hole, Mickey Mouse never really kissed Minnie, and Gumby never really waved good-bye. The movements of these imaginary creatures occurred only on film.

Because animation is not limited to recording things that really happened, it can show viewers many things that live action cannot, from the movements of a single atom to a view of an entire galaxy. An animated character can fly without wings, fall off a cliff without getting hurt, or be squashed flat as a pancake and pop back into shape. The only limits to what animation can show are the limits of the artist's imagination.

▶ ANIMATION TECHNIQUES

There are two basic types of animation. In one technique, two-dimensional (flat) drawings are animated. The other technique involves the animation of three-dimensional objects such as puppets or clay figures. (A third type of animation, done with computers, is discussed in the box "Computer Animation" on page 322.)

To make an animated film, a series of drawings—or an object placed in a series of positions—is photographed, one picture at a time, by a motion picture camera. In each picture, or **frame**, the subject's position is changed slightly. When the completed film is run, the subject appears to move.

Artists and writers first prepare a **storyboard**, which is an illustrated script. The storyboard looks like a giant comic strip, with sketches showing the action of the story and dialogue (the characters' spoken lines) written under each sketch. Next, the music and the dialogue are recorded. Then the work of animation begins.

Two-Dimensional Animation. The animation of drawings is the technique most often used to create animated films and television shows.

The animators follow a chart listing the length of time and number of frames needed for each word, sound, and action in the entire script. To look smooth and natural, a single action that takes one second of screen time may require as many as 24 drawings. For example, if a script calls for a character to raise his hand, the first picture the animators draw shows the character with his hand at his side. In the next drawing, his hand is raised slightly, and a third drawing shows his hand still higher. Drawing after drawing is made in this way until, in the 24th drawing, the action is completed. More than a million drawings may be used in an animated feature film. Most television cartoons use fewer drawings per second. As a result, the characters' movements may not look as lifelike.

The animators draw every movement of every character that will appear in the film. When the drawings are completed, they are traced onto sheets of clear plastic called **cels**. Colors are then painted on the reverse sides of the cels. Other artists paint the backgrounds in the film. The finished cels are laid over the backgrounds and photographed with a special camera that shoots one frame of film at a time. The camera operator follows a chart that tells the proper sequence of the cels and which background is needed for each frame. The operator takes a picture, removes the cel and replaces it with the next one, then takes another picture. The soundtrack, containing the music, dialogue, and sound effects, is added after the photography is completed.

Some animated films are made without using cels. Instead, the drawings themselves are photographed. Pencil, charcoal, and colored pencil can produce subtle, shaded effects that are very different from the bright colors of the painted cels.

Three-Dimensional Animation. Three-dimensional figures and objects can be animated using a process called **stop-motion photography**. Animators often work with special puppets, which are made of flexible plastic

Below: Three favorite animated characters are Elmer Fudd, Bugs Bunny, and Daffy Duck. *Below right:* In the film *Who Framed Roger Rabbit?*, humans appeared to interact with cartoon characters. *Right:* Animated clay figures enliven a television ad for California raisins.

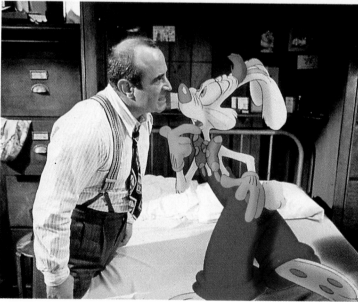

The title character from the computer-animated film *Tin Toy*, which won an Academy Award in 1989.

Computer Animation

Some of the most exciting developments in animation are taking place in the field of computer graphics, in which artists use computers to produce images and animate them. Computer animation is used to create video games and films, as well as graphics and special effects for television and movies.

Computer graphics techniques vary, depending on the kind of equipment and the software (instructions that tell the machine what to do) that are used. But most computer graphics systems have certain features in common.

The inside surface of a computer screen is coated with thousands of tiny dots of light-sensitive chemicals called phosphors. Each dot is called a picture element, or **pixel**. The pixels are arranged in clusters of three, with each pixel responsible for producing one of the three primary colors of light: red, blue, and green. These colors can be combined to produce all the colors an artist might need. Using a computer graphics program, the artist tells the computer which pixels to light up. The glowing pixels create the image on the screen.

The amount of detail in the image depends on the number of pixels on the screen. Most home computer screens have comparatively few pixels, and pictures drawn on them often show little detail. But a powerful computer used by an animator may have millions of pixels on the screen. With these machines it is possible to produce highly detailed images.

Once the artist has produced an image and stored it in the computer, the machine can be instructed to calculate all the slight adjustments in position that are needed to give the appearance of motion. It can also make all the necessary changes in light, shading, and perspective. Each succeeding computer-generated image is photographed and used to make a single frame of film. When the film is run, the effect is one of movement.

Computer animation can be used to create effects that would be difficult or impossible to achieve using drawings. For example, surfaces such as metal, glass, and plastic can be given extremely lifelike textures. For this reason, computer animation is often used to create realistic settings and backgrounds. However, some filmmakers continue to use traditional animation techniques to bring characters to life.

molded around a jointed metal "skeleton." In recent years, figures and objects made of clay have become popular subjects of stop-motion animation.

Using a special motion picture camera, animators film the figure or object. After each frame is photographed, the camera is stopped, and the animators adjust the figure's position slightly. When the film is developed and projected, the figure appears to move.

Stop-motion photography is used to make short animated films and television commercials. It is also used to animate the imaginary creatures that appear in live-action fantasy and science-fiction movies. The giant ape King Kong, as well as some of the creatures in the *Star Wars* series, were animated using stop-motion techniques.

▶ HISTORY OF ANIMATION

The first animated film, *Humorous Phases of Funny Faces*, was made in 1906 by J. Stuart Blackton, an American newspaper illustrator. Blackton filmed a series of faces that had been drawn on a blackboard and also used a variety of other techniques. Another early animated film, *Gertie the Dinosaur*, was created by the American cartoonist Winsor McCay in 1914. In this film, for the first time, a character drawn of lines seemed to live and breathe on the screen.

Audiences liked these animated cartoons. Soon many American film studios were producing animated films, which were shown in movie theaters before the feature films. The Pat Sullivan studio produced one of the most famous characters of the silent-film era, Felix the Cat. The Fleischer studio produced cartoons featuring the character Ko-Ko the Clown and later created Betty Boop, Popeye, and Superman cartoons.

The first successful animated cartoon with sound was *Steamboat Willie* (1928), which introduced the character Mickey Mouse. This film was produced by Walt Disney, who was to become the most famous American producer of animated films. Disney's series of Mickey Mouse cartoons and another series called *Silly Symphonies* were very popular.

The success of his early cartoons enabled Disney to launch an ambitious training program for his artists. They studied anatomy, drawing, acting, and motion to improve their animation. The results of this training can be

Right: Snow White and the Seven Dwarfs, released by the Walt Disney studio in 1937, was the first feature-length animated film made in the United States.

Below: The beloved Disney character Mickey Mouse made his first appearance in 1928 in *Steamboat Willie*, the first successful animated cartoon with sound.

seen in Disney's *Snow White and the Seven Dwarfs* (1937), which was the first feature-length animated film made in the United States. Other important Disney films followed, including *Pinocchio* (1940), *Fantasia* (1940), *Dumbo* (1941), and *Bambi* (1942).

By the end of World War II (1939–45), leadership in the field of animation had passed to two major film studios, Metro-Goldwyn-Mayer (MGM) and Warner Brothers. At MGM, William Hanna and Joseph Barbera made cartoons featuring Tom and Jerry, a cat and a mouse. Warner Brothers cartoons, directed by Tex Avery, Chuck Jones, and Friz Freleng, starred Bugs Bunny, Daffy Duck, and many other characters. These cartoons owed much to the early Disney films, but they were faster-paced, with a slapstick humor. During the 1950's, United Productions of America (UPA) introduced a flat, modernistic drawing style in cartoons featuring Gerald McBoing-Boing and Mr. Magoo.

During the 1960's, television networks began broadcasting children's cartoons on Saturday mornings. Some cartoons were shown in the evenings, during prime time. The most successful television animation studio was Hanna-Barbera, which introduced the Flintstones, the Jetsons, Yogi Bear, and hundreds of other characters.

During the 1980's, feature-length animated films again became popular. *An American Tail* (1986) was the first animated film from the producer Steven Spielberg. The Disney studio released *Oliver and Company* (1988) and *The Little Mermaid* (1989). *Who Framed Roger Rabbit?* (1988), produced jointly by Disney and Spielberg, combined animation with live action. Animation returned to prime-time television with the Fox Network's *The Simpsons*. These developments, along with experiments in computer animation, promised to bring about the most exciting period in animation since its heyday some 50 years earlier.

CHARLES SOLOMON
Author, *Enchanted Drawings: The History of Animation*

INDIA, ART AND ARCHITECTURE OF

From at least 3000 B.C. to the present day, many civilizations have flourished on the subcontinent of India (which includes today's countries of India, Pakistan, and Bangladesh). Each has made valuable contributions to India's rich artistic heritage.

Several of the world's major religions—including Buddhism and Jainism, Hinduism, and Islam—either began in India or flourished there. India has also been home to small communities of Jews, Christians, and Parsis (Persian fire-worshipers who moved to India in the early A.D. 700's). Much Indian art, therefore, has religious content.

► SCULPTURE

The earliest examples of Indian art come from the Indus Valley, an area in present-day Pakistan. The Indus Valley civilization flourished from about 2500 to 1700 B.C. Many small sculptures of metal and clay survive from this period. They usually represent human or animal figures. Other objects include soapstone seals engraved with writing

and animal forms. The seals may have been used to stamp trade goods or as a means of personal identification.

Four larger bronze statues—of a buffalo, a rhinoceros, an elephant, and a bull with chariot driver—have been found near Bombay. They are thought to date from about 1300 B.C.

About 1500 B.C., nomads from the Russian steppes (plains) invaded India. The era that followed is known as the Vedic period, after the religious hymns called Vedas that were brought by the nomads to India. Except for some pottery and metal figures, few works of art remain from the Vedic period.

Buddhist Sculpture. Indian sculpture flourished during the Mauryan dynasty (about 321–184 B.C.). Much of the surviving art is Buddhist. Among the most important monuments of the Mauryan period are large stone pillars that stood at crossroads and important sites. A pillar often had a lotus-shaped top bearing the figure of a lion, a symbol of imperial rule borrowed from Persian art. Many pillars also featured important Indian symbols, including the elephant, the bull, and the lotus itself.

Asoka (Ashoka), the most famous Mauryan ruler, made Buddhism the state religion. But he tolerated the worship of such traditional vil-

Above: A bronze statue from the Chola period depicts the Hindu god Shiva in one of his characteristic forms, as Lord of the Dance. *Right:* A sculpture of a meditating Buddha is among the earliest images showing the god in human form. *Opposite page:* A fragment of a wall painting from the Ajanta caves contains a realistic portrait of a princely couple.

lage gods as yakshas and yakshis, male and female nature spirits. Many larger-than-life stone images of these spirits were made during Asoka's reign, and smaller versions began to be placed on Buddhist monuments.

During the Mauryan period and the following Shunga dynasty, burial mounds (**stupas**) were built. Often, ornately carved gateways surrounded the stupas. Reliefs (raised carvings) on the gateways used symbols rather than a human image to represent Buddha.

During the Kushan dynasty (about A.D. 50–250), Buddhism spread to areas outside India. To teach new followers the story of Buddha's life on earth, relief carvings began to show Buddha in human form. Early images of Buddha had staring eyes and a tense smile. By the Gupta period (A.D. 320–475), images of Buddha had a more inward, meditative look, with downcast eyes and a graceful pose.

Hindu Sculpture. Small images of Hindu gods were also carved of stone. Although made in human form, the images were also meant to show the many different forms taken by Hindu gods. Some gods were given many arms or heads and were always shown carrying certain emblems.

In northern India during the Gupta dynasty, images of Hindu gods were carved into the rock in man-made caves or housed in specially built temples. Such temples appeared across India after A.D. 400. Elaborate relief carvings were made on the temple walls, representing a variety of gods and their attendants.

In southern India after 800, bronze figures of Hindu gods were made. It was believed that the spirit of a temple god could be transferred to the statue, which was then carried in a religious procession. Outstanding bronzes were made in the Chola period (800–1200).

During the period from 900 to 1500, Hindu sculpture in the north tended to emphasize rich decoration. Much of this sculpture was used to ornament religious buildings. Sculpture of figures decreased after 1200 when northern India was ruled by Islamic leaders, whose religion forbade the use of human images for worship. Figural sculpture was produced for Hindu rulers, however.

Traditional sculpture continues to be made in modern India, mainly for an international tourist market. Other sculptors have experimented with modern styles and techniques.

▶ **PAINTING**

The people of ancient India made little distinction between artists who made images in paint and those who carved in stone. Each brought reality into being through art.

Wall Painting. In the first centuries A.D., large Buddhist temples and monasteries were cut into cliffs near Bombay. The walls of these cave-halls are decorated with both carved and painted images. Some of the paintings date from the first century and earlier, but most were made in the 400's, when support for the arts came mainly from the royal court of the Vakataka dynasty. The painting style used at one site, Ajanta, later spread from India into Afghanistan and Central Asia. Figures are realistically painted and firmly outlined. Color is used for shading and to suggest the body's solidity. The scenes seem to project out from the painted wall.

Manuscript Illustration. Illustrated manuscripts were made in India beginning in the 1000's. Early manuscripts had writing surfaces made from palm leaves. Some schools of manuscript illustration tried to imitate the complex colors and solidly modeled shapes of earlier wall paintings. In western India, however, a different style of manuscript painting developed. There, manuscripts that told the life stories of saints of the Jain religion were used as offerings in temples. Their illustrations had flattened shapes and areas of pure, bright color. Illustrations made in this style stand out from the text, and can be easily understood by the viewer.

Left: An illustration from a Rajput manuscript shows the Hindu gods Krishna and Radha.
Below: A painting by modern-day artist Amrita Sher-Gil depicts a scene from Indian life.

The Mogul (Mughal) dynasty came to power in the 1500's and ruled much of India until the British took control in the 1850's. Mogul rulers, who followed the Islamic faith, brought Islamic artists from Persia to train talented Indian painters. The literary works commonly illustrated in the Islamic world were very different from the religious texts illustrated by Indian artists. Many were myths or histories of kings. Akbar, one of the most famous Mogul rulers, encouraged painters to record the world around them. During his rule, Mogul painting combined Islamic, Hindu, and European elements into an original and expressive style.

Another style of manuscript painting developed in the courts of the Rajput rulers in northern India. These works continued to follow older Hindu themes but also adopted some Mogul traditions, such as portrait painting.

Some Mogul court-painters went to Rajput kingdoms in the Pahari hills when Mogul power declined in the 1600's. A Pahari school of manuscript illustration developed in the 1800's that used pastel colors rather than the bright colors of earlier Rajput paintings.

Modern Painting. The observation of nature encouraged by some Mogul rulers continued under the British, who first went to India as traders in the 1700's. Paintings made for the British East India Company include detailed studies of birds that resemble the works of the American painter and naturalist John James Audubon (who painted the birds of North America). European painters who worked in oils also went to India and painted for local Hindu rulers. In the late 1800's, art schools modeled on European institutions were established in Calcutta and Bombay. They trained a number of talented Indian painters.

Early in the 1900's, a South Indian artist, Ravi Varma, made large oil paintings of Hindu gods in the style of British portrait paintings of the 1800's. These works had a strong influence on modern images of Hindu gods. A painter from eastern India, Jamini Roy, used the simple lines of modern European painters such as Henri Matisse to cast traditional folk images in a new light.

The writer Rabindranath Tagore, who won the Nobel prize for literature in 1913, was also a painter. Tagore's followers tried to combine Indian painting traditions with other Asian styles. Their work has had little influence on modern Indian art, however.

The oil paintings of Amrita Sher-Gil, on the other hand, continue to influence many Indian painters. Sher-Gil, who was half Hungarian, studied in Europe, but her paintings have a well-observed Indian content.

Other modern painters have followed a variety of international models. Most seek in personal ways to find a means of expression that can be both modern and Indian.

Right: A Buddhist temple at Ellora is carved into the mountainside. *Below:* Clusters of curved towers characterize this Hindu temple at Khajuraho. *Below right:* A marble pillar inlaid with gemstones is from the Taj Mahal, an elaborate tomb built by a Mogul ruler.

▶ ARCHITECTURE

During the Indus Valley period, cities were built according to a grid pattern of intersecting streets. Buildings were made of brick. Later Hindu cities seem less organized, although similar rules of planning were laid down in Hindu architectural manuals. In Buddhist India small trading towns formed as centers of commerce, linked by trade routes. Structures were built of brick or mud. They often had pillared halls, balconies, and vaulted roofs with dormer windows.

Cave Architecture. The design of Buddhist cave-halls carved into the mountainsides near

Bombay was based on the free-standing structures built in towns. Cave architecture continued at least into the 800's at such sites as Ajanta and Ellora. They were created by Hindus and Jains as well as Buddhists. In some cases, whole temples were carved out of the rock. The most famous rock-cut temple at Ellora is called the Kailasa temple, after the mountain on which the Hindu god Shiva was said to have his palace.

Temples. Large free-standing temples were built in India from the 500's onward, mainly by Hindus and Jains. In the north, these temples had curving towers. The architecture of the temple was used to symbolize many things: an altar, a residence for a god, a shelter for the worshiper seeking enlightenment. Many such temples were built in northern India. Outstanding examples are also found at Khajuraho in central India, Bhubaneswar on the eastern coast, and Somnath in the west.

In southern India, temples were more like palaces. Great walls with tall gateways were built to include much of the surrounding city within the temple grounds.

Islamic Architecture. Islamic rulers gained political control over northern India in the 1190's. Long before this period, Islamic merchants along the coasts of India had hired local craftsmen to build structures for their use. One common type of Islamic building is the mosque, where the faithful gather for prayer. Most mosques have an open courtyard surrounded by a covered hallway and are oriented toward the sacred city of Mecca. (In India, this would be to the west-southwest.)

Under the patronage of sultans and emperors, a variety of Indo-Islamic architectural styles developed. Some were based on local styles, while others borrowed from Islamic traditions. Mosques, tombs, and palaces all survive from this era, known as the Sultanate period, and from the period of Mogul rule that followed it.

A masterpiece of Indo-Islamic architecture is the Taj Mahal. This large marble structure was built in the 1600's by Shah Jahan, a Mogul emperor, as a tomb for his wife. It combines architectural conventions from Central Asia with uniquely Indian craftsmanship and materials.

Modern Architecture. Architecture in modern India draws on a variety of contemporary styles. For example, buildings in the capital, New Delhi, were designed by the British architect Edward Lutyens in the early to mid-1900's. They were built by Indian craftsmen, however, and are decorated with a variety of Indian designs.

After the creation of the nations of India and Pakistan in 1947, the Indian government asked the great French architect Le Corbusier to create a plan for the new capital of the Punjab State at Chandigarh. Le Corbusier also designed many buildings in the city of Ahmedabad in western India. One of his supervising architects, B.K. Doshi, founded India's premier school of architecture there in the early 1960's.

Doshi and other architects built major projects for the Indian government and for industrial housing. Their designs follow many of the conventions of the modern international style. Doshi also established a foundation for the study of India's traditional architecture. He and other modern Indian architects have sought to design buildings in a style based on India's past rather than on forms adopted from European traditions.

MICHAEL W. MEISTER
University of Pennsylvania

The three marble domes of the Pearl Mosque rise above the massive sandstone walls of the Red Fort in Delhi. Mosques were built throughout India by Islamic rulers.

INDIA, LITERATURE OF

The term "Indian literature" refers to literature of the geographic area that includes today's countries of India, Pakistan, and Bangladesh. This entire region was known as India until 1947, when it was divided into two nations, India and Pakistan. Bangladesh separated from Pakistan in 1971.

The constitution of modern India recognizes 15 official languages, and many more are spoken throughout the country. Sanskrit, the most ancient language of India, is spoken by relatively few people today. However, most modern Indian languages come from Sanskrit, just as the modern European languages French, Italian, and Spanish developed from Latin. The languages that developed from Sanskrit are spoken mainly in northern India. The languages that are spoken in the south belong to a different language family, called Dravidian.

Another language, Urdu, developed in the 1500's as a result of contact with Persian-speaking Muslims. Urdu is similar to Hindi, a language of northern India, but contains many Persian and Arabic words.

English is spoken throughout India by a small percentage of the people. Most of them speak English as a second language, in addition to their mother tongue.

Each of these languages and language groups has its own literary tradition. Much of what is considered classical Indian literature was written in Sanskrit or in Tamil, a Dravidian language. After A.D. 500, literature written in the modern languages of India began to emerge. Beginning in the 1800's, some Indian literature was written in English.

▶ VEDIC LITERATURE

The first period of Indian literature, from 1200 to 500 B.C., is known as the Vedic period. It was during this time that the Vedas, collections of hymns and other sacred lore, were composed. There are four Vedas. The oldest is known as the *Rig Veda*, and it contains more than 1,000 hymns. The Vedas were not written down but were passed on orally, from memory. Because the texts were sacred, every word had to be memorized accurately.

▶ SANSKRIT LITERATURE

The earliest examples of written Sanskrit are inscriptions that were carved on stone pillars in the early centuries A.D. Literature was probably first written down at about the same time. However, few manuscripts from before 1400 survive. Most of the texts were written on strips of palm leaves or birch bark, which soon decayed in India's hot, humid climate. Thus people had to make new copies of any piece of literature that they wanted to save. This process of copying and recopying preserved many works.

Epics. During the classical period (500 B.C.–A.D. 1200), two great Hindu epics were composed: the *Mahabharata* ("The Great Bharata"), by Vyasa, and the *Ramayana* ("The Wanderings of Rama"), by Valmiki. Scholars may never be able to determine exactly when these long narrative poems were completed. Although each text is attributed to one poet, they were most likely composed over several centuries, with later poets adding to the main story. The dates of composition for the epics are usually given as 400 B.C. to A.D. 400 for the *Mahabharata* and 200 B.C. to A.D. 200 for the *Ramayana*.

The *Mahabharata* tells of the war between two groups within one large family. It is one of the longest poems in the world, with about 100,000 verses. One part of the poem consists of a conversation between the warrior Arjuna and his chariot driver Krishna. Arjuna is counseled on the duties of a soldier by Krishna, who reveals himself to be the Lord. This conversation, called the *Bhagavad Gita* ("The Song of the Lord"), is considered by many to express the basic beliefs of the Hindu faith.

The *Ramayana* is one of the most famous stories in Indian literature. It is the tale of Prince Rama and his wife Sita and of the adventures that follow Sita's capture by Ravana, a demon with ten heads. Sita is rescued with the help of Hanuman, a monkey general, and his army.

Puranas ("Old Lore") are another form of Sanskrit literature. These huge collections of knowledge contain myths and legends about Hindu gods and descriptions of the ways to worship them.

Kavya describes a type of written literature as well as a style of writing, either prose or verse. It was composed at India's royal courts. The language of kavya is very ornate and descriptive, with many puns and other kinds of wordplay. The standard of excellence for kavya was established by early works of literary criticism. These works stated that all good literature must have a special quality called *rasa*. The literal meaning of *rasa* is "juice." In literature, *rasa* is the essential part of the work, the "juices" that give the literature its distinctive flavor.

The most famous kavya poet was Kalidasa, who wrote during the 300's or 400's. His best-known work is the play *Sakuntala*. It tells the story of the marriage of a young girl, Sakuntala, to a king and the misadventures that result from a curse. Another work by Kalidasa is the narrative poem *Meghaduta* ("The Cloud Messenger"). It recounts the thoughts of an exiled Yaksa, a semi-divine being. The Yaksa asks a passing cloud to carry a message to his beloved in the Himalaya Mountains.

A fine example of prose kavya is *Kadambari*, a long tale of love and reincarnation by Banabhatta, who wrote in the 600's. A song of devotion in the kavya style is the *Gitagovinda* ("The Cowherd's Song"), written in the 1100's by Jayadeva in praise of Lord Krishna.

Fables and Stories. Some Sanskrit prose concentrated on storytelling, both to educate and to entertain. Two examples are the *Pancatantra* ("The Five Books") and the *Kathasaritsagara* ("The Ocean of Story"). Other tales, called *Jatakas* ("Birth Tales"), were written in Pali, a language similar to Sanskrit that was used by Buddhists. The *Jatakas*, which contain moral lessons, tell of the earthly forms—both human and animal—assumed by the Buddha.

▶ **TAMIL LITERATURE**

The Tamil language, although not as old as Sanskrit, has a rich literary tradition that has continued to the present day. One important

Sita is captured by the ten-headed demon Ravana in this scene from the *Ramayana*.

group of Tamil writings consists of more than 2,000 poems organized into eight collections. The poems are known as samgam literature because, according to legend, they were composed in academies called samgams. Thought to have been written during the first to the third centuries A.D., the poems are the oldest examples of non-Sanskrit literature in India.

One of the most famous Tamil epics is *Silappatikaram* ("The Jeweled Anklet"), by Ilanko Atikal. It tells the story of a man who is wrongly accused of stealing a jeweled anklet. The man is executed, and his faithful widow destroys the city in which he died. Another epic, a Tamil version of the *Ramayana*, was composed in the 1000's or 1100's by a writer named Kamban. In this version, Ravana is portrayed in a more positive fashion than in the Sanskrit version.

▶ **MEDIEVAL LITERATURE**

During the first half of India's medieval period (500–1800), the modern languages of India began to emerge, although Sanskrit literature continued to be composed. At the beginning of this period, a religious movement known as *bhakti* ("devotion") occurred within the Hindu faith. It started in the south and soon swept across all of India. Followers of *bhakti* believed that worshipers could communicate directly with their chosen god or goddess, without the help of a Brahmin priest.

The *bhakti* revolution gave rise to poetry written in all the modern Indian languages—wonderful poems that speak directly to God. In the south, the Saiva poets addressed the god Shiva, and the Vaishnavas composed poems to Vishnu. In Hindi-speaking northern India, notable poet-saints included Surdas, who sang to Krishna, and Kabir, who sang passionately to his own personal god. Kabir's god was neither

Hindu nor Muslim but encompassed both faiths. Another poet, Miribai, lived in Rajasthan in western India. She composed her devotional lyrics to Krishna. Miribai was the best-known woman saint of the later Middle Ages. In Bengal, in the northeast, the poet Ramprasad composed emotion-filled songs to the mother goddess Kali.

From the Muslim poets of medieval India came the *ghazal*, a form of poetry written in Urdu. Poems written in this form consist of couplets, or pairs of lines, each containing a complete thought. The couplets can also be linked together; the last line of each couplet must rhyme. The subject matter of the poems concerns all aspects of life and love. Two of the finest *ghazal* poets were Mir and Ghalib.

▶ **MODERN LITERATURE**

The modern period began in the 1800's. During this period, India came increasingly under the control of the British, who ruled the region until India and Pakistan won their independence in 1947. The British presence greatly affected all aspects of Indian life, including literature. The sonnet form of poetry came into Indian literature as a result of contact with the British, as did two forms of prose fiction, the novel and the short story. Today, however, all of these literary forms are as much Indian as they are British.

Literature in all the modern languages of India blossomed during this period. The following discussion, however, focuses on the development of literature written in Bengali, a language of northern India.

Michael Madhusudan Dutt is considered the father of modern Bengali poetry. His most famous narrative poem is *Meghanadavadha Kavya* ("The Slaying of the Meghanada"; 1861). It is based on an episode in the *Ramayana* in which Rama slays Meghanada, the son of Ravana. In Dutt's version, Ravana, not Rama, is presented as the sympathetic hero. Dutt's many sonnets are the first examples of that form of poetry in Bengali literature. The sonnet continued to be a popular form among later Bengali poets.

The first novels in Bengali were written by Bankim Chandra Chatterjee. Before Chatterjee, most Indian literature had been written in verse. Chatterjee's novels were immensely popular in his day. Many, such as *Durgesnandini* ("The Chieftain's Daughter"; 1864),

were historical romances set in India. Others reflect his interest in social issues.

Rabindranath Tagore is without a doubt the best-known Indian author worldwide. Tagore wrote all kinds of literature: poetry, plays, novels, and short stories. He received the Nobel prize for literature in 1913. The award was based mainly on his collection of religious poems, *Gitanjali* ("Song Offerings"), which he translated into English in 1912. Tagore was knighted by the British crown in 1915 but gave back his knighthood four years later to protest an incident in which Indian demonstrators were killed by the British. Tagore was also an accomplished musician and composer. Two of his songs were chosen as the national anthems of India and Bangladesh.

The novels of Sarat Chandra Chatterjee depict life in the villages of Bengal, especially the social interactions of the villagers. One such work is *Pallir Samaj* ("Village Society"; 1916). Almost all his novels have been translated into other Indian languages, and many have been made into motion pictures.

Kazi Nazrul Islam is known as "the rebel poet," after his most famous poem, "Bidrohi" ("The Rebel"; 1922). He was a Muslim who lived in Calcutta, a city with a largely Hindu population. An important theme in his work is the need for brotherhood between Muslims and Hindus.

Jibanananda Das is best known for his collection of poems on rural Bengal, *Rupasi Bamla* ("Bengal the Beautiful"; 1957). The beauty of his language makes the Bengal countryside come alive for the reader. In his later works, Das focused on the problems of modern society. The novels and short stories of Mahasweta Devi are also concerned with social ills. Her writings forcefully and compassionately express the point of view of the poor and the tribal peoples of India.

Other Bengali writers have chosen English as their literary language. Bharati Mukherjee became a permanent resident of the United States in 1980. Her writings, including *Wife* (1975), concern the experience of living in a different culture. The works of R. K. Narayan, including *Talkative Man* (1986), are set in the fictional town of Malgudi.

CLINTON B. SEELY
Department of South Asian Languages
and Civilizations
The University of Chicago

HEDGEHOGS

As dusk falls, it ambles out of its resting place. It is beginning its nightlong journey searching for food. Even though it is as likely to live in city suburbs as in fields or pastures, you will never see this night prowler unless you live in Europe, Asia, Africa, or New Zealand. Only those places are home to the hedgehog.

The hedgehog belongs to a group of mammals known as insectivores ("insect-eaters"). It is a trusting animal, but it can afford to be trusting: It is covered with a dense coat of brownish spines that acts as a spiky shield. The thousands of spines cover the entire back and sides. When a hedgehog feels threatened, it rolls up into a tight ball and tucks its face, legs, tail, and other soft parts inside. Only a very daring—or dumb—enemy will attack it.

One of the most common kinds, or species, of hedgehog is the European hedgehog. It is only 10 to 12 inches (25 to 30 centimeters) long and weighs less than 2 pounds (1 kilogram). Like other hedgehogs, it has very poor vision. It relies on excellent hearing and a keen sense of smell to lead it on its nighttime journeys. It also uses its sense of smell to find food, recognize its environment, identify mates and babies, and learn that enemies are near.

The Life of a Hedgehog. Except during the breeding season, hedgehogs live alone. Most daylight hours are spent sleeping curled up in a ball. Their nests may be under bushes, in dense hedges, or in thick, tall grass.

In mild climates, hedgehogs are active all year. But in northern Europe, hedgehogs hibernate during the winter. Before hibernating, the hedgehog eats a lot of food and becomes very fat. Then it burrows into the nest and stays until spring, when it wakes up and becomes active again.

Hedgehogs and Their Young. European hedgehogs court and mate during the spring and summer. After five to six weeks, the female gives birth to a litter containing five to seven babies. A newborn hedgehog is 2 to 3½ inches (5 to 9 centimeters) long and weighs ⅖ to ⅘ ounce (11 to 23 grams). Its eyes and ears are closed. Tiny white spines cover its back. (During birth these spines are pushed back against the baby's skin, so they do not hurt the mother.) The white spines are like a person's baby teeth. They drop out as the hedgehog's colored adult spines develop. As soon as the young hedgehogs can care for themselves, the mother chases them out of the nest.

The Hedgehog and its Environment. Hedgehogs do not have many enemies. Their spines protect them against most predators. Occasionally, large owls, polecats, and foxes will attack and kill hedgehogs. The greatest danger to hedgehogs is traffic. Large numbers of hedgehogs are killed on highways each year.

In some places, such as Britain, hedgehogs have become very popular. Images of hedgehogs appear on toys and clothing, people often put food out for the hedgehogs, and there is even a special hedgehog care unit in a wildlife hospital. But it is dangerous for hedgehogs to live near people. Land that once provided homes for many hedgehogs has been cleared and developed. Farming methods such as spraying with insecticides have decreased the hedgehogs' food supply.

Concerned scientists study the hedgehog as an example of what can happen to other animals and plants as the environment changes. With knowledge and interest, efforts can be made that will help make it possible for the hedgehog to continue to survive in a changing world.

JENNY TESAR
Author, *Introduction to Animals*
Reviewed by DOUGLAS FALK
Assistant Curator
New York Zoological Society

During its daily search for food, the hedgehog uses its sensitive nose to seek out insects, earthworms, slugs, spiders, and snails.

SHREWS

It may not often be seen in meadows and fields, but hidden in the long grass or in burrows just under the surface of the ground lurks one of the most ferocious creatures alive. It feeds almost all the time, day and night, with only short rest periods between hunting trips. Each day it devours more than its own weight in food. This creature is the shrew—the smallest mammal on land.

All shrews are very small, usually about 5 inches (10 centimeters) long and about 1.2 ounces (34 grams) in weight. The smallest of all—Savi's pygmy shrew—is only 2.5 to 3 inches (6 to 8 centimeters) long, including its tail. It weighs less than a penny, only $\frac{1}{14}$ ounce (2 grams). Shrews are found throughout the world except the polar regions, Australia, New Zealand, and most of South America.

The Life of a Shrew. The shrew is a nervous creature with a body that functions at an incredibly fast rate—its heart may beat 1,000 times a minute. Highly active, the shrew works continually to satisfy its enormous appetite. If left without food, a shrew would starve to death within hours.

Generally, shrews are found near streams or other moist places. Some, called water shrews, spend much of their life in water. They build dens along the banks of ponds, lakes, and streams. Water shrews are excellent swimmers, and catch fish, insects, and frogs while swimming underwater.

Homes for land shrews may be under stones or bushes, in networks of tunnels they have dug, or even in vacant burrows made by mice or other animals. When winter comes, shrews may move into barns and other buildings. They use their long snouts and excellent sense of smell to hunt insects, spiders, and other invertebrates. Some shrews have a poisonous substance in their saliva that allows them to kill animals much larger than themselves.

Shrews and Their Young. Most shrews in northern lands court and breed from spring to autumn. In warmer regions, shrews mate all year round. Sometimes males fight each other for mates. The winner courts the female, calling to her with low twittering sounds. A female shrew may have three or four litters of babies during just one mating season.

About three weeks after breeding, the fe-

The short-tailed shrew is just one of the more than 200 different kinds of shrews. Most shrews have dark fur, tiny eyes and ears, and long, pointed snouts.

male prepares a nest of grass or dry leaves under a log or in an abandoned burrow. Here she gives birth to a litter of four to seven babies. The babies are born blind and hairless. They weigh only $\frac{1}{28}$ ounce (1 gram) and are about the size of a jelly bean.

Even before their eyes open, the babies begin to crawl out of the nest. The tiny shrews follow their mother in a train, each using its teeth to hold onto the tail of the one in front. By 2 weeks of age their eyes are open. They are fully grown by the time they are 5 or 6 weeks old. If the young shrews are not killed by other animals or by disease, they usually live for about a year.

The Shrew and its Environment. Although two or more kinds of shrews may be found living in the same area, most shrews are solitary animals. They come together only during the breeding season. At other times, shrews are fierce fighters quick to defend their territory against one another. They rise up on their back legs as they attack one another.

The most dangerous time of year for the shrew is the winter. Shrews do not hibernate, and their constant search for food often drives them into the open where they are easy prey for birds such as owls and hawks. Weasels and other small meat-eating animals also attack shrews. However, the skin glands of the shrew produce a bad-tasting substance that stops most predators from eating the tiny creatures.

JENNY TESAR
Author, *Introduction to Animals*
Reviewed by DOUGLAS FALK
Assistant Curator
New York Zoological Society

The Russian ruler Ivan III is known as the Great. During his reign (1462–1505), he established a unified rule over what had been a divided Russia.

IVAN

Ivan was the name of six rulers of Russia, who lived between the 1300's and the 1700's. They are sometimes referred to by the equivalent English name, John.

Ivan I (1304?–40) ruled the principality of Moscow from 1328 to 1340 and served as grand prince of Russia (from 1331). Ivan owed this throne to the khan (ruler) of the Mongols, who controlled the lands of Russia at the time. He paid considerable attention to courting the khan, and was quick to join in crushing any movement hostile to the Mongols among other Russian princes. A wise money manager, Ivan earned the nickname *Kalita*, or Moneybag. He used his money-making talent to buy other territories, increasing the size of his own principality of Moscow by nearly seven times.

By the time of Ivan I's death, Moscow had emerged as the political and religious capital of all Russia, although it was still subject to the overall control of the Mongols. Ivan established the tradition that princes of Moscow had first claim on the position of Russian grand prince. His heirs held that title almost without interruption.

Ivan II (1326–59), a son of Ivan I, served as Russian grand prince from 1353 to 1359. Known as *Krotkii*, or the Meek, he was not a strong ruler, and was inept as both a political and military leader. He continued to give obedience to the Mongols. Ivan II was strongly influenced by a capable and energetic metropolitan of the Russian Orthodox Church, Alexis. Alexis, in effect, ruled Russia for most of Ivan's reign.

Ivan III (1440–1505), known as the Great, was Russian grand prince from 1462 to 1505. One of only three Russian rulers to be called the Great, he began the unification and centralization of the Russian lands under Moscow. During Ivan III's reign, Mongol rule in Russia declined. In 1480 he repelled an invasion of Moscow by the Mongols, finally freeing Russia from their domination.

During the 1470's and 1480's, Ivan absorbed Moscow's old rivals to the north, the principalities of Novgorod and Tver, as well as other territories, and established a unified rule over what had been a divided Russia. He also fought Lithuania (1492–94 and 1500–1503) in an attempt to reconquer the Ukraine, which Lithuania had occupied. But in this he was only partly successful.

One of the most important accomplishments of Ivan III's reign was the introduction of a new law code in 1497. This made legal procedures uniform throughout Russia and helped to curb widespread corruption among officials. During Ivan's reign, Moscow was the site of an impressive building campaign, directed by Italian architects and artists.

After the death of his first wife in 1467, Ivan married Sophia, niece of the last Byzantine emperor, in 1472. Following the marriage, Ivan developed a court ceremony based on that of the Byzantine Empire. He also began to use the title of czar, a variation of the Roman title caesar. By the time of his death, Russia had become a strong nation-state.

Ivan IV (1530–84), known as the Terrible, was crowned czar in 1547, the first Russian ruler officially to hold this title. That same year he married Anastasia Romanov. Although Ivan remarried a number of times after her death, he was never able to recapture the happiness he had enjoyed with Anastasia. The Romanov dynasty, which ruled Russia from 1613 to the overthrow of the monarchy in 1917, traces its claim to the throne from their

Ivan IV was the first Russian ruler to be crowned czar. The first part of his reign (1533–60) was a period of great accomplishment. The second part (1560–84), however, was a time of repression and terror that gave him his nickname of the Terrible. His last years were marked by tragedy. In a fit of anger, he killed his eldest son, Ivan (shown being held by his father).

union—through Anastasia's brother, Nikita.

Historians often divide Ivan IV's reign into two periods. The first, from 1533 to 1560, was a period of constructive policies. The second, from 1560 to his death in 1584, was a time of repression and terror that gave Ivan his nickname of the Terrible.

During the first period, Ivan instituted reforms in local government, drew up a new law code, and standardized the duties and responsibilities of the nobility. Russia also began its expansion to the east, beyond the Ural Mountains, and before Ivan's death, had established itself in Siberia. In addition, Ivan opened trade contacts with the English, French, and Dutch.

Anastasia's death in 1560 marked the end of this period of accomplishment. Increasingly powerful, Ivan turned against his advisors. He became convinced that they, backed by the prominent nobility (the boyars), had caused Anastasia's death. By threatening to abdicate (give up the throne), Ivan was given the authority to punish those whom he considered traitors and wrongdoers, executing them if necessary and confiscating their property. His bodyguard, the *oprichniki*, destroyed most of the wealthy old boyar families. Those who were not killed were ruined by Ivan's political and economic policies.

Ivan also began a series of disastrous wars during this period, in an attempt to gain access for Russia to the Baltic Sea. His last years were marked by turmoil and tragedy. In 1581,

in a fit of anger, he lashed out at his eldest son, also called Ivan, and killed him. He probably never fully recovered from the guilt he felt for this act, and he died a broken man.

Ivan V (1666–96) served as co-ruler of Russia from 1682 to 1696. Ivan was feeble-minded and partially blind. But he was installed on the throne, along with his half brother Peter I, by his sister Sophia, who governed as regent. When Peter (the future Peter the Great) overthrew Sophia in 1689, he allowed Ivan to continue sharing the throne. Ivan, however, had virtually no power, serving merely as a ceremonial figure.

Ivan VI (1740–64) was emperor of Russia from 1740 to 1741, while still an infant. The great nephew of the Empress Anne (who ruled from 1730 to 1740), Ivan was only 2 months old at the time of Anne's death. Several groups contended for control of the throne. A group centered around Ivan's mother, Anna Leopoldovna, eventually won out.

However, in 1741 a coup led by Elizabeth, Peter the Great's only surviving daughter, overthrew the ''baby emperor,'' and he was imprisoned. A plot to free Ivan in 1764, during the reign of the Empress Catherine II (the Great) failed, and the former emperor was murdered. He had spent 23 of his 24 years in prison.

DONALD L. LAYTON
Indiana State University

Edison's light bulb, 1879.

INVENTIONS

An invention is a new device or a new method for making things.

Popular stories give the idea that invention is a simple matter. Someone has a sudden inspiration while strolling in the woods or working at a job, and the idea is an instant success. Nothing could be further from the truth. Flashes of inspiration usually come only after an inventor has been at work on a problem for a long time. Then a great deal more work must be done to turn the idea into a working reality.

The process of invention goes through many stages. First, some new knowledge makes possible the idea of doing or building something. Then, someone has such an idea and proposes it, but cannot put it into practice. Later, more knowledge is acquired, often from the experience of people trying to make the idea work. Finally, someone succeeds, and he or she becomes known as the inventor.

The process of invention does not stop when the first successful model is built and tested. Other inventors continue to make improvements on the original idea. A modern jet with kitchens and comfortable seats in an air-conditioned cabin is a far cry from the Wright brothers' original biplane.

Sometimes one invention leads to another. The invention of the steam engine led to the invention of many machine tools needed to make metal parts for engines. An automobile is a combination of hundreds of inventions. Every part, from the engine and transmission to the nuts and bolts, had to be invented.

Who Is the Actual Inventor?

It is often difficult to decide who really deserves the credit for an invention. Often two people work separately on the same invention at the same time. One might be quicker to patent the invention, or register it with the government. Who should get the credit? Sometimes an inventor fails to make a business success of an invention. Years later someone else does succeed with the same invention. Which of these people is the true inventor? Sometimes a well-known inventor takes credit for an invention that is really the work of an assistant. For these reasons historians often prefer not to single out any one person as the inventor of a device or process.

Many inventors have failed because the

What is the difference between an invention and a discovery?

It is often hard to tell the difference between an invention and a discovery, but we usually speak of **inventing** something that did not exist before and of **discovering** something that did exist before but was not known.

Thus we say that Galileo discovered the spots on the face of the sun. Sunspots had always existed, but no one knew about them until Galileo found them. We say that Thomas Edison invented the phonograph, since there was no such thing as a phonograph until Edison created the first one.

Invention involves an act of creation. But discoveries, too, often involve a creative act. Long before Alexander Fleming discovered penicillin in mold in 1928, biologists knew that molds would sometimes destroy bacteria. But it was Fleming who created the idea that a substance that destroyed bacteria could be extracted from the mold. It was this idea that led him to the discovery of penicillin. Without Fleming's idea of looking for a bacteria-killing substance in mold, penicillin might not have been discovered.

technical knowledge of their time was not enough to allow them to carry out their ideas. A number of inventors made electric light bulbs years before Edison did, but their efforts failed because they had no good material for the filament (the tiny wire that glows and makes light when the electric current passes through it). One English inventor produced a successful light bulb before Edison but failed to patent it in time.

▶ THE INCANDESCENT LIGHT

The case of the incandescent light, or electric light bulb, is a good example of the stages in the development of an invention.

In the 1700's many people became interested in electricity and began conducting experiments. However, they had no way of producing a steady stream, or current, of electricity. Then, in 1800, an Italian scientist named Alessandro Volta (1745–1827) invented the electric battery. With the battery an electric current could be obtained.

A few years later, in 1808, the famous British scientist Sir Humphry Davy (1778–1829) used electricity to make light. Using a battery, Davy made electricity jump between two carbon rods, or electrodes. The electricity leaping across the gap made a continuous spark, or arc, which glowed brilliantly. Scientists began using the new arc lamp for laboratory experiments, but the best batteries of that day could not keep going for long. There was no source of electric current good enough to make the arc lamp practical for lighting purposes.

The invention of the electric generator was another important step in making electric lighting possible. It is also one of the early examples of an invention based on scientific research. The electric generator is based on a discovery made about 1831 by another British scientist, Michael Faraday (1791–1867). He found that when a wire is moved near a magnet, electricity moves in the wire. During the years that followed, many inventors from many different countries helped to develop this idea into the electric generator. By the middle of the century steam-powered generators were being used to run arc lamps in lighthouses. In 1870 Zénobe Théophile Gramme (1826–1901), a Belgian engineer and inventor, developed the first really practical generator. With this source of current, arc lamps came into wide use for lighting city streets. The arc lamp gave a very bright light, but it was not suitable for indoor use. It was very noisy, it was dangerous, and it produced serious eyestrain.

But many engineers and scientists had been working for years on another idea—an idea that was the basis of the electric light bulb. They were experimenting with the use of a fine wire, or filament, heated white-hot by an electric current. In 1845 an American named J. W. Starr (1822?–47) patented an electric lamp that used a piece of metal or carbon in a vacuum. In 1860 an English chemist and inventor, Joseph Swan (1828–1914), also made such a lamp. It used a strip of carbon in a bulb from which much of the air had been pumped out. The carbon burned up very quickly, however, because Swan was unable to remove enough of the air. It was not until the German chemist Hermann Sprengel (1834–1906) invented the mercury air pump in 1865 that a good enough vacuum was possible. Swan then built better lamps.

After 1865 all the discoveries and inventions necessary to make an incandescent light bulb were known. Scientists had discovered that an electrically heated filament could give light. The carbon filament had been invented. The need for a vacuum had been realized, and the means to produce it had been invented.

Lamps were being made in both England and the United States, but they wore out quickly. Then, in 1879, Thomas Edison (1847–1931) made a practical incandescent lamp. He patented it in both Britain and the United States.

Credit for inventing the incandescent lamp is usually given to Edison, but his invention was partially the result of many earlier inventions and the work of many other people.

Edison's invention of 1879 was not the last step in the development of the electric light bulb. Other inventors contributed their ideas and their work to its improvement. One of the most important of these improvements was the use of tungsten instead of carbon for the filament. Tungsten is a metal with a very high melting point. A filament of tungsten glows more brightly than one of carbon, and it lasts much longer. But tungsten filaments had to wait until an American scientist named William D. Coolidge (1873–1975) discovered a way of treating tungsten metal so that it could be formed into wires. In its natural state, tungsten is too brittle to be shaped.

Another important improvement was made by Irving Langmuir (1881–1957), an American scientist. He filled the light bulb with an inert gas (a gas that does not react chemically with other substances, even at very high temperatures). This gas helped make light bulbs last longer by keeping the white-hot filament from evaporating as it did in a vacuum.

A third improvement was to frost the inside of the bulb to reduce glare and cause the light to spread more evenly.

In 1938 fluorescent lights, which last longer than standard bulbs and use less energy, were invented. Instead of a filament, the tube is coated with a chemical that fluoresces, or gives off light, when electricity is passed through the inert gas inside. Improvements of the light bulb are still being made.

▶ INVENTIONS IN THE PRODUCTION OF ENERGY

Today vast amounts of energy are available for doing work. This was not always so. During much of history the only source of energy was human muscle power. Many early inventions were devices for helping people make better use of their muscular energy. For example, a person can raise a heavy object by sliding it up an inclined plane, or sloping ramp, even though he or she could not possibly lift it straight up by hand. The Egyptians used inclined planes to raise the great stone blocks of the pyramids into position.

When humans learned to tame animals such as cattle and horses, they began to use animals' muscle power for carrying loads. Later, the invention of harnesses, enabling animals to pull loads, made animal power much more useful. A horse or an ox can pull a heavier load along the ground than it can carry on its back. With the harness, animals could also be used to turn early water scoops and mills that ground grain into flour.

Around the 100's B.C., the invention of the nailed horseshoe gave the horse a better grip on the ground and so increased its pulling power. The type of horseshoe that is used today dates from about the A.D. 800's. The invention of the horse collar about the 900's enabled the horse to pull a heavy load without being choked by the harness. These two seemingly minor inventions made the horse more useful as a work animal.

Another advance was made when people learned to use the energy of natural forces such as running water, wind, and burning fuel. The invention of the waterwheel about 2,000 years ago gave humans the first source of energy that did not depend on muscle power. Animals get tired and must rest, just as human beings do. But a waterwheel keeps on running as long as there is water to turn it. The waterwheel was probably first used in the Roman Empire. By the 300's the waterwheel was in widespread use from Ireland to China. During the Middle Ages many different kinds of machinery that could be driven by waterpower were invented.

The windmill, another source of nonmuscular energy, was invented in Persia perhaps 1,300 years ago. By the 900's Persians were using windmills to pump water and grind flour. When the windmill became known in Europe, it came into wide use, especially in broad, flat areas like eastern England, the Low Countries (Belgium, Luxembourg, the Netherlands), and northern Germany, where there is nearly always some wind. With the great amounts of energy made available by the windmill and the waterwheel, people could accomplish greater physical tasks than ever before. Pumps run by wind or waterpower irrigated fields and supplied cities with water.

The invention of the steam engine brought a new source of energy—the energy of burn-

The Grove Battery, 1839.

ing fuel. A steam engine uses the heat energy of burning fuel to boil water and turn it into steam. During the 1600's and 1700's a number of engineers and inventors, of whom Scotsman James Watt (1736–1819) is the most famous, contributed ideas for the steam engine. Each of these inventors improved on the work of those who had gone before. By 1800 steam engines were in general use. Although waterwheels and windmills were still used, the invention of the steam engine made it possible to have large quantities of power wherever and whenever it was needed. During the 1800's the internal-combustion engine was developed. This engine is more efficient—that is, it wastes less energy—than the steam engine. The automobile engine is an example of an internal-combustion engine.

The electric motor was invented during the 1830's. A number of people in different countries took part in its development. But the electric motor could not be put to practical use until a good source of electrical energy became available. For years batteries were the only source of electricity. But batteries were heavy, clumsy, and expensive. In 1870 the electric generator was perfected. Together the electric generator and motor provided a new way of transmitting power from one place to another. Before the invention of the electric motor and generator, factories were usually built close to sources of energy, such as coalfields or waterfalls. Bringing coal or other fuel to the factories was inconvenient and expensive. Today only the electric generator plant has to be near the source of energy. The factory may be many miles away.

The electric generator in itself is not a new source of energy. It must be driven by another power producer, such as a steam engine, a water turbine, or an internal-combustion engine. Burning fuel or running water is still the original source of energy. But electrical energy is easier to transmit, control, and use.

Since the mid-1900's the nuclear reactor has provided a new source of energy. Nuclear reactors use the energy created by splitting atoms and convert that energy into electrical energy. Their use is widespread, but there is great controversy over their safety and their effects on the environment.

Land Transportation. The earliest forms of transportation—walking and carrying—used muscle power. The litter, or barrow (a device like a hospital stretcher), is a prehistoric invention. So is the sled, which was used to ease the moving of heavy objects. Before 3000 B.C., people had domesticated animals and used them to carry and pull heavy loads.

One of the greatest inventions was the invention of the wheel about 3500–3000 B.C. In fact, the wheel was the last major development in land transportation for thousands of years. Wheeled vehicles, which could be pulled by people or animals, were improved by inventions like spoked wheels for lightness and springs for a smoother ride. But land transportation was almost the same in George Washington's time as it had been in the time of the Babylonian Empire, thousands of years before. Then, in the 1800's and 1900's the steam engine and later the internal-combustion engine were used to drive wheeled vehicles. The development of these two inventions made possible locomotives, automobiles, trucks, and buses.

Water Transportation. The first "boat" was probably a floating log used as an aid in swimming. The next step was tying a number of logs together to make a raft. Rafts were also made from other materials that floated well, such as bundles of reeds and inflated animal skins. Though rafts could carry heavy loads, they were slow and hard to steer. The change from a raft to a true boat came long before history was recorded, when someone thought of hollowing out a log. Like many basic inventions, this simple idea made a great difference. A hollow log floats better than a solid log and can carry a bigger load.

Rafts and boats had to be propelled. The current could carry them downstream. Traveling upstream, people would have to tow their craft from the shore or, if the water was not too deep, push them with poles. With the invention of the paddle, another very old device, boats or rafts could be handled even in deep water. Oars were developed from paddles. Sails, too, were invented before the beginning of written history.

Over the centuries boat design was improved by additional inventions. One of these inventions was building boats with planks instead of hollowing them out of single logs; another invention was the keel, or plate, extending along the length of the bottom of the boat in the center to give it strength and stability. By the time of the Phoenicians (about 1200 B.C.), whose ships traded all around the Mediterranean Sea, boat design had become standardized into two types. The broad-beamed merchant ship, usually driven by a sail, was slow but seaworthy, and it could carry large cargoes. The long, slim galley, or warship, propelled by a large crew of oarsmen, moved swiftly, but it had little room for cargo and was not designed to ride out storms at sea. These two basic designs hardly changed for hundreds of years.

In the late Middle Ages a number of inventions revolutionized water travel and made possible worldwide voyages and exploration. One was the sternpost rudder, a flat, moveable piece of wood attached at the back of a ship, which greatly increased control over steering. Before this a ship was steered by a large oar attached to its side. This gave poor control. The sternpost rudder made it possible to steer even sailing ships in almost any direction.

Another important invention was the tun, a wooden cask for water. With a supply of fresh water stored in tuns, a ship could make long voyages far from land. So important was the tun that a ship's carrying capacity was measured in "tunnage," meaning the amount of space in the ship. Today the word is spelled "tonnage," but in shipping the ton is still a unit of space rather than a measure of weight.

Late in the 1700's, several inventors applied the power of the steam engine to boats. Practical designs were worked out in the early 1800's, and steamboats were soon in widespread use. Although at first steamboats were slower than sailboats, they were completely independent of winds and currents, and by the end of the 1800's steamboats had replaced sailboats for most purposes. Steam engines in turn were replaced by internal-combustion engines. Today nuclear energy is used to drive some naval vessels and some cargo ships.

Air Transportation. For thousands of years people have dreamed of traveling through the air. One famous person who designed a flying machine was the Italian artist and inventor Leonardo da Vinci (1452–1519). However, none of the early flying machines worked. In 1783 the first successful flight was made by a lighter-than-air craft, the balloon, in France.

The Wright brothers' first flight at Kitty Hawk, December 17, 1903.

Jacques Cousteau (left) shows his Aqua-lung, October 30, 1950.

Marine chronometers used by Captain James Cook on his second voyage in 1772.

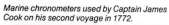

Printout of a modern electrocardiograph of three normal heartbeats.

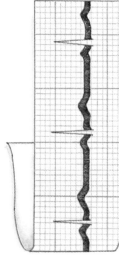

Mauchly and Eckert, co-inventors of ENIAC, the first electronic digital computer, show how it works, February 8, 1946.

SOME SIGNIFICANT INVENTIONS

Invention	Date	Place	Inventor
Adding machine	1642	France	Blaise Pascal
Air brake	1869	United States	George Westinghouse
Air conditioning	1902	United States	Willis H. Carrier
Airplane	1903	United States	Orville and Wilbur Wright
Air pump	1654	Germany	Otto von Guericke
Aqualung	1943	France	Jacques Yves Cousteau; Emile Gagnan
Arc Lamp	1808	England	Humphry Davy
Automobile	1769	France	Nicolas Cugnot
(first self-propelled vehicle — crashed on trial run)			
	1801	England	Richard Trevithick
(first successful steam-powered road vehicle)			
	1865	Austria	Siegfried Marcus
(self-propelled carriage with liquid-fuel internal-combustion engine)			
	1885	Germany	Karl Benz
(first practical gasoline-powered automobile)			
Bakelite	1909	United States	Leo H. Baekeland
Balloon	1783	France	Jacques Étienne Montgolfier; Joseph Michel Montgolfier
Ball-point pen	1888	United States	John Loud
Barometer	1643	Italy	Evangelista Torricelli
Battery, electric	1800	Italy	Alessandro Volta
Bessemer process	1855	England	Henry Bessemer
	1851	United States	William Kelly
(not patented until 1857)			
Bicycle	1840	Scotland	K. MacMillan
Canning of food	1804	France	Nicolas F. Appert
Cash register	1879	United States	J. Ritty
CAT scanner	1968	England	Godfrey N. Hounsfield
(advanced X-ray)	1968	United States	Allan M. Cormack (working independently)
Celluloid	1870	United States	J. W. Hyatt
Clock:			
Mechanical clock	1300's	Europe	Uncertain
(sometimes credited to Henry de Vick of Württemberg, Germany, about 1360)			
Pendulum clock	1656	Netherlands	Christiaan Huygens
Marine chronometer	1735	England	John Harrison
Computer:			
Punch-card machine	1890	United States	Herman Hollerith
Electronic digital computer	1946	United States	J.P. Eckert; J.W. Mauchly
Cotton gin	1793	United States	Eli Whitney
Cyclotron	1931	United States	Ernest O. Lawrence
Diesel engine	1898	Germany	Rudolf Diesel
(principle patented 1892)			
Diving suit	1825	England	William H. James
Dynamite	1865	Sweden	Alfred Nobel
Electric motor	1821	England	Michael Faraday
(demonstrated basic principle — the electric motor is the work of many inventors)			
Electrocardiograph	1903	Netherlands	Willem Einthoven
Electromagnet	1828	United States	Joseph Henry
Elevator	1853	United States	Elisha G. Otis
Escalator	1891	United States	Jesse Reno
Ether	1846	United States	W.T.G. Morton and J.C. Warren
Force pump	200's B.C.	Egypt	Ctesibius
Generator, electric	1831	England	Michael Faraday
(discovered basic principle)			
	1870	France	Zénobe T. Gramme
(first really practical generator)			
Gyrocompass	1911	United States	E. A. Sperry
(patent issued 1915)			
Gyroscope	1852	France	Jean B. L. Foucault
Hall-Héroult process	1886	United States	Charles M. Hall
	1886	France	Paul Héroult (working independently)

SOME SIGNIFICANT INVENTIONS

Invention	Date	Place	Inventor
Harvester	1858	United States	Charles and William Marsh
Helicopter	1939	United States	Igor Sikorsky
Hypodermic syringe	1853	France	Charles Gabriel Pravaz
Incandescent lamp	1879	United States	Thomas A. Edison
Internal-combustion engine	1860	France	Jean J.E. Lenoir
Jet engine	1936	England	Frank Whittle
Kite	About 1000 B.C.	China	Unknown
Laser	1960	United States	T.H. Maiman
Lightning rod	1752	American colonies	Benjamin Franklin
Linotype machine	1884	United States	Ottmar Mergenthaler
Lock, pin-tumbler cylinder	1865	United States	Linus Yale, Jr.
Magnetic compass	About 1100	Possibly China	Unknown
Magnetic tape-recorder	1898	Denmark	Valdemar Poulsen
Mechanical refrigeration	1834	England	Jacob Perkins
Microscope	About 1590	Netherlands	Uncertain

(Zacharias Janssen is known to have built an early microscope; Anton van Leeuwenhoek was first to use microscope for scientific observations)

Invention	Date	Place	Inventor
Microscope, electron	1932	Belgium	L. L. Marton
Motion-picture camera	1888	France	E. J. Marey
Motion-picture projector	1888	United States	Thomas A. Edison
Nuclear reactor	1942	United States	Enrico Fermi and others
Nylon	1936	United States	Wallace H. Carothers

(patented 1937)

Invention	Date	Place	Inventor
Paper	1st century A.D.	China	Tsai Lun, a Chinese court official
Phonograph	1877	United States	Thomas A. Edison
Photography	1826	France	Joseph Nicéphore Niépce
Pneumatic drill	1871	United States	S. Ingersoll

(uses air pressure)

Invention	Date	Place	Inventor
Pneumatic tire	1845	United States	R.W. Thompson
Polaroid Land Camera	1947	United States	Edwin H. Land
Polio vaccine	1954	United States	Jonas Salk
Portland cement	1824	England	Joseph Aspdin

(the kind of cement used in modern construction)

Invention	Date	Place	Inventor
Power loom	1786	England	Edmund Cartwright

(for weaving cloth)

Invention	Date	Place	Inventor
Printing with movable type	About 1440	Germany	Usually credited to Johann Gutenberg; sometimes credited to Laurens Coster of the Netherlands
	About same time		
Quick-freezing of food	1924	United States	Clarence Birdseye
Radar	1936	England	R. A. Watson-Watt
Radio	1896	England	Guglielmo Marconi

(wireless telegraph)

Invention	Date	Place	Inventor
Razor, electric	1923	United States	Jacob Schick
Razor, safety	1895	United States	King Camp Gillette
Reaper	1834	United States	Cyrus McCormick

(harvester)

Invention	Date	Place	Inventor
Revolver	1835	United States	Samuel Colt

(patented 1836)

Invention	Date	Place	Inventor
Rocket, liquid-fuel	1926	United States	Robert Goddard
Rotary printing press	1847	United States	Richard M. Hoe

(press actually built in 1846)

Invention	Date	Place	Inventor
Safety match	1844	Sweden	Gustaf Erik Pasch
Safety pin	1849	United States	Walter Hunt

(modern)

Daguerreotype Camera, 1840.

Otis presents his first elevator at the Crystal Palace, New York City, in 1853.

Thomas A. Edison in 1915 in his laboratory with the "Edison Effect" lamp.

Hypodermic syringe, 1860.

A lithograph of Robert Fulton's steamboat, Clermont, done in the 1830's.

April, 1941: Igor Sikorsky keeps the helicopter he invented airborne and stationary for over an hour.

Alexander Graham Bell makes the first long-distance telephone call, New York to Chicago, in 1893.

The first modern typewriter was sold by its designers to Remington to be manufactured. This model is from 1873.

Telegraph key used in 1844 by Samuel F.B. Morse, the inventor of Morse Code.

Vladimir Zworykin shown in 1929 holding the cathode ray tube used in the television process he invented in 1923.

Guglielmo Marconi and his wireless telegraph, which led to the development of radio.

SOME SIGNIFICANT INVENTIONS

Invention	Date	Place	Inventor
Sewing machine	1830	France	Barthelemey Thimonnier
	1845	United States	Elias Howe
(patented 1846)			
Spinning jenny	1764	England	James Hargreaves
Steamboat	1783	France	Claude F. D. Jouffroy d'Abbans
(first boat propelled by steam)			
	1787	United States	John Fitch
(first steamboat capable of sustained operation)			
	1807	United States	Robert Fulton
(first commercially successful steamboat)			
Steam engine, reciprocating	1712	England	Thomas Newcomen
	1769	Scotland	
(working with back-and-forth motion of a piston in a cylinder) (first steam-powered engine)			
	1782	England	James Watt
(separate condenser, double-acting rotary engine)			
Steam hammer	1839	England	James Nasmyth
(patented 1842)			
Steam locomotive	1804	England	Richard Trevithick
Steam shovel	1838	United States	William S. Otis
Steam turbine	1884	England	Charles A. Parsons
Stethoscope	1817	France	René Théophile Hyacinthe Laennec
Submarine	1776	United States	David Bushnell
(first boat to move underwater — hand powered)			
	1887	United States	J. P. Holland
(first power-driven submarine)			
Telegraph	1837	United States	Samuel F. B. Morse
(others had invented telegraphs earlier, but Morse's worked better)			
Telephone	1876	United States	Alexander Graham Bell
Telescope	Late 1500's	Probably Italy or Netherlands	Unknown
(an early telescope maker was Zacharias Janssen, of the Netherlands, who made a telescope in 1604)			
Television	1923	United States	Vladimir J. Zworykin
Thermometer	1593	Italy	Unknown
(one of the earliest inventors of a thermometer, however, was Galileo Galilei)			
Threshing machine	1786	Scotland	Alexander Meikle
Transistor	1948	United States	John Bardeen; Walter H. Brattain; William Shockley
Transmission, automatic	1940	United States	General Motors
Typewriter	1868	United States	Christopher L. Sholes; Carlos S. Glidden; Samuel W. Soulé
Vacuum tube	1904	England	John A. Fleming (the diode)
	1907	United States	Lee De Forest (the triode)
Videotape recorder	1956	United States	Charles Ginsberg; Charles E. Anderson; Ray Dolby; Alex Maxey; Fred Pfost; Shelby Henderson
Vulcanization of rubber	1839	United States	Charles S. Goodyear
Washing machine	1851	United States	J. T. King
Water screw	200's B.C.	Greece	Archimedes
(for raising water)			
Watch	1504	Germany	Peter Heinlein
(first portable timepiece)			
Waterwheel	1st century B.C.	Roman Empire	Unknown
Windmill	About 600's A.D.	Persia	Unknown
X-ray tube	1895	Germany	Wilhelm Konrad Roentgen
Xerography	1942	United States	Chester Carlson
Zipper	1896	United States	W.L. Judson

NOTE: Whenever possible, date given is that of the patent. In some cases, however, the invention was completed several years before the patent was issued. In other cases, the idea was patented before the inventor had a working model. Dates before 1700 are in many cases approximations, since records are not reliable.

Steady improvements led to the invention of the airship. However, airships are not successful, because they are easily damaged.

The first successful airplane was invented in the United States in 1903 by the Wright brothers, Wilbur (1867–1912) and Orville (1871–1948). But many earlier inventions went into the making of the first airplane. One of the most important of these was the glider, a motorless heavier-than-air craft that depended on air currents in order to stay up for any length of time. A leading inventor of gliders was the German engineer Otto Lilienthal (1848–96).

The invention of the airplane had to wait until a suitable source of power was available. Steam engines were too heavy, as were battery-driven electric motors. The internal-combustion engine, the first engine that was both light enough and strong enough, finally made the airplane possible. There have been many developments since then, most importantly, the jet engine.

The helicopter, perfected in 1939 by the Russian-American engineer Igor Sikorsky (1889–1972), uses many of the same principles as the airplane. One basic difference is that the helicopter's rotor wing moves, while the airplane's wing does not move.

A very old invention, the rocket, used before the 1300's in China to launch weapons and fireworks, has become important in the 20th century. Rocket engines are used to launch spacecraft into orbit around the earth as well as to other planets. Robert H. Goddard (1882–1945), an American physicist, was a pioneer in the development of modern rockets. He patented 214 inventions. Every rocket today uses some of his many ideas.

▶ INVENTIONS OF COMMUNICATION

Humans probably first communicated with gestures and grunts. Gradually they developed language and used pictures to communicate ideas. The earliest writing we know of is about 5,500 years old. Writing made knowledge more permanent—it no longer had to be passed down from generation to generation by word of mouth. The knowledge stored in the millions of books in modern libraries and in computer databases is available to us because of the invention of writing.

Early writing was done on rock, bone, ivory, clay tablets, animal hides, and wood. The writing was carved, scratched, or painted on these materials. The Egyptians invented papyrus, a paperlike material made from the stems of the papyrus plant, on which to write. They pasted sheets of papyrus edge-to-edge to form one long sheet, which was then rolled up into a scroll for ease of storage. These scrolls were the first books. The book as we know it today, with one page on top of another, was invented about 2,000 years ago.

Papyrus was used for hundreds of years in many countries. Another writing material, parchment, a thin-scraped piece of sheepskin, was invented about 2,000 years ago. This was stronger and lasted longer than papyrus. Also, mistakes could be erased more easily.

Paper, a Chinese invention, reached Europe by the A.D. 1100's. It was made from such plant fibers as linen and cotton. In the 1800's paper made from wood pulp was invented. Wood-pulp paper is much cheaper than other kinds. But it does not last as long because of chemical changes that take place in the paper as it ages. In fact, documents from 500 years ago are often in better condition than those written 20 years ago.

When books had to be written out by hand, it took a very long time to produce a single copy and books were very expensive. With the invention of the printing press and movable type in the 1400's, many copies could be made, books became much cheaper, and more people were able to buy them. One of the first people to print books was the German printer Johannes Gutenberg (1400?–68). For centuries he and other printers used muscle power to press paper against inked type to transfer the ink to the paper. Then electric motors were used to operate printing presses at very high speeds. In 1884 the invention of the Linotype, a machine that was used to set type for printing presses, eliminated the slow process of setting type by hand. It was invented by the German-American inventor Ottmar Mergenthaler (1854–99). Today, the photocomposition process uses computers and photography to set type.

Even with the invention of writing and printing, communication was slow. Speedier methods of communication grew out of discoveries about electricity that were made during the 1700's. One was that electricity will move along a wire. Another was that electricity moves very quickly. A third was the invention of the Leyden jar, in which electricity can be stored. These discoveries led people to think about the possibility of sending messages along wires by electricity. If a Leyden jar was connected to one end of a long wire, that fact would be known very quickly at the other end. In 1837 the British inventors William F. Cooke (1806–79) and Charles Wheatstone (1802–75) designed an electric telegraph. The next year a 13-mile telegraph line was built between two English railway stations. In that same year an American painter, Samuel F. B. Morse (1791–1872), invented a better type of telegraph. He also invented a code system of dots and dashes that is called Morse code.

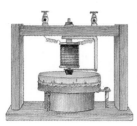

Bell's first telephone, 1876.

After the invention of the telegraph many inventors tried to find a way to send spoken words, instead of just a coded message, through a wire. Several successful telephones were invented. In 1876 the Scottish-American inventor Alexander Graham Bell (1847–1922) was the first to patent the telephone.

After many years of research by many inventors, the Italian electrical engineer Guglielmo Marconi (1874–1937) invented the wireless telegraph, which he patented in 1896. In 1904 the British scientist Sir John Ambrose Fleming (1849–1945) invented the vacuum tube. With improvements made by the American scientist Lee De Forest (1873–1961), the vacuum tube proved to be of great importance for controlling and amplifying electrical signals in wireless telegraphy. It also made the development of radio possible. Marconi's wireless could only send beeps; radio could send voice or music. Radio broadcasts began in the early 1920's. Within a few years many inventors had begun work on the development of television and radar. Today communications satellites orbiting the earth relay telephone calls and television signals around the world. Thus the vacuum tube led to the growth of a new branch of engineering: electronics.

In 1948 transistors were invented and began to replace vacuum tubes. Transistors have since been miniaturized enough to fit thousands onto a tiny silicon chip for use in pocket calculators and personal computers.

▶ INVENTIONS AND SCIENCE

The instruments with which we observe and measure the world around us make up another important group of inventions. Some of the most important instruments are very simple. Many date back thousands of years. The invention of the measuring rod made it possible to measure length in standard units. This was important because measurements based on the human body, such as length of the foot, vary from person to person. When land had to be divided up or when large buildings were built, exact measurements were essential. Scales, another ancient invention of importance, helped trade by measuring weight. Later, scales became useful in scientific work.

Prehistoric people told the time of day by the sun's shadow. They used this idea for the sundial. By 1500 B.C. water clocks and hourglasses were also in use. In the A.D. 1300's mechanical clocks were invented in Europe. The pendulum clock was invented in the 1600's. The pendulum made clocks more accurate than they had ever been before. In the 1700's a British instrument maker, John Harrison (1693–1776), invented the marine chronometer, the first clock accurate enough to tell ships' captains the time in their homeland when they were far out at sea. This was essential in calculating the ship's position.

A number of very important scientific instruments were invented in the 1600's. Most of these used ideas that had been known for a long time but were applied in a new way. For example, eyeglasses had been invented by the 1200's. Early in the 1600's some unknown inventor—probably in the Netherlands—put two lenses in a tube and invented the telescope. In 1609 the Italian scientist Galileo Galilei (1564–1642) invented the astronomical telescope—he had the idea of using the telescope to look at the stars, sun, and planets. With it he discovered mountains on the moon, the satellites of Jupiter, the phases of Venus, sunspots, and many new stars. The microscope, important in biology, was invented by using lenses to look closely at small objects.

Two other important scientific instruments that were invented in the 1600's are the thermometer and the barometer. Both were developed slowly, in a number of stages. These instruments, which measure temperature and atmospheric pressure, are important in meteorology, the science of weather.

Today many thousands of instruments, from the simple ruler to giant particle accelerators for atomic research, are used in science and engineering. Scientists are interested in understanding the natural world; engineers and inventors are concerned with controlling it. Today these two interests overlap. However, until about 200 years ago science was not important in engineering. Since the late 1700's a new branch of engineering has developed: applied science. Applied science uses scientific knowledge to help control natural phenomena and has been very useful to inventors. The science of chemistry is used to make better steel. Knowledge from biology is used in medicine. Physics is used in aircraft design.

▶ **OTHER INVENTIONS**

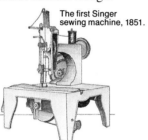
The first Singer sewing machine, 1851.

Many inventions throughout the centuries have had to do with food, clothing, or shelter—our basic needs. For example, the idea of salting or drying foods to preserve them was a very early invention. So was the idea of preserving food by keeping it cold. In the early 1800's the French chef Nicolas Appert (1750–1841) invented canning, a major advance in food preservation. The development of refrigeration equipment by the American inventor John Gorrie (1803–55) made it easier to keep food cold. Clarence Birdseye (1886–1956), also an American, invented still another method of preserving foods: quick-freezing.

Clothing is an ancient invention, so old that we cannot say when it was first used. The earliest clothing was probably made from animal skins. About 10,000 years ago weaving was invented, making cloth possible. The invention of dyeing has helped make clothing more attractive. In the 20th century artificial fibers, such as nylon and rayon, have made it easier to take care of clothing. The practical sewing machine invented by an American, Elias Howe (1819–67), made clothing easier to manufacture and therefore less expensive. Many small inventions help to hold clothing together. Some are quite old, such as the safety pin, which was invented over 3,000 years ago. Others are 20th-century inventions, such as the zipper and Velcro.

Early humans took shelter in caves from storms and cold. Then they began to build shelters. When people started to live in villages and towns, larger and more permanent structures were built. Those involved many new inventions. The earliest builders used rocks and dead trees, but even in prehistoric times people had begun to shape the building materials to suit their desires. Tools were invented for cutting down trees and making planks from them and for cutting and shaping stone. At first these tools were themselves wood or stone. Later, metal tools were invented. The Egyptian pyramids show us how long ago people learned to build massive structures. The Great Pyramid of Cheops at Giza, Egypt, was built over 4,500 years ago. It is still one of the largest structures in the world. Some of the stone blocks in this pyramid weigh over 50 tons. To cut such large pieces of stone, shape them, and move them into position required many inventions.

Today the construction of any building requires the use of many different inventions. Hammers, saws, drills, planes, and pulleys are used. The construction of large buildings requires the use of cranes and power shovels run by gasoline or diesel engines. Many of the materials used are ancient inventions, while others were invented quite recently. Bricks have been used since prehistoric times. Mortar was an invention of the Romans. Iron and steel were not used for building until the 1800's. The 20th century brought the use of reinforced concrete, aluminum, plastics, and many other materials.

▶ **INVENTIONS TODAY**

Millions of inventions are in use today. Some date from prehistoric times; others are quite recent. Every year there are thousands more. These new inventions in turn will lead to other inventions and improvements.

Many of today's inventions are the work of teams of inventors and engineers, working in well-equipped laboratories, developing complex devices such as space labs and high-definition television. Many inventions are still being made by individuals working alone. Each of these involves thousands of earlier inventions as well as new ideas.

Though many conditions have changed over the years, the basic process of invention is the same as ever.

DUANE H. D. ROLLER
The University of Oklahoma

AZTECS

The Aztecs were an American Indian people of central Mexico, best known as the builders of an empire that swiftly fell under Spanish control during the years 1519 to 1521.

The defeat of the Aztecs was no ordinary conquest. The capital of their empire was a city larger than Rome. In its beauty it resembled Venice, set in the middle of a lake with canals for streets.

Although the city was demolished in the final battle of 1521, its fame has endured. Aztec civilization is remembered today for its elaborate religious life, complex social organization, elegant literature, and monumental works of sculpture.

► SOCIAL ORDER

What made Aztec society run smoothly? How was it organized?

Such questions cannot be answered fully. Yet there is a wealth of information in the writings of conquerors and missionaries. Aztecs themselves learned to use alphabetic script, and some of them wrote descriptions of life as it had been before the Spanish Conquest. These early accounts are our sources.

Family and Community

When a man tied the end of his cloak to the corner of a woman's blouse, she became his wife and he could marry no other. Although he might take one or more secondary ''wives,'' only the children of his actual wife could inherit his property.

A man's duties included farming, soldiering, and the various trades, such as carpentry and metalwork. A woman took care of the home, wove cloth, or practiced medicine.

Children also had responsibilities. Girls helped with the weaving. Boys fetched firewood or went to the marketplace for scraps of maize (corn) and beans left by the merchants.

Settlements. Families lived in villages, towns, or cities. Every town had neighborhoods, each with its chief. A city with many neighborhoods might be divided into four quarters, each quarter with its chief. These divisions made it easy to recruit people for military service or large work projects.

In the Valley of Mexico, the center of the Aztec world, there were dozens of cities. The largest was the capital, called Tenochtitlán, which may have had a population of 200,000. Tenochtitlán and its twin city, Tlatelolco, were located on islands in the middle of a shallow lake. The islands were connected to the mainland by earthen causeways.

Today the capital of the republic of Mexico is Mexico City. It is on the same site, but the lake, over the years, has been mostly drained.

Social Classes. Like cities today, the Aztec capital was a place of bustling activity, filled with people of all kinds. Everybody, however, fit into one of three categories: nobles, commoners, and *tlatlacotin*. The *tlatlacotin* were poor people who had sold themselves as permanent workers. Their children, however, were born free.

This drawing by Ignacio Marquina shows the Aztec capital Tenochtitlán as it appeared in 1519. It is based on the descriptions of Spanish conquerors and the remains of Aztec monuments.

High officials were usually chosen from the noble class. Commoners were also selected, if of proven ability.

Government

Each city was ruled by a king, who gave orders to neighborhood chiefs and to kings of cities under his control. There was no single chain of command but several, each ending with one of the important kings. These kings made alliances among themselves. Since Tenochtitlán was the strongest of the cities, its ruler can be called emperor or king of the empire.

The reason for controlling other cities was to make them pay taxes, or tribute. Tribute goods included cloaks, hides, timber, stone, precious feathers, jewels, gold, and various foods.

Warfare. People did not like giving tribute to a king in a distant city. They were loyal to their own town. But if they refused to pay, they were threatened with armed attack.

Aztec armies were well equipped with bows and arrows, spears, and a kind of wooden sword, called *macana*, which was edged with sharp bits of stone.

If the kings or emperor heard of a faraway city rich in goods, they sent warriors to conquer it. Afterward they divided up the tribute and made sure that it kept coming regularly. This is how the empire grew.

▶ WAY OF LIFE

Traditional Aztec wisdom preached caution. The saying "The world is slick and slippery" meant it is easy to make mistakes in life. Aztecs also said, "Not twice on earth," meaning you only live once, so enjoy life while you can.

From Birth to Death

When a girl was born, she was presented with a tiny sewing basket. A boy was given a miniature shield and four little arrows. Before the age of 4, children had their ears pierced. At 5 or 6, children could go out to play, if they had finished their chores.

Education. At 10, children were legally responsible for their actions and could be sentenced to punishment. At this age all boys and girls were sent to neighborhood boarding schools. Some students learned trades. Others studied history, music, the art of speaking, and the interpretation of dreams.

Fragment of an Aztec Song

We merely come to stand sleeping,
we merely come to dream. It
is not true, not true that
we come to live on earth.
We come to do as herbs in spring:
and though our hearts come
sprouting, come green, those
few flowers of our flesh
that open wither away.

— translated by John Bierhorst from *Cantares Mexicanos*, a manuscript written in the 1500's.

At 15, a young woman was ready for marriage. The typical young man became a warrior and would marry later.

Dress. Men wore loincloths and simple cloaks knotted over one shoulder. Women wore sleeveless blouses and wrap-around skirts of cotton cloth.

Shelter and Food. Houses were of one story and might have several rooms, each facing a central courtyard. The kitchen with its fireplace was in the rear. A young family often lived in a single room in the house of the husband's father.

Maize, beans, squash, and turkey were important foods. Crops were grown on island gardens called *chinampas*, made of fertile soil scooped from the lake bottom.

Commerce. More unusual foods, such as cacao, pineapples, and vanilla, were brought by merchants from the lowlands. Cacao beans, the source of chocolate, were often used as money in the great marketplaces, where goods from all over the Aztec world were traded.

Goods came to market on the backs of porters. There were no beasts of burden and no wheeled vehicles. Water transport was by dugout canoe.

Old Age. Alcohol was restricted by law. But the elderly could drink as much as they wanted. This, along with retirement from work, was a privilege of old age.

Aztec statues are noted for their massive size and mysterious details. *Left:* The great statue of the earth goddess Snake Skirt wearing a carved necklace of human hands and hearts. *Above:* The famous "calendar stone." In the center is the face of an Aztec earth god.

Funerals. Long prayers were said for a dead person. The corpse was either buried or cremated, together with a sewing basket and weaver's tools (for a woman) or weapons (for a man).

It was believed that most people went to the dead land beneath the earth. Those who had drowned went to the paradise of the rain god. The most honored dead were men killed in battle and women who had died in childbirth. They went to the sky to live with the sun.

Religion

Aztecs worshipped many gods in addition to the rain god and the sun. There was the fire god, called Old God. There was an earth goddess, called Snake Skirt, and a goddess of love, named Flower Plume.

Merchants and hunters had special gods who received their prayers. The city of Tenochtitlán had a tribal god, Huitzilopochtli (wee-tseel-oh-POACH-tlee), who protected the city's warriors.

Feasts and the Calendar. The year was divided into 18 "months," each with 20 days. In each of these months there was a feast in honor of one or more gods. The rain god and the maize god were remembered in the spring. One of the fall months was devoted to Cloud Snake, god of hunting. Religious feasts were marked by parades and music. At the end of the year were five unlucky days, when people stayed indoors.

At the close of every 52 years a special ceremony was held. All fires were put out. Then a priest kindled a new fire using a drilling stick. Runners with torches carried the new fire to each of the settlements in the Valley of Mexico.

The Payment. Aztecs believed that the gods demanded payment, perhaps an offering of food or a sacrifice of quail. For the new fire ceremony and other important feasts it was necessary to make the "human payment"— the sacrifice of a human being.

Arts

Architects, painters, and musicians were skilled professionals who enjoyed prestige in Aztec society.

The most impressive works of architecture were the pyramids, built in tiers like a wedding cake. At the top of a pyramid were one or more temples, housing statues of gods.

Gods were also depicted in books, made from long sheets of bark paper, rolled or folded. There were no words, only numbers and pictures. The books were used to record history, to explain the functions of gods, and to list the tribute each city had to pay.

Aztec literature as we know it today was not preserved in these old-style books. It was written after the Spanish Conquest, using the alphabetic script learned from missionaries. It includes poetic speeches, myths, histories, and the texts of songs.

Songs, both before and after the Conquest, were accompanied by two kinds of drums: a skin drum, played with the hands, and a two-toned log drum, played with mallets. Songs, as well as speeches, often touch upon historical incidents that are explained more fully in other longer works of literature.

▶ HISTORY

Traditional Aztec histories begin with myths of world creation. They continue with legends about the Aztecs' predecessors, the Toltecs, who archeologists have determined flourished between A.D. 900 and 1200. Their capital, Tula, now in ruins, is located 45 miles (75 kilometers) north of Mexico City. These legends are followed by historical accounts of the kings who built the Aztec empire.

Origin of the Aztecs

Aztecs claimed to have come from a region far to the north, migrating south toward Tula and into the Valley of Mexico. At about this time—according to legend—Tula's last ruler, the priest-king Quetzalcoatl (keh-tsahl-KOH-ahtl) broke his priestly vows and fled in disgrace to the eastern seashore. He disappeared over the water, promising one day to return. After he had gone, an Aztec tribe called the Mexica founded Tenochtitlán, in 1325.

The Rise and Fall of the Aztec Empire

After years of warring with its neighbors, Tenochtitlán formed an alliance with two other cities, Texcoco and Tlacopán. This occurred about 1430. The new alliance, or empire, grew rapidly. By the time of the emperor Montezuma II, Aztecs controlled a territory stretching from the Pacific Ocean to the Gulf of Mexico and south to the present border of Guatemala.

A close-up view of the tiers of a Teotihuacan pyramid located outside Mexico City. Teotihuacan means "Palace of the Gods."

Spanish Conquest. It was Montezuma II who greeted the conqueror Hernando Cortes in 1519 (or the year 1 Reed by the Aztec calendar). At first Montezuma believed Cortes was the legendary Quetzalcoatl, who was to return in the year 1 Reed. Hesitant to give offense, Montezuma was taken prisoner by the Spaniards and mysteriously killed. Unable then to restrain the populace by peaceful means, Cortes resorted to force. Firearms, horses, and steel armor gave the Spaniards an edge. But they could not have won without the help of Aztec cities that sided with them, eager to see Tenochtitlán humbled. The capital was reduced to rubble during the fierce battle of the summer of 1521. A new Spanish city began to rise in its place.

Aftermath. Smallpox and other diseases brought from Europe greatly diminished the Aztec population. The Aztecs, however, did not disappear. The succession of kings continued through the 1500's. Now known as *gobernadores* (governors), they served under Spanish authority. Although the *gobernadores* eventually lost what remained of their powers, people continued to read and write the Aztec language through the 1700's and to keep up many of the ancient customs.

Legacy of the Aztecs

The modern Aztec language, known as Nahuatl or *mexicano*, is still spoken by more than a million Nahua, who continue to plant maize, weave cotton cloth, and play instruments like the log drum. The Nahua live mostly in small towns and villages in central Mexico.

Nationally, Aztec art is recognized as an essential feature of Mexico's heritage. Aztec painting and sculpture have influenced Mexican artists such as Diego Rivera and Miguel Covarrubias. Modern poets such as Octavio Paz have been inspired by Aztec literature.

Perhaps the most widely known legacy of Aztec culture is in the realm of foods and recipes. *Avocado, chili, chocolate,* and *tomato* are all Aztec words. If you have been to a Mexican restaurant or have prepared Mexican food at home, you may have had *enchiladas, guacamole, tacos,* and *tamales.* These are dishes made with ingredients that go back to Aztec times.

JOHN BIERHORST
Author, *The Mythology of Mexico and Central America*

Sprawled out on branches, often high above the ground, iguanas warm themselves and feed on buds, leaves, and flowers. They may also eat small insects.

IGUANAS

Although it looks like a small, fierce dinosaur with its claws and spines, the shy iguana's main pleasure is lounging in the treetops nibbling on tender shoots and leaves. The green iguana, which is the largest lizard in the Americas, may weigh up to 30 pounds (13.6 kilograms) and reach a length of 6 feet (1.8 meters). Its whiplike tail makes up almost two thirds of its length. The green-scaled body has a crest of soft spines running along the middle of the back. Hanging on the throat is a fold of loose skin called a dewlap.

Green iguanas can be found basking in the sun of tropical and subtropical forests from Mexico to Brazil. They belong to the group of reptiles, called Squamata, that includes all lizards and snakes. Its large family includes horned and spiny lizards, chuckwallas, anoles, and basilisks. While most of its relatives live in the Americas, some live as far away as Madagascar and Fiji.

The Life of an Iguana. Iguanas, like all reptiles, are cold-blooded: Their blood is the same temperature as the outside environment. They still need heat for their bodies to function normally, so much of their time is spent soaking up heat energy from the sun. During cold weather, the animals move to the forest floor and seek warm places under logs or in holes.

Each male iguana marks out its own territory. It produces a waxy, scented substance and leaves traces of it among the leaves and branches of its treetop home. It defends this territory against other male iguanas. Rising up on its front legs, it snaps its tail and hisses to scare off an intruding iguana. The best fighter has the largest territory—and mates with the most females.

Iguanas and Their Young. Green iguanas court and breed in January or February. When an iguana mates or is being aggressive, parts of its body, such as the head and shoulders, change color. From its greenish color, the iguana changes to orange or pink.

About two months after breeding, the female digs a tunnel in soft ground and lays 20 to 90 round, white-shelled eggs in a chamber at the tunnel's end. Each egg is about 1 inch (2.5 centimeters) in diameter.

If the nest is not disturbed, the eggs hatch about five months after they are laid. The baby iguanas are about 10 inches (25 centimeters) long. Often, they leave the nest hole together and stay in groups. They clean one another, rub chins, and sleep together.

The young animals are bright green. As they get older, dark bands of scales begin to develop across the shoulders and tail. The iguanas grow rapidly. By the time iguanas are a year old, they are about 3 feet (about 1 meter) long. Although iguanas can live up to ten years, most are killed by predators before their second birthday.

The Iguana and its Environment. At one time the iguana flourished in the lowland forest, but much of the forestland has been cleared to raise crops and cattle. Animals and people eagerly hunt the iguana, killing almost 95 percent of the iguana population for food. Iguana meat is considered such a tasty treat that it is often called "chicken of the trees." The fat of the iguana is also used as a salve for burns.

Today, efforts are being made to establish iguana ranches in tropical forests. The successful breeding of captive iguanas will not only help save the threatened iguana, but it will also save the vanishing tropical forests.

JENNY TESAR
Author, *Introduction to Animals*

Reviewed by DOUGLAS FALK
Assistant Curator
New York Zoological Society

MOLES

If there were a contest for the hardest working animal, the first prize would surely go to the mole—a small mammal that spends most of its life digging underground tunnels. Using its powerful front limbs and spade-shaped front feet, the mole digs through the dirt pushing a mass of earth, sometimes 20 times its own weight, upward to form a heap on the surface. The mole can dig at the rate of over 18 feet (5.5 meters) an hour. In less than a day, this champion builder can dig a tunnel over 300 feet (91 meters) long!

The mole has very poor eyesight; it relies on keen senses of touch and hearing to find its way underground. Even the thick, soft brown fur of the mole is well suited to its digging existence. The fur can lie flat in any direction, which is very helpful as the mole moves back and forth in the narrow tunnels.

All moles are part of a group of mammals known as insectivores, or "insect-eaters." The more than 20 different kinds of moles are found in mild climates throughout North America, Europe, and Asia. Moles are small animals, about the size of mice. They range in length from 2½ to 8½ inches (6 to 22 centimeters), plus a tail of ⅗ inch to 8½ inches (1.5 to 22 centimeters). The average weight of a mole is between ³⁄₁₀ ounce and 6 ounces (9 and 170 grams).

The Life of a Mole. Moles generally live alone, tirelessly digging tunnels and searching for food. They stay active all year long and do not hibernate. As winter approaches, however, moles do collect more food and store it in special underground chambers. Their diet consists of large amounts of food—mainly insect larvae and earthworms. They also eat adult insects, snails, and baby birds.

One North American mole spends part of its time burrowing beneath the ground and part swimming in water. It is the starnose mole. It gets its name from the fleshy starlike ring of feelers around the end of its nose. As the mole hunts, the feelers wave back and forth, helping the animal find its way.

Moles and Their Young. During the spring, moles court and mate. Males will search on the surface and travel through tunnels looking for females. Sometimes a male will wander into the burrow of another male by mistake; then a fight occurs.

With its strong claws, the eastern mole scrapes out underground tunnels, leaving scattered mounds of dirt (or molehills) on the surface to mark its path.

After the male and female find each other and mate, the female prepares a nest. Six weeks later two to five baby moles are born. The babies are pink and hairless at birth. Their eyes are closed. Hair soon grows, and in three weeks the eyes open. In a very short time, at about 5 weeks, the young moles are ready to leave the nest and begin independent lives.

The Mole and its Environment. Moles have few natural enemies. Birds such as owls, ravens, and eagles hunt the mole, but they must wait for the mole to come to the surface. Even though other animals may kill it, the mole has a built-in protection against becoming some animal's dinner—it tastes bad.

The main danger to moles is from people. At one time moles were hunted for their fur, which was used to make clothing. Today, moles are mainly hunted and killed because they destroy the appearance of lawns and gardens and can cause damage to machinery used to tend yards and farm fields. People use a variety of methods to try and get rid of moles —from flooding the tunnels with water to putting mothballs in their burrows. When left to roam under gardens and fields, moles are very helpful. They eat vast quantities of the insects that feed on crops and garden plants.

JENNY TESAR
Author, *Introduction to Animals*

Reviewed by DOUGLAS FALK
Assistant Curator
New York Zoological Society

ISLAM

Islam is one of the world's major religions with close to 1 billion followers. It is also one of the fastest growing religions in the world. The word "Islam" means submission in Arabic, which is the religion's main language of prayer. The "submission" refers to obedience to God. In Arabic, God is called Allah, an all-powerful, all-forgiving, merciful, and compassionate God.

A person who believes in Islam is called a **Muslim**. Muslims are found on every continent, but their greatest concentration is in South Asia, the Middle East, and Africa. The largest Muslim population is in Indonesia. Large numbers of Muslims are also found in Pakistan, India, Bangladesh, Turkey, Egypt, Iran, Nigeria, and the Soviet Union. Over 3 million Muslims live in the United States.

▶ THE BEGINNINGS OF ISLAM

Muslims believe that their religion is based on divine statements, or revelations, from God. These divine revelations came from God through a long line of **prophets**—people chosen by God to speak for Him. Among these prophets are Abraham and Moses from the Old Testament of the Bible. Muslims also believe that Jesus was a great prophet. However, they reject the Christian belief that Jesus is the son of God.

According to Islam, the teachings of the prophets were sometimes misinterpreted or distorted by their followers until the appearance of a prophet named Mohammed (or Muhammad). Muslims believe that Mohammed's teachings are the most accurate and complete.

Mohammed

Mohammed was born about A.D. 570 in the city of Mecca, an important commercial and cultural center in Arabia. Mecca was also the site of an important annual fair that attracted people from many different Arabian tribes. Each tribe worshiped a different idol-god.

When Mohammed was about 40 years old, he had an experience that changed the course of his life. According to Islamic tradition, the angel Gabriel appeared to Mohammed one night while he was meditating and commanded him to tell the word of God to the people.

For more than twenty years, the angel Gabriel continued to appear to Mohammed and give him the word of God. These revelations became the foundation of Islam. They included matters related to religious beliefs, human conduct, government, and relationships among people. They also included a narrative of events similar to those in the Bible.

Mohammed's Preaching

Several years after Mohammed received his first revelation, he began to preach among the people of Mecca. He preached the ideas of equality and charity, and criticized the worshiping of idols. He also spoke against the practice of making large sums of money from interest on loans to needy people.

At first the wealthy leaders of Mecca ignored Mohammed. But as he began to attract more followers, they became alarmed. They threatened Mohammed and persecuted his followers. Because of this persecution, Mohammed and his followers decided to leave Mecca. Their destination was the city of Yathrib, some of whose residents had invited the Prophet to come and help resolve a dispute. Mohammed and his followers went to Yathrib in the year A.D. 622. This became known as the year of **Hegira** or "migration." It was made the year 1 of the Islamic calendar.

In Yathrib, Mohammed became a political and religious leader. In time, the city's name was changed to al-Madinah al-Munawwarah (the enlightened city) or Madinat al-Nabi (the city of the Prophet). Today, it is known as Medina.

352

Mohammed and his followers stayed in Medina for about eight years. During that time Mohammed had more revelations, many of which dealt with rules about organizing Muslim society. Then in 630 Mohammed returned to Mecca, where many people had begun to accept the ideas of his preaching. With the support of the people of Mecca, major tribes throughout Arabia soon converted to Islam. For the first time, many tribes were united in their allegiance to one religion and one God. By the time Mohammed died in 632, Islam was the major religion in Arabia.

▶ ISLAM AFTER THE DEATH OF MOHAMMED

After the death of Mohammed, the Muslims selected Abu Bakr, a close associate of Mohammed, to be their leader. He was given the title of **caliph**, which means "the successor." The caliph was Mohammed's successor only as the leader of the faithful, however, not as a prophet. Muslims considered Mohammed to be the last of the prophets.

The faith of some Muslims was badly shaken with the death of the Prophet. A number of tribes even abandoned Islam. However, Abu Bakr was able to restore the supremacy of the religion in Arabia.

After Abu Bakr's death in 634, Muslim leaders selected a new caliph, Umar Ibn al-Khattab. Under Umar's leadership, the Muslims of Arabia invaded Syria and North Africa, which were part of the Christian Byzantine empire. The Muslims defeated the Byzantine armies there and continued their advance northward until they were stopped in southern Anatolia (the country of Turkey today). Muslim armies also went east and defeated the Persians and took over their empire. These invasions and conquests were part of a Muslim *jihad*, or holy war, to expand the influence of Islam.

Opposite page: A Muslim reads the Koran in the Wazir Khan Mosque in Lahore, Pakistan. The Koran is the holy book on which Islamic religion and law are based. *Below left:* The dome of the Masjid-i-Shah Mosque in Isfahan, Iran, a striking example of arabesque decorative art. *Below:* The Prophets Mosque in Medina, Saudi Arabia.

353

A mosque from the 1500's made of mud and wooden poles at Agadez, Niger.

Two Muslims of the Hausa sect in northern Nigeria. Both countries are in West Africa.

Disagreements About Choosing a Caliph

In 656 Umar was assassinated. This time, Muslim leaders disagreed about the selection of a successor. Some wanted Uthman Ibn Affan, an elderly Muslim from a wealthy and influential family, to become caliph. Others preferred Ali the son of Abu Talib, a cousin and son-in-law of the Prophet Mohammed.

Although Ali was smart, strict, and a devout Muslim, many influential Muslim leaders did not favor him as caliph. They chose Uthman instead. Ali accepted this decision, but some of his followers did not. One of these followers killed Uthman twelve years later.

After the death of Uthman, Ali was chosen to succeed him as caliph. Uthman's relatives and supporters, however, tried to arouse opposition to Ali. The most powerful person to oppose him was Mu'awiyah, the governor of Damascus. Mu'awiyah tried to defeat Ali in battle, but failed. Ali ruled for five years before he too was assassinated.

After Ali's death, Mu'awiyah quickly gathered enough support to declare himself the new caliph. As caliph, he made Damascus the capital of the Muslim empire and suppressed all opposition. When he died in 680, his son Yazid was named caliph. From then on, the position of caliph became hereditary (passed from one ruler to the next of kin). Mu'awiyah's family, the Umayyad, became the ruling **dynasty**, or family of rulers.

A Major Split Develops

When Yazid was made caliph, a major split began to develop in Islam. A group called the Shi'ites refused to accept Yazid as caliph. In-stead, they wanted Ali's son Husayn to be made caliph. But Husayn and a small group of relatives and followers were killed by members of an Umayyad army.

The Sunnites and Shi'ites. The division that formed between the Shi'ites and a group called the Sunnites remains to this day. The Shi'ites believe that Muslim leadership was restricted to descendants of Ali, Mohammed's son-in-law. The Sunnites believe that Muslim leadership could be passed to elected members of the Muslim community.

The Shi'ites have a special place for Ali and his descendants in their faith. They consider Ali to be the first **imam**, or leader in prayer. The Shi'ites believe that Ali and eleven imams who followed were especially suited to interpret Mohammed's revelations and lead the Muslim community since they were descendants of the Prophet. According to Shi'ites, the twelfth imam disappeared around the year 873. They believe that God hid him from humans, and that someday he will return to lead the Muslim community and the world.

Today the Shi'ites account for about 12 to 15 percent of all Muslims, and they are spread throughout the Islamic world. The largest concentration is in Iran, where they form a majority. The Shi'ites rank their religious leaders, or **mullahs**, according to religious learning, piety, and leadership. The highest rank is that of **ayatollah**. Shi'ite leaders have great prestige, and their judgments have the status of law.

The Sunnites represent the great majority of Muslims in the world today. They accept the historical order of caliphs and other elected successors as the true and rightful line of authority. Although the position of caliph no longer exists, the King of Saudi Arabia is responsible for guarding and preserving the holy cities of Mecca and Medina. Sunnite religious leaders have less authority than Shi'ite leaders, and some Sunnite and Shi'ite laws are different. Despite their differences, however, Shi'ites and Sunnites agree on most major matters of faith and worship.

▶ THE RISE AND DECLINE OF THE ISLAMIC EMPIRE

Under the Umayyad dynasty, Islamic conquests greatly expanded the territory ruled by Muslims. The Muslims conquered North Africa and even moved into Europe through Spain and Portugal. Although their advance into western Europe was finally stopped, parts of Spain were ruled by the Muslims for about seven hundred years. The last of the Muslims were finally expelled from Spain in 1492.

In 750 the Umayyad dynasty was overthrown by the Abbasids, a dynasty descended from Abbas, one of Mohammed's uncles. The Abbasids moved the capital of the Islamic empire to Baghdad, a new city that they built on the Tigris River. (Today, Baghdad is the capital of Iraq.)

Independent Islamic States

With the fall of the Umayyad dynasty, the Muslims in Spain set up an independent state and separated from the Islamic empire to the east. During a period of decline beginning in the 800's other regions of the empire also became independent under their local dynasties.

As different local governments emerged, the Islamic empire lost much of its unity. But Muslims continued to control a vast area. Muslims in India, for example, founded an empire that remained in power until the British took control in the 1700's. The Ottoman Turks, who originally came from central Asia, defeated the Byzantine Empire in Greece and Turkey. In time, their Muslim empire expanded to embrace a vast area including southeastern Europe, the Middle East, and most of North Africa. The Ottoman Turks remained in power until the 1900's. Another Muslim empire based in Persia was very powerful during the 1500's and the 1600's.

The Muslims ruled in other places as well. Areas of Southeast Asia, east and west Africa, and central Asia remained largely in Muslim control until they were invaded and occupied by European colonial powers in the 1700's and 1800's.

The Non-Muslim Threat

From the late 1000's to the 1200's, European Christians invaded the Middle East to recover the Holy Land from the Muslims and to gain land and wealth. These Christian invasions were known as the Crusades. By the 1200's, the Muslims had succeeded in getting rid of the Christian Crusaders.

Far left: **The minaret of the Kadhimain Mosque in Baghdad, Iraq. Note the arabesque decoration on the lower portion of the tower.**

Left: **A street scene in Iran. At left, note the three women in chadors, long veils that cover their bodies and faces.**

Above: A Muslim woman in Manila, Philippines. *Above right:* The Grand Sultan Mosque in the Arab quarter of Singapore. *Right:* A Muslim from Luxor in Egypt.

The Muslims were not so successful in other places. In the western part of the Islamic empire, the Christians of Spain were gradually reclaiming the country from the Muslims. By the end of the 1400's this reconquest was complete, and Muslims were forced either to convert to Christianity or to leave Spain.

The Treatment of Non-Muslims

According to Islamic belief, non-Muslim peoples are supposed to be tolerated and protected when they are within the Islamic state. In most cases in the past, they were. Nevertheless, when the Muslims felt threatened by foreign powers, they often limited the freedom of their non-Muslim subjects. During the time of the Crusades, for example, the Christians were suppressed. In later years, life for Christians within the Ottoman Empire was difficult because of wars between the Ottoman Turks and European powers. In most cases, however, Christians and Jews were allowed to worship freely and run their own affairs.

The Mosque in Moroni, the capital city of Comoros, an island country off the southeastern coast of Africa.

▶ THE IMPACT OF ISLAM

By the 800's, Islamic influence was greater than that of any other empire in history up to that time. Muslims ruled from Spain and Morocco in the west to India in the east. Most of this expansion had been achieved through conquest. During the centuries that followed, however, the expansion of Islam was accomplished primarily through trade and the conversion of people by Islamic missionaries.

As a result of Islamic expansion, people of many different ethnic groups, speaking many different languages, intermingled with each other. Arabic became a common language for trade and communication. In much of the Middle East the population was Arabized, meaning that their language and culture became Arabic. In other areas, people retained their own language and culture, although they often used Arabic script for writing.

The interior of the Great Mosque in Cordoba, Spain.

Three Muslim girls in white prayer robes study the Koran. They are from Maldives, an island located in the Indian Ocean.

Mathematics, natural sciences, literature, and art flourished in the Islamic empire. The Arabs invented algebra. Art and architecture were blended together in the building of beautiful **mosques**, or houses of worship, and palaces. The unique art of **arabesque**, a special type of decoration with intricate floral and geometric patterns, was used in building, painting, and embroidery. **Calligraphy**, the art of writing in artistic styles, was often included in arabesque designs as well.

Islamic civilization influenced many aspects of European culture such as the use of irrigation, new types of plants, and the Arabic system of numbers. The Muslims also translated many books from ancient Greek and were responsible for the transmission of Greek ideas to Europe.

▶ ISLAMIC BELIEFS

Islam views life on earth as a brief, passing phase that leads to eternal life after death. This eternal life can be filled with bliss and happiness or torment and anguish depending on how one's life was lived on earth. If people obey the teachings of Islam, they will be rewarded with eternal life in Paradise. If they do not obey, they will suffer the agonies of Hell.

The Koran

The teachings of Islam are based on the book known as the **Koran**. After Mohammed's death, Muslim leaders collected and preserved the Prophet's revelations in the Koran. Muslims believe the Koran to be the words of God spoken through Mohammed. Although they accept the Bible as a holy book, they believe that the Koran is the ultimate source of divine instruction and information. Many familiar biblical events and people, such as the Creation, the Flood, the Exodus, Abraham, Moses, David, Solomon, and Jesus, are also found in the Koran.

The Koran is divided into 114 *suras*, or chapters. Each *sura* is divided into *ayat*, or verses. People with beautiful voices are trained to chant the *suras*. Each morning, radio and television stations in virtually all Muslim countries begin with chanting. Happy or sad occasions usually include chanted selections from the Koran as well. Since the revelations of the Koran were originally in Arabic, all Muslims, whether Arabic-speaking or not, try to learn parts of it in that language. The Arabic of the Koran is considered the most eloquent form of the language.

Islamic Laws

The Koran is also the main source for Islamic law. Another source is the **Hadith**, a collection of sayings and decisions of the

Prophet Mohammed. Occasionally, the Koran and the Hadith may not provide clear guidance about a specific situation. In such cases, Islamic judges will try to base their decision on a similar situation in the Koran or Hadith, or by general agreement among learned leaders. The judges may also be guided by their own interpretation if necessary. The body of Islamic laws based on the Koran and the decisions of Islamic judges is called **Shariah**, or ''God's Way.'' Among these laws are prohibitions against stealing, lying, killing, adultery, and alcoholic beverages. The laws also instruct Muslims to be charitable and modest, and to treat each other fairly.

Islamic Duties

Besides following Islamic laws and accepting its beliefs, a Muslim must fulfill five important duties called the **Five Pillars of Islam**. These five duties are:

1. **Shahadah**, or profession of faith. Every Muslim must believe that there is only one God, and that Mohammed is His messenger and the Prophet. The belief that Mohammed is God's prophet and messenger distinguishes Islam from Judaism and Christianity, which believe in the same God as Islam.

2. **Salat**, or prayer. Muslims must pray five times every day: at daybreak, at noon, at mid-afternoon, at sunset, and at night before going to sleep. At noon on Friday, the Islamic holy day, Muslims go to the mosque to pray. After the noon prayer, an imam gives a sermon.

The duty of prayer can be done at work, at home, in school, or anywhere else. Before praying, Muslims must wash their faces, necks, hands, arms, and feet as a means of purification. Prayer consists of reciting short selections from the Koran, bowing, kneeling, and touching the ground with the forehead, an expression of submission to God. Some Muslims carry a small prayer rug that they use to stand and kneel on during their prayers.

When praying, Muslims must face the direction of the holy city of Mecca. In Mecca's

Left: The word ''Mecca'' written in Arabic calligraphy. *Below:* Muslims celebrate the Feast of Sacrifice at the Great Mosque in Mecca, Saudi Arabia. In the center is the Kaaba, a small building built to enclose the Black Stone, Islam's most holy object. *Right:* A close-up of the Kaaba.

main house of worship, the Great Mosque, there is a small stone building called the **Kaaba**. The Kaaba was built to enclose the Black Stone, Islam's most holy object. According to Islamic tradition, the black stone was given to the prophet Abraham by God.

3. **Zakat**, or almsgiving. Unless they are poor, Muslims must give a portion of their wealth to the needy. The normal amount is 2.5 percent of one's yearly income or 10 percent of revenue from crops or businesses. Wealthy people are encouraged to give more. It is considered *sadaqah*, or a good deed, to give more than the recommended amount.

For centuries, most of the zakat money of each country was given to special endowments called *waqf* to support schools and hospitals, to aid the needy, to maintain mosques, and to fund other charitable activities. In recent years a number of governments in Muslim countries have made the zakat part of their tax system, and the revenue is still used for different types of social welfare programs.

4. **Sawm**, or fasting. All Muslims, except children, pregnant women, and sick people, must fast from daybreak to sunset each day during the month of *Ramadan*. They are not allowed to eat or drink anything, including water, during those hours. At the end of the month, Muslims end their fast and celebrate *Id al-Fitr*, or the Feast of Ramadan. *Id al-Fitr*, a three-day holiday, is one of the two most important Muslim feasts. The dates for this feast and other Islamic holy days are determined by a lunar calendar based on the phases of the moon. This calendar is different from the one you use, which is based on the solar year. Muslims use both types of calendar.

5. **Hajj**, or pilgrimage. Muslims who are able to travel and can afford it must make a pilgrimage to the city of Mecca at least once in their lifetime. This pilgrimage must take place during *Id al-Adha*, or the Feast of Sacrifice, which is the other great feast in the Islamic lunar calendar. It commemorates the prophet Abraham's willingness to sacrifice his son as an offering to God. When God saw Abraham's faith, he was merciful and sent an angel with a lamb to be sacrificed instead.

Each year nearly 2 million people travel to Mecca to commemorate *Id al-Adha*. Dressed in plain white robes, the pilgrims pray at the Great Mosque and walk around the Kaaba seven times while praying. They also visit other holy sites nearby. Muslims of all racial, national, and ethnic groups make this pilgrimage. A man who makes the pilgrimage may be called **hajji**. A woman may be called **hajjah**. These terms mean that the people have fulfilled their hajj duty. Upon their return home, they are greeted with special celebrations.

▶ **ISLAM TODAY**

The past hundred years have brought about many changes in the Muslim world. These changes extend from politics and government to the personal lives of Muslim individuals.

A hundred years ago, most of the Muslim world was under the control of European colonial powers. Over time, the Muslims resisted European rule and resistance led to independence. But instead of the formation of one or two large Islamic states as in the past, these movements led to the formation of more than forty independent nations. Ethnic and national feelings were often as important as religion in causing the independence movements and in deciding the borders of the new nations. Nevertheless, religion is still a very important part of these countries, and Islam remains a strong force throughout the world.

The Muslim countries of the world today have a variety of governments, including kingdoms, republics, democracies, and dictatorships. In some of these countries, such as Saudi Arabia and Iran, traditional Islamic rules and customs are strictly enforced by the government. In other countries, such as Turkey and Albania, there is a separation between religion and the state.

Muslim countries differ in other ways as well. In some, women cannot vote in elections. Yet in Pakistan, the country with the second largest Muslim population, a woman served for more than a year as prime minister, the most powerful position in the country. Some Muslim countries have great wealth, such as those around the Persian Gulf that are rich with oil. But others are very poor, as in the case of Bangladesh, and most of the Muslim countries of western Africa. Although the Muslims of today have differences that divide them, they also have a common heritage and a strong bond in their religion.

DR. MOUNIR A. FARAH
President, The Middle East Outreach Council
Reviewed by TALAT SAIT HALMAN
New York University

نَ الفَن

Above: Calligraphy, or beautiful handwriting, is an important element in Islamic art and architecture. Arabic, the language of most Islamic texts, can be written in a variety of beautiful scripts. The Arabic word for "art" is written here.

Right: Calligraphy and elaborate designs called arabesques decorate a wall in a mosque in Iran. The prayer niche in the wall orients the worshiper toward Mecca. *Opposite page middle:* Glazed earthenware tiles bear an Arabic inscription.

ISLAMIC ART AND ARCHITECTURE

Islam is the religious faith preached by the Arab prophet Mohammed. During the five hundred years after Mohammed's death in A.D. 632, Islam spread far beyond its place of origin in the Arabian Peninsula. The followers of Mohammed, called Muslims, conquered the rest of the Middle East, as well as North Africa, Spain, central Asia, and north and central India. Most of the conquered people accepted the Islamic religion.

As Islam spread, a distinctive style of Islamic art gradually developed. It was used mainly for religious architecture, book illustrations, and the decoration of pottery, metalware, and other useful objects. Islamic art was influenced by the artistic styles of the conquered regions. These styles included late Roman, Byzantine, and Persian art.

The development of Islamic art was also influenced by two religious restrictions. Mohammed warned artists not to imitate God, the creator of all life, by making images of living things. Most religious art therefore consisted of ornamental designs that did not represent people or animals. The second restriction discouraged the use of costly materials. Islamic artists, therefore, worked mainly with brass, clay, and wood. They learned to decorate objects made of these less expensive materials so skillfully that they looked as beautiful as silver and gold.

▶ DESIGN CHARACTERISTICS

The restriction on making images led to the development of one of the most outstanding features of Islamic art. Artists avoided depicting lifelike forms. Instead, they developed a special kind of decoration, called **arabesque**. An arabesque is a very complicated design. It can consist of twisting patterns of vines, leaves, and flowers. It can be made up of geometric shapes and patterns of straight lines, or

▶ ARCHITECTURE

The religious buildings known as mosques, where Muslims worship, are among the most important examples of Islamic architecture. Other kinds of buildings include madrasahs, or religious schools; tombs; and palaces.

Mosques. The first mosques were simple buildings made of wood and clay. Then, as the world of Islam grew in size and power, large mosques of cut stone and brick were built. Because no Islamic building tradition yet existed, these early mosques were modeled after Christian churches. The oldest existing mosque, the Dome of the Rock in Jerusalem, was built in 691. It has many features of Byzantine Christian churches, including Grecian-style columns and mosaic decorations.

Muslim architects soon began to develop a new type of religious building, designed spe-

it can have curving lines that twist and turn over each other. Sometimes animal shapes were used, but they were always highly stylized and not lifelike.

Another important characteristic of Islamic art is the use of **calligraphy**, or beautiful handwriting. Arabic, the language of most Islamic texts, can be beautifully written in several different kinds of script. These include the straight, geometric Kufic script and the rounded, flowing Naskhi. Islamic artists used Arabic script (which is read from right to left) as part of their designs for religious books, wall decorations, and art objects. Especially beautiful calligraphy and decoration were used for copies of the Koran, the holy book of the Islamic faith.

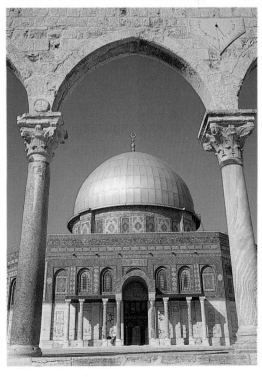

Right: The Dome of the Rock in Jerusalem, built in A.D. 691, is the oldest existing mosque. Some of its features were modeled after early Christian churches.

cifically for Islamic worship. An early example of the new design is the Great Mosque in Damascus, begun about 705. It is entered through a rectangular court with covered passageways on three sides. In the court is a fountain for washing before prayer. The fourth wall of the court is closest to Mecca, the holy city of Islam. All Muslims face in the direction of Mecca when they pray. The wall is marked by a small, arched prayer niche. Over the aisle leading to this niche is a dome. A tower, or **minaret**, is used to call the faithful to prayer.

Other architects developed variations on this basic style. Some mosques have domes over each end of the aisle leading to the prayer niche. Other mosques have a large central dome. Some domes are ridged on the outside and resemble large melons. Inside, the ceilings of domes are often covered with decorative forms that resemble honeycombs, scales, or stalactites (icicle-like formations found in caves). Many mosques, especially those in

Spain, North Africa, and Persia, are covered with tiles. In the 1500's and 1600's mosques became more complex, with many domes and minarets. The Sultan Ahmed Mosque (also called the Blue Mosque), in Istanbul, Turkey, is a typical example.

Madrasahs and Tombs. Madrasahs, or religious schools, were often built next to mosques. They are four-sided structures built around a central court. Each side has a large arched hall that opens onto the courtyard. Students attended lectures in the large halls and lived in smaller rooms within the structure.

Sometimes the tomb of a ruler was part of a complex of buildings that also included a mosque and a madrasah. The tomb-mosque of Sultan Hasan, built in the mid-1300's in Cairo, Egypt, is such a complex. It is laid out like a cross, with four halls opening off a large square court.

Another well-known tomb is that of the Tatar warrior Tamerlane, which was built in the city of Samarkand about 1400. (Today Samarkand is part of the Soviet Union.) This building has a melon-shaped dome covered with brilliant blue and gold tiles. The tiles are made of glazed earthenware cut into various sizes and arranged in elaborate patterns. Perhaps the most famous Islamic tomb of all is the Taj Mahal in Agra, India. It was built in the 1600's by the ruler Shah Jahan as a tomb for

Islamic art is found in many parts of the world. *Left:* The tomb of Tamerlane, in the present-day Soviet Union, is notable for its tiled, melon-shaped dome. *Below left:* The Court of the Lions is one of three courtyards of the Alhambra palace in Granada, Spain. *Below right:* The Blue Mosque in Istanbul, Turkey, has the tall minarets (towers) and clustered domes typical of later mosques.

his wife. The Taj Mahal is so renowned that its very name calls up images of almost unreal splendor and beauty.

Palaces. The early Muslim rulers, or caliphs, were used to desert life; they did not like living in crowded cities. They built palaces in the desert where they could go to relax and hunt. The palaces looked like Roman fortresses, for they were built of stone and surrounded by walls with big towers. The throne rooms, prayer rooms, baths, and living quarters were decorated with murals and mosaics.

In the 700's the capital of the Muslim world moved from Damascus, Syria, to Baghdad, Mesopotamia (now Iraq). The architecture of palaces changed as a result of the move. Domed palaces were built of brick covered with thick layers of stucco, and the interiors were decorated with stucco reliefs. In the Jawsaq Palace, built about 850 in Samarra, Mesopotamia, the stucco ornament was of three distinct styles. One type showed deeply carved vine forms, and another added patterns to the surface of the main design. The third style used more abstract patterns, as in the metalwork of Central Asian nomads. These three styles contributed to the development of arabesque decoration, which became typical of Muslim art all over the world.

Of later palaces, the Alhambra at Granada, Spain, built in the 1300's, is the best known. Its many rooms are built around three open courts. The Court of the Myrtles features a long rectangular pool flanked by hedges. In the center of the inner Court of the Lions is a fountain depicting twelve lions. The lower part of the palace walls are decorated with colored tiles set in geometric patterns. Painted and gilded plaster designs cover the upper walls. Arabic inscriptions in the midst of the ornament say there is "no conqueror but Allah."

▶ **BOOK ILLUSTRATION**

Islamic painting developed mainly in the form of book illustration. Islamic artists produced many beautiful **illuminated manuscripts** (handwritten books decorated with painted pictures and designs). These paintings were created to help explain a scientific text or to add to the pleasure of reading a work of history or literature. Because of the restrictions on making images, illustrations for the Koran and other religious manuscripts often consisted of intricate ornamental designs.

Islamic book illustration reached a high point with the work of Persian artists. This page from a famous Persian epic contains detailed and realistic images.

Nonreligious manuscripts sometimes contained images of human and animal figures. Figures in early illustrations were simple and painted to look flat or two-dimensional. These qualities can be seen in the illustrations for a famous book of fables, *Kalilah and Dimnah*. Later illustrators painted more detailed and realistic works. Especially skilled were artists working in Persia from the 1300's to the 1700's. One of the best-known Persian painters was Kamal ad-Din Bihzad. This artist combined the ornamental style of Persian illustration with realistic observation of people and animals.

By the end of the 1200's, parts of the Islamic world, including Persia, had been invaded by Mongols from the East. From this time on, the influence of Chinese ink paintings, especially landscapes, can be seen in Islamic painting. The last of the great invaders from central Asia was Tamerlane. He and his followers ignored the dictates of their new religion and encouraged artists to paint pictures of people. These pictures still appeared mainly in nonreligious books, however. Most Islamic

illustration remained ornamental, uniting many design elements into an intricate pattern.

The Muslims greatly respected the knowledge contained in books, especially in the Koran. Their book covers nearly always include a flap to cover and protect the page edges. The covers were made of beautifully tooled leather, often with added decorations of gold and bright colors.

▶ DECORATIVE ARTS

Many different arts were used in the decoration of Islamic mosques and palaces. Arabesque carvings in stone, wood, and plaster adorn the doorways, prayer niches, and pulpits of mosques. The borders of the decorations were often inscribed with quotations from the Koran. Both mosques and palaces were decorated with mosaics—pictures made by pressing tiny pieces of colored glass into wet cement. Painted and glazed tiles covered interior and exterior wall surfaces. Glass lamps decorated with arabesques and Arabic letters hung by long chains from ceilings.

Beginning in the 1000's, a new class of wealthy merchants arose in cities throughout the Islamic world. They traded ceramics, leather goods, metalware, and textiles as far east as India and China and as far west as Europe. The tastes and spending power of the merchants, as well as the increased contact with other cultures, led to new developments in the decorative arts. Scenes of everyday and popular stories were realistically portrayed on all kinds of objects. These decorative scenes greatly influenced the development of book illustration.

Left: Islamic potters were skilled at making lusterware, pottery covered with a shining metallic glaze. *Below:* A bronze candlestick is engraved with intricate designs.

Metalware. Islamic metalworkers created beautifully worked brass and bronze objects, including pitchers, boxes, and trays. Sometimes they inlaid these objects with intricate designs of gold or silver. Arabesques, scenes with figures, and Arabic writing were all used as decoration. The designs began as detailed drawings, which were then skillfully adapted to a particular object and material.

Ceramics. By the 800's Islamic potters had developed many different techniques for making ceramics and pottery. A major center of pottery production was the city of Kashan, in Iran. The Kashan potters were especially skilled at making **lusterware**, a kind of pottery that is covered with a shining metallic glaze. Luster glaze was also used on tiles that covered prayer niches, wall surfaces, and the outsides of domes and minarets.

Rugs. Luxurious rugs were made by knotting single strands of wool or silk to create intricate patterns. Fine woolen rugs have more than one hundred knots per square inch, while some silk rugs have as many as eight hundred.

Rugs were used in both mosques and homes. Muslims often kneel on rugs to pray. The designs on these prayer rugs were made to resemble the arch of the prayer niche in a mosque. Nonreligious rugs often were decorated with geometric patterns. Other designs featured arabesques of flowers and plants in imitation of gardens. Animal and hunting scenes sometimes were added to the floral patterns. Dragons and other fantastic creatures frequently were part of the design.

▶ **LATER ISLAMIC ART**

During the Middle Ages, Christians and Muslims fought wars known as the Crusades. The nations of Islam were united in religion and in their common wars against the Christian Europeans. Islamic art was also unified. From Spain to India, the art of the countries of Islam was almost identical.

By the 1400's there was less to unify the Islamic world. Many people in Islamic nations belonged to other religions. The Crusades were over, and Muslim countries sometimes fought against each other.

Artistic activity in the Islamic style continues to flourish. Mosques are still being built; objects of metal, clay, and leather are still ornamented with arabesques; books are illuminated with miniatures; and rugs are still woven in the traditional way. However, after 1500, some Islamic artists began to add elements of European art to their work. Today the art of many Islamic countries has an international character, although the scenes or subjects may relate to a single Islamic nation.

GULNAR K. BOSCH
Florida State University

MAYA

The Maya are an American Indian people who have lived in western Central America for at least 3,000 years. Today, with a population of nearly 5 million, they continue to speak Maya languages and to carry on traditions that go back to the time of their famous ancestors.

During their Classic period, A.D. 200–900, the ancient Maya made advances in painting, sculpture, astronomy, and writing. They built magnificent cities, then abandoned them. In the mid-20th century, many of the palaces and pyramids were cleared of jungle growth and could again be appreciated for their beauty. More recently, scholars have begun to decipher Maya writing and to read the inscriptions on the ancient walls. As a result, the Maya of the Classic period are better known now than they were just a few years ago.

▶ SOCIAL ORDER

Maya cities were built with the co-operation of thousands of people. At the top of the social order stood the king, whose power was granted by the gods. From him, authority flowed downward through the many layers of society.

The King

No pains were spared to establish the dignity of the ruler. His official title was "Great Sun," and his royal ancestry could be traced back to legendary kings or even to the gods. Ordinarily, rulership was passed from father to son. In rare cases the ruler was a woman.

To impress his subjects, the king had a stone pillar, called a **stele**, carved with his portrait. Sometimes he was shown wearing the costume of a god. Surrounding the portrait were inscriptions telling of his deeds, along with the dates of important events in his life. These free-standing steles are one of the most typical features of ancient Maya culture. When the king died, a pyramid might be erected over his tomb, with a small temple at the very top. Evidently there was a close connection between the respect paid to kings and the worship of gods.

The City-State

There was never a single Maya empire. Rather, there were dozens of cities, each with its own government. Among the largest were Tikal in Guatemala, Copán in Honduras, and Palenque (pah-LAYNG-kay) in southern Mexico. In the hope of increasing his power, the king of one of these cities might marry off his sister or daughter to the king of another city. More often, however, a city's influence was extended by conquest.

Warfare. The king himself was the leader of his warriors. His greatest achievement was to capture a rival king and bring him home to be sacrificed. In close combat the warriors wore armor of quilted cotton and used axes, clubs, and long spears. The Maya of the Classic period did not use the bow and arrow.

A conquered city was ruled in the king's name by a group of nobles called governors.

A drawing of how the city of Copán—one of the most important Maya cities—would have looked in late Classic times.

Social Classes. The governors formed one of several classes that were close to the king. Those who served him at home as personal servants, including musicians, formed another class. Still another was the priestly class in charge of religious ceremonies.

An aerial view of one of the larger cities shows a central plaza, surrounded by palaces, pyramids, and temple structures. Behind these are smaller plazas. Farther removed are yet smaller courtyards and smaller buildings. Such arrangements suggest that the ruling classes were ranked so that the most important lived nearest the king.

Beyond the stone buildings are the remains of outlying settlements. These were occupied by the common people whose main business was farming. The entire population, including the residents of these suburbs, might have reached as many as 50,000 for a great city like Tikal.

Temple I at Tikal, Guatemala. This is a good example of Maya architecture.

▶ WAY OF LIFE

The vast region stretching from central Mexico to northwest Costa Rica is known to archaeologists as Mesoamerica. Within this area, ancient Indian cultures built cities, traded with each other, and shared customs. It is not surprising, therefore, to find that the Maya have much in common with the Aztecs and other Mesoamerican peoples, even though they developed their own particular way of life.

▶ WORK

The main work of the ancient Maya was farming. Without large food supplies their cities could not have been built. In the swampy lowlands, raised fields were made by scooping up the rich, wet soil. In hilly country, the slopes were terraced to hold moisture and prevent erosion.

Maize (corn) was the most important crop. Beans, squash, tomatoes, chili peppers, cacao (chocolate), and avocados were also grown.

Weaving. Another important crop was cotton. Women wove cloth from the fiber, using a long loom strapped around the middle of the body and attached at the far end to a post or tree.

For themselves they made long wraparound cotton skirts and loose-fitting blouses; for the men, loincloths and capes. Among the nobles, fancy dress might include a turban wound around the head or necklaces and ear ornaments of jade and feathers, as well as other precious materials.

House Construction. The simpler houses were made of wooden poles set closely together and roofed with thatch. Wooden beds were covered with kapok-filled mattresses. In the stone palaces of the nobles, sleeping platforms were built into the walls.

Transportation. Most men, if they were commoners, were farmers. But many men worked as porters, carrying goods from town to town. There were no beasts of burden and no wheeled vehicles. Yet the Maya were great merchants, bringing goods from as far away as central Mexico and setting up markets in all the cities.

Religion

The Sun God, the Maize God, the planet Venus, and numerous Death gods were among the deities that watched over the Maya world. The Moon Goddess was the most important of the female deities. Often she is shown spinning or weaving.

Blood Offerings. The gods were worshiped, or ''nourished,'' with gifts of blood. Men and women pierced their earlobes or their tongues and ran strips of bark paper through the wound. The blood-soaked paper would then be burned as an offering. Prisoners of war were bled for the same purpose, and some were sacrificed.

Death Gods. The gods of the underworld were among the most feared. When a king died, his tomb was furnished with painted vases showing mythical heroes who had outwitted the lords of death. Following the example of the heroes, the king himself, it was believed, might survive the trials of the underworld and achieve everlasting life.

Arts and Learning

The ancient Maya are celebrated for their artistic and intellectual accomplishments. Few Maya books survive, but Maya artworks are prized possessions in museums around the world.

Books and Writing. Books that open like a folding screen were made of bark paper and painted in red and black. The symbols, found also in stone carvings and on painted vases, can be read more or less like letters in the modern alphabet. They make up the only true writing system developed in ancient America.

Astronomy. A folding-screen book now called the Dresden Codex is the finest of the surviving Maya books. It was written after the Classic period, and parts of it are thought to have been adapted from a Classic source. In this codex is a table for predicting the phases of the planet Venus: when it appears as evening star and when as morning star. The Maya were keen observers of the planets, especially Venus, which they held to be a god that guided them to victory in war.

The Long Count. Many of the peoples in Mesoamerica had accurate calendars, but the calendars ran out after 52 years and had to be started all over again. The Maya had this kind of calendar, too. But they also had a Long Count, which started from a fixed point in the distant past—like our modern calendar, which counts years from the birth of Christ.

Pottery and Painting. Figurines and vases made of fired clay are among the most admired of Maya artworks. Some vases have a carved surface. Others are painted with lifelike scenes. The Maya painters, using a fine brush, achieved a delicacy of line that was well suited to depicting human figures.

Architecture and Sculpture. Stone buildings were roofed by means of the corbel arch, not a true arch but a steep peak made by laying stones closer and closer together. Thus the interiors were dark and narrow and had to be lit by torches. Sometimes painters working in a bold style filled interior spaces with scenes of battles and ceremonies. But inside walls were usually left bare and were probably darkened by smoke.

The exteriors of important buildings were sometimes completely covered with sculpture. Today the exteriors are the color of natural stone. To visualize them as the Maya saw them, one must imagine them as they originally were, vividly tinted with reds, blues, yellows, and greens.

▶ HISTORY

Unlike the Aztecs, the Maya have a long history, spanning thousands of years. Although their time of greatest fame may have passed, they remain a vital people with prospects for the future.

Pre-Columbian Era

It is not known where or when Maya civilization began. The Maya kings themselves traced their origin to the Olmecs, who had built cities along the Gulf of Mexico between 1200 and 100 B.C. The Olmecs are known to have had the Long Count and evidently invented the bar-and-dot method of writing numbers.

Classic Period. During the last years of the Olmecs, the Maya were already building cities of their own. Their writing system and art style matured about A.D. 200, which marks the beginning of the Classic period.

Suddenly, about the year 900, many of the cities were abandoned. No one knows the reason for this Maya "collapse." Disease, food

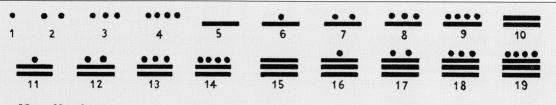

Maya Numbers   Higher numbers are written by placing these symbols for the first 19 numbers in different positions.

A special photograph of a Maya painted vase showing a palace scene. All sides of the vase can be seen in one picture.

shortages, rebellions, and a foreign invasion have all been suggested as the cause.

Postclassic Period. The collapse did not spell the end of Maya civilization. Cities continued to thrive in the Guatemala highlands and in Yucatán. The important Yucatec city of Chichén Itzá belongs to this period. Typical of the Postclassic, the architecture of Chichén Itzá shows strong influences from central Mexico.

Colonial Era

By the time the Spaniards arrived, in the 1520's, the Maya were living in smaller, more hastily built cities than those their ancestors had known. As in the past, they were divided into rival factions. In 1523 the Guatemalan Maya were conquered by Pedro de Alvarado with the help of Indian allies. The conquest of Yucatán was accomplished in the 1540's by Francisco de Montejo and his son.

As a conquered people, the Maya were brought into the Spanish *encomienda* system. This meant that the land was now owned by Spaniards, for whom the Indian people were forced to work.

Burning of the Books. Hoping to end the worship of Maya gods, Christian missionaries collected the ancient books and burned them. But the Maya promptly learned to use the alphabetic script that had been brought from Europe and prepared new books to preserve their traditions. Among these are the *Popol Vuh*, written in Guatemala in the 1550's, and the *Books of Chilam Balam*, written in Yucatán.

The Modern Maya

The Maya of today speak about 30 closely related languages. Among the best-known groups are the Tzotzil and Yucatec of southern Mexico and the Ixil, Quiché, and Kekchi of Guatemala. Christianity has been accepted, but prayers are still made to Maya gods. Maize is grown in small family plots. Yet, as they did during the Colonial era, many Maya still work on large plantations that are owned by non-Indians.

Crisis in Guatemala. Fearing revolution, the government of Guatemala began to attack Indian villages in the early 1980's. Entire communities were massacred and as many as a million people were driven from their homes. For the Maya of Guatemala it was the worst crisis since the Spanish Conquest.

The Maya, however, have shown a remarkable ability to survive as a people and to continue their ancient traditions. Sacred stories, or myths, that go back to the Classic period are still told in many communities. In Guatemala, scholars who themselves are Maya have prepared new Spanish translations of the *Popol Vuh*.

Meanwhile, in Yucatán, copies of the *Books of Chilam Balam* are still kept in a few villages, where they are read publicly in annual ceremonies. A thousand years after the abandonment of Tikal and Palenque, the Maya have not lost their respect for the written word.

JOHN BIERHORST
Author, *The Mythology of Mexico and Central America*

369

IMAGING, DIAGNOSTIC

For centuries, it was a mystery: What did the inside of the human body look like? How did it work? Doctors developed ideas about pain and disease and their treatment by examining the outside of the body. It wasn't until the 1800's that a way to "see" inside the body was discovered.

▶ THE FIRST IMAGE

It was in 1895, while experimenting with a simple device called a cathode-ray tube, that the German physicist Wilhelm Conrad Roentgen discovered a new form of energy. To his astonishment, Roentgen found when he turned the tube on and placed his hand between the tube and a piece of chemically treated cardboard, he could see an image of the bones of his hand on the cardboard. He reasoned that unseen rays must have passed from the tube through his hand to make the image on the cardboard. Roentgen named the rays from this mysterious form of energy X rays, "X" standing for the unknown. Within months after his work became known, other doctors were using the X-ray procedure to diagnose broken bones and other ailments.

▶ X-RAY IMAGING

X rays are no longer a mysterious force; they are known to be very short wavelengths of electromagnetic radiation. The X-ray examinations performed today use the same process developed by Roentgen almost a hundred years ago. A person is placed between an X-ray source and an X-ray image recorder (a piece of film), and the X rays are passed through the body. An image is produced because the body is made up of all different kinds of tissues, and each kind of tissue allows a different amount of X rays to pass through to the film. Bone tissue is very dense and is able to stop more X rays than muscle and fat. So on X-ray film, bones appear white, while less dense tissues range from black to shades of gray. And the lungs, which are filled with air and thus readily allow X rays to pass through, appear almost black.

Although X rays are helpful in diagnosing disease, too much exposure to X rays can damage body tissue and cause cancer. Because of this danger, doctors set limits on the amount of X ray any one person receives during an examination.

▶ COMPUTED TOMOGRAPHY (CT)

In 1972, a new diagnostic tool was developed that combined the computer and X-ray techniques. British scientist Godfrey Hounsfield first documented this exciting new technique, calling it **computerized axial tomography** (CAT) scanning. Now it is simply called **computed tomography**.

When a CT image is made, a thin X-ray beam is passed through a very small, well-defined area of the body as the body travels through a large tubelike machine. A series of detectors opposite the X-ray source collects the X rays that have passed through the body. The tube revolves, so that the same small slice of the body is viewed from a different angle. The detectors then feed this information to a computer. The computer is able to store and compare the slices and then produce a cross-sectional image of what has been "seen." Although this technique was originally used to produce images of the brain, all parts of the body can now be imaged showing the subtle differences between bone and soft tissue detail.

▶ DIGITAL SUBTRACTION ANGIOGRAPHY (DSA)

Another imaging technique that uses X rays is **digital subtraction angiography**. The arteries of the heart and other body vessels (or ducts), such as the ducts within the liver, can be examined using DSA. DSA starts with the making of an X-ray image of the area to be examined. Then a radiopaque dye, a substance that does not allow the passage of X rays, is injected into the area's arteries or veins. As the dye is being injected, a second image is made. A computer compares the two images

Early X-ray pictures, such as the one made by Roentgen of his wife's hand (*left*), are hazy images compared to the detailed, colored X rays now possible (*right*).

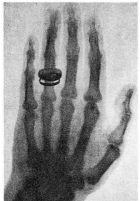
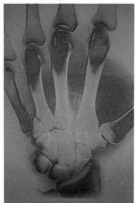

and produces a final image with everything removed except the dye-filled vessels within the small well-defined area of interest.

▶ MAGNETIC RESONANCE IMAGING (MRI)

Many people view the development of **magnetic resonance imaging** to be as important as the development of X-ray imaging. MRI uses powerful magnets placed in the outer walls of a tunnel-like machine to create a magnetic field. When a human body is placed in this magnetic field, the hydrogen atoms in the body become magnetized and line up in an organized pattern. Radio waves are released by the machine, changing the order of the hydrogen atoms. When the radio waves are turned off, the hydrogen atoms move back into order and emit an electrical signal. The signals are collected, fed to a computer, and used to produce an image.

Not only are the images more finely detailed than CT images, but MRI better distinguishes between certain kinds of similar body tissues, such as the white matter and gray matter of the brain. Although not everyone can be placed in a magnetic field—the strong field can interfere with heart-pacing devices—there are no known harmful effects of MRI.

▶ SONOGRAPHY

The technique known as **sonography** owes its development to the use of sonar during the two world wars. During wartime, sonar (a system of underwater detection using sound waves) was used to search out underwater objects—submarines and icebergs.

Like sonar, sonography uses sound waves; but the fluid environment is the human body. High-frequency sound, or ultrasonic, waves are sent out from a device called a transducer, which acts as both the source and the receiver of the ultrasonic waves. The transducer is placed against the skin and moved over the area to be studied. The waves penetrate the body, strike the structures within, and bounce back to the surface, where they are captured by the transducer. A computer analyzes these echoes and builds an image that is projected onto the computer screen.

Sonography is used to image soft body structures such as the heart. Because it is considered to be a relatively safe form of imaging, it is the only recommended body scanning technique used on expectant mothers.

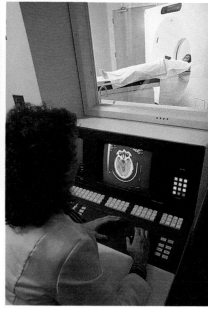

As the body is scanned, a variety of CT images, such as the cross-sectional image (*right*) and the three-dimensional image (*above*), can be produced.

▶ RADIOISOTOPE IMAGING

Some types of imaging use **radioisotopes**, chemical elements that give off energy particles. Very small amounts of a radioisotope are combined with a substance the body processes, such as sugar or protein, and is then injected into the body. Because energy is given off, or emitted, by the radioisotope, its path through the body can be tracked by detectors. Information is gathered about where the chemical collects, how it is processed by the body, and how or if it is eliminated from the body. The information is fed into the computer and an image results.

Two types of imaging that use radioisotopes are **positron emission tomography** (PET) and **single photon emission computed tomography** (SPECT). Radioisotope imaging may be used to study the flow of blood through the body, the activity of specific organs, or the spread of tumor cells.

Diagnostic imaging has given new eyes to medicine—eyes that not only help diagnose disease but detect it at an early stage when preventative steps can still be taken. With each new technology the vision improves, bringing more understanding of the body and the chance for a longer, healthier life.

RONALD L. RAGLAND, M.D.
Chief, Neuroradiology
University of Massachusetts Medical Center

INCOME TAX

Part of the money people earn is paid to the government as an income tax. Most forms of income—wages, business profits, interest from savings accounts, and earnings from investments—are taxed. The income tax is paid by individuals and by businesses from small shops to giant corporations.

For governments in the United States, Canada, and many other countries, the income tax is the biggest source of **revenue**, or money received. It is also one of the easiest taxes to collect. Often, before giving workers their paychecks, an employer will **withhold**, or take out, a portion of the workers' wages to pay to the government toward their annual income taxes. That way, most of the income taxes the workers owe are paid as they earn their salaries, and the government receives a steady flow of money.

▶ HOW THE TAX BEGAN

As long as people have had governments, they have had some form of income tax. In ancient times, money was not widely used, but grain was considered income, and people gave part of their crops to the government. Ancient Greeks and Romans imposed a form of tax on money earned by citizens. The first modern income tax was adopted by the British Parliament in 1799. The United States imposed an income tax in 1862 to help pay for the costs of the Civil War. In 1894 the United States Supreme Court declared income taxes unconstitutional. Because the revenues it provided were needed, however, Congress was urged to amend the Constitution to make the tax legal. In 1913 the 16th Amendment went into effect, and that year Congress passed a law that imposed an income tax on individuals and corporations. Many changes have been made in the law since then, but the tax remains.

▶ PURPOSE OF THE TAX

Governments provide services that cannot be done by individuals, such as building roads, defending against foreign attacks, protecting national boundaries and forests, and providing mail services. The main purpose of the income tax is to raise money so that governments can pay the costs of these services and the salaries of the people who perform them. (Government workers also pay income taxes on the money they earn.) The costs of law enforcement, the courts, education, space exploration, and even weather reports are at least partly paid for by income taxes.

The government uses part of the money to provide social services, such as health care, supplemental old-age pensions, benefits for the unemployed, food stamps, welfare payments, and housing, as well as public works projects, such as road building, that create jobs. In Sweden and other European democracies, the use of the income tax is very important. Tax rates are higher in these countries than in the United States and their governments spend more on social services.

Most taxes are **graduated**, or progressive. That is, people who earn high wages generally pay a bigger part of every dollar to the government than people who earn low wages. People who earn more are asked to pay a higher percentage. Besides paying different tax rates, some taxpayers are allowed to **exempt** (exclude) a part of their income or **deduct** (subtract) certain expenses from it. For example, some taxpayers can deduct the amount they give to charity.

▶ MULTIPLE TAXATION

A person's income may be taxed more than once. In the United States and Canada, people pay income taxes to the federal government. In addition, many American states and all Canadian provinces impose their own income taxes. Some American city and county governments collect income taxes as well. Some of these cities tax income earned in that city, no matter where the taxpayer lives. As a result, a worker can owe an income tax to the city in which he or she works, and also owe income taxes to the city, state, and country where he or she resides. But nearby, another person might live and work in a city and state that have no income tax. This person, then, would pay an income tax only to the federal government.

By April 15 every year, each worker fills out at least one form called a federal tax **return**, and sends it to the Internal Revenue Service (IRS). If the amount of tax withheld during the year is more than the tax owed, the taxpayer will receive a refund from the IRS.

Reviewed by LEONARD SLOANE
Author, *The New York Times Book of Personal Finance*

Auguste Renoir portrayed a festive moment in *The Luncheon of the Boating Party* (1881). The informal, light-filled scene is characteristic of impressionist art.

IMPRESSIONISM

In Paris during the late 1860's, a small group of artists began to produce paintings that were beautiful to look at, but that were very different from most art of the period. The new paintings were lighter and more colorful than traditional paintings, and their subject matter often was informal. Many depicted scenes of sidewalk cafés, seaside resorts, and other popular spots. Others showed tranquil views of the French countryside. Most unusual of all was the artists' painting technique. Instead of mixing paint on a palette to create a range of color combinations, the artists daubed pure, unmixed pigments directly onto the canvas in what seemed to be a hodgepodge of brightly colored dashes.

The new form of painting, which came to be called impressionism, was the first modern art movement. Misunderstood at first, it later was widely accepted, changing the way artists painted and the way people looked at art.

▶ **FRENCH IMPRESSIONISM**

Although impressionism later became an international art movement, it originated in Paris, the major European art center of the late 1800's. The first group of French impressionists consisted of about thirty artists, including Claude Monet, Auguste Renoir, Alfred Sisley, Camille Pissarro, Edgar Degas, and Berthe Morisot. A better-known and slightly older artist, Édouard Manet, worked with the group but did not exhibit with them. All the artists shared similar beliefs about art, although their individual styles differed.

The artists held their first exhibition in 1874, calling themselves an "anonymous group." The show drew a storm of criticism from the press and the public. One critic mockingly called the artists' work "impressionism," taking the term from the title of Monet's painting *Impression: Sunrise*. The critic meant that the paintings were only impres-

Claude Monet tried to capture the effects of changing light on color and form. This work, one of his many paintings of water lilies, shows the play of sunlight and shadow on the pond at his home in Giverny.

sions, sketchy and incomplete. Later, supporters of the movement also adopted the name.

Style and Techniques. Impressionist paintings were unpopular at first mainly because they were so different from the paintings people were used to seeing. Traditional paintings often depicted people and scenes that were familiar to everyone—subjects from myth and legend, famous historical events, or biblical stories. Artists usually worked in their studios and made many preliminary drawings before producing a finished painting.

Impressionists, in contrast, chose to paint ordinary people and everyday scenes. To them, the subject of a painting was not as important as the portrayal of light and color. For this reason, they preferred to work outdoors, painting quickly to capture rapidly changing qualities of light and atmosphere. Shapes were no longer carefully modeled and clearly outlined. Instead, they were painted as masses of vibrating color. Even shadows, usually painted gray or black, were tinged with color. Using what is called a "broken-color" technique, impressionist painters applied pure color to the canvas in many small brushstrokes. When viewed from a slight distance, the strokes of color seemed to merge, forming a complete image.

Each of the French impressionists used these techniques in different ways. Monet was especially interested in the effects of changing

Édouard Manet influenced the impressionists but did not use their bright colors. *The Balcony* (1868) has strongly contrasting areas of light and dark tones.

The Bridge at Sevres (1877), by Alfred Sisley, captures the atmospheric conditions of a cloudy day by the water. A detail of the painting (*above*) shows the loosely painted brushstrokes that combine to form the image.

The Tub is a pastel drawing made by Edgar Degas about 1886. The informal subject matter, gracefully defined figure, and indoor setting are typical of the artist's style.

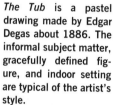

light on color and form. He frequently painted the same scene at different times of day. The changes in light and atmosphere caused the subject to look different in each painting.

Renoir portrayed the effects of flickering light by painting softened forms that appeared slightly out of focus. Manet did not use the bright colors of the impressionists, but his preference for everyday subjects greatly influenced the younger artists. Degas, too, painted informal subjects, such as women bathing and dancers stretching. Unlike other impressionists, he painted indoors and used outlines to define the shapes of his figures.

Although impressionism was considered to be a revolutionary art movement, earlier artists had experimented with similar techniques. The English painters John Constable and J. M. W. Turner skillfully portrayed light and atmosphere. The Spanish painters Diego Velázquez and Francisco Goya used color and brushwork to create the appearance of movement. The French artist Eugène Delacroix had observed that shadows contain elements of color. The work of all these artists influenced the impressionists, as did the forms and composition of Japanese woodblock prints.

▶ **SPREAD AND INFLUENCE OF IMPRESSIONISM**

After 1875, impressionism became widely accepted and began to influence artists in other European countries. Prominent painters outside France, including the German artist Max Liebermann, the Italian artist Giuseppi De Nittis, and the English artist Wilson Steer, added elements of impressionism to their work.

Left: Allies Day, May 1917, by American impressionist Childe Hassam. *Right: Mont Sainte-Victoire* (1906), by postimpressionist Paul Cézanne, whose style led to cubism.

By the end of the 1800's, impressionism had spread to the United States. Many American artists, including Theodore Robinson, William Glackens, and Mary Cassatt, visited France and became closely associated with French impressionists. Cassatt, who studied with Degas, specialized in portraits of mothers and their children. Among other American impressionists were Childe Hassam and John Henry Twachtman.

Postimpressionism. By 1890, impressionism had begun to fade as a movement. Differences in individual styles increased as artists moved in separate directions. Some artists wanted to preserve the bright color of the impressionists but create art with more structure, using strong outlines and solidly modeled forms. Others wanted to use color not just to capture an image but to express emotion. Together, the various styles that grew out of impressionism are called postimpressionism. Many important ideas in modern art developed from postimpressionism.

One of the postimpressionists, Georges Seurat, developed **pointillism**, a much more scientific version of the impressionist broken-color technique. His paintings were composed of many small dots of different colors calculated to produce an exact color effect. Another artist, Paul Cézanne, tried to demonstrate the solidity of objects by showing that they were made up of many intersecting planes (flat surfaces). Cézanne's technique led directly to the modern art style called cubism. It also influenced the development of abstract art. Abstract paintings may consist only of lines, planes, and shapes.

Other postimpressionists, such as Vincent van Gogh, Henri de Toulouse-Lautrec, and Paul Gauguin, were particularly interested in expressing emotion with color and design. Their work looked forward to the art movement known as expressionism, in which artists tried to reveal their inner feelings through art.

Impressionism in Literature and Music. Impressionist ideas also appeared in literature and music. Like impressionist artists, impressionist writers, such as Stéphane Mallarmé, and composers, such as Claude Debussy, tried to capture and portray in their work a fleeting moment in time. Elements in their works often seem disconnected and unformed. The parts are brought into an integrated whole by the imagination of the reader or listener, just as the separate strokes of color in an impressionist painting form a complete image in the eye of the viewer.

HOWARD E. WOODEN
Director Emeritus
The Wichita Art Museum

SUPPLEMENT

Deaths

Independent Nations of the World

The United States

Senate

House of Representatives

Cabinet

Supreme Court

State Governors

Canada and Its Provinces and Territories

DEATHS

Abernathy, Ralph David. American civil rights leader; died April 17, at the age of 64. An aide to the late Martin Luther King, Jr., Abernathy helped organize the Montgomery bus boycott of 1955— an important event in the civil rights movement.

Arden, Eve. American actress and comedienne; died on November 12, at the age of 83. Arden appeared in some 100 movies but was best known as the ironic but sympathetic English teacher in the radio and television series *Our Miss Brooks* (1948–57).

Bailey, Pearl. American singer and musical star; died on August 17, at the age of 72. Bailey, who was noted for her throaty singing style, appeared in several movies and played the title role in an all-black Broadway version of *Hello, Dolly!* (1967–69).

Bennett, Joan. American actress; died December 7, at the age of 80. During her 50-year career, Bennett appeared in 75 movies. She also starred on television and the stage.

Bernstein, Leonard. American musician; died on October 14, at the age of 72. Best known as a conductor, Bernstein, at age 40, became the youngest music director of the New York Philharmonic Orchestra (1959–69). He led many other orchestras and was known for his exuberant con-

Leonard Bernstein

ducting style. He was also a composer of both serious and popular music. His works included symphonies, ballets, movie scores, and Broadway musicals, including *West Side Story.*

Bettelheim, Bruno. Austrian-born psychoanalyst; died on March 13, at the age of 86. Bettelheim was best known for his pioneering work in treating emotionally disturbed children.

Blakey, Art. American jazz drummer and band leader; died on October 16, at the age of 71. Blakey established his band, the Jazz Messengers, in the 1940's and greatly influenced the development of modern jazz.

Copland, Aaron. American composer; died on December 2, at the age of 90. Copland, who had been called the founder of modern symphonic music, used folk songs and jazz in his compositions. Among his best-known works were his ballet scores *Appalachian Spring* and *Rodeo.*

Cugat, Xavier. Spanish-born band leader; died on October 27, at the age of 90. Known for his showmanship, Cugat introduced the rumba, tango, and other Latin American dance rhythms to North American audiences in the 1930's and 1940's.

Cullen, William ("Bill"). American television personality; died on July 7, at the age of 70. Cullen was the host of such game shows as *The Price Is Right*, *Name That Tune*, and *$25,000 Pyramid.*

Cummings, Robert. American actor; died on December 2, at the age of 82. Cummings starred in numerous movies and four television comedy series in the 1950's and 1960's.

Davis, Jr., Sammy. American singer, dancer, and actor; died May 16, at the age of 64. Davis, who began his professional career at age 3 in vaudeville, was one of the first black performers to gain

Pearl Bailey

widespread popularity. He appeared in Broadway musicals, movies, and television shows. Among his hit recordings were "Candy Man," "What Kind of Fool Am I?," and "Mr. Bojangles."

Duff, Howard. American actor; died on July 8, at the age of 76. Duff played private detective Sam Spade on radio during the 1940's and later appeared in many movies and television shows.

Dunne, Irene. American actress; died on September 4, at the age of 91. Dunne appeared in more than 40 movies, mostly in the 1930's and 1940's. Among her best-known roles was as the mother of a Norwegian immigrant family in *I Remember Mama* (1948).

Durrell, Lawrence. British author and poet; died on November 7, at the age of 78. Durrell's best-known work was the four-novel collection *The Alexandria Quartet*.

Edgerton, Harold E. American scientist and inventor; died on January 4, at the age of 86. In 1931, Edgerton invented the stroboscope, an electronic device that emits brief flashes of light, enabling photographers to "freeze" objects in motion.

Erté (born Romain de Tirtoff). Russian-born designer; died on April 21, at the age of 97. Erté was known for his Art Deco designs in fashion, theater sets, and the graphic arts.

Greta Garbo

Sammy Davis, Jr.

Forbes, Malcolm. American publisher of *Forbes* business magazine; died on February 24, at the age of 70. Forbes was a colorful multimillionaire known for his art collections and his love of yachting, motorcycling, and hot-air ballooning.

Garbo, Greta. Swedish-born actress; died April 15, at the age of 84. The legendary Garbo, who was celebrated for her classic beauty, appeared in 27 films including *Mata Hari* (1931) and *Camille* (1936). She ended her film career in the 1940's and became a recluse, greatly valuing her privacy.

Gardner, Ava. American actress; died January 25, at the age of 67. Gardner was one of Hollywood's most famous movie stars from the 1940's through the 1960's. She appeared in about 60 films, including *Mogambo* (1953) and *On the Beach* (1959).

Gilford, Jack. American actor and comedian; died June 4, at the age of 82. Gilford appeared in theater, movies, and television. His best-remembered film roles included *A Funny Thing Happened on the Way to the Forum* (1966) and *Cocoon* (1985).

Goddard, Paulette. American movie actress; died on April 23, at the age of 78. Goddard was a popular film star of the 1930's and 1940's. Her best-known roles were in Charlie Chaplin films.

Goldberg, Arthur J. American lawyer and public figure; died on January 19, at the age of 81. Goldberg served as U.S. Secretary of Labor (1961–62), Supreme Court justice (1962–65), and representative to the United Nations (1965–68).

Graziano, Rocky. American boxing champion; died on May 22, at the age of 71. Noted for his brawling style, Graziano compiled a record of 67 wins, 10 ties, and 6 losses from 1942 to 1952. He held the world middleweight title for 11 months in 1947–1948. His autobiography, *Somebody Up There Likes Me*, was made into a 1956 film starring Paul Newman.

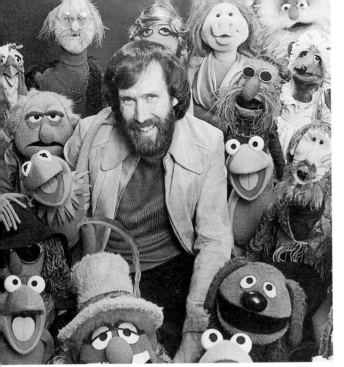

Jim Henson

Hale, Jr., Alan. American actor; died on January 2, at the age of 71. Hale was best known for his role as the skipper of a shipwrecked charter boat on the television series *Gilligan's Island*.

Halston (born Roy Halston Frowick). American fashion designer; died on March 26, at the age of 57. Halston, noted for his classic styles, was one of the top American designers of the 1960's and 1970's. Among his most famous creations was the "pillbox" hat worn by former First Lady Jacqueline Kennedy.

Hammer, Armand. American industrialist; died on December 10, at the age of 92. Hammer, chairman of Occidental Petroleum Corporation, was a long-time crusader for international peace.

Harrison, Rex. British film and stage actor; died on June 2, at the age of 82. During his long career, Harrison specialized in playing witty, sophisticated characters. He is best remembered for his portrayals of Professor Henry Higgins in the Broadway and film versions of *My Fair Lady*, winning both a Tony Award (1957) and an Academy Award (1964).

Henson, Jim. American puppeteer; died on May 16, at the age of 53. Henson created the popular Muppet characters, including Miss Piggy, Kermit the Frog, Big Bird and the Cookie Monster. The Muppets are the main characters on *Sesame Street*, a television program for preschoolers that is watched by millions of children all over the world.

Kahane, Meir. American-born Israeli rabbi; assassinated on November 5, at the age of 58. In 1968, Kahane founded the militant Jewish Defense League. He moved to Israel in 1971 and from 1984 to 1988 served in that nation's parliament. He was barred from running for re-election because of his racist, anti-Arab political platform.

Kliban, Bernard. American cartoonist; died on August 12, at the age of 55. Kliban was best known for his drawings of plump, striped cats who often engaged in human activities such as roller skating.

Martin, Mary. American musical comedy star; died on November 3, at the age of 76. Martin starred in many Broadway musicals, including *South Pacific* (1948) and *The Sound of Music* (1959). Her best-remembered stage role was of the boy who wouldn't grow up, in *Peter Pan* (1954), which later aired on television.

Matsunaga, Spark M. U.S. Senator from Hawaii; died on April 15, at the age of 73. Matsunaga, a Democrat, was a Senator since 1977 and House Representative from 1963—76. He was an advocate for peaceful resolutions of conflicts and for Soviet-American cooperation in space exploration.

McCrea, Joel. American actor; died on October 20, at the age of 84. McCrea appeared in more than 80 movies, many of them Westerns.

Menninger, Karl. American psychiatrist; died on July 18, at the age of 96. Menninger is credited with explaining psychiatry to the general public. Together with his father and brother, he founded the world-renowned Menninger Clinic for the emotionally disturbed in 1925.

Moravia, Alberto. Italian writer; died on September 26, at the age of 82. Moravia's many novels and short stories have been translated into some 30 languages and are read around the world. His works explored the search for personal values.

Mumford, Lewis. American philosopher, cultural critic, and historian; died on January 26, at the age of 94. Mumford was an authority on architecture and city planning, and he believed that people were being dehumanized by large-scale urban development and the spread of technology.

Mary Martin

Barbara Stanwyck

Noyce, Robert. American physicist; died on June 3, at the age of 62. Noyce, along with Jack Kilby, invented the computer microchip, which revolutionized the electronics industry. In 1968, Noyce founded the Intel Corporation, which developed the first microprocessor, the integrated circuit that is the basis of personal computers.

Paley, William S. American founder of CBS; died on October 26, at the age of 89. Paley bought a small radio network in 1928 and turned it into one of the world's most powerful communications companies.

Percy, Walker. American author; died on May 10, at the age of 74. Percy's six novels are set in the South and focus on people's search for love and faith in the modern world. His first and best-known novel was *The Moviegoer*, which won a National Book Award in 1962.

Peter, Laurence J. Canadian-born author; died January 12, at the age of 70. He was best known for having popularized the "Peter Principle," which states that in a bureaucratic organization every employee tends to rise to his or her level of incompetence.

Porter, Eliot. American photographer and conservationist; died on November 2, at the age of 88. Porter's best-known photographs were of wilderness landscapes, birds, and plants.

Ray, Johnnie. American singer; died on February 24, at the age of 63. Ray, who was popular in the 1950's, was known for his emotional vocal technique that included simulated sobs. His biggest hit was the ballad "Cry."

Skinner, B. F. American psychologist; died on August 18, at the age of 86. Skinner was noted for his studies of human and animal behavior. He believed that people could be taught to act in specific ways by rewarding or punishing certain behavior.

Stanwyck, Barbara. American actress; died on January 20, at the age of 82. Stanwyck appeared in more than 80 films during her 60-year career, including *Stella Dallas* (1937) and *Sorry, Wrong Number* (1948). She also starred in television, winning particular acclaim for her portrayal of the matriarch Victoria Barkley in the 1960's Western series *The Big Valley*.

Tayback, Victor. American actor; died on May 25, at the age of 60. Tayback was best known for his role as Mel, the diner owner in the television series *Alice*.

Terry-Thomas. British comedian and actor; died on January 8, at the age of 78. Known for his gap-toothed grin, he performed on stage, radio, and television. He also appeared in some 40 movies.

Vaughan, Sarah. American jazz singer; died on April 3, at the age of 66. Known as the "Divine One," Vaughan was noted for the unusually wide range of her voice (three octaves) and for her versatile vocal style. Her memorable songs included "Misty" and "Send in the Clowns."

Wallace, Irving. American author; died on June 29, at the age of 74. Wallace's novels, which sold more than 120 million copies worldwide, included such best-sellers as *The Chapman Report* (1960), *The Prize* (1962), and *The Fan Club* (1974).

White, Ryan. American teenager who symbolized the problems faced by children with AIDS; died on April 8, at the age of 18. White, a hemophiliac who contracted AIDS from a blood transfusion, was shunned by his classmates. When he was barred from school, he and his parents brought the case to court and won. White served as a spokesman for AIDS education and became a symbol of courage and a leader in building understanding and compassion for victims of the disease.

Ryan White

INDEPENDENT NATIONS OF THE WORLD

NATION	CAPITAL	AREA (in sq mi)	POPULATION (estimate)	GOVERNMENT
Afghanistan	Kabul	250,000	15,800,000	Najibullah—communist party secretary and president
Albania	Tirana	11,100	3,200,000	Ramiz Alia—communist party secretary and president Adil Carcani—premier
Algeria	Algiers	919,595	24,600,000	Chadli Benjedid—president
Angola	Luanda	481,354	9,750,000	José Eduardo dos Santos—president
Antigua and Barbuda	St. John's	171	85,000	C. Vere Bird—prime minister
Argentina	Buenos Aires	1,068,297	32,000,000	Carlos Saúl Menem—president
Australia	Canberra	2,967,895	16,800,000	Robert Hawke—prime minister
Austria	Vienna	32,374	7,600,000	Kurt Waldheim—president Franz Vranitzky—chancellor
Bahamas	Nassau	5,380	249,000	Lynden O. Pindling—prime minister
Bahrain	Manama	240	489,000	Isa ibn Salman al-Khalifa—head of state
Bangladesh	Dhaka	55,598	106,500,000	Shahabuddin Ahmed—president
Barbados	Bridgetown	168	256,000	Lloyd Erskine Sandiford—prime minister
Belgium	Brussels	11,781	9,900,000	Baudouin I—king Wilfried Martens—premier
Belize	Belmopan	8,867	178,000	George Price—prime minister
Benin (Dahomey)	Porto-Novo	43,484	4,600,000	Mathieu Kerekou—president
Bhutan	Thimbu	18,147	1,500,000	Jigme Singye Wangchuck—king
Bolivia	La Paz Sucre	424,165	7,200,000	Jaime Paz Zamora—president
Botswana	Gaborone	231,804	1,300,000	Quett Masire—president
Brazil	Brasília	3,286,478	147,400,000	Fernando Collor de Mello—president
Brunei Darussalam	Bandar Seri Begawan	2,226	249,000	Hassanal Bolkiah—head of state
Bulgaria	Sofia	42,823	9,000,000	Zhelyu Zhelev—president Dimitar Popov—premier
Burkina Faso (Upper Volta)	Ouagadougou	105,869	8,800,000	Blaise Compaoré—president
Burma (Myanmar)	Rangoon	261,218	40,800,000	Saw Maung—head of government
Burundi	Bujumbura	10,747	5,300,000	Pierre Buyoya—president

NATION	CAPITAL	AREA (in sq mi)	POPULATION (estimate)	GOVERNMENT
Cambodia (Kampuchea)	Pnompenh	69,898	8,100,000	Heng Samrin—communist party secretary Norodom Sihanouk—president
Cameroon	Yaoundé	183,569	11,500,000	Paul Biya—president
Canada	Ottawa	3,851,809	26,600,000	Martin Brian Mulroney—prime minister
Cape Verde	Praia	1,557	368,000	Aristides Pereira—president
Central African Republic	Bangui	240,535	2,800,000	André Kolingba—president
Chad	N'Djemena	495,754	5,500,000	Idris Deby—president
Chile	Santiago	292,257	13,000,000	Patricio Aylwin—president-elect
China	Beijing	3,705,390	1,130,000,000	Jiang Zemin—communist party secretary Li Peng—premier
Colombia	Bogotá	439,736	31,200,000	César Gaviria Trujillo—president
Comoros	Moroni	838	500,000	Mohammed Djohar—president
Congo	Brazzaville	132,047	1,900,000	Denis Sassou-Nguesso—president
Costa Rica	San José	19,575	2,900,000	Rafael Calderón Fournier—president
Cuba	Havana	44,218	10,500,000	Fidel Castro—president
Cyprus	Nicosia	3,572	700,000	George Vassiliou—president
Czechoslovakia	Prague	49,370	15,600,000	Vaclav Havel—president Marian Calfa—premier
Denmark	Copenhagen	16,629	5,100,000	Margrethe II—queen Poul Schlüter—premier
Djibouti	Djibouti	8,494	394,000	Hassan Gouled Aptidon—president
Dominica	Roseau	290	100,000	Mary Eugenia Charles—prime minister
Dominican Republic	Santo Domingo	18,816	7,000,000	Joaquín Balaguer—president
Ecuador	Quito	109,483	10,500,000	Rodrigo Borja Cevallos—president
Egypt	Cairo	386,660	53,100,000	Mohammad Hosni Mubarak—president Atef Sedky—premier
El Salvador	San Salvador	8,124	5,200,000	Alfredo Cristiani—president
Equatorial Guinea	Malabo	10,831	340,000	Obiang Nguema Mbasogo—president
Ethiopia	Addis Ababa	471,777	49,500,000	Mengistu Haile-Mariam—president
Fiji	Suva	7,055	738,000	Ratu Sir Penaia Ganilau—president
Finland	Helsinki	130,120	5,000,000	Mauno Koivisto—president Harri Holkeri—premier
France	Paris	211,207	56,200,000	François Mitterrand—president Michel Rocard—premier
Gabon	Libreville	103,346	1,100,000	Omar Bongo—president
Gambia	Banjul	4,361	835,000	Dawda K. Jawara—president
Germany	Berlin	137,744	78,600,000	Richard von Weizäcker—president Helmut Kohl—chancellor

NATION	CAPITAL	AREA (in sq mi)	POPULATION (estimate)	GOVERNMENT
Ghana	Accra	92,099	14,600,000	Jerry Rawlings—head of government
Greece	Athens	50,944	10,000,000	Constantine Karamanlis—president Constantine Mitsotakis—premier
Grenada	St. George's	133	100,000	Nicholas Brathwaite—prime minister
Guatemala	Guatemala City	42,042	8,900,000	Vinicio Cerezo Arévalo—president
Guinea	Conakry	94,926	6,700,000	Lansana Conté—president
Guinea-Bissau	Bissau	13,948	966,000	João Bernardo Vieira—president
Guyana	Georgetown	83,000	1,000,000	Hugh Desmond Hoyte—president
Haiti	Port-au-Prince	10,714	5,600,000	Jean-Bertrand Aristide—president-elect
Honduras	Tegucigalpa	43,277	5,000,000	Rafael Leonardo Callejas—president
Hungary	Budapest	35,919	10,600,000	Arpad Goncz—president Jozsef Antall—premier
Iceland	Reykjavik	39,768	250,000	Vigdis Finnbogadottir—president Steingrimur Hermannsson—prime minister
India	New Delhi	1,269,340	811,800,000	Ramaswamy Venkataraman—president Chandra Shekhar—prime minister
Indonesia	Jakarta	735,358	179,100,000	Suharto—president
Iran	Teheran	636,294	54,200,000	Ayatollah Ali Khamenei—religious leader Ali Hashemi Rafsanjani—president
Iraq	Baghdad	167,925	18,300,000	Saddam Hussein—president
Ireland	Dublin	27,136	3,500,000	Mary Robinson—president Charles Haughey—prime minister
Israel	Jerusalem	8,019	4,500,000	Chaim Herzog—president Yitzhak Shamir—prime minister
Italy	Rome	116,303	57,500,000	Francesco Cossiga—president Giulio Andreotti—premier
Ivory Coast	Yamoussoukro	124,503	12,100,000	Félix Houphouët-Boigny—president
Jamaica	Kingston	4,244	2,400,000	Michael Manley—prime minister
Japan	Tokyo	143,751	123,100,000	Akihito—emperor Toshiki Kaifu—premier
Jordan	Amman	35,475	4,100,000	Hussein I—king Mudar Badran—premier
Kenya	Nairobi	224,959	24,900,000	Daniel arap Moi—president
Kiribati	Tarawa	264	67,000	Ieremia Tabai—president
Korea (North)	Pyongyang	46,540	22,400,000	Kim Il Sung—president Yon Hyong Muk—premier
Korea (South)	Seoul	38,025	42,400,000	Roh Tae Woo—president Ro Jai Bong—premier
Kuwait	Kuwait	6,880	2,000,000	Jabir al-Ahmad al-Sabah—head of state
Laos	Vientiane	91,429	3,900,000	Phoumi Vongvichit—president Kaysone Phomvihan—premier
Lebanon	Beirut	4,015	2,900,000	Elias Hrawi—president Omar Karami—premier

NATION	CAPITAL	AREA (in sq mi)	POPULATION (estimate)	GOVERNMENT
Lesotho	Maseru	11,720	1,700,000	Moshoeshoe II—king Justin Lekhanya—prime minister
Liberia	Monrovia	43,000	2,500,000	In midst of civil war
Libya	Tripoli	679,362	4,200,000	Muammar el-Qaddafi—head of government
Liechtenstein	Vaduz	61	28,000	Hans Adam—prince
Luxembourg	Luxembourg	999	367,000	Jean—grand duke Jacques Santer—premier
Madagascar	Antananarivo	226,657	11,600,000	Didier Ratsiraka—president
Malawi	Lilongwe	45,747	8,000,000	H. Kamuzu Banda—president
Malaysia	Kuala Lumpur	127,317	17,000,000	Azlan Muhibuddin Shah—king Mahathir Mohammad—prime minister
Maldives	Male	115	200,000	Maumoon Abdul Gayoom—president
Mali	Bamako	478,765	8,000,000	Moussa Traoré—president
Malta	Valletta	122	350,000	Vincent Tabone—president Eddie Fenech Adami—prime minister
Mauritania	Nouakchott	397,954	2,000,000	Maouya Ould Sidi Ahmed Taya—president
Mauritius	Port Louis	790	1,100,000	Aneerood Jugnauth—prime minister
Mexico	Mexico City	761,602	84,300,000	Carlos Salinas de Gortari—president
Monaco	Monaco-Ville	0.6	28,000	Rainier III—prince
Mongolia	Ulan Bator	604,248	2,200,000	Gombojavyn Ochirbat—communist party secretary
Morocco	Rabat	172,413	24,500,000	Hassan II—king Azzedine Laraki—premier
Mozambique	Maputo	309,494	15,300,000	Joaquím A. Chissano—president
Namibia	Windhoek	318,260	1,400,000	Sam Nujoma—president
Nauru	Yaren District	8	8,000	Bernard Dowiyogo—president
Nepal	Katmandu	54,362	18,400,000	Birendra Bir Bikram Shah Deva—king Krishna Prasad Bhattarai—prime minister
Netherlands	Amsterdam	15,770	14,800,000	Beatrix—queen Ruud Lubbers—premier
New Zealand	Wellington	103,736	3,300,000	Jim Bolger—prime minister
Nicaragua	Managua	50,193	3,700,000	Violeta Barrios de Chamorro—president
Niger	Niamey	489,190	6,900,000	Ali Saibou—president
Nigeria	Lagos	356,667	109,200,000	Ibrahim Babangida—president
Norway	Oslo	125,056	4,200,000	Olav V—king Gro Harlem Brundtland—premier
Oman	Muscat	82,030	1,400,000	Qabus ibn Said—sultan
Pakistan	Islamabad	310,404	108,700,000	Gulam Ishaq Khan—president Nawaz Sharif—prime minister
Panama	Panama City	29,761	2,400,000	Guillermo Endara—president

NATION	CAPITAL	AREA (in sq mi)	POPULATION (estimate)	GOVERNMENT
Papua New Guinea	Port Moresby	178,260	3,600,000	Rabbie Namaliu—prime minister
Paraguay	Asunción	157,047	4,200,000	Andrés Rodríguez Pedotti—president
Peru	Lima	496,222	21,800,000	Alberto Fujimori—president
Philippines	Manila	115,830	60,100,000	Corazon C. Aquino—president Salvador H. Laurel—vice-president
Poland	Warsaw	120,725	37,900,000	Lech Walesa—president Tadeusz Mazowiecki—premier
Portugal	Lisbon	35,553	10,500,000	Mário Alberto Soares—president Aníbal Cavaco Silva—premier
Qatar	Doha	4,247	420,000	Khalifa ibn Hamad al-Thani—head of state
Rumania	Bucharest	91,700	23,100,000	Ion Iliescu—president Petre Roman—premier
Rwanda	Kigali	10,169	7,000,000	Juvénal Habyarimana—president
St. Christopher and Nevis	Basseterre	105	50,000	Kennedy Simmonds—prime minister
St. Lucia	Castries	238	148,000	John Compton—prime minister
St. Vincent and the Grenadines	Kingstown	150	110,000	James F. Mitchell—prime minister
São Tomé and Príncipe	São Tomé	372	115,000	Manuel Pinto da Costa—president
Saudi Arabia	Riyadh	830,000	14,400,000	Fahd ibn Abdul-Aziz—king
Senegal	Dakar	75,750	7,200,000	Abdou Diouf—president
Seychelles	Victoria	107	67,000	France Albert René—president
Sierra Leone	Freetown	27,700	4,000,000	Joseph Momoh—president
Singapore	Singapore	224	2,700,000	Wee Kim Wee—president Goh Chok Tong—prime minister
Solomon Islands	Honiara	10,983	317,000	Solomon Mamaloni—prime minister
Somalia	Mogadishu	246,200	7,300,000	Mohammed Siad Barre—president
South Africa	Pretoria Cape Town Bloemfontein	471,444	34,500,000	F. W. de Klerk—president
Soviet Union	Moscow	8,649,512	285,900,000	Mikhail S. Gorbachev—president
Spain	Madrid	194,897	38,800,000	Juan Carlos I—king Felipe González Márquez—premier
Sri Lanka (Ceylon)	Colombo	25,332	16,800,000	Ranasinghe Premadasa—president
Sudan	Khartoum	967,500	24,500,000	Omar Hasan Ahmad al-Bashir—prime minister
Suriname	Paramaribo	63,037	400,000	Dési Bouterse—military leader
Swaziland	Mbabane	6,704	763,000	Mswati III—king

NATION	CAPITAL	AREA (in sq mi)	POPULATION (estimate)	GOVERNMENT
Sweden	Stockholm	173,731	8,500,000	Carl XVI Gustaf—king Ingvar Carlsson—premier
Switzerland	Bern	15,941	6,600,000	Flavio Cotti—president
Syria	Damascus	71,498	11,700,000	Hafez al-Assad—president Mahmoud Zubi—premier
Taiwan	Taipei	13,885	19,400,000	Lee Teng-hui—president Hao Po-tsun—premier
Tanzania	Dar es Salaam	364,898	24,800,000	Ali Hassan Mwinyi—president
Thailand	Bangkok	198,457	55,400,000	Bhumibol Adulyadej—king Chatichai Chunhawan—premier
Togo	Lomé	21,622	3,350,000	Gnassingbe Eyadema—president
Tonga	Nuku'alofa	270	118,000	Taufa'ahau Tupou IV—king Prince Tu'ipelehake—prime minister
Trinidad & Tobago	Port of Spain	1,980	1,300,000	Noor Hassanali—president A.N.R. Robinson—prime minister
Tunisia	Tunis	63,170	8,000,000	Zine el-Abidine Ben Ali—president
Turkey	Ankara	301,381	56,700,000	Turgut Ozal—president Yildirim Akbulut—prime minister
Tuvalu	Funafuti	10	9,000	Bikenibeu Paeniu—prime minister
Uganda	Kampala	91,134	17,800,000	Yoweri Museveni—president
United Arab Emirates	Abu Dhabi	32,278	1,500,000	Zayd ibn Sultan al-Nuhayan—president
United Kingdom	London	94,226	57,200,000	Elizabeth II—queen John Major—prime minister
United States	Washington, D.C.	3,618,467	248,000,000	George H. Bush—president James Danforth Quayle—vice-president
Uruguay	Montevideo	68,037	3,100,000	Luis Alberto Lacalle—president
Vanuatu	Vila	5,700	160,000	Walter Lini—prime minister
Venezuela	Caracas	352,143	19,200,000	Carlos Andrés Pérez—president
Vietnam	Hanoi	128,402	65,700,000	Nguyen Van Linh—communist party secretary Do Muoi—premier
Western Samoa	Apia	1,097	167,000	Malietoa Tanumafili II—head of state
Yemen (Sana)	Sana	203,849	10,200,000	Ali Abdullah Saleh—president Haider Abu Bakr al-Attas—premier
Yugoslavia	Belgrade	98,766	23,700,000	Borisav Jovic—president Ante Markovic—premier
Zaïre	Kinshasa	905,565	34,500,000	Mobutu Sese Seko—president
Zambia	Lusaka	290,585	7,800,000	Kenneth D. Kaunda—president
Zimbabwe	Harare	150,333	9,100,000	Robert Mugabe—executive president

THE CONGRESS OF THE UNITED STATES

UNITED STATES SENATE

(56 Democrats, 43 Republicans, 1 vacancy)

Alabama
Howell T. Heflin (D)**
Richard C. Shelby (D)

Alaska
Ted Stevens (R)**
Frank H. Murkowski (R)

Arizona
Dennis DeConcini (D)
John S. McCain III (R)

Arkansas
Dale Bumpers (D)
David H. Pryor (D)**

California
Alan Cranston (D)
vacant

Colorado
Timothy E. Wirth (D)
Hank Brown (R)*

Connecticut
Christopher J. Dodd (D)
Joseph I. Lieberman (D)

Delaware
William V. Roth, Jr. (R)
Joseph R. Biden, Jr. (D)**

Florida
Bob Graham (D)
Connie Mack (R)

Georgia
Sam Nunn (D)**
Wyche Fowler, Jr. (D)

Hawaii
Daniel K. Inouye (D)
Daniel K. Akaka (D)*

Idaho
Steve Symms (R)
Larry E. Craig (R)*

Illinois
Alan J. Dixon (D)
Paul Simon (D)**

Indiana
Richard G. Lugar (R)
Dan Coats (R)**

Iowa
Charles E. Grassley (R)
Thomas R. Harkin (D)**

Kansas
Robert J. Dole (R)
Nancy Landon Kassebaum (R)**

Kentucky
Wendell H. Ford (D)
Mitch McConnell (R)**

Louisiana
J. Bennett Johnston (D)**
John B. Breaux (D)

Maine
William S. Cohen (R)**
George J. Mitchell (D)

Maryland
Paul S. Sarbanes (D)
Barbara A. Mikulski (D)

Massachusetts
Edward M. Kennedy (D)
John F. Kerry (D)**

Michigan
Donald W. Riegle, Jr. (D)
Carl Levin (D)**

Minnesota
David F. Durenberger (R)
Paul Wellstone (D)*

Mississippi
Thad Cochran (R)**
Trent Lott (R)

Missouri
John C. Danforth (R)
Christopher S. Bond (R)

Montana
Max Baucus (D)**
Conrad Burns (R)

Nebraska
J. James Exon, Jr. (D)**
J. Robert Kerrey (D)

Nevada
Harry Reid (D)
Richard H. Bryan (D)

New Hampshire
Warren B. Rudman (R)
Robert C. Smith (R)*

New Jersey
Bill Bradley (D)**
Frank R. Lautenberg (D)

New Mexico
Pete V. Domenici (R)**
Jeff Bingaman (D)

New York
Daniel P. Moynihan (D)
Alfonse M. D'Amato (R)

North Carolina
Jesse Helms (R)**
Terry Sanford (D)

North Dakota
Quentin N. Burdick (D)
Kent Conrad (D)

Ohio
John H. Glenn, Jr. (D)
Howard M. Metzenbaum (D)

Oklahoma
David L. Boren (D)**
Donald L. Nickles (R)

Oregon
Mark O. Hatfield (R)**
Bob Packwood (R)

Pennsylvania
John Heinz (R)
Arlen Specter (R)

Rhode Island
Claiborne Pell (D)**
John H. Chafee (R)

South Carolina
Strom Thurmond (R)**
Ernest F. Hollings (D)

South Dakota
Larry Pressler (R)**
Thomas A. Daschle (D)

Tennessee
James R. Sasser (D)
Albert Gore, Jr. (D)**

Texas
Lloyd Bentsen (D)
Phil Gramm (R)**

Utah
Jake Garn (R)
Orrin G. Hatch (R)

Vermont
Patrick J. Leahy (D)
James M. Jeffords (R)

Virginia
John W. Warner (R)**
Charles S. Robb (D)

Washington
Brock Adams (D)
Slade Gorton (R)

West Virginia
Robert C. Byrd (D)
John D. Rockefeller IV (D)**

Wisconsin
Robert W. Kasten, Jr. (R)
Herbert H. Kohl (D)

Wyoming
Malcolm Wallop (R)
Alan K. Simpson (R)**

(D) Democrat
(R) Republican

*elected in 1990
**re-elected in 1990

UNITED STATES HOUSE OF REPRESENTATIVES

(267 Democrats, 167 Republicans, 1 Independent)

Alabama
1. H. L. Callahan (R)
2. W. L. Dickinson (R)
3. G. Browder (D)
4. T. Bevill (D)
5. B. Cramer (D)*
6. B. Erdreich (D)
7. C. Harris, Jr. (D)

Alaska
D. Young (R)

Arizona
1. J. J. Rhodes III (R)
2. M. K. Udall (D)
3. B. Stump (R)
4. J. L. Kyl (R)
5. J. Kolbe (R)

Arkansas
1. W. V. Alexander, Jr. (D)
2. R. Thornton (D)*
3. J. P. Hammerschmidt (R)
4. B. F. Anthony, Jr. (D)

California
1. F. Riggs (R)*
2. W. W. Herger (R)
3. R. T. Matsui (D)
4. V. Fazio (D)
5. N. Pelosi (D)
6. B. Boxer (D)
7. G. Miller (D)
8. R. V. Dellums (D)
9. F. H. Stark, Jr. (D)
10. D. Edwards (D)
11. T. P. Lantos (D)
12. T. Campbell (R)
13. N. Y. Mineta (D)
14. J. Doolittle (R)*
15. G. Condit (D)
16. L. E. Panetta (D)
17. C. Dooley (D)*
18. R. H. Lehman (D)
19. R. J. Lagomarsino (R)
20. W. M. Thomas (R)
21. E. W. Gallegly (R)
22. C. J. Moorhead (R)
23. A. C. Beilenson (D)
24. H. A. Waxman (D)
25. E. R. Roybal (D)
26. H. L. Berman (D)
27. M. Levine (D)
28. J. C. Dixon (D)
29. M. Waters (D)*
30. M. G. Martinez, Jr. (D)
31. M. M. Dymally (D)
32. G. M. Anderson (D)
33. D. Dreier (R)
34. E. E. Torres (D)
35. J. Lewis (R)
36. G. E. Brown, Jr. (D)
37. A. A. McCandless (R)
38. R. K. Dornan (R)
39. W. E. Dannemeyer (R)
40. C. C. Cox (R)
41. W. D. Lowery (R)
42. D. Rohrabacher (R)
43. R. Packard (R)
44. R. Cunningham (R)
45. D. L. Hunter (R)

Colorado
1. P. Schroeder (D)
2. D. Skaggs (D)
3. B. N. Campbell (D)
4. W. Allard (R)*
5. J. M. Hefley (R)
6. D. Schaefer (R)

Connecticut
1. B. B. Kennelly (D)
2. S. Gejdenson (D)
3. R. DeLauro (D)*
4. C. Shays (R)
5. G. Franks (R)*
6. N. L. Johnson (R)

Delaware
T. R. Carper (D)

Florida
1. E. Hutto (D)
2. P. Peterson (D)*
3. C. E. Bennett (D)
4. C. T. James (R)
5. B. McCollum, Jr. (R)
6. C. B. Stearns (R)
7. S. M. Gibbons (D)
8. C. W. B. Young (R)
9. M. Bilirakis (R)
10. A. Ireland (R)
11. J. Bacchus (D)*
12. T. Lewis (R)
13. P. J. Goss (R)
14. H. A. Johnston (D)
15. E. C. Shaw, Jr. (R)
16. L. J. Smith (D)
17. W. Lehman (D)
18. I. Ros-Lehtinen (R)
19. D. B. Fascell (D)

Georgia
1. R. L. Thomas (D)
2. C. F. Hatcher (D)
3. R. B. Ray (D)
4. B. Jones (D)
5. J. R. Lewis (D)
6. N. Gingrich (R)
7. G. B. Darden (D)
8. J. R. Rowland (D)
9. E. L. Jenkins (D)
10. D. Barnard, Jr. (D)

Hawaii
1. N. Abercrombie (D)*
2. P. Mink (D)*

Idaho
1. L. LaRocco (D)*
2. R. H. Stallings (D)

Illinois
1. C. A. Hayes (D)
2. G. Savage (D)
3. M. Russo (D)
4. G. E. Sangmeister (D)
5. W. O. Lipinski (D)
6. H. J. Hyde (R)
7. C. Collins (D)
8. D. Rostenkowski (D)
9. S. R. Yates (D)
10. J. E. Porter (R)
11. F. Annunzio (D)
12. P. M. Crane (R)
13. H. W. Fawell (R)
14. J. D. Hastert (R)
15. E. R. Madigan (R)
16. J. Cox, Jr. (D)*
17. L. Evans (D)
18. R. H. Michel (R)
19. T. L. Bruce (D)
20. R. Durbin (D)
21. J. F. Costello (D)
22. G. Poshard (D)

Indiana
1. P. J. Visclosky (D)
2. P. R. Sharp (D)
3. T. Roemer (D)*
4. J. Long (D)
5. J. P. Jontz (D)
6. D. L. Burton (R)
7. J. T. Myers (R)
8. F. McCloskey (D)
9. L. H. Hamilton (D)
10. A. Jacobs, Jr. (D)

Iowa
1. J. Leach (R)
2. J. Nussle (R)*
3. D. R. Nagle (D)
4. N. Smith (D)
5. J. R. Lightfoot (R)
6. F. L. Grandy (R)

Kansas
1. C. P. Roberts (R)
2. J. C. Slattery (D)
3. J. Meyers (R)
4. D. Glickman (D)
5. D. Nichols (R)*

Kentucky
1. C. Hubbard, Jr. (D)
2. W. H. Natcher (D)
3. R. L. Mazzoli (D)
4. J. Bunning (R)
5. H. D. Rogers (R)
6. L. J. Hopkins (R)
7. C. C. Perkins (D)

Louisiana
1. R. L. Livingston, Jr. (R)
2. W. Jefferson (D)*
3. W. J. Tauzin (D)
4. J. McCrery (R)
5. T. J. Huckaby (D)
6. R. H. Baker (R)
7. J. A. Hayes (D)
8. C. C. Holloway (R)

Maine
1. T. Andrews (D)*
2. O. J. Snowe (R)

Maryland
1. W. Gilchrest (R)*
2. H. Delich Bentley (R)
3. B. L. Cardin (D)
4. C. T. McMillen (D)
5. S. H. Hoyer (D)
6. B. B. Byron (D)
7. K. Mfume (D)
8. C. A. Morella (R)

Massachusetts
1. S. O. Conte (R)
2. R. E. Neal (D)
3. J. D. Early (D)
4. B. Frank (D)
5. C. G. Atkins (D)
6. N. Mavroules (D)
7. E. J. Markey (D)
8. J. P. Kennedy II (D)
9. J. J. Moakley (D)
10. G. E. Studds (D)
11. B. J. Donnelly (D)

Michigan
1. J. Conyers, Jr. (D)
2. C. D. Pursell (R)
3. H. E. Wolpe (D)
4. F. S. Upton (R)
5. P. B. Henry (R)
6. B. Carr (D)
7. D. E. Kildee (D)
8. B. Traxler (D)
9. G. Vander Jagt (R)
10. D. Camp (R)*
11. R. W. Davis (R)
12. D. E. Bonior (D)
13. B. Collins (D)*
14. D. M. Hertel (D)
15. W. D. Ford (D)
16. J. D. Dingell (D)
17. S. M. Levin (D)
18. W. S. Broomfield (R)

Minnesota
1. T. J. Penny (D)
2. V. Weber (R)
3. J. Ramstad (R)*
4. B. F. Vento (D)
5. M. O. Sabo (D)
6. G. Sikorski (D)
7. C. Peterson (D)*
8. J. L. Oberstar (D)

Mississippi
1. J. L. Whitten (D)
2. M. Espy (D)
3. G. V. Montgomery (D)
4. M. Parker (D)
5. G. Taylor (D)

Missouri
1. W. L. Clay (D)
2. J. K. Horn (D)*
3. R. A. Gephardt (D)

4. I. Skelton (D)
5. A. D. Wheat (D)
6. E. T. Coleman (R)
7. M. D. Hancock (R)
8. W. Emerson (R)
9. H. L. Volkmer (D)

Montana
1. P. Williams (D)
2. R. C. Marlenee (R)

Nebraska
1. D. Bereuter (R)
2. P. Hoagland (D)
3. B. Barrett (R)*

Nevada
1. J. H. Bilbray (D)
2. B. Farrell Vucanovich (R)

New Hampshire
1. B. Zeliff (R)*
2. D. Swett (D)*

New Jersey
1. R. Andrews (D)*
2. W. J. Hughes (D)
3. F. Pallone, Jr. (D)
4. C. H. Smith (R)
5. M. S. Roukema (R)
6. B. J. Dwyer (D)
7. M. J. Rinaldo (R)
8. R. A. Roe (D)
9. R. G. Torricelli (D)
10. D. M. Payne (D)
11. D. A. Gallo (R)
12. R. A. Zimmer (R)*
13. H. J. Saxton (R)
14. F. J. Guarini (D)

New Mexico
1. S. Schiff (R)
2. J. R. Skeen (R)
3. W. B. Richardson (D)

New York
1. G. J. Hochbrueckner (D)
2. T. J. Downey (D)
3. R. J. Mrazek (D)
4. N. F. Lent (R)
5. R. J. McGrath (R)
6. F. H. Flake (D)
7. G. L. Ackerman (D)
8. J. H. Scheuer (D)
9. T. J. Manton (D)
10. C. E. Schumer (D)
11. E. Towns (D)
12. M: R. O. Owens (D)
13. S. J. Solarz (D)
14. S. Molinari (R)*
15. B. Green (R)
16. C. B. Rangel (D)
17. T. Weiss (D)
18. J. Serrano (D)*
19. E. L. Engel (D)
20. N. M. Lowey (D)
21. H. Fish, Jr. (R)
22. B. A. Gilman (R)
23. M. R. McNulty (D)
24. G. B. Solomon (R)
25. S. L. Boehlert (R)
26. D. O. Martin (R)

27. J. T. Walsh (R)
28. M. F. McHugh (D)
29. F. Horton (R)
30. L. M. Slaughter (D)
31. B. Paxon (R)
32. J. J. LaFalce (D)
33. H. J. Nowak (D)
34. A. Houghton, Jr. (R)

North Carolina
1. W. B. Jones (D)
2. T. Valentine (D)
3. H. M. Lancaster (D)
4. D. E. Price (D)
5. S. L. Neal (D)
6. H. Coble (R)
7. C. Rose (D)
8. W. G. Hefner (D)
9. J. A. McMillan (R)
10. C. Ballenger (R)
11. C. Taylor (R)*

North Dakota
B. L. Dorgan (D)

Ohio
1. C. Luken (D)*
2. W. D. Gradison, Jr. (R)
3. T. P. Hall (D)
4. M. G. Oxley (R)
5. P. E. Gillmor (R)
6. B. McEwen (R)
7. D. Hobson (R)*
8. J. Boehner (R)*
9. M. C. Kaptur (D)
10. C. E. Miller (R)
11. D. E. Eckart (D)
12. J. R. Kasich (R)
13. D. J. Pease (D)
14. T. C. Sawyer (D)
15. C. P. Wylie (R)
16. R. Regula (R)
17. J. A. Traficant, Jr. (D)
18. D. Applegate (D)
19. E. F. Feighan (D)
20. M. R. Oakar (D)
21. L. Stokes (D)

Oklahoma
1. J. M. Inhofe (R)
2. M. Synar (D)
3. B. Brewster (D)*
4. D. McCurdy (D)
5. M. H. Edwards (R)
6. G. English (D)

Oregon
1. L. AuCoin (D)
2. R. F. Smith (R)
3. R. L. Wyden (D)
4. P. A. DeFazio (D)
5. M. Kopetski (D)*

Pennsylvania
1. T. M. Foglietta (D)
2. W. H. Gray III (D)
3. R. A. Borski, Jr. (D)
4. J. P. Kolter (D)
5. R. T. Schulze (R)
6. G. Yatron (D)
7. W. C. Weldon (R)
8. P. H. Kostmayer (D)
9. B. Shuster (R)

10. J. M. McDade (R)
11. P. E. Kanjorski (D)
12. J. P. Murtha (D)
13. L. Coughlin (R)
14. W. J. Coyne (D)
15. D. L. Ritter (R)
16. R. S. Walker (R)
17. G. W. Gekas (R)
18. R. Santorum (R)*
19. W. F. Goodling (R)
20. J. M. Gaydos (D)
21. T. J. Ridge (R)
22. A. J. Murphy (D)
23. W. F. Clinger, Jr. (R)

Rhode Island
1. R. K. Machtley (R)
2. J. Reed (D)*

South Carolina
1. A. Ravenel, Jr. (R)
2. F. D. Spence (R)
3. B. C. Derrick, Jr. (D)
4. E. J. Patterson (D)
5. J. M. Spratt, Jr. (D)
6. R. M. Tallon, Jr. (D)

South Dakota
T. Johnson (D)

Tennessee
1. J. H. Quillen (R)
2. J. J. Duncan, Jr. (R)
3. M. Lloyd (D)
4. J. H. S. Cooper (D)
5. B. Clement (D)
6. B. J. Gordon (D)
7. D. K. Sundquist (R)
8. J. S. Tanner (D)
9. H. E. Ford (D)

Texas
1. J. Chapman (D)
2. C. Wilson (D)
3. S. Bartlett (R)
4. R. M. Hall (D)
5. J. W. Bryant (D)
6. J. L. Barton (R)
7. B. Archer (R)
8. J. M. Fields (R)
9. J. Brooks (D)
10. J. J. Pickle (D)
11. C. Edwards (D)*
12. P. M. Geren (D)
13. B. Sarpalius (D)
14. G. Laughlin (D)
15. E. de la Garza (D)
16. R. D. Coleman (D)
17. C. W. Stenholm (D)
18. C. Washington (D)
19. L. E. Combest (R)
20. H. B. Gonzalez (D)
21. L. S. Smith (R)
22. T. D. DeLay (R)
23. A. G. Bustamante (D)
24. M. Frost (D)
25. M. A. Andrews (D)
26. R. K. Armey (R)
27. S. P. Ortiz (D)

Utah
1. J. V. Hansen (R)
2. D. W. Owens (D)
3. W. Orton (D)*

Vermont
B. Sanders (I)*

Virginia
1. H. H. Bateman (R)
2. O. B. Pickett (D)
3. T. J. Bliley, Jr. (R)
4. N. Sisisky (D)
5. L. F. Payne, Jr. (D)
6. J. R. Olin (D)
7. D. F. Slaughter, Jr. (R)
8. J. Moran (D)*
9. F. C. Boucher (D)
10. F. R. Wolf (R)

Washington
1. J. R. Miller (R)
2. A. Swift (D)
3. J. Unsoeld (D)
4. S. W. Morrison (R)
5. T. S. Foley (D)
6. N. D. Dicks (D)
7. J. McDermott (D)
8. R. Chandler (R)

West Virginia
1. A. B. Mollohan (D)
2. H. O. Staggers, Jr. (D)
3. R. E. Wise, Jr. (D)
4. N. J. Rahall II (D)

Wisconsin
1. L. Aspin (D)
2. S. Klug (R)*
3. S. C. Gunderson (R)
4. G. D. Kleczka (D)
5. J. Moody (D)
6. T. E. Petri (R)
7. D. R. Obey (D)
8. T. Roth (R)
9. F. J. Sensenbrenner, Jr. (R)

Wyoming
C. Thomas (R)

(D) Democrat
(R) Republican
(I) Independent

*elected in 1990
all others: re-elected in 1990

UNITED STATES SUPREME COURT

Chief Justice: William H. Rehnquist (1986)
Associate Justices:
  Byron R. White (1962)
  Thurgood Marshall (1967)
  Harry A. Blackmun (1970)
  John Paul Stevens (1975)
  Sandra Day O'Connor (1981)
  Antonin Scalia (1986)
  Anthony M. Kennedy (1988)
  David H. Souter (1990)

UNITED STATES CABINET

Secretary of Agriculture: Clayton K. Yeutter
Attorney General: Richard L. Thornburgh
Secretary of Commerce: Robert A. Mosbacher
Secretary of Defense: Richard B. Cheney
Secretary of Education: Lamar Alexander
Secretary of Energy: James D. Watkins
Secretary of Health and Human Services:
  Louis W. Sullivan
Secretary of Housing and Urban Development:
  Jack F. Kemp
Secretary of the Interior: Manuel Lujan, Jr.
Secretary of Labor: Lynn Martin
Secretary of State: James A. Baker III
Secretary of Transportation: Samuel K. Skinner
Secretary of the Treasury: Nicholas F. Brady
Secretary of Veteran Affairs: Edward J. Derwinski

In a surprise victory for the Democrats, State Treasurer Ann Richards was elected governor of Texas.

STATE GOVERNORS

Alabama	Guy Hunt (R)**	**Montana**	Stanley G. Stephens (R)
Alaska	Walter J. Hickel (I)*	**Nebraska**	Ben Nelson (D)*
Arizona	runoff elections to be held in 1991	**Nevada**	Bob Miller (D)**
Arkansas	Bill Clinton (D)**	**New Hampshire**	Judd Gregg (R)**
California	Pete Wilson (R)*	**New Jersey**	James J. Florio (D)
Colorado	Roy Romer (D)**	**New Mexico**	Bruce King (D)*
Connecticut	Lowell P. Weicker, Jr. (I)*	**New York**	Mario M. Cuomo (D)**
Delaware	Michael N. Castle (R)	**North Carolina**	James G. Martin (R)
Florida	Lawton Chiles (D)*	**North Dakota**	George Sinner (D)
Georgia	Zell Miller (D)*	**Ohio**	George V. Voinovich (R)*
Hawaii	John Waihee (D)**	**Oklahoma**	David Walters (D)*
Idaho	Cecil D. Andrus (D)**	**Oregon**	Barbara Roberts (D)*
Illinois	Jim Edgar (R)*	**Pennsylvania**	Robert P. Casey (D)**
Indiana	Evan Bayh (D)	**Rhode Island**	Bruce Sundlun (D)*
Iowa	Terry E. Branstad (R)**	**South Carolina**	Carroll A. Campbell, Jr. (R)**
Kansas	Joan Finney (D)*	**South Dakota**	George S. Mickelson (R)**
Kentucky	Wallace Wilkinson (D)	**Tennessee**	Ned R. McWherter (D)**
Louisiana	Charles E. Roemer III (D)	**Texas**	Ann Richards (D)*
Maine	John R. McKernan, Jr. (R)**	**Utah**	Norman H. Bangerter (R)
Maryland	William Donald Schaefer (D)**	**Vermont**	Richard Snelling (R)*
Massachusetts	William F. Weld (R)*	**Virginia**	L. Douglas Wilder (D)
Michigan	John Engler (R)*	**Washington**	Booth Gardner (D)
Minnesota	Arne Carlson (R)*	**West Virginia**	Gaston Caperton (D)
Mississippi	Ray Mabus (D)	**Wisconsin**	Tommy G. Thompson (R)**
Missouri	John Ashcroft (R)	**Wyoming**	Mike Sullivan (D)**

*elected in 1990 **re-elected in 1990

(D) Democrat (R) Republican (I) Independent

CANADA

Capital: Ottawa
Head of State: Queen Elizabeth II
Governor General: Ramon John Hnatyshyn
Prime Minister: Martin Brian Mulroney (Progressive Conservative)
Leader of the Opposition: Jean Chrétien (Liberal)
Population: 26,600,000
Area: 3,851,809 sq mi (9,976,185 km²)

PROVINCES AND TERRITORIES

Alberta
Capital: Edmonton
Lieutenant Governor: W. Helen Hunley
Premier: Donald R. Getty (Progressive Conservative)
Leader of the Opposition: Ray Martin (New Democratic Party)
Entered Confederation: Sept. 1, 1905
Population: 2,469,800
Area: 255,285 sq mi (661,188 km²)

British Columbia
Capital: Victoria
Lieutenant Governor: David C. Lam
Premier: William N. Vander Zalm (Social Credit)
Leader of the Opposition: Michael F. Harcourt (New Democratic Party)
Entered Confederation: July 20, 1871
Population: 3,131,700
Area: 366,255 sq mi (948,600 km²)

Manitoba
Capital: Winnipeg
Lieutenant Governor: George Johnson
Premier: Gary Filmon (Progressive Conservative)
Leader of the Opposition: Gary Doer (New Democratic Party)
Entered Confederation: July 15, 1870
Population: 1,089,900
Area: 251,000 sq mi (650,090 km²)

New Brunswick
Capital: Fredericton
Lieutenant Governor: Gilbert Finn
Premier: Frank McKenna (Liberal)
Leader of the Opposition: None
Entered Confederation: July 1, 1867
Population: 723,900
Area: 28,354 sq mi (73,436 km²)

Newfoundland
Capital: St. John's
Lieutenant Governor: James A. McGrath
Premier: Clyde Wells (Liberal)
Leader of the Opposition: Thomas Gerard Rideout (Progressive Conservative)
Entered Confederation: March 31, 1949
Population: 573,000
Area: 156,185 sq mi (404,517 km²)

Nova Scotia
Capital: Halifax
Lieutenant Governor: Lloyd Crouse
Premier: Roger Bacon (Progressive Conservative)
Leader of the Opposition: Vincent J. MacLean (Liberal)
Entered Confederation: July 1, 1867
Population: 891,600
Area: 21,425 sq mi (55,491 km²)

Ontario
Capital: Toronto
Lieutenant Governor: Lincoln M. Alexander
Premier: Bob Rae (New Democratic Party)
Leader of the Opposition: Bob Nixon (Liberal)
Entered Confederation: July 1, 1867
Population: 9,731,200
Area: 412,582 sq mi (1,068,582 km²)

Prince Edward Island
Capital: Charlottetown
Lieutenant Governor: Marion Reid
Premier: Joseph A. Ghiz (Liberal)
Leader of the Opposition: Leone Bagnall (Progressive Conservative)
Entered Confederation: July 1, 1873
Population: 130,400
Area: 2,184 sq mi (5,657 km²)

Quebec
Capital: Quebec City
Lieutenant Governor: Martial Asselin
Premier: Robert Bourassa (Liberal)
Leader of the Opposition: Jacques Parizeau (Parti Québécois)
Entered Confederation: July 1, 1867
Population: 6,762,200
Area: 594,860 sq mi (1,540,700 km²)

Saskatchewan
Capital: Regina
Lieutenant Governor: Sylvia Fedoruk
Premier: Grant Devine (Progressive Conservative)
Leader of the Opposition: Roy Romanow (New Democratic
  Party)
Entered Confederation: Sept. 1, 1905
Population: 1,000,300
Area: 251,700 sq mi (651,900 km²)

Northwest Territories
Capital: Yellowknife
Commissioner: Daniel L. Norris
Government Leader: Dennis Patterson
Reconstituted as a Territory: Sept. 1, 1905
Population: 54,000
Area: 1,304,896 sq mi (3,379,684 km²)

Yukon Territory
Capital: Whitehorse
Commissioner: J. Kenneth McKinnon
Premier: Tony Penikett (New Democratic Party)
Leader of the Opposition: Willard Phelps
  (Progressive Conservative)
Organized as a Territory: June 13, 1898
Population: 26,000
Area: 186,299 sq mi (482,515 km²)

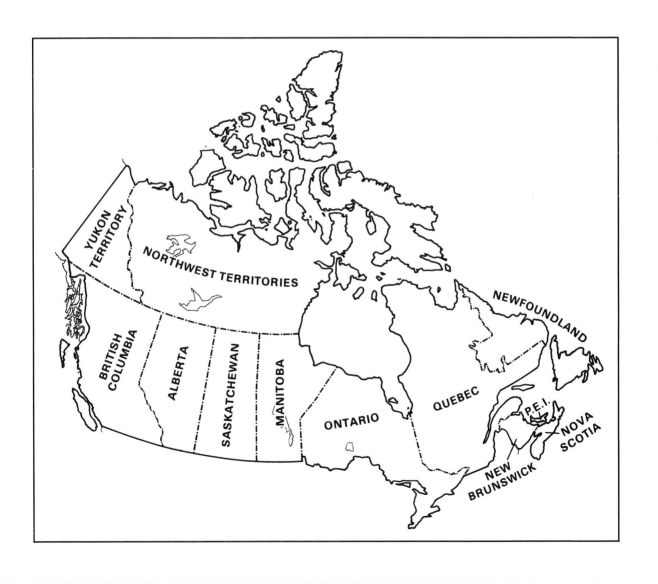

INDEX

B

D

E

F

G

H

I

J

K

N

O

Q

Qatar 43, 385
Quebec, province, Canada 393
    Canadian Museum of Civilization, Hull, picture 259
    Meech Lake accord and separatism issue 46–47
    Mohawk Indian land claims 31
Quilts, fabric folk art 247
    Earth Day 114

R

Railroads
    Channel Tunnel trains between Britain and France
        39
    coins 159
    high-speed trains 112–13
Rain forests, jungles
    environmental concerns 115–16, 119, 121
Rap, music with pounding beat and spoken rhymes 266,
    268
Ray, Johnnie, American musician 381
Reagan, Ronald, president of the United States 58
Redouté, Pierre Joseph, French artist 110
Reed, Frank, American hostage in Lebanon 23
Reid, Vernon, American musician 267
Religion
    American Indian Ghost Dance 194; picture 195
    Aztec 348
    Buddhist sculpture, India 324–25
    golden calf archeological find, Israel 28; picture 29
    Hinduism 324–25, 329, 330–31
    Inca 318
    Islam 28, 214, 215, 328, 352–59, 360–65
    Kahane, Rabbi Meir, death of 380
    Maya 367–68
    violence at Palestinian Arab-Israeli holy site 34
Remora, fish, picture 78
REM (rapid eye movement) sleep, period during sleep
    cycle when dreams occur 106
Renoir, Auguste, French artist 373, 375
Reptiles
    iguanas 350
    turtle endangerment, picture 89
Rhinoceros, animal, picture 79
Rice, Jerry, American athlete 172
Richards, Ann, governor of Texas
    elected, picture 391
Richards, Richard N., American astronaut 35
Rijo, Jose, American athlete, picture 166
Road Runner, cartoon character, picture 320
Robinson, David, American athlete 171
Robinson, Mary, president of Ireland
    elected 36
Robotic dinosaurs, computerized models 84–85
Rock and Roll Hall of Fame Awards 269
Roller-blading, recreational sport
    183; picture 162–63
Roller coasters, amusement park rides 196–201
Roman calendar 212–15

Roy, Jamini, Indian artist 327
Rumania 385
    elections 24, 51
    Nobody's Child album fund-raiser for orphans 268
Running, sport
    Junior Bloomsday road race, picture 225
    track and field 182–83
Russia, republic, Soviet Union 49
Russia (pre-1917)
    Ivan I through VI, rulers (1328–1741) 334–35
    roller coaster development 196–97
    see also Soviet Union
Rutherford, Margaret, British actress, picture 255
Rwanda 385

S

Sabah, Sheik Jabir al-Ahmad al-, ruler of Kuwait 30, 41,
    43
Sabatini, Gabriela, Argentinian athlete 181
Sachets, small scent bags,
    construction directions 148–51
St. Christopher and Nevis 385
St. Lucia 385
St. Vincent and the Grenadines 385
Saleh, Ali Abdullah, president of Yemen 24–25
Sampras, Pete, American athlete 181; picture 180
Sana *see* Yemen
Sanders, Summer, American athlete 186
Sand sculpture, artform 272–73
Sanskrit literature, India 329–30
Sao Tomé and Principe 385
Sartzetakis, Christos, president of Greece 24
Saskatchewan, province, Canada 393
Saturn, planet
    Hubble telescope pictures 129
Saudi Arabia 385
    Islam 43, 44, 359
    Mecca accident 28
    Mecca, Grand Mosque, 358, 362
    U.S. troop contingents, 30, 37, 41–45; pictures 12–
        13, 30–31, 36
Savings and loan associations, thrift institutions
    failure crisis 57–58
Scalia, Antonin, American Supreme Court justice 33
Scholastic Art Awards, photography, pictures 236–
    39
Schwartz, Amy, American illustrator
    The Lady Who Put Salt in Her Coffee, book by Lucretia
        Peabody Hale, picture 289
Science
    botanical illustration 108–11
    computer aids 99
    dream research 104–07
    Edgerton, Harold E., death of 379
    Exploratorium, San Francisco museum, 220, 222–
        223; pictures 221
    inventions 344–45
    kite experiments 135
    Nobel Prizes 35
    Noyce, Robert, death of 381
    Skinner, B.F., death of 381
    space exploration 128–31

T

U.S.S.R. *see* Soviet Union
Ustinov, Peter, Russian-British actor, picture 255

V

Vagin, Vladimir, Soviet artist
  Here Comes the Cat!, book with Frank Asch, picture 284
Van Gogh, Vincent, Dutch artist 24, 376
Vanuatu 387
Vaughan, Jimmie, American musician 268
Vaughan, Sarah, American musician 267
Vaughan, Stevie Ray, American musician 267–68
Vedic literature, India 329
Velázquez, Diego, Spanish artist 375
Venezuela 387
Venus, planet
  Magellan space probe 130; pictures 130–31
Video *see* Television
Videodiscs, computer display of both still and motion photos 100–01
Vietnam 387
  Cambodian involvement 62–63
Viktorenko, Alexander S., Soviet astronaut 131
Virginia
  Civil War 205; pictures 206, 208
  Wilder, L. Douglas, first black governor 64
Virginia, Confederate Civil War naval ship, picture 207
Volta, Alessandro, Italian scientist 336

W

Wahlberg, Donnie, American musician, picture 261
Walesa, Lech, president of Poland
  elected 38, 51
Wallace, Irving, American writer 381
Wallinger, Karl, American musician 265
Warner Bros. Inc., American movie studio
  animated cartoons 262–63, 323
Warsaw Pact, Eastern European defense organization 50
Washington, Denzel, American actor 248, picture 249
Washington, state
  Goodwill Games 186
Washington, D.C.
  Earth Day demonstration 115
  Smithsonian Institution Kite Festival 137
Waste disposal
  environmental pollution 119–20, 121
Waterloo, battle of, Belgium
  defeat of Napoleon Bonaparte 216–17
Watt, James, Scottish engineer 338
Weathervane, decorative device that shows direction of wind flow
  folk art 245–46
Week, seven-day period in calendar
  days of 213–15
Weizsäcker, Richard von, president of Germany 34

Wellington, Duke of, British military leader 216–17
Western Samoa 387
Westinghouse Science Talent Search winner, picture 229
Wetherbee, James D., American astronaut 17
Wetlands, swamps, marshes, and bogs
  pollution effects 116–17
Whale, marine mammal
  scrimshaw carvings 245
  symbiotic partnership 78
Wheatstone, Charles, British inventor 344
White, Ryan, American teenage AIDS victim 381
Who Framed Roger Rabbit?, animated movie 323; picture 321
Wilder, L. Douglas, governor of Virginia, picture 64
Wildlife *see* Nature and wildlife preservation; specific kinds
Wile E. Coyote, cartoon character, picture 320
Wilson, Ann and Nancy, American musicians 267
Wilson, Carnie and Wendy, American musicians 265
Wilson Phillips, music group 265
Wood, Danny, American musician, picture 261
World Cup, soccer 164–65
World Series, baseball 166–67
  Little League 169
World Summit for Children, United Nations-sponsored conference 33; picture 32
World War I
  kite use 134
  sinking of *Lusitania* 25
World War II
  Cold War following 36–37, 48
  commemorative coins 159
  German defeat and division 32, 52
  kite use 134
Wounded Knee, battle of, South Dakota 194–95
Wovoka, American Indian prophet 194
Wrasse, cleaner, fish
  symbiotic partnership 78; picture 77
Wright, Orville and Wilbur, American inventors 343

X

X-ray imaging, diagnostic pictures made with X-rays 370–71

Y

Yeltsin, Boris, president of Russian republic, Soviet Union 49
Yemen (Sana) 387
  Persian Gulf crisis 43
  unification 24–25
Yolen, Jane, American writer
  Best Witches, book, picture 287
Young, Ed, American illustrator and translator
  Lon Po Po, book, picture 288

Z

ILLUSTRATION CREDITS AND ACKNOWLEDGMENTS

The following list credits or acknowledges, by page, the source of illustrations and text excerpts used in this work. Illustration credits are listed illustration by illustration—left to right, top to bottom. When two or more illustrations appear on one page, their credits are separated by semicolons. When both the photographer or artist and an agency or other source are given for an illustration, they are usually separated by a dash. Excerpts from previously published works are listed by inclusive page numbers.

12– © Dennis Brack—*Time* magazine
13
16 © Robert T. Bakker
17 © Robert D. Tonsing—Picture Group
18 © William K. Sacco—Courtesy Yale University
19 © Ron Haviv—SABA
21 © Gerry Ellis—Ellis Wildlife Collection
22 © Wayne Stayskal—Tampa Tribune
23 NASA
24 Courtesy Christie's New York
25 The Bettmann Archive
26 Eslami Rad—Gamma/Liaison
27 Diana Walker—*Time* magazine
29 David Rubinger—*Time* magazine
30– © Dennis Brack—*Time* magazine
31
32 Chester Higgins, Jr.—NYT Pictures
33 Peter Aaron—Esto
34 © B. Bisson—Sygma
36 © T. Graham—Sygma
37 © J. L. Atlan—Sygma
38 AP/Wide World Photos
39 Sygma
40 AP/Wide World Photos
41 J. Langevin—Sygma
44 © P. Robert—Sygma
45 © Anthony Suau—Black Star
46 © Steve Liss—*Time* magazine
48 © David Burnett—Contact Press Images/ Woodfin Camp & Associates
49 © Robert D. Tonsing—Picture Group
50 © Robert D. Tonsing—Picture Group; © Pacha —Eastlight/Picture Group
51 Gad Gross—JB Pictures
52 © Thomas Hoepker—Magnum
54 Chesnot—SIPA Press
55 © P. Habans—Sygma
56 UPI/Bettmann
57 Artist, Michèle A. McLean
59 © Bill Foley—*Time* magazine
60 © Mark Peters—SIPA Press
61 Reuters/Bettmann
63 Reuters/Bettmann
64 UPI/Bettmann
65 Ian Turner—FSP, Gamma/Liaison; © Juraj Groch—Sygma
66 © John W. Emmons; © Ken Regan—Camera 5
67 © Abe Frajndlich—Sygma; © Bill Finney— Sygma
68– © George Marler
69
70 Stephen J. Krasemann—DRK Photo
72 Stephen J. Krasemann—DRK Photo
73 Bruce Coleman Inc.
74– Jackie Geyer—Ranger Rick
75
76 © Dave B. Fleetham—Tom Stack & Associates
77 © Denise Tackett—Tom Stack & Associates; © Larry Lipsky—DRK Photo
78 © James H. Carmichael—Bruce Coleman Inc.
79 © Stephen J. Krasemann—DRK Photo
80 © Clem Haagner—Bruce Coleman Inc.
81 © Ed Robinson—Tom Stack & Associates
82 © Fred Bavendam—Valan Photos; © Zig Leszczynski—Animals Animals
83 © Michael Fogden—DRK Photo
84 © Jean-Marc Giboux—Gamma/Liaison
85 Lawrence A. Lambert
86 AP/Wide World; © Karen Jettmar—Gamma/ Liaison

87 © Zoological Society of San Diego
88 © Pat & Tom Leeson—Photo Researchers, Inc.
89 © Zig Leszczynski—Animals Animals; © Bernhard Meier, courtesy Conservation International
90– John Running—Black Star
91
92 © Robert A. Tyrell
93 © Clayton A. Fogle; © Robert A.Tyrell
94 Artist, Michèle A. McLean
95 © Clayton A. Fogle
96– © Don Landwehrle—The Image Bank
97
98 © Stephen Hunt—The Image Bank
99 © D. Kirkland—Sygma
100 © Philip Marcus, University of California, Berkeley, *Discover* magazine; NASA
101 © Hank Isen, *Discover* magazine
102 © Dan McCoy—Rainbow ("Missile Command," "Super Mario Bros. II"); Courtesy Bohle Company for NEC ("Psychosis")
103 © George Steinmetz
104– John Pack
105
106 © Charles Moore—Black Star
108 General Research Division, The New York Public Library, Astor, Lenox and Tilden Foundations
109 General Research Division, The New York Public Library, Astor, Lenox and Tilden Foundations; Illustration by Sydenham Edwards from *Botanical Magazine*, plate 2388 (1823), The Royal Botanic Gardens, Kew; General Research Division, The New York Public Library, Astor, Lenox and Tilden Foundations
110 Giraudon—Art Resource; General Research Division, The New York Public Library, Astor, Lenox and Tilden Foundations
111 Illustration by Stella Ross-Craig from *Botanical Magazine*, plate 122 (1950), The Royal Botanic Gardens, Kew; Print Collection, Miriam & Ira D. Wallach Division of Art, Prints and Photographs, The New York Public Library, Astor, Lenox and Tilden Foundations; Hunt Institute, Carnegie-Mellon University, Pittsburgh, Pennsylvania
112 © A. Wolf—Publiphoto
113 Artist, Daniel Forster
114 © 1989 Children's Television Workshop. Used courtesy *3-2-1 Contact* magazine
115 R. Azoury—Sipa Press; © Michael Fogden— DRK Photo
116 © M.P. Kahl—DRK Photo; © Nathan Farb
117 © W. Meltzen—Southern Stock Photos; © Stephen J. Krasemann—DRK Photo
118 © Jeffry Myers—Southern Stock Photos; © Alan Oddie—Photo Edit
119 © Thomas A. Schneider—F-Stop Pictures; © Jim Brandenburg—DRK Photos
120 © Tom Bean—DRK Photos; © Frank S. Balthis
121 © Norma Sullivan
122– Peach Reynolds
123
124– © Tobey Sanford
125
125 © Martin Rogers—Stock Boston
126 © John P. Kelly—The Image Bank

127 © Nathan Bilow—Allsport USA
128 NASA
129 JPL
130– AP/Wide World Photos
131
132– © Chris Luneski
133
134 Douglas Faulkner—Photo Researchers
135 Artist, Michèle A. McLean
136 © Chris Luneski—Image Cascade; Theodore L. Manekin; © Chris Luneski—Image Cascade
137 Theodore L. Manekin
138 SOLUTION: The Queen of Hearts
138 Artist, Michèle A. McLean
139 Designed and created by Jenny Tesar
140– Designed and created by Michèle A. McLean
141
146 Designed and created by Jenny Tesar
147 Artist, Michèle A. McLean
148– Designed and created by Jenny Tesar
151
153 Artist, Leslie Dunlap
154– Courtesy, *Crafts 'n Things* magazine
157
158– Courtesy, Krause Publications, Inc.
159
160– From *Many Friends Cooking: An International*
161 *Cookbook for Boys and Girls.* Text © 1980 by Terry Touff Cooper and Marilyn Ratner. Illustrations © 1980 by Tony Chen. Used by permission of Philomel Books, a division of the Putnam Publishing Group
162– © Nathan Bilow—Allsport USA
163
164 © Billy Strickland—Allsport USA
165 © Focus on Sports
166 © Chris Corr—Focus on Sports
167 © Don Smith—Allsport USA
169 UPI/Bettmann
170 Focus on Sports
172– © Focus on Sports
173
174 © Mike Powell/Allsport USA
175 Focus on Sports; UPI/Bettmann
176 © Bruce Bennett
178 © Allsport USA
179 © Claus Anderson—Allsport USA
180 © Focus On Sports
181 © Bob Martin—Allsport USA
182 © Dan Smith—Allsport USA; © Tim DeFrisco —Allsport USA
183 © Allan Laidman
184 UPI/Bettmann
185 © Trippett—Sipa Press
186 Reuters/Bettmann
187 © David Madison—Duomo
188– The Granger Collection
189
190 Jon A. Rembold—*Insight* magazine
191 By permission of Mike Luckovich and Creators Syndicate
192 © John Giordano—SABA
195 The Granger Collection
196– © Co Rentmeester
197
197 The Granger Collection
198 © Linda Hill
199– © Chad Slattery
200
201 © Paul Ruben
202 The Granger Collection

203 The Bettmann Archive; Historical Picture Service
204 Illinois State Historical Library; Culver Pictures
205 Culver Pictures; Museum of the Confederacy
206 Library of Congress; The Granger Collection
207 The Bettmann Archive; Culver Pictures
208 North Wind Picture Archive; Historical Picture Service
209 The Bettmann Archive
210 Camera Hawaii
211 © The Friends of 'Iolani Palace
212– Artist, Charles Varner
215
217 Giraudon—Art Resource
218– © DRS Productions—The Stock Market
219
220 © The Exploratorium
221 © The Exploratorium, photo by S. Schwartzenberg; © The Exploratorium, photo by Nancy Rodger; © The Exploratorium
222– © The Exploratorium
223
224 © 1988 MWS, Inc. Program: © 1987, 1988, 1989, 1990 MWS, Inc. Teenage Mutant Ninja Turtles (R) Mirage Studios. Leonardo ©, Donatello ©, Michelangelo © and Raphael © are trademarks of Mirage Studios. Based upon comics originally created by Kevin Eastman and Peter Laird, © 1985 Mirage Studios. Artwork, © 1987, 1988, 1989, 1990 MWS, Inc.
225 Photofest; Photography Unlimited, courtesy Boulevard Consulting
226 © Stacy Pick—Stock Boston; © E. Bernager—Photo Researchers, Inc.
227 © Evelyn Floret—People weekly; © Rob Kinmoth
228 © Tess Steinkolk
229 Courtesy Westinghouse; Courtesy The Walt Disney Company
230 © Lorimar Television
231 John R. Hamilton—Globe Photos
232 Danny Sanchez—Shooting Star
233 Close Encounters of the Third Kind; Globe Photos
234 Alan Oddie—Photo Edit
235 © Charles Gupton—The Stock Market
236– Courtesy Scholastic Art Awards, conducted by
239 Scholastic Inc.
240– National Gallery of Art, Washington, gift of
241 Edgar William and Bernice Chrysler Garbisch
242 The Abby Aldrich Rockefeller Folk Art Center —Colonial Williamsburg Foundation
243 The Abby Aldrich Rockefeller Folk Art Center —Colonial Williamsburg Foundation; Collection of the Museum of American Folk Art
244– The Abby Aldrich Rockefeller Folk Art Center
247 —Colonial Williamsburg Foundation
248– Photofest
249
250 © James R. Hill III
251 Courtesy Cooper-Hewitt Museum, Smithsonian Institution—Art Resource
252 © Mick Hales; © James R. Hill III
253 © Mick Hales
254 Black Star
255 Kobal Collection—Super-Stock; Photofest
256 Howard Frank Archives
257 © Conrad Collette—Shooting Star; Martha Swope
258 Philadelphia Museum of Art, bequest of Anne Thomson as a memorial to her father, Frank Thomson and her mother, Mary Elizabeth Clarke Thomson; Metropolitan Museum of Art, bequest of Mrs. H. O. Havemeyer, 1929. The H. O. Havemeyer Collection
259 © Ron Kocsis—Publiphoto
260 © A. Montaine—Globe Photos; Art Resource
261 Shooting Star; Retna
262 © 1990 Warner Bros. Inc.
264 © John Roca—LGI
265 © Eddie Malluk—Retna

266 © Michael Benabib—Retna
267 © Andy Freeberg—Retna
268 © Frank Micelotta—Outline Press
269 © Neal Preston—Outline Press
270 Photofest
271 NBC; Courtesy of Lippin Group
272 © Chad Slattery
273 © Jerry Howard—Positive Images; Jerry Howard—Positive Images; © Chad Slattery
274– Illustration from Tony's Bread by Tomie
275 dePaola, © 1989 by Tomie dePaola. Reprinted by permission of G. P. Putnam's Sons
276 Oscar Gustave Rejlander, collection of Arthur A. Houghton, Jr., The Pierpont Morgan Lib.
278– Artist, Elizabeth Miles
283
284 From Here Comes the Cat!, illustrations © 1989 by Vladimir Vagin. Reprinted by permission of Scholastic Inc.
285 From Helen Creswell's, Time Out, illustrated by Peter Elwell. Illustrations © 1990 by Peter Elwell. Reprinted by permission of Macmillan Publishing Company
286 Illustration from The Magic Paintbrush, by Robin Muller. © 1989 by Robin Muller. Published in Canada by Doubleday Canada Limited. Reprinted by permission of the publisher
287 From Best Witches, by Jane Yolen, published 1989 by G. P. Putnam's Sons, illustration by Elise Primavera. Reprinted by permission of G. P. Putnam's Sons
288 From Lon Po Po, by Ed Young, published in 1989 by Philomel Books. Illustrations by Ed Young. Reprinted by permission of Philomel Books
289 Illustration from The Lady Who Put Salt in Her Coffee, by Lucretia Hale. Illustrated by Amy Schwartz. Illustrations © 1989 Amy Schwartz. Published in 1989 by Harcourt Brace Jovanovich. Reprinted by permission of the publisher
290 Photograph from Number the Stars, by Lois Lowry, published in 1989 by the Houghton-Mifflin Company. Reprinted by permission of the publisher
291 Illustration from Princess Furball, by Charlotte Huck. Illustrated by Anita Lobel. Illustrations © 1989 by Anita Lobel. Reprinted by permission of Greenwillow Books, a division of William Morrow & Co., Inc.
292– Artist, Daisy de Puthod
293
295 Artist, Al Leiner
297 Artist, Daisy de Puthod
298– Artist, Al Leiner
299
301 Artist, Daisy de Puthod
302 Artist, Al Leiner
305 Artist, Daisy de Puthod
306– Artist, Michèle A. McLean
307
308– Artist, Anne Feiza
314
316 © Grant Heilman
317 Metropolitan Museum of Art, gift of George D. Pratt, 1933
318 © Bert Schmid
320 © Warner Bros.—Photofest
321 © 1951 Warner Bros. Inc.; © Will Vinton Productions, The California Raisins (TM), © CALRAB; © Touchstone Pictures—Amblin Entertainment, Inc.
322 © 1988 Pixar
323 © The Walt Disney Company; © Walt Disney Productions
324 Lauros-Giraudon—Art Resource; Borromeo—Art Resource
325 Giraudon—Art Resource
326 Giraudon—Art Resource; Lauros-Giraudon—Art Resource

327 Art Resource; © Randa Bishop; © Cameramann Int.
328 © Tim Gibson—Envision
330 Freer Gallery of Art
332 © Hans Pretschinger—Peter Arnold Inc.
333 © Runk Schoenberger from Grant Heilman
334 The Granger Collection
335 © Sovfoto
340 The Granger Collection; UPI/Bettmann; The Granger Collection; UPI/Bettmann
341 UPI/Bettmann; UPI/Bettmann; The Granger Collection; The Granger Collection; Culver Pictures
342 The Granger Collection; The Granger Collection; The Granger Collection; UPI/Bettmann; UPI/Bettmann
346 Courtesy Department of Library Services, American Museum of Natural History
348 © Buddy Mays; © Comstock
349 © George H. Harrison—Grant Heilman
350 © Zig Leszczynski—Animals Animals
351 © James F. Parnell
352 © Viviane Moos—The Stock Market
352– Art Resource
353
353 © Nabeel Turner—TSW Click/Chicago, Ltd.
354 © George Holton—Photo Researchers, Inc.; © Lawrence Manning—TSW Click/Chicago, Ltd.
355 Art Resource; Pascal Maitre—Gamma/Liaison
356 © Hernandez—Sygma; © David Austen—TSW Click/Chicago, Ltd.; © David Ryan—Photo 20-20; © George Holton—Photo Researchers, Inc.
357 © Peter Scholey—TSW Click/Chicago, Ltd.; © Hilary Kavanagh—TSW Click/Chicago, Ltd.
358 Mehmet Biber—Photo Researchers, Inc.; © M. I. Dunes—Gamma/Liaison
360 SEF—Art Resource
361 Victoria and Albert Museum, London; © Nathan Benn—Woodfin Camp & Associates
362 Lauros-Giraudon—Art Resource; Sasaki Scanlon—Comstock; Zeynep Sumen—TSW Click/Chicago, Ltd.
363 The Metropolitan Museum of Art, collection of Arthur A. Houghton, Jr.
364 © Francis G. Mayer; Courtesy Freer Gallery of Art, Smithsonian Institution, Washington, D.C.; Kuwait National Museum, the Al-Sabah Collection
365 The Royal Collection, Stockholm
366 Field Museum of Natural History; © President and Fellows of Harvard College 1982. All rights reserved. Peabody Museum, Harvard University. Photograph by Hillel Burger
367 © Justin Kerr
369 © Justin Kerr
370 The Granger Collection; © Howard Sochurek
371 © David York—Medichrome; © Howard Sochurek—The Stock Market
373 The Phillips Collection, Washington, D.C.
374 Giraudon—Art Resource; Musée d'Orsay from the Metropolitan Museum of Art
375 Tate Gallery, London, from Art Resource; Hill-Stead Museum, Farmington, Connecticut
376 National Gallery of Art, gift of Ethelyn McKinney in memory of her brother, Glenn Ford McKinney; Philadelphia Museum of Art, the George W. Elkins Collection
378 AP/Wide World Photos; © Bob Noble—Globe Photos
379 Sygma; © Nade Cutler—Globe Photos
380 Photofest
381 AP/Wide World Photos; © Brian Reynolds—Sygma
391 AP/Wide World Photos

Grolier Enterprises, Inc. offers a varied selection of both adult and children's
book racks. For details on ordering, please write:

Grolier Enterprises, Inc.
Sherman Turnpike
Danbury, CT 06816
Attn: Premium Department